The Nashville and Decatur
in the Civil War

The Nashville and Decatur in the Civil War

History of an Embattled Railroad

Walter R. Green, Jr.

McFarland & Company, Inc., Publishers
Jefferson, North Carolina

LIBRARY OF CONGRESS CATALOGUING-IN-PUBLICATION DATA

Names: Green, Walter R., 1949– author.
Title: The Nashville and the Decatur in the Civil War : history of an embattled railroad / Walter R. Green.
Description: Jefferson, North Carolina : McFarland & Company, Inc., Publishers, 2022 | Includes bibliographical references and index.
Identifiers: LCCN 2022030524 | ISBN 9781476688527 (paperback : acid free paper) ♾ ISBN 9781476646510 (ebook)
Subjects: LCSH: United States—History—Civil War, 1861–1865—Transportation. | Nashville and Decatur Railroad—History—19th century. | Railroads—Tennessee—History—19th century. | Railroads—Alabama—History—19th century. | Confederate States of America—Transportation. | BISAC: HISTORY / United States / Civil War Period (1850–1877) | HISTORY / United States / State & Local / South (AL, AR, FL, GA, KY, LA, MS, NC, SC, TN, VA, WV)
Classification: LCC E491 .G74 2022 | DDC 973.7/8—dc23/eng/20220629
LC record available at https://lccn.loc.gov/2022030524

BRITISH LIBRARY CATALOGUING DATA ARE AVAILABLE

ISBN (print) 978-1-4766-8852-7
ISBN (ebook) 978-1-4766-4651-0

© 2022 Walter R. Green, Jr. All rights reserved

No part of this book may be reproduced or transmitted in any form or by any means, electronic or mechanical, including photocopying or recording, or by any information storage and retrieval system, without permission in writing from the publisher.

Front cover: sketch of Federal Train at North End of Madry's Ridge Tunnel, Giles County, Tennessee (Ben Johnson, Franklin, Tennessee)

Printed in the United States of America

*McFarland & Company, Inc., Publishers
Box 611, Jefferson, North Carolina 28640
www.mcfarlandpub.com*

Table of Contents

Acknowledgments   vii
Preface   1
Introduction   3

1. Going Home to Michigan   5
2. Harnessing the Iron Horse   7
3. Innes and the 1st Michigan Build Their Reputation   29
4. Raids and Stockades   46
5. Dodge and Boomer Rebuild Trestles and Bridges   61
6. U.S. Colored Troops, Contraband Camps and Tunnel Hill   81
7. Relying on Merrill's and Innes' Blockhouses   91
8. Forrest Comes Calling   103
9. Hood Looks for a Fight   121
10. The Battles of Franklin and Nashville   135
11. Chasing Hood: The Battle of Bridge Builders   145
12. In the Wake   160
13. After the War   164

Appendices
    A—Early History of the Three Railroads Composing the N&D   177
    B—Civil War–Era Railroads, Communications and Pontoon Bridges   185
    C—Locating the Crossings and Fortifications in Mid–1864   193
    D—Troops Protecting the Railroad   212
    E—The Southern Claims Commission   219
    F—The 1901 Franklin, Tennessee, L&N Passenger Depot   224

Chapter Notes   227
Bibliography   235
Index   239

Acknowledgments

Two people provided the spark that compelled me to create this book. My wife, Weezie (Louise), saw how much time I was spending on research of the 1901 Franklin passenger depot and the railroad to its immediate north and south and asked why I didn't write a book about the entire railroad. Soon after that, while discussing with Calvin Lehew the books he had written, he asked me what *my* book was going to be about. My book? I had never intended to write one but now the fire was lit and I could see myself doing it. It is fascinating what lies unrecognized within us and how strong the power of suggestion can be.

I am very grateful for the people who contributed their time and knowledge to this project. Like any other large venture, book writing involves a team. Most of the many people with whom I worked I had never met before. Developing those new relationships was one of the most wonderful aspects of the book writing journey.

In addition to Weezie (who also provided me the time and space to do the work) and Calvin were my primary editor Leslie LaChance and secondary editors Pam Horne and Amy O'Connor, mapmaker Hal Jespersen and advisor Dr. John Selby at Roanoke College. Andy Blair in Nashville and David Meagher in Giles County provided a great deal of information and inspiration. It is a pleasure and a privilege to be able to share David's drawings in the book, as well as Ben Johnson's wonderful sketch of the train and tunnel.

Research was the backbone of the effort. The National Archives and Records Administration and the Library of Congress were exciting places to visit and hunt for information. I owe special gratitude to Cornell University for its "Making of America" which made accessible and searchable through digital technology *The War of the Rebellion* compilation; I spent countless hours searching for numerous key words.

Many thanks to Jerry Barksdale, Richard Martin and Rebekah Davis (Limestone County Archives) in Athens; David Breland, Robert Parham and John Allison (Morgan and Limestone County Archives) in Decatur; Kelly Hamlin and John Lancaster (Giles County Archives) in Giles County; Bob Duncan at the Maury County Archives; Jim Ogden at Chickamauga and Chattanooga National Military Park; Dr. Joan Markel at the University of Tennessee; John Scales in Huntsville; Tim Turner in Lynnville and Allen Stanley (Railroad Data Exchange). I am grateful for the help from Nashville: the Nashville Public Library; Dr. Wayne Moore, Myers Brown and the staff at the Tennessee State Library and Archives; Ralcon Wagner and Harry Wade. In Franklin, I so appreciate my fellow Franklin History Boys—Rick Warwick, Brian Laster and Paul Clements—who reviewed the book and inspired me through their own significant literary efforts—Mary Pearce, Jack Monckton, Tina Jones, Rod Heller, Sam Gant, the Williamson County

Archives and the Williamson County Library (especially Marcia Fraser in Special Collections and other staff—especially Lindsey Roseberry—who helped me get the many books via Interlibrary Loan).

Special thanks to my brother, Dr. Ewing (Bo) Green in Shanghai (who inspires and encourages me in a unique manner); McFarland for choosing to publish the book; and God, without whom I would not be and, therefore, could do nothing.

Preface

The passion for writing this book originated in my preteen years. I grew up in Nashville, Tennessee, and spent many childhood weekends at my paternal grandparents' house on their farm 20 miles to the south in Franklin. My four-great grandfather, Alexander Ewing, a Revolutionary War soldier, had purchased the land near the Harpeth River from the heirs of a fellow Revolutionary soldier from North Carolina. The farm was a wonderful place to go to balance my suburban life. That was in the early 1960s, which now seems like a long time ago. The farm and wood-frame house, however, represented an even earlier time. There, I was introduced to the original log structure built in the 1790s and coal-burning fireplaces. I loved exploring the fields, barns and creek, but the garage held a special treasure. I saw a 12-pound cannon ball there that my grandmother said she had found in her garden. Wow, I didn't know that more than great food came from her garden! Seeing and holding that piece of iron provided my first sensual connection to the Civil War. She gave it to me and I still cherish it.

My high school years were spent at Battle Ground Academy in Franklin. In those days the school was located, as the name implies, on the field of the Battle of Franklin. The campus was only a quarter mile south of the famous Carter House. Spending four years on those grounds reinforced my connection to local history. I would not realize until much later that experiencing Franklin nourished my love and respect for the past more than any other influence in my life.

After retirement, I moved from Nashville to Franklin to become part of the community where my relatives had been, and still were, so involved. My wife, Weezie, and I bought the house in the historic district where my dad and his brother were raised. It was built in 1895 by Confederate veteran Merideth P.G. Winstead who lost most of his left leg at Perryville, Kentucky. The house had been in my family since 1920 and I felt fortunate to be the third generation in my family to reside there. Because I loved trains and waterways, I was delighted that the railroad and the Harpeth River were nearby.

The desire to create the book was fueled by more than my love of Franklin, trains and rivers. My training and work as a professional civil-structural engineer had exposed me to many projects involving rivers and bridges. This book might not exist, however, if Franklin's 1901 Louisville and Nashville (L&N) passenger depot had not been demolished. I was interested in seeing it rebuilt and started researching Franklin's old depots, then expanded the study to include the entire 122-mile rail line between Nashville and Decatur, Alabama.

I am excited that this book seems to be the first major work regarding the Nashville and Decatur Railroad during the Civil War. I limited research primarily to the war years because there appeared to be enough history along the Nashville-to-Decatur corridor during that period of time, including Forrest's raids and the Battles of Franklin and Nashville, to warrant a book. The main topics are the railroad; its bridges, trestles and protective blockhouses and the four key federal men and their design and construction of those structures; the most significant military actions between Nashville and Decatur; freed Blacks, the U.S. Colored Troops and contraband camps; and my concept for locations of the blockhouses. Though the book's focus is on the war years, I provide some pre-war background and discuss the railroad in the years immediately following the war.

Railroads and their bridges, trestles and fortifications, as well as wagon and pontoon bridges, are given little attention in many history books. This book is different in that it gives those features the visibility they deserve. Additionally, I present recent research about the contraband camp and the railroad timber supply complex at Tunnel Hill on Madry's Ridge, and I provide mini biographies of the major characters and six appendices that are relevant to the subject but do not fit within the main text.

I tried to make the book as factual as possible, relying upon substantial research and providing notes for much of the text. Research included visiting the National Archives and Library of Congress, thoroughly searching the *War of the Rebellion*, visiting numerous libraries and archives and obtaining materials from many archives in other states, using Interlibrary Loan extensively, searching old newspapers and consulting historians. I treated the subject with respect and professionalism, spending more than 3,000 hours researching and writing. My hope is that the book will expand the knowledge about the railroad and encourage further study by others.

Introduction

By the mid-nineteenth century, the Industrial Revolution had created many changes in how things were done and what could be done in America, just as the Digital Revolution is doing now. One of the advancements was the development of the steam engine and, subsequently, the steam-powered locomotive. In the 1850s, the American railroad industry was booming. Several railroads to Nashville, Tennessee, and a railroad through Decatur, Alabama, were being completed. Then, to connect the two cities, the Nashville and Decatur (N&D) Railroad, which actually consisted of three separate railroads, was built. It would be open along its entire 122-mile length in November 1860, a short five months before the start of the Civil War and only 17 months before the Federals would take control of Nashville and, soon thereafter, the railroad.

That alone creates an interesting story but is only the beginning. A multitude of men, animals and locomotives would converge upon South Central Tennessee and Northern Alabama to create perhaps the richest chapter in the history of the region. The war would provide the first opportunity for railroads to be both a tool and a target in a large conflict. The N&D would be highly contested. It ran due south from Nashville, a federal stronghold, well into Confederate territory. This made it important to the Union for supplying their troops and strengthening their foothold in Alabama. In essence, the N&D—a Southern railroad—had been captured by the Federals and was being used as a weapon against the Confederacy. The Confederate Army and its sympathizers resented this and tried incessantly to disrupt the railroad's operation. The number of times the railroad's bridges, trestles and protective blockhouses were destroyed and rebuilt is startling. Though the wartime period was sad and violent, its story—and that of the N&D—is important. The war would shape the new South and the N&D would become part of the famous Louisville & Nashville (L&N) Railroad, now CSX Transportation.

Four federal men—Colonel William P. Innes, General Grenville M. Dodge, Lucius B. Boomer and Colonel William E. Merrill—are the key figures in the book because their design and construction efforts are central to the story. Without the work of these men and the many others who supported them, the N&D would not have remained in operation as much as it did, and the Federals would have been less successful in the South.

Wagon and pontoon bridges are often mentioned only in passing in books about the Civil War. However, they could play huge roles in the successes and failures of the armies. Prime examples are the Federals' inability to cross the Harpeth River before the Battle of Franklin, their crossing of it after the battle, and both armies' crossing of waterways during Hood's retreat. The structures that allowed the railroads and the armies to cross natural obstacles did not magically appear. It took a lot of planning, materials and labor to put them in place. This book brings some clarity to how that was done.

Another fascinating story is that, as enslaved Blacks were being freed and leaving their owners in 1863, many of them were drawn to the safety of the Union camps or contraband camps or joined the U.S. Colored Troops (USCTs). Recent research has revealed much about the contraband camp and military activities in the vicinity of the Madry's Ridge railroad tunnel in Giles County, Tennessee. The chapter on those subjects explanation of the relatively unknown roles that the 1st Michigan Engineers and Mechanics had in building blockhouses, bridges and trestles and the Boomer Bridge Works played in rebuilding the railroad's bridges; and the appendix devoted to locating the railroad blockhouses are components of the book of which I am especially proud.

My primary goal was to create a thorough study of the wartime N&D railroad and its crossings and fortifications. The book is intended to bring these features, as well as the important wagon and pontoon bridges and the contraband camp and other facilities at Madry's Ridge, out of the shadows and give them and the men who played a major role with them the visibility they deserve. I give some attention to Franklin's L&N passenger depot and hope it can be rebuilt as a beneficial feature for the city and as a monument to the rich history of the embattled railroad. And I would love to see the story of the railroad increasingly woven into the larger story of the Civil War that is being told in Franklin and elsewhere between Nashville and Decatur. I am very grateful to the publisher for its help in making this book available to you and hope that you will find it worthwhile and interesting.

1

Going Home to Michigan

The train would be arriving at the Grand Rapids station in the next hour or so. Brevet Brigadier General William P. Innes, a Civil War hero, was among the passengers. Though the conflict was never waged in Michigan, the lives of all of those aboard had been changed by the war. Some of the other travelers were likely to be former soldiers, entrepreneurs and immigrant farmers coming to try their luck in the Upper Midwest. It was the fall of 1868, and the nation was still trying to mend from four years of internal military conflict.

Innes had departed Nashville, Tennessee, and was coming home to his wife, Arianna, and four children, Robert, Eliza, Sarah and William. Most of the men in the regiment he commanded had returned home four years earlier. There had been a lot of time to think during the trip. This last segment was on the Detroit and Milwaukee Railroad (D&M). The railroad company was a little behind the times with regards to their passenger cars. His was not enclosed so he was riding in an open coach with only a roof to protect him from the elements, much like a long stagecoach on wheels. Occasional breeze blew against his signature long beard. As the train crossed the Thornapple River, he recalled some of the bridges his men rebuilt for the Union Army or that he later repaired while working for the Nashville and Chattanooga Railroad (N&C).

Before he entered the war in 1861, Innes had been a respected surveyor and civil engineer in Michigan. He had built bridges and trestles and, in fact, helped build the D&M. Like many other men from the North, joining the army gave him the opportunity to fight for a cause while applying his leadership skills and experience. In Grand Rapids, he had raised a regiment of 1,000 men, the 1st Michigan Engineers and Mechanics, a regiment that proved crucial in supporting the Union Army in Tennessee. He was proud that during the three years the regiment was under his command, his men had contributed in so many ways.

There had been attacks by Confederates and Mother Nature on the bridges, trestles, blockhouses and other fortifications along the N&C and the embattled Nashville and Decatur Railroad (N&D). The 1st Michigan had built or rebuilt many of them. Those structures helped the Federals keep the railroads operating, so the army could create and maintain footholds in, and expand control of, the South. Most importantly, the blockhouses his regiment had built on the N&C helped General William T. Sherman receive the supplies he needed for his advance into Georgia, culminating in the capture of Atlanta.

Control of the railroads in Tennessee had been returned to their owners in September 1865 and the companies needed new leaders who were experienced and loyal to the Union. Innes' successes with the Union-controlled military railroads had made him a prime candidate. He was offered and accepted the position of Superintendent of the N&C and Nashville and Northwestern Railroad (N&NW). He was also Receiver of the N&NW under Tennessee Governor William Brownlow, helping the company to continue operating in spite of financial difficulties. Innes held those positions for three years—the same length of time that he had been in the military—and labored for the railroads' success during the early years of Reconstruction. In December 1867, he was also elected President of the new Tennessee and Pacific Railroad.

Innes was proud that he had helped to lead the railroad companies through difficult times, but those times had been difficult for him, as well. The pressures of being a northerner in the post-war South and running two railroads that his Union Army had captured from the Confederacy and converted into weapons used against the Confederacy had taken their toll on him. He may have had health issues, as well, that needed attention. When he was accused of mismanaging money and state bonds for the N&NW—though claiming innocence—it became impossible for him to stay.

He had served his country extremely well and remained in the South to provide for his family. Now, he was finally returning home to Grand Rapids, leaving work in railroads to start a new career in insurance and real estate. More importantly, he would be with his loved ones and in a community where he would be respected.

2

Harnessing the Iron Horse

Long before the N&D and N&C were running trains through Tennessee, the cars of the Tuscumbia Railway were rolling, pulled initially by horses. Chartered in 1830, it was the first railroad built west of the Allegheny Mountains. Financed largely by cotton planters to move cotton, the Tuscumbia ran 2.1 miles from downtown Tuscumbia, Alabama, to the Tennessee River. The primary purpose of most of the railroads in the South was the same—moving cotton to port. From that beginning, visionaries in northern Alabama and Middle Tennessee would dream of other, grander lines that would provide better access to outside markets for their crops. For instance, a railroad from Decatur, Alabama, to Nashville, Tennessee, should it be built, promised to connect central Tennessee and northern Alabama with trade-rich gulf ports.

In the succeeding decades, three new railroads would be built to Nashville and one through Decatur, but none yet between the two towns.

Construction of the Nashville and Chattanooga (N&C) Railroad had begun in 1849 and was completed between Nashville and Chattanooga in February 1854, and the Louisville and Nashville Railroad (L&N) reached Nashville from Louisville on October 27, 1859. By 1861, construction of the Nashville and Northwestern Railroad had taken it from Nashville only 24 miles to the west to Kingston Springs. The Edgefield and Kentucky Railroad (E&K) was nearby, though it did not run to Nashville. It ran from Central Kentucky to its junction with the L&N at Edgefield, just across the Cumberland River from Nashville. The E&K was allowed to use the L&N bridge over the Cumberland.[1]

The Memphis and Charleston (M&C) Railroad was chartered in 1846. Its construction was completed from Memphis through Decatur to Stevenson, Alabama, in 1857. In 1834, the Tuscumbia Railway had been extended to Decatur, becoming the Tuscumbia, Courtland and Decatur (T, C &D) Railroad. The T, C &D was incorporated into the M&C. The town of Stevenson was named for Vernon K. Stevenson, who had been a very active proponent of the N&C and was elected its president in 1848.

The line from Nashville to Decatur finally became a reality in late 1860 after three new railroad companies spent seven years constructing 122 miles of continuous track between the two towns.

The northern section, the Tennessee and Alabama Railroad (T&A), ran 44 miles from Nashville to Columbia and had an additional 12-mile leg from Columbia to Mount Pleasant. Its construction took place between late 1852 and about early 1857, so it was started at about the time the N&C was finished and was completed before the L&N reached Nashville. The southern section, the Tennessee and Alabama Central (T&AC), ran twenty-nine-and-a-half miles from the Tennessee state line to where it met the M&C

at Decatur Junction. The junction was across the Tennessee River from Decatur, not far from the north bank. The T&AC was built between about 1856 and 1859, so it was completed to Decatur Junction after the M&C was already serving Decatur. The middle piece was the last to be completed. The Central Southern Railroad (CS) connected to the T&A in Columbia and ran forty-eight-and-a-half miles to meet the T&AC at the state line. It was built on about the same schedule as the T&AC, from about 1856 to late 1860. However, its completion was delayed because of difficulty in finishing the tunnel through Madry's Ridge in southern Giles County.[2]

The total length of the three lines is sometimes reported as 119 or 120 miles, as well as 122. The discrepancy is probably due in part to how the length is rounded to the nearest mile and whether it was measured to include the northernmost mile—later removed—from the T&A's freight yard to its passenger depot in Nashville.

On July 1, 1861, the three companies agreed to operate independently yet cooperatively as the Nashville and Decatur Railroad (N&D). It would not be until after the war, on March 8, 1867, that the three became a single corporation officially named the Nashville and Decatur Railroad. The company began service under that name on January 1, 1868. Additional history of the three railroads is presented in Appendix A and a general discussion of Civil War–era railroads is in Appendix B.

Federal Train at North End of Madry's Ridge Tunnel, Giles County, Tennessee (Ben Johnson, Franklin, Tennessee).

2. Harnessing the Iron Horse

Map 1 shows the alignment of the N&D (referred to as such, rather than the T&A, for convenience) and the limits of each of the three railroads. Maps 2 through 6 show some detail along the track, including the bridges and trestles that are thought to have been in place at the end of the war and the large forts along the railroad. For even more detailed information, Table 3 in Appendix C lists the main features along the track, including the most significant waterways. It is interesting that the section between Swan Creek and Decatur Junction is not a straight line. Map 7 shows the original track alignment near the junction. The company seems to have shifted the track to the east to avoid the large swampy area that it would have encountered if it had continued southward. This segment was later relocated to the west and is the only known section of track that was subsequently moved.[3]

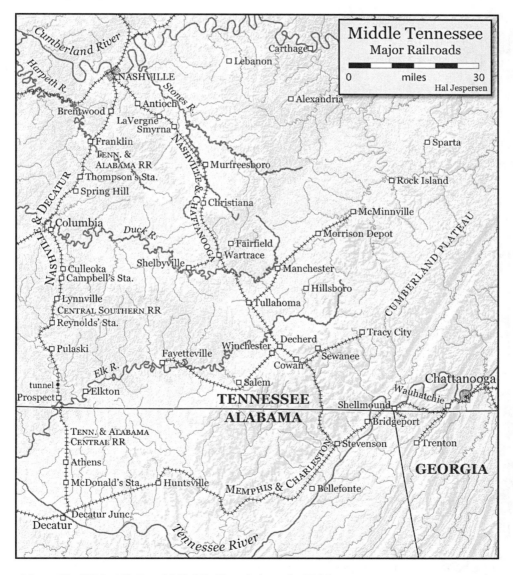

Map 1, The N&D, N&C and M&C Railroads (map by Hal Jespersen, www.cwmaps.com).

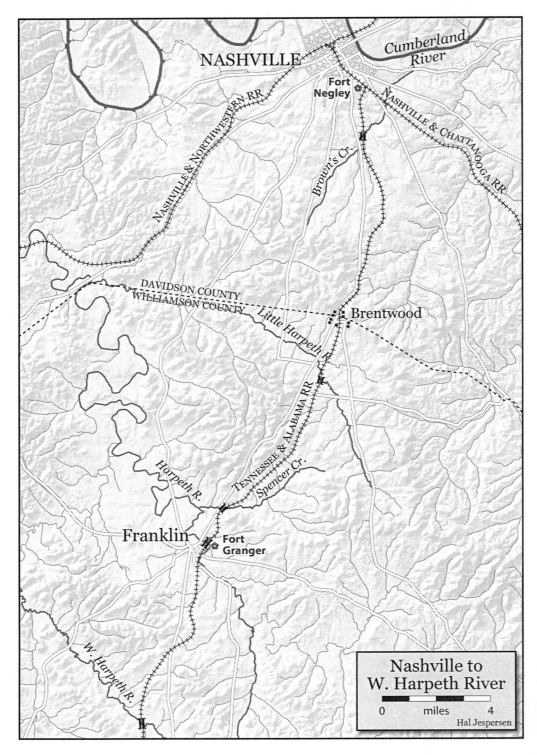

Map 2, N&D from Nashville to the West Harpeth River (map by Hal Jespersen, www.cwmaps.com).

2. Harnessing the Iron Horse

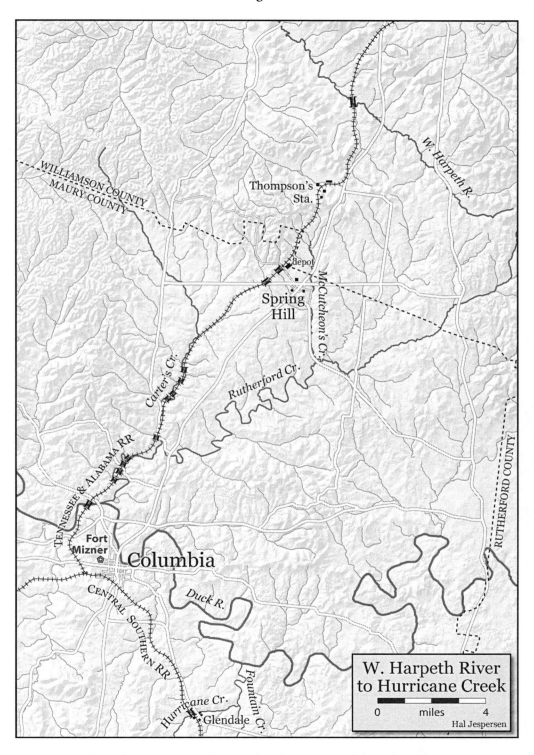

Map 3, N&D from the West Harpeth River to Hurricane Creek (map by Hal Jespersen, www.cwmaps.com).

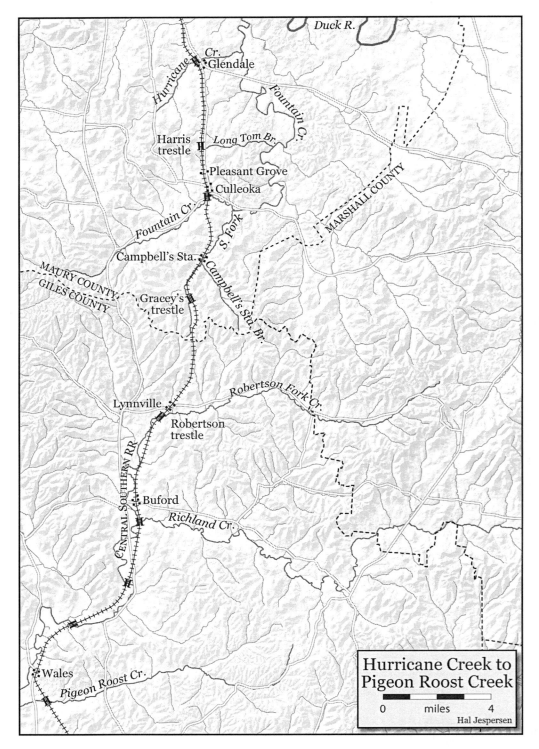

Map 4, N&D from Hurricane Creek to Pigeon Roost Creek (map by Hal Jespersen, www.cwmaps.com).

2. Harnessing the Iron Horse 13

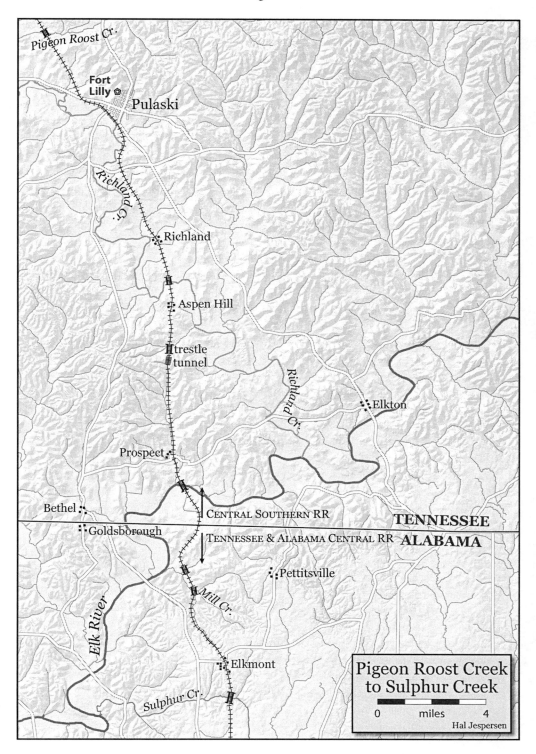

Map 5, N&D from Pigeon Roost Creek to Sulphur Creek (map by Hal Jespersen, www.cwmaps.com).

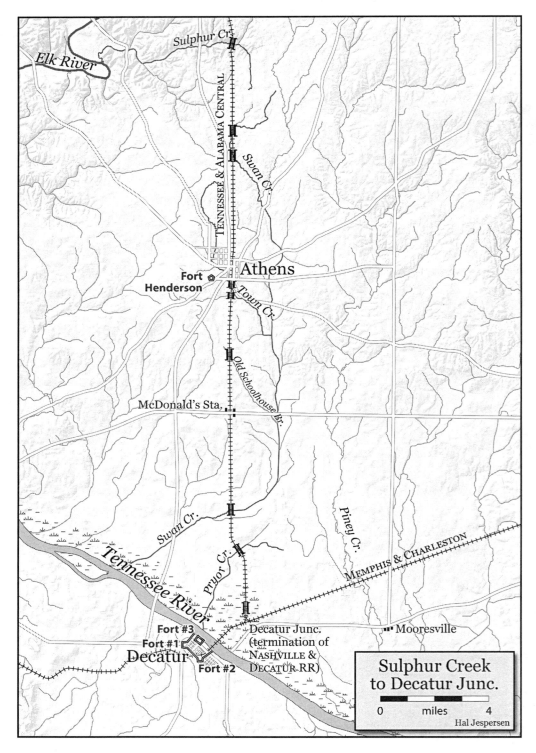

Map 6, N&D from Sulphur Creek to Decatur Junction (map by Hal Jespersen, www.cwmaps.com).

2. Harnessing the Iron Horse 15

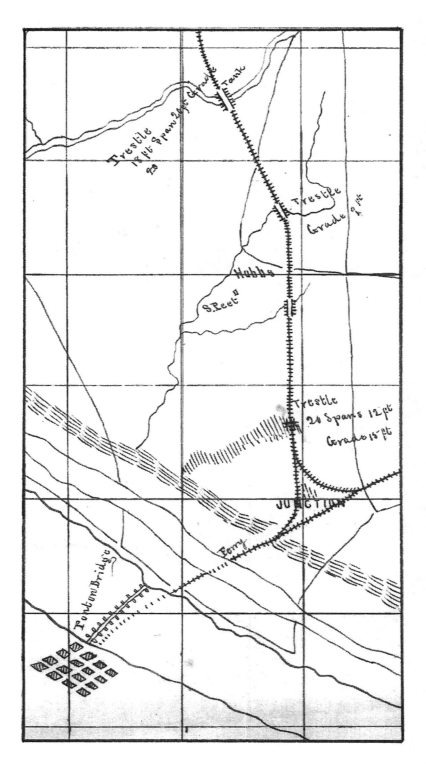

Map 7, Decatur Junction (National Archives and Records Administration).

It was a big day for the N&D and a cause for celebration when, after the track was finally laid through the Madry's Ridge tunnel, the first train ran all the way from Nashville to Decatur on November 22, 1860. The next couple of months, several of the Southern states were celebrating for a very different reason. South Carolina seceded from the Union on December 20. Mississippi followed on January 9, and Florida on the tenth. Alabama became the fourth state to do so, seceding on January 11. Georgia, Louisiana and Texas followed. On February 8, 1861, representatives of those seven states announced the formation of the Confederate States of America (CSA). The nation was divided.

The relationship between the United States of America and the new CSA was fairly calm until April 12 when the Confederates fired upon Union-held Fort Sumter at Charleston, South Carolina. The fort surrendered the next day and on April 15 President Abraham Lincoln, who had just been inaugurated on March 4, issued a proclamation calling for 75,000 volunteers to stop the Southern uprising. The number of men from each Union state was apportioned to its population. The nation seemed headed toward war. Then, Virginia, Arkansas and North Carolina also voted to secede, followed by Tennessee on June 8, the last of the 11 states to do so.[4]

During the remainder of 1861, a number of minor battles took place, none of which affected the three young railroads. Confederate regiments were being organized and some used the N&D to help them do so. The Maury Light Artillery, for example, was formed in Santa Fe, Tennessee. It left there on October 3 and traveled to the Duck River Station, just north of the Duck. They took a train on the N&D to Nashville, crossed the Cumberland River and were sworn in at Camp Weakley. Into very early 1862, the three railroad companies continued operating cooperatively.

At this time, most Southerners were optimistic about a favorable outcome to the war even though they had many reasons to think otherwise. The Confederacy had entered the conflict with numerous disadvantages. The South's share of national manufacturing was only 16 percent. Compared to the North, it had about one-fourth as many White males between the ages of 14 and 40. This discrepancy is reflected in the enlistment during the war of about 2.5 million men into the Union forces as opposed to about a million for the Confederacy. With the money to be made in Southern cotton, hemp, rice, sugar and tobacco increasing in the decades leading up to the war, most of the farming acreage in the South was put to use in growing those products for export rather than food crops. Though the southerners would later shift to planting more crops for food, this created a relatively food-deficient region. Also, with most of the South's wealth tied up in land and enslaved people, cash for diversified investment, like the war, was hard to find. The North did not have that problem, partly because of the great banking houses in New York and Philadelphia. Finally, there was a discrepancy in the railroad as an asset. This would be the world's first large war in which the railroad played a significant role, and the North had twice the mileage of track, about 21,276 miles as compared to about 9,000 in the South. Compounding this relative shortage of rails would be the Southern variation in gauges, gaps in their network and a shortage of iron to replace worn or damaged rail. The Confederacy would also struggle with its depreciating paper money which made it difficult to maintain the railroads' workforce and equipment. Later, on May 26, 1866, Daniel C. McCallum, Brevet Brigadier General, Director and General Manager, U.S. Military Railroads, summed up the importance of railroads in the war when he reported to Bvt. Maj. Gen. Montgomery C. Meigs, Quartermaster-General U.S. Army, that as the war progressed, the nature, capacity and value of railroads were better understood on both sides. He added that, because of the value of the roads to the Federals, a great number of systematic and determined efforts were made by the Confederates to damage the rails used for transporting supplies to the Union Armies.

> Montgomery C. Meigs (1816–1892) was born in Augusta, Georgia, but grew up in Pennsylvania. He excelled at West Point. Most of his early military years were spent building forts with the Corps of Engineers. In the 1840s, he served under then–Lieutenant Robert E. Lee making navigational improvements to the Mississippi River. He later helped construct the Washington Aqueduct and supervised the building of the dome and wings of the U.S. Capitol. In May 1861, he was appointed Brigadier General and Quartermaster General of the Army, headquartered in Washington and responsible for supplying all of the essential items. He held that position through the entire war, retiring from it in 1881 after 46 years. In 1864, he was in charge of purchasing land for national cemeteries for the military dead. His staff recommended Arlington Estate, the home of Robert E. Lee, for a large, new national military cemetery, a fitting political message in the minds of many.
>
> Robert E. Lee (1807–1870) was born at Stratford Hall Plantation in Westmoreland County, Virginia. His father was Maj. Gen. Henry Lee III, Governor of Virginia. Lee attended West Point and was superintendent there from 1852 to 1855, educating many of the young men who would later serve under or against him in the Civil War. In April 1861, President Lincoln offered Lee command of the federal forces, but he declined, saying after his home state of Virginia seceded that same month that he could not fight against his own people. Instead, he accepted a general's commission in the new Confederate Army. In January 1865, just two months before Lee's surrender to Grant at Appomattox, Confederate President Jefferson Davis finally put Lee in charge of the Confederate forces. His pre-war family home, the Custis-Lee mansion, had been seized by Union forces during the war and became part of Arlington National Cemetery. From October 1865 until his death at age 63, he was president of Washington College, which became Washington and Lee University.

Though most southerners dreamed of victory in the new war, Gen. William Tecumseh Sherman wrote about the South: "Only in your spirit and determination are you prepared for war. In all else you are totally unprepared." Those were harsh words that would largely be proven true.[5]

As the months passed in 1862, the number and magnitude of battles escalated. Though the Battle of Nashville would wait until December 1864, there could well have been an earlier one in February 1862 if the Confederates had fortified the city. However, no position on the north side of the Cumberland River had been found that was adequate for a large enough number of troops to provide a defense. Being situated on the river, Nashville was vulnerable to attack by watercraft. Fort Donelson, 85 miles to the west and overlooking the Cumberland River near the Tennessee-Kentucky state line, prevented Union gunboats and other enemy vessels from reaching the city by water. With no fortifications in Nashville, the fort was critical for protection against the Federals. On Sunday, February 16, the city lost that protection when the fort and 15,000 Confederates surrendered to Gen. Ulysses S. Grant. Vague rumors about Fort Donelson and federal plans were sweeping through the streets of Nashville. It was being said that the fort had been captured and the Confederate forces taken prisoner, that Gen. Don Carlos Buell and 38,000 men were at Springfield—only 25 miles away—and that a fleet of federal gunboats had passed Clarksville and would be at Nashville by 3:00 that afternoon. There was fear that Buell would be arriving on the north side of the Cumberland at about the same time and that he and the gunboats would begin shelling the city. This threw the defenseless, predominantly secessionist city into a state of panic and evacuation. To add to the confusion in the city, that same day Confederate Gen. Albert S. Johnston and his Army of Central Kentucky were pouring through Nashville, retreating to Murfreesboro. With him he was withdrawing the defenses from the north bank of the Cumberland River. The Confederates were abandoning Nashville where about 15,000 Whites and 3,800 enslaved and free Blacks lived. Gen. Washington Burrow and Mayor Richard B. Cheatham visited Gen. Johnston at his headquarters in Edgefield. They learned that he would not put up a stand at Nashville so as not to damage the city.[6]

Don Carlos Buell (1818–1898) was born in Lowell, Ohio. He graduated from West Point. In May 1861, he succeeded Sherman as commander of the newly formed Army of the Ohio. Buell's plan for Union forces to move along the Tennessee and Cumberland Rivers toward Nashville was essentially adopted, allowing Grant to capture Forts Henry and Donelson and Buell to move his army into Nashville with almost no opposition. He was one of the few federal officers who had enslaved people. Already under suspicion as somewhat sympathetic to Southerners, the suspicion grew because of his policy of non-interference toward citizens in the South. He was also considered too cautious. Buell's downfall came after he failed to aggressively chase Bragg's retreating force at Perryville, Kentucky, in October 1862. He was relieved of his command of the Army of the Ohio and was replaced by Gen. William Rosecrans, who renamed the organization the Army of the Cumberland. Buell did not receive further assignment. When Grant later offered Buell a possible assignment, he refused to serve under either Sherman or Thomas because he outranked them.

Albert S. Johnston (1803–1862) was born in Washington, Kentucky. He graduated from West Point and, when the Civil War broke out, joined the Confederate Army. Johnston was promoted to general in August 1861. In February 1862, he moved his force, the Army of Central Kentucky, to Nashville and also reinforced Fort Donelson on the Cumberland River with 12,000 more men. On the sixteenth, Fort Donelson was surrendered. Johnston was criticized for the weak defense of the fort, especially as its fall and that of Fort Henry exposed Nashville. To avoid being captured, he removed his forces from Nashville. He took command of the Army of the Mississippi at Corinth, Mississippi, and on April 6 launched a massive surprise attack against Grant at Shiloh. Johnston was wounded in the right leg, probably from friendly fire that clipped an artery, and bled to death with no tourniquet applied, though he had one in his pocket. He was the highest-ranking officer on either side to be killed in the war.

Panic had set in around the city. Burrow and Cheatham addressed the people gathered at the Public Square, advising them to try to stay calm. However, the untrue rumors about the troops and boats had control. Late that morning, it was also falsely rumored that Tennessee Governor Isham Harris had recommended that all women and children leave the city by 2:00 that day. The depots were overwhelmed with hopeful travelers. Approximately 1,000 Nashville residents left by whatever means were available—by foot, horse, wagon or rail—taking with them their small valuables. Governor Harris, his legislators and the state archives were taken to Memphis on a special train. The train ran south on the N&D through Maury County. At Spring Hill, it stopped long enough for a government official to suggest that Spring Hill residents burn their homes, fields and any belongings they did not want the enemy to have. It does not seem, however, that anyone did that. Though Confederates had torn up the L&N between Bowling Green and Nashville, the N&D was still functional. An estimated seven trains were loaded to the maximum with people leaving the city in every direction except northward. General Johnston had told Mayor Cheatham that the people should remain calm and go about their business. However, that did not start to happen until 3:00 came and there were no troops or gunboats. Although the vast majority decided to stay, thousands more fled over the next several days.

Government officials in Nashville realized that there was time to send a large part of their accumulated supplies south to support the Confederacy. On Monday the seventeenth, stores in Nashville were closed and shipments of food and supplies started flowing southward, largely by rail. A large number of wagons from the city and country were pressed into service and men on the streets were marched to the warehouses to load stores onto the wagons for transport to the depot. Because many of the rail cars were being used to transport these supplies, the few cars available to residents were filled to capacity. That day, officials started distributing the Confederate stores to the public. All day, in the rain, and continuing on Tuesday, Johnston's men were pouring through the city streets. Johnston had reminded the people that there would be no fight and that the Confederates would be gone before the Federals arrived. Food and supplies were still being distributed and Gen. Nathan Bedford Forrest arrived with his command to join Johnston.[7]

Nathan Bedford Forrest (1821–1877) was born to a poor family near Chapel Hill, Tennessee. He was named Nathan for his grandfather and Bedford for the county in which he was born. By the start of the war, he had become wealthy from his two cotton plantations, horse and cattle trading and the business of trading enslaved people in Memphis. Most often called "Bedford," at 6'1½" and 210 pounds he stood much larger than most men at that time. In July 1861, he joined the Confederate Army as a private but was quickly commissioned as a lieutenant colonel. Though he had no formal military training or experience, he was given command of the 3rd Tennessee Cavalry Regiment. He generally succeeded in battle and was promoted to brigadier general in July 1862 and given a cavalry brigade. Forrest was promoted to major general in 1863. His record is stained by his men's involvement in war crimes at Fort Pillow, where he seems to have done nothing to prevent them from massacring Union soldiers, many of whom were USCTs, after the battle. Forrest's greatest victory came at Brice's Crossroads in June 1864. For his helping Hood escape across the Tennessee River, he was promoted to lieutenant general. Gen. Sherman considered him to be "the most remarkable man the Civil War produced on either side." After the war, he returned to planting and managing his plantation and was an early member of the Ku Klux Klan. Forrest became president of the Marion and Memphis Railroad which eventually went bankrupt. He ran out of money trying to repay his debts and spent his final days running a prison work farm on the Mississippi River. He died from complications of diabetes at the Memphis home of his brother Jesse and was buried in Memphis. His remains were later moved to Columbia, Tennessee.

When Johnston left Nashville, he put Gen. John B. Floyd, who had escaped from Fort Donelson, in command of the city. Floyd ordered that the cable suspension wagon bridge and the L&N railroad bridge over the Cumberland be burned. This was done late on the night of the eighteenth. Confederate supplies that could not be sent out were now being distributed first to the unpaid women who had worked in support of the Confederacy and then to the needy. The residents became unruly over the distribution of food, so Floyd tasked Forrest with bringing the city to order. Forrest was largely successful. He stationed cavalry in front of the warehouses to control the crowds and cleared paths to the railroad depots so that supplies and the hundreds of sick and wounded soldiers in the hospitals could be moved. At one point, the huge, unruly crowd had to be dispersed by use of a fire department steam engine that came in to give them a cold bath. On the afternoon of February 20, Floyd and his soldiers departed for Murfreesboro, with Forrest left in command. The following day, the flow of shipments to the South continued, with several million dollars' worth of heavy ordnance machinery going to Atlanta. On the twenty-third, the N&C was shut down because of some damaged bridges but the N&D was still open and being put to good use, moving large quantities of meat and other supplies. That day, federal pickets arrived at Edgefield.[8]

Another train took residents and soldiers to Decatur on the N&D and Forrest sent about 30 wagonloads of ammunition, taken from the Confederate arsenal, along the N&D or by wagon to Murfreesboro. About 40 pieces of light artillery had to remain, but they were spiked. Forrest and his 40 men departed that night for Murfreesboro. On the evening of the twenty-fourth, Gen. Buell arrived at Edgefield. The next morning, Tuesday the twenty-fifth, the 1st Michigan Engineers and Mechanics Regiment, which would play a major role in keeping local railroads open for the Federals, arrived at about 9 a.m. Their procession of boats had come up the Cumberland, led by a gunboat, and they were first to take possession of the city. Mayor Cheatham and a citizens' committee crossed the river on a steamer. They met with Buell at 11 a.m. and surrendered. This made Nashville the first capital of an insurgent state in which federal authority was reestablished. Cheatham proclaimed to the citizens that the Federals would protect the people and property of Nashville. The Union gunboat *Cairo* arrived, as did the 36th Indiana and the 24th, 41st and 51st Ohio Infantry Regiments on a steamboat

Gen. Nathan Bedford Forrest (Library of Congress).

flotilla from the west. The men disembarked and entered the city. This made the federal presence about 10,000 men. They took possession of the remaining Confederate food and supplies, valued at $1 million to $3 million. The 6th Ohio Volunteer Infantry and Gen. William "Bull" Nelson, commander of Buell's Fourth Division, took military possession of Nashville at 8:45 p.m. and the Confederate flag over the Capitol was replaced by the stars and stripes at 9:15. That initial American flag was temporarily replaced by William Driver's famous "Old Glory." Also that day, the Federals captured two of the T&A's locomotives, the *Nashville* and the *Williamson*. They were taken to Nashville and became U.S. Military Railroad (USMRR), Division of the Mississippi, engines No. 22, still named the *Nashville*, and No. 6, still the *Williamson*.[9]

> William "Bull" Nelson (1824–1862) was born in Maysville, Kentucky. After five years in the Pacific Ocean as a midshipman, he joined the first class to attend the newly formed Naval Academy at Annapolis, Maryland. He was involved in several engagements in the Gulf of Mexico and was acting master of the USS *Scourge*. Nelson later joined the Mediterranean Squadron and attained the rank of lieutenant. After more than 20 years in the Navy, he was released in July 1861 and was promoted to brigadier general that September. In November 1861, Nelson joined the Army of the Ohio under Buell. He was shot and killed in Louisville on September 29, 1862, by fellow officer Brig. Gen. Jefferson C. Davis because Nelson had dismissed him for his lackadaisical behavior in the defense of Louisville that month and insulted him in front of witnesses. Davis was never prosecuted.

For the past 10 days, Nashville had been isolated—no mail or papers and no businesses open. A form of civilization was returning, though. For three more days, troops continued to arrive by steamboat. The 51st Ohio remained in Nashville as provost guard under the command of Col. Stanley Matthews. The city would remain under federal control for the remainder of the war.

Private Ezra Stearns of Company H, 1st Michigan Engineers and Mechanics, was with his regiment in Nashville on February 25. They and apparently 1st Michigan companies D, F and G had been under the command of Lt. Col. Kinsman A. Hunton at the Battle of Mill Springs, Kentucky, on January 19, though only guarding the camps during the battle and burying the dead. Several of his letters provide first-hand accounts of action in Nashville and along the T&A. According to Stearns, about 80 Texas Rangers saw Union soldiers coming off the first boat and attacked them but were driven back. Stearns also reported that the Federals had found about $100,000 worth of provisions hidden within the asylum and other locations in Nashville.[10]

The Federals controlled the city with a large number of troops and the Confederates were not in a position to put up a defense in the region. This made it easy for the Federals to expand their realm of control to the south. They quickly captured the N&D between Nashville and Franklin, then moved south of Franklin and seized the roadbed into northern Alabama. While the Federals were marching south and taking over the railroads, the Confederates moved rolling stock down the track to save it.

Now that their track had been taken by the enemy, the three railroad companies were no longer in business a short 17 months after that first train had run from Nashville to Decatur. By the end of April 1862, the entire length of the N&D, including Nashville, Franklin, Columbia, Pulaski and Athens, would be controlled by the Federals. Even the N&C and the 83-mile portion of the M&C between Decatur and Stevenson, Alabama, had come under Union control. Except for a few periods of time and some sections of track, the N&D would be operated by the Federals until the end of the war. The same applied generally to other lines in Middle Tennessee.

The N&D, M&C and N&C created a rail circuit that the Federals used to deliver supplies to Stevenson, Alabama, about 35 miles west of Chattanooga. In April 1864, with the N&C in poorer condition than the other two roads, they started running their loaded trains counter-clockwise along the loop—south on the N&D through Decatur Junction, east on the M&C from the Junction to Stevenson. After unloading, the lightened cars that were empty or loaded with the wounded came northwestward back to Nashville along the N&C. Although the distance via Decatur along the loop was about 85 miles longer than going back and forth along the 120 miles of the N&C alone, using that longer route was necessary to keep troops and supplies moving until mid-1864 when the N&C was able to carry the load by itself between Nashville and Stevenson. Supplies that went to Stevenson were warehoused there or sent on by rail via the N&C to Chattanooga. Just as the N&D could use the M&C's track on the Tennessee River Bridge at Decatur, the N&C had agreed to allow the M&C to use the 38 miles of their track from Stevenson to Chattanooga.[11]

In August 1861, Thomas A. Scott, Vice President of the Pennsylvania Railroad, had been appointed Assistant Secretary of War and became responsible for the federal government's railroad and telegraph systems. Early in the war, the rail lines captured by the Federals were run by the department of the Army that was in charge of that area. The first examples of this were Scott's seizures of the Annapolis and Elk Ridge Railroad and the Washington Branch of the Baltimore & Ohio Railroad.

On January 31, 1862, before the N&D was captured, Congress passed the Railways and Telegraph Act authorizing the president to take military possession of all railroads in the U.S., including their telegraph systems, rolling stock, buildings, shops and offices. To the exclusion of all other business, the railroad companies were to be ready to transport troops and munitions of war as was ordered by the Union military authorities. The companies were to be reimbursed for their service. The authorization created the USMRR which, rather than some other department of the Army, would oversee the federally controlled military railroads. The USMRR would be effective in this capacity until the fall of 1865 when the captured railroads were transferred to the original owners. The act encouraged northern railroads to join in the war effort and allowed for the Southern railroads that were in territory captured by the Union, including the N&D, to be pressed into Union service. The USMRR was effective in getting full cooperation from the northern railroads and allowed them to continue performing their commercial business along with the military business with little government interference. Most of the Northern railroad companies complied without coercion and proved to be quite efficient in handling the new military business. In fact, Quartermaster Meigs reported in November 1864 that there had been no need to impose military control on any of the railroads in the loyal states. This was good for the Federals because they did not want to forcefully take control of the companies. Also, the act was not necessary for the Federals to take control of lines in the Confederate states because the rights of war were ample authority for their seizure without an act of Congress. It is important to note that, with the authorization not essential to the seizure of railroads, its primary effect was that it allowed the USMRR to operate the railroads in the South that the Federals had captured. Ultimately, about 50 Southern railroads with a total length of 2,639 miles, including the N&D, would be operated by the Union. That was about 30 percent of the Confederate track and seems like a lot of railroads, but many were short, as evidenced by the average of about 50 miles of track per company.[12]

The USMRR was organized into the Transportation Corps and Construction Corps. The Transportation Corps was responsible for conducting and managing movement of the trains and maintenance of the rails, structures and rolling stock. The Construction Corps handled reconstruction of the lines that were damaged. It employed civilians and was organized in six original stand-alone divisions, with a maximum of seven. To allow multiple simultaneous deployments, each division had the proper personnel and was equipped with tools, camping gear and field transportation. Each was ready to travel via rail, wagon or foot. A complete division had over 775 men. Each division was to have: a track crew and a bridge crew, each with 365 men, including a quartermaster, surgeon, blacksmith and 12 cooks; a water station crew with 15 men; an ox brigade with 20 men, including a foreman, 18 drivers and a cook; a train crew with 11 men, including two conductors, four brakemen, two engineers, two firemen and a cook; and a masonry crew with 13 men. The Construction Corps grew from 300 in 1863 to nearly 10,000, with about 6,000 in the Military Division of the Mississippi alone. That division included the Armies of the Ohio, the Tennessee and the Cumberland which had responsibility for the region between the Appalachians and the Mississippi River.[13]

While the USMRR operated and maintained the railroads, the Quartermaster Department was critical to successful utilization of the railroads. That department worked in conjunction with the USMRR by providing everything the railroads needed, plus managing what went on the trains. It was the federal government's largest business operation and, per Army Regulations, was to provide the quarters and transportation of the army, storage and transportation of all army supplies, clothing, camp and garrison equipment, horses for the cavalry and artillery, fuel, forage, straw, material for bedding and stationery. The department employed about 1,500 men as federal quartermasters during the war, plus thousands of civilians, both men and women. Having the rails, steamships and telegraphs gave the department additional resources but required the development of management techniques.[14]

The military had relatively few men who were experts in railroad transportation, so the Federals would need to fill most of the USMRR's leadership positions with civilian executives who had managed railroads as a profession. Going a step further, they sometimes commissioned civilian railroad men and placed them in positions of great responsibility. On January 20, 1862, President Lincoln had named Edwin M. Stanton Secretary of War. Stanton made two such appointments when he named railway architect Daniel C. McCallum as Colonel, Military Director and Superintendent of the USMRR with the staff rank of Colonel and civil engineer Herman Haupt as Colonel, Chief Railroad Engineer for the Federals. That gave the organization a quasi-military look, with uniformed men at the top and civilians filling the positions of director/superintendent and operating personnel.

> Edwin M. Stanton (1814–1869) was born in Steubenville, Ohio. He became a well-known and successful lawyer and on December 20, 1860, was sworn in as President Buchanan's Attorney General, a position he held until March 4, 1861. Stanton replaced Secretary of War Simon Cameron who had become embroiled in controversy, accused of corruption and became ineffective. Before Stanton, military promotions were most often given to individuals favorable to the administration rather than based upon merit. He changed that. Stanton worked to create an effective transportation and communication network in the North, focusing on the railroads and telegraph lines. On March 11, 1862, Lincoln replaced General-in-Chief of the U.S. Forces McClellan with Stanton, a position he held simultaneously as Secretary of War until July 22 of that year when he was replaced by Henry W. Halleck. Stanton, Grant and their wives would later be invited to Ford's Theatre for a show on April 14, 1865, the night of Lincoln's assassination, but opted out. Lincoln went with Maj. Henry Rathbone and his fiancée. After the assassination, Stanton earned his reputation as organizer of the manhunt for John Wilkes Booth. He ordered a lockdown of Washington. Several of Booth's coconspirators were taken into custody, while Booth was shot at a barn in Virginia and died soon after. Stanton was nominated by Grant as an Assistant Justice of the Supreme Court but died four days after the nomination was confirmed by the Senate.
>
> Daniel C. McCallum (1815–1878) was Scottish born. Prior to the war he had been an accomplished architect in Rochester, New York. He developed a truss bridge design for railroads and built and maintained railway bridges as a subcontractor for the New York and Erie Railroad, then was an engineer and general superintendent at that railroad. While at the New York and Erie, he introduced new management methods, including development of the first modern business organizational chart and communication protocol using the telegraph. He was also founder of the McCallum Bridge Company in Cincinnati, specializing in railroad bridges. McCallum was largely responsible for the efficient operation of the Union railroads and was promoted to major general in 1865. He was mustered out of the service in July 1866.
>
> Herman Haupt (1817–1905) was born in Philadelphia, a civil engineer with a strong railroad background. At age 22, he designed and patented a new bridge construction technique called the Haupt Truss. He worked as general superintendent and then as chief engineer of several railroads. On April 27, 1862, he was put in charge of the military railroads in the Virginia Theater. That September, he was promoted to brigadier general but did not officially accept it, saying he did not want his military rank to limit what he wanted to accomplish in private business. Again offered a promotion in the fall of 1863, Haupt's conditions for accepting were not approved, his appointment was rescinded, and he left his position on September 14. He was replaced by Adna Anderson who had been chief engineer of the USMRR railroads in Virginia. Though only in the service for one-and-a-half years, Haupt greatly impacted the Union war effort by improving its efficiency. One of his primary contributions was in the Gettysburg Campaign where he organized trains to keep the Union well supplied and to carry thousands of wounded Union soldiers to hospitals. After the war, he returned to railroad, bridge, pipeline and tunnel construction.

McCallum had authority to "enter upon, take possession of, hold and use all railroads, engines, cars, locomotives, and equipment that may be required for the transport of troops, arms, ammunition, and military supplies of the United States, and to do and perform all acts ... that may be necessary and proper ... for the safe and speedy transport aforesaid." He appointed Adna Anderson, one of Haupt's best lieutenants, as general superintendent of transportation and maintenance of the rails. Anderson had been chief engineer for the T&A. McCallum was authorized to procure whatever he required to be successful. In one instance, he anticipated the need for 200 locomotives as compared to the 47 available and got them. McCallum saw his organization as a great construction and transportation machine that would carry out the missions of the commanding generals. He proved to be a great asset to the Union effort, with his greatest success in the war perhaps being the coordination of rail support during 1864 for Gen. Sherman's army of 100,000 men and 60,000 animals in the Western Theater, which was the territory south and west of Virginia. Sherman's capture of Atlanta would seal the fate of the Confederacy. Sherman underscored the importance of the rails and the USMRR by stating that his final campaign and the taking of Atlanta would not have been possible without the railroads. His forces had fought for more than six months, supplied by the 473 miles of track from Louisville through Nashville and Chattanooga to Atlanta.[15]

Though he was the top man in the USMRR, McCallum confined his responsibilities to the railroads in the North because control of some regions had been delegated to others. For example, on November 2, 1861, Gen. Sherman appointed John B. Anderson as Railroad Director of the Department of the Ohio which consisted of several states to the north of Tennessee. Also, Haupt was in charge of the military railroads in Virginia.[16]

> John B. Anderson (1817–1897) and his wife opened two private schools for boys and girls in New Albany, Indiana. While operating his schools, he supervised construction of a railroad, was chief engineer on another proposed railroad and then was general superintendent of another. In 1858, he quit teaching and devoted himself to railroading, working his way up through two jobs as superintendent before becoming superintendent of the Louisville and Nashville Railroad. Holding that position at the beginning of the Civil War made him an excellent candidate in railroad management for the Union. He was Railroad Director for the Department of the Ohio, then Union superintendent of the railroads for the Army of the Cumberland. Anderson was Master of Transportation and overseer of repairs for the T&A and N&C until November 1862, at which time he became railroad superintendent for what was next called the Department of the Cumberland. In October 1863, he was appointed general manager of the railroads in the new Military Division of the Mississippi, which included the N&D, the Mount Pleasant Branch, the N&C and the eastern division of the M&C which ran between Decatur and Stevenson. He held that position until February 1864. Following the war, he became financially involved in the Union Pacific Railroad.

In early 1864, as Grant and Sherman planned the march into Georgia, they realized the important role the railroads would play and knew the N&C, M&C and N&D would have to be kept open and functioning efficiently. They, especially Grant, were not impressed with the way John Anderson, General Manager of the railroads in the Military Division of the Mississippi, was running the railroads and felt that he was not up to the task of supporting the armies. On February 4, Grant removed Anderson and replaced him, on the tenth, with Adna Anderson. W.W. Wright became chief engineer of construction of that division. After the war had ended, Wright submitted a report which included a list of the bridges and trestles that were along the N&D at the end of the war. That list is in Appendix C, Table 2. Adna seems to have held his position until the following November. On February 11, Grant put McCallum as general manager of the USMRR, giving him authority beyond the North. He would hold that position for the remainder of the war. The USMRR had been suffering from inefficient management because of inconsistent supervision of the various departments around the country. The Department of the Military Division of the Mississippi in Nashville operated autonomously and fell into that category.

McCallum turned the USMRR into an effective machine. He reorganized it, giving each department a general superintendent of transportation to operate and maintain the captured Confederate lines and a chief engineer of construction to repair the damaged lines and maintain lines of communication. Under each general superintendent and chief engineer were division superintendents and superintendents for each road. Unlike many contemporary entities, the organizational structure of the USMRR was streamlined such that no one answered to more than one immediate superior. Also, because promotions were awarded based upon competency and length of service, most employees stayed. That gave the organization additional stability, staff with experience and an organizational history.[17]

On November 1, 1864, Adna Anderson was made chief superintendent and engineer of all of the USMRR, second only to McCallum. It is not clear how long he held that position. Sometime in 1864, W.J. Stevens was appointed superintendent of all the Nashville railroads. The next year, Stevens was named General Superintendent of the Military Division of the Mississippi. A.W. Dickerson succeeded him as superintendent of Nashville railroads and W.R. Gifford became superintendent of the Nashville-Decatur-Stevenson line.

Soon after McCallum took on the role as general manager of the USMRR in February 1864, he toured the lines in Tennessee. At that time, the N&D, the portion of the M&C between Decatur and Stevenson, Alabama, and the N&C between Nashville and Charleston, South Carolina, had 47 military locomotives plus three borrowed from the L&N, a total of 50. Eleven of those were disabled, leaving 39 fit for service. They also had 437 military cars plus about 100 borrowed from the L&N, for a total of 537. Of those, about 400 were in operating condition. Another source of rolling stock for the Tennessee railroads became available on January 27, 1864, when it was announced that the M&C would be broken up. The cars, locomotives and machinery that would be useful to the N&D were to be sent by steamboat to Nashville and delivered to John Anderson, who at that time was still General Superintendent in the Military Division of the Mississippi.[18]

The USMRR proved to be a large and effective military organization for the Federals. By the end of the war, it controlled and operated about 2,600 miles of track with about 425 engines and 6,500 cars, much of that being, of course, in the South. The Southern states were never able to organize their railroads in a similar manner. Fresh from their secession and yearning for independence, they were opposed to integration of state resources or centralized control by President Jefferson Davis' government. This reluctance to pool and leverage its limited resources, including consolidation of the railroads, limited their ability to meet the logistical demands of war. Unlike the Federals, early in the war Davis did not have the power to commandeer the railroads in the South. He had appointed William Ashe, president of the Wilmington and Weldon Railroad, as an assistant quartermaster and Superintendent of Railroads. Ashe was the first in a

2. Harnessing the Iron Horse 27

The *Genl. J.C. Robinson* (Library of Congress).

series of appointees who attempted without success to centralize the Southern railroad capability. The Confederate Railroad Bureau was established, but it did not sufficiently consolidate the southern railroad companies. This lack of success was largely due to the decentralized, States-rights government in the South and the railroad companies' general disrespect for government. Not until February 28, 1865, did a bill pass for regulation of the Confederate railroads. By that time, however, it was too late to make a difference in the outcome of the war and the bill was never put into effect.[19]

Jefferson Davis (1808–1889) was born in Kentucky. His middle name was "Finis," Latin for "final," because he was the tenth and last child in his family. He graduated from West Point and married future president Zachary Taylor's daughter, Sarah, against Taylor's wishes. She died of malaria only three months later. He was a U.S. Congressman from Mississippi, U.S. Senator and President Franklin Pierce's Secretary of War in 1853. In February 1861, the Confederate Congress selected him as provisional President of the Confederacy. He was elected for a six-year term in November 1861 and inaugurated in February 1862. On April 3, 1865, with Union troops about to capture Richmond, Davis and his cabinet and staff escaped to Danville, Virginia. After the assassination of President Lincoln, President Andrew Johnson accused Davis of helping to plan the murder and offered a $100,000 reward for his capture. On May 5 in Washington, Georgia, Davis officially dissolved the Confederate government. On May 10, Union forces caught him and his small party near Irwinville, Georgia, and he was imprisoned at Fort Monroe, Virginia, for two years. Davis was released on $100,000 bail and moved to Quebec, Canada, to join his family. He remained under indictment until President Johnson issued a pardon on Christmas Day, 1868 and his case was dismissed in February 1869. He became president of the Carolina Life Insurance Company in Memphis and died in New Orleans of acute bronchitis complicated with malaria. His remains are buried in Richmond.

Early in the war, the Confederate railroads played an important role in aiding the Southern armies. The Federals became determined to take control of Southern railroads like the N&D, M&C and N&C because doing so deprived the Confederacy of its use of the roads and benefited the Union as it moved deeper into the South. The Union used captured railroads, including the N&D, quite effectively to meet their military objectives, moving supplies and troops relatively quickly to where they were most needed and transporting the wounded rapidly to safer locations.

Rail resources allowed them to maintain an almost constant pressure on Confederate forces, which contributed to the Union victory in the war. By 1864, the Federals would have control of all of the railroads in Tennessee, operating nearly all of them for use by the military.

On November 10, 1862, federal orders were sent out which proved to be crucial to the successful operation of the military railroads. It was directed that commanding officers of troops along the railroads would do all they could to help the officers of the railroads and quartermasters to unload the cars so as to minimize delays. Upon arrival at a depot, whether at day or night, the cars were to be unloaded "instantly." Working parties were to be always ready for that duty and sufficient to unload the entire train at once. Commanding officers were charged with guarding the track, sidings, wood, water tanks and other features. Any military officer found negligent of those duties would be reported and his name stricken from the rolls of the Army. Anyone who interfered with the running of the cars would be dismissed from the service for disobedience of orders. Also, under the direction of the commanding general, supply depots were to be established at suitable points and properly guarded.[20]

The old saying, "It's hard to find good help" certainly applied to the USMRR. Because of its specialized nature and the rapid expansion of the nation's railroads, there was a national shortage of competent railroad men for both the transportation and construction departments in the USMRR. Another reason for the difficulty in obtaining men for the USMRR was that there was a huge difference between civilian and military rail work. Military railroad work was very hard. It was not unusual for the operators to be out with their trains for five to 10 days with no sleep except that which they could grab on their engine or cars while the train was standing to be loaded or unloaded. The workers, especially the engineer, crew and others aboard the trains, were exposed to great danger from the Confederates, guerrillas and scouting parties. The N&D was an attractive target for the Confederates and could not, of course, be guarded along its entire length all the time. It was not uncommon for a train to be attacked and the crew shot at or for the rails to be damaged or moved so the train would wreck. Raids and wrecks occurred frequently, as did the efforts to repair the tracks. As an example of the danger, in the first six months of 1865 a wrecking train picked up from the railroads around Nashville and delivered to the city 16 wrecked locomotives, 530 wrecked freight cars and 294 carloads of car wheels, bridge iron and other railroad materials. With the work so dangerous, it was sometimes only through the force of military authority that the rail men would continue their service.[21]

3

Innes and the 1st Michigan Build Their Reputation

The three railroad companies, the Confederate government and the majority of the citizens along the 122 miles of track resented that their railroads had been taken by the Federals to use as a weapon against them. Throughout the war, if they were in retreat, the Confederates would do their best to burn the railroad bridges and trestles, tear up the track, destroy water stations and wood yards, take or destroy locomotives and rolling stock and do whatever else they could to put the railroads out of operation. In his March 1, 1865, report to President Johnson, Secretary of War Stanton stated, "As the rebel armies are beaten back they burn all important railroad bridges, tear up the railroad tracks, destroy the water stations, carry off the machinery and rolling-stock, and do all that is in their power to render the railroads useless to our armies." They first did this on the N&D immediately after the evacuation of Nashville in February 1862, when the track and its crossing structures were still in great condition. Confederate Col. John Simms Scott's 1st Louisiana Cavalry destroyed all the bridge and trestle work on the N&D from Nashville to and including the bridge at the Elk River. While they were at it, they destroyed a number of wagon bridges in the region, including the one at Huey's Mill near Columbia. Scott had been ordered not to burn the bridges between the Elk and Decatur, which included the grand Sulphur Creek Trestle in Alabama. In response to this destruction, on March 12 the presidents of the railroads wrote Gen. A.S. Johnston, commander of the Western Division of the Army of the Confederate States, telling of the losses they had sustained and asking that they be reimbursed. We can assume that Johnston was sympathetic but not financially supportive. Scott's destruction of the bridges and trestles would be the first of many, mostly smaller, attacks by the Confederates or guerrillas that would affect the operation of the N&D and require repair or rebuilding of its structures.[1]

Most of the original bridges and trestles along the N&D did not stand very long. With Scott destroying virtually all of them along the T&A in early 1862, those lasted about seven-and-a-half years. Because the CS was built a bit later, most of its structures stood only about two-and-a-half. The lifetimes of the original structures on the T&AC varied but were generally longer than those on the CS.

As the months passed, the railroads had an ever-increasing role in the war. Both the Federals and Confederates were learning what a great implement of war the railroads could be. Trains were very proficient at moving men and materials to where the armies needed them. From the time of its capture by the Union in March and April of 1862 through the remainder of the war, the Federals controlled and operated most of the railroad. However, the tracks passed through territory in which the Confederates were generally free to travel and damage it if not deterred from doing so. Because of this, the N&D would become one of the most contested and embattled railroads in the South.

With the Confederates and their sympathizers often damaging the railroads, repairing them quickly and keeping the line open was key to success of the rails. Many a Confederate later stated that he was amazed at the rapidity with which railroad breaks were repaired by the Federals.

Scott's damage would be repaired, but sections of the railroad would continue to be shut down. Having use of only portions of the railroad would not have a significant impact on the war, but would affect local operations, especially in the Federals' rapid movement of troops and animals, and delivery of food, forage, ammunition, clothing, building materials and other supplies to the south. The greatest hardship in this regard on the N&D would be in the spring and summer of 1862 when the federal forces in Northern Alabama were in short supply of essentials. On the other hand, the supreme success in the region related to adequate and timely movement of trains would be the period of several months beginning in June 1864 when Sherman and his vast army were supplied by the N&C for their march into Georgia.

Both the Federals and Confederates became effective at shutting down sections of the railroads that were benefiting the enemy. Along the N&D, it would be the Confederates and heavy rains that did almost all of the damage. The Confederates' most common methods of shutting down a section of railroad were by destroying a bridge or trestle or tearing up the track by removing and twisting the rails and burning the cross ties. Culverts could be blown up. The wood and water stations and turntables were targets, as well. The threat of this happening along the N&D was almost constant. To keep the road open, the Federals initially sent troops to the key locations, especially the bridges, trestles, stations, tunnel and perhaps some of the culverts. They must have been very protective of the tunnel because a derailment inside it would have been difficult and time-consuming to clear. There is no evidence of such a wreck.

The war would teach the Federals that the most efficient way to shut down a stretch of track was perhaps not by tearing it up, but by placing fence rails or similar combustible material on the track at intervals and firing it in such a way as to heat the rails and burn off the ends of the cross ties. Doing so would cause the rail to expand and be bent into shapes that could not be straightened and reused. This technique left no solution except the time-consuming one of clearing the road and replacing everything above the soil or ballast.[2]

The manner in which the Federals protected the railroad evolved over time. At first, troops occupied encampments and wood and earthen fortifications at strategic locations, but that did not prevent the Confederates, guerrillas and uncooperative citizens from inflicting major damage. To provide the best protection for the N&D, the troops themselves needed to be well protected. With that in mind, the Federals then built wooden stockades which were an improvement but were still vulnerable to artillery. Finally, heavy wooden blockhouses replaced the stockades. Compared to the stockades, the houses offered superior protection and helped to keep the railroads open, but even they had their limitations because the Confederates adapted their tactics to deal with whatever form of protection the Union provided. There were various types of blockhouses. Those constructed to protect the bridges and trestles were typically square with sides about 20 to 30 feet long. Larger houses were built at various strategic locations for purposes other than just protection of a railroad.

3. Innes and the 1st Michigan Build Their Reputation

The Federals intended to guard the key sites at all times and to patrol the track periodically. Troops were shuttled in and out of the sites as needed, spending generally two or three months at any one location. A large number of regiments and companies spent time doing guard duty; some of them are presented in Appendix D. The N&D was generally well guarded until July 1865 when, due to the absence of Confederate troops, it was found that the need was no longer urgent. At that time it was ordered that the sites be guarded by smaller numbers of troops.

The rebuilding of damaged bridges and trestles was expensive and time-consuming but essential to keeping the N&D and the other local railroads open. John Anderson's civilians were adept at replacing and repairing track but slow at replacing bridges and trestles. Early in the war, the Construction Corps of the USMRR was still in its infancy and very small. The Corps of Engineers was a potential source of technical and construction expertise for the Federals; however, it had expanded only slightly during the war, from one company to four. As late as January 1865, it still numbered only about 600. The Union Army needed more men than those two Corps could provide, so other sources were needed. The 1st Michigan Engineers and Mechanics and Rosecrans' Pioneer Brigade would satisfy most of that need locally.[3]

Bridges, trestles and fortifications along the N&D were repaired or rebuilt throughout the war by a number of different forces. Four key builders, however, deserve special recognition—Col. William P. Innes of the 1st Michigan, Gen. Grenville M. Dodge, Lucius B. Boomer and Captain William E. Merrill. It must be stated as an obvious reminder, however, that these men did not do the work alone. Recognition goes also to the thousands of individuals—officers, troops, employees and former enslaved people—who managed or performed the physical work.

William P. Innes (1826–1893) was born in New York City. He left home at age 16 to help provide for his widowed mother and two siblings, working for and learning about engineering from the Erie Railway. At age 27, he moved to Michigan, became a respected railroad surveyor and civil engineer and made a name for himself building railroads in the state. Innes worked for the Detroit, Grand Haven and Milwaukee Railroad Company, then as a civil engineer on the Oakland & Ottawa Railroad and as chief engineer for the prospective Grand Rapids & Indiana Railroad. He was commissioned Colonel and took command of the 1st Michigan Engineers and Mechanics in September 1861 at the age of 35. In August 1863, he was appointed Military Superintendent of Railroads of the Department of the Cumberland, which put him in charge of the N&D, N&C and other railroads. Innes left the 1st Michigan when he mustered out on October 26, 1864.[4]

In mid–1861, a group of prominent men from Grand Rapids was eager to form an engineering regiment entirely from the State of Michigan. Wright Coffinberry, Baker Borden, Perrin Fox and James W. Sligh were well acquainted with the construction field but needed an advocate to push the concept through the appropriate channels. They turned to Innes and offered him command of the unit if he could get it approved. Though he had no military experience, Innes accepted. He contacted Secretary of War Cameron for authority to move forward with the plan. Cameron approved, as did Michigan's Governor Blair, and an agreement was struck. Blair gave Innes authority to raise a regiment of 10 companies, A through K but without J (because of the chance that "J" could be mistaken in writing for "I"), to be known as the 1st Michigan Engineers and Mechanics. They would be similar to the Corps of Engineers, officered and equipped as infantry but provided with the implements for engineering and construction service. The men were to be paid as engineers of the regular army. On September 12, 1861, Innes was commissioned Colonel and the next day Special Order No. 76 was issued from the Governor's office calling for only mechanics or engineers to fill the rolls. The rally point for the enrolled men was at Camp Owen at the Fair Grounds in Marshall, Michigan. On October 29, the 10 companies were mustered into service by Capt. Henry R. Mizner.[5]

Innes is the first of four highlighted builders in this book. He and his quartermaster officer, Maj. Enos Hopkins, provided 1,000 coats, shirts, pants, hats, and sets of mess utensils, 2,000 flannel shirts and drawers, 300 mess pans, 120 kettles, 10 mess chests, 12 company desks, 10 drums and bugles, 55 axes, 50 hatchets and 25 shovels and picks. The engineer-specific equipment, weapons, and transportation that were to be provided by the federal government were much harder to

Col. William P. Innes after the war (RG 2019-4, AOM#003580, Archives of Michigan).

A company of the 1st Michigan Engineers and Mechanics (RG 218-82, AOM#003581, Archives of Michigan).

procure. The overworked supply system created delays. By November only enough obsolete Belgian muskets were on hand to allow one company to drill at a time. Ammunition for live firing was not available until later and the regiment had only 80 of the 280 horses required to fully equip them.[6]

All of the original 1,032 recruits were volunteers and most had no military experience. At least half were skilled craftsmen or artisans and nearly a third were carpenters, joiners or cabinetmakers. Many had experience as carriage or wagon makers, wheelwrights or blacksmiths, or had worked in the railroad industry. A large number were farmers, familiar with the clearing of forests for timber. Because the men were relatively skilled, they were an average of about three years older than the original members of other Northern regiments. At Camp Owen, the young men trained for three months to be disciplined military men with reasonable skills in weaponry. This was essential because they would sometimes be called upon to fight. Because their role was not primarily combat-related, however, they were often not included in the orders of battle for engagements they supported. Possibly more than any other organization, the 1st Michigan worked in detachments, often at widely varying locations. They built pontoon bridges, boats, forts, blockhouses and sawmills and destroyed enemy railroads. With little outside help, they built bridges and trestles using trees from nearby forests. The 1st Michigan's most noteworthy roles related to the N&D would be as the premier builders of bridges and trestles in 1862 and 1863 and as the builders of blockhouses in 1864. The men who served in the regiment played a critical role for the Union Army in the Western Theater, enabling the armies of Generals William S. Rosecrans, Sherman, George H. Thomas and others to move and attack.[7]

The regiment departed camp on December 17, reported to Gen. Buell at Louisville, Kentucky, and was divided into four detachments assigned to the four divisions of Buell's Army of the Ohio scattered throughout Kentucky. They remained with the divisions through the winter. Buell arrived at Nashville in late February and soon some companies of the 1st Michigan started rebuilding the damaged bridges and trestles along the N&D and some on the N&C.

By the end of May, about half of the original 1,032 enlistees were sick in Union hospitals, discharged or dead. In one of the engagements, three companies were at Perryville, Kentucky, on October 8, 1862, where 17 of their men were wounded. They then returned to Nashville and went to the N&C to build bridges. From January through late June 1863, the regiment was stationed at La Vergne, Tennessee, on the N&C and a point near Nashville on the N&D. During that time, they built nine bridges and several other structures and re-laid and repaired a large amount of track. In late June, the regiment moved to the N&C to work between Murfreesboro and Bridgeport. On January 1, 1864, 391 of them saw action at La Vergne in the Battle of Stone's River. About a mile south of La Vergne, at 2:00 in the afternoon, the wagon train they were moving and protecting was surrounded by 1,200 men of Brig. Gen. John A. Wharton's cavalry. An even larger force was not far away under Confederate Gen. Joseph Wheeler. The 1st Michigan was protected only by the wagons and light brush. The Confederates charged seven times with cavalry and soldiers afoot and pillaged and burned 30 wagons. During the fight, Wharton sent flags of truce and surrender four times, to which Col. Innes replied sarcastically, "We don't surrender much." That saying became the regiment's motto. Sometime after 5:00, Wharton retreated. Though heavily outnumbered, Innes and his men had beaten back the enemy, suffering only 15 casualties, including two dead.

As the war took its toll in various ways, there was attrition. On August 10, 1863, the 1st Michigan had 779 men total, including 23 officers and 688 men present for duty. That winter, they obtained 913 recruits, allowing them to fill out the existing 10 companies plus two new ones, L and M, to 150 men each. This allowed them to reach the authorized size of 1,800 men. For much of 1864, the regiment worked on the N&D, especially its bridges and blockhouses. Nine companies served with Gen. Sherman as he went to Atlanta. The 1st Michigan built for him 3,500 feet of pontoon bridges, seven trestle bridges and five double-track trestles.[8]

After Sherman took Atlanta in September 1864, his chief engineer Capt. Orlando M. Poe issued orders for many of the scattered companies of the 1st Michigan to report to Atlanta. On October 27, William H. Kimball and most of Company H marched to Atlanta to join the other nine original companies. Kimball kept a diary that survived the decades and is a valuable record of some of his experiences. Many of the men, including Innes, were officially mustered out on November 2, though by re-enlistments the regiment maintained its full strength for the remainder of the war. Kimball and a few others were assigned to help fill out the voluminous paperwork while the majority of the 10 companies were building defenses and destroying nearby track, military facilities and public property that was useful to the Confederates. Because Southern guerrillas were still attacking Union troop trains, the men who had been mustered out received weapons for personal defense while traveling home.[9]

During the war, the regiment would participate in nearly a dozen serious engagements with the enemy. It is estimated that, of the 2,920 total who had enrolled, six were killed, two died while in Confederate prisons, 280 died of disease and 279 were discharged for wounds or disease. Several of the dead are buried at the National Cemetery in Nashville.[10]

Pay issues would plague the 1st Michigan and nearly all volunteer engineer organizations. Many of the men were angry that they were offered the pay of infantry instead of engineers. They typically rejected that offer and sometimes threatened not to work unless paid properly. The men were given the option to leave the regiment and approximately 30 chose to do so. Innes and his officers took severe action against the ringleaders, reducing some in rank and sending others to the guard house. On April 2, 1862, the regiment, still at Nashville, was ordered to march but the majority refused to do so and signed a protest document. Nashville post Commander Ebenezer Dumont threatened to have the mutiny leaders shot. Kimball was one of the men who refused to sign the protest document. The malcontents had a night to think it over and most decided to march as ordered. The severity of the pay problem prompted Innes to travel to Washington to plead the case. The War Department showed little sympathy, however, stating that no authority existed to pay volunteer engineers. Innes was steered to President Lincoln and, as a result of his personal meeting with the President, that authority was finally given in July. Unfortunately, it would still be several months after that before the regiment was paid properly. This created outright mutiny that November, leading to several arrests and demotions.

It is important to remember that many of the troops in the 1st Michigan were young and still had a lot of "boy" in them. Early in the war, there was chaos in the procurement of supplies and equipment and difficulty in converting the independent-minded young civilians into soldiers. An example of both was that in October 1861 two companies overturned tables loaded with unacceptable food, one inside their tent and the other carried outside and dumped onto the ground. Rather than receiving punishment, however, the young men quickly received rations of higher quality. The fellows needed fun and enjoyed playing cards but were told not to drink. And getting their target practice was important, though it was not supposed to be while aboard a train. Regardless, some entertained themselves by firing their rifles at rabbits, dogs or other four-legged creatures that were unfortunate enough to be near the tracks when the troops rolled by. The officers often frowned at the activity, threatening to arrest them if they continued the practice.

To add to the controversy within the regiment, on May 17, 1862, Brig. Gen. C.P. Buckingham wrote Maj. Gen. Halleck, commander of the Department of the Mississippi, that Innes "had practiced great fraud" as well as cruelty to his men. He directed that Innes be immediately mustered out and discharged from the service. However, the order was suspended because of questionable evidence and the importance of Innes to the military. On June 17, an investigation cleared Innes of all charges.[11]

March of 1862 was a busy month in Middle Tennessee and for the N&D. Sometime in late February or early March, Gen. John Mitchell and Companies A and K of the 1st Michigan, headquartered in Nashville, performed the regiment's initial work on the N&D. They started rebuilding "temporary" replacement structures for the railroad bridges that Scott had burned between Nashville and Columbia. On March 8, it was reported that the N&D should be open again to Franklin on the ninth and, in few more days, to Columbia. The track and new structures, however, became fresh targets for Southern raiders and guerrillas even before the railroad could be reopened. This was such a problem for the Union that those caught burning bridges or tearing up track were sometimes executed on the spot.[12]

Also that month, with the bridge over the Little Harpeth rebuilt and the N&D intact from Nashville to Franklin, a temporary Union supply depot was established at Franklin, probably on the north side of the Harpeth where it would be protected by the encampment of Union troops. Soon after, when the rail was open to Columbia, another supply depot was built there. These depots were used to temporarily store and then funnel supplies to the Union Army farther south. At that time, only nine locomotives and about 50 cars were available for sending troops and supplies out of Nashville along the N&D and N&C. The shipments included rations, munitions, ordnance, clothing, horses and mules, mail, tools, garrison equipment and a great deal of forage. Coal cars that normally hauled coal for steamships and blacksmiths were sometimes used, in addition to box cars, for carrying the forage.[13]

While the new depots and replacement bridges were being built, Buell's Army was under orders to report to Gen. Grant at Savannah, Tennessee, and was heading southwest from Nashville to Shiloh, near Savannah. On March 16–18, Buell's 20,000 to 25,000 infantrymen passed through Franklin, crossing the Harpeth River on the wagon bridge on Nashville Pike. Gen. "Bull" Nelson and his Fourth Division were the first to enter Maury County. Getting to the Duck before Buell, Nelson needed to cross the swollen river and had been at a ford on the north bank for several days while troops were building a bridge of trees felled in the Duck River peninsula. On the twenty-sixth, Buell inspected the bridge and, thinking it was not sturdy enough, ordered that a pontoon bridge be built. With the river calming a bit and the pontoon bridge still not complete, Nelson was tired of waiting and insisted that his 8,000 to 10,000 men wade across and enter Columbia, which they did on the twenty-ninth. In crossing, Nelson had his men fix their bayonets, take off their pants and blouses, bundle everything onto their bayonets, wade in their drawers and shirts with bayonets held high and dress as quickly as possible once on the other side. A large contingency of town folk had gathered to witness, cheer and laugh at the spectacle. Later that day, Mayor J.P. McGaw surrendered Columbia to Nelson. The wooden bridge was reinforced, and the pontoon bridge was finished and braced against the river current by tying it off to trees along the banks. Then the remainder of the troops crossed. While at Columbia, the Federals rebuilt the Duck River railroad bridge that had been burned by Scott. By March 31, the army was headed south of Columbia. Buell left Gen. William Negley in charge of the town with a garrison of 5,000 men. Columbia and Maury County were now in their early days of Union occupation.[14]

On April 3, Col. Innes, his staff and Companies B, C, E, H and I left Nashville and were joined at Columbia by Companies D, F and G. This combined force (all but Companies A and K) marched with Buell to re-enforce Grant at Shiloh. On the fourteenth, they quickly built several bridges to help Buell reach his destination on schedule. Later, on June 1, the companies started a march toward Decatur and built about 3,000 feet of bridges on the M&C along the way.

The first Federals to visit Pulaski in any significant number came in April when a detachment of Gen. Negley's brigade under Col. Marcellus Mundy was sent in to drive off Confederate Gen. John Hunt Morgan. On May 1, Morgan's cavalry again burst into town and confiscated the goods of a sutler. Federal authorities demanded that the town compensate the man in gold coin. The gold was collected quickly. A long-standing story is that Mr. Thomas Martin, founder in 1870 of Martin Female College, the forerunner of Martin Methodist College that is there today, was a major contributor of the gold and saved the town. This part of the story might be more local legend than historical fact. What is known for certain about the Union presence is that the Federals would go on to build Fort Lilly (on what is now called Fort Hill), an earthwork overlooking Pulaski. It was a fairly strong fortification, with deep trenches down the sides of the hill for some distance. It was named after Major Eli Lilly, the engineer in charge of the work. The Union Army went on to occupy Pulaski for most of the war.

Eli Lilly (1838–1898) was born in Baltimore, Maryland. He opened a drugstore in Indiana in January 1861 and enlisted in the 21st Indiana Infantry that July. Later that year, he resigned, recruited 150 men and formed the 18th Battery, Indiana Light Artillery. He was captain of the unit and its commander for two years, serving under Rosecrans in several engagements. Earthen Fort Lilly at Pulaski was named for him. In 1864, he left the 18th Battery and joined the 9th Indiana Cavalry, being promoted to major. That September, he was captured by Forrest at the Battle of Sulphur Creek Trestle and held prisoner at Enterprise, Mississippi, until January 1865. He was promoted to Colonel in June and mustered out that August. After the war, he tried to run a cotton plantation in Mississippi. His wife died there, and he returned to Indiana, filing for bankruptcy. Lilly opened a drug manufacturing operation in Indianapolis in January 1874. That business was modestly profitable. In May 1876, he started a laboratory and began manufacturing drugs with three employees under the name "Eli Lilly, Chemist." His first innovation was gelatin-coated pills and capsules, then came fruit flavorings and sugar-coated pills which made the medicines easier to swallow. Lilly's manufacture of quinine to treat malaria brought a 10-fold increase in sales. After the business had experienced even more growth, it was incorporated as "Eli Lilly and Company" in 1881. Lilly pioneered the concept of giving addictive or dangerous drugs only after a physician had determined the need.

> Ormsby Mitchel (1810–1862) was born in Kentucky and grew up in Ohio. He was a multi-talented man—an attorney, chief engineer of the Little Miami Railroad and professor at Cincinnati College. Mitchel was also an astronomer, credited with publishing the first magazine in the U.S. devoted to astronomy and helping to establish several observatories. When the war started, he turned soldier, entering as Brigadier General of Volunteers. Mitchel took command position of the Department of the Ohio in late 1861. In that role, he ordered the raid later known as the Great Locomotive Chase in which espionage agent James J. Andrews, a Union civilian scout and secret agent, and about 23 others conspired to steal the Confederate locomotive *General* and damage the track, bridges and telegraph on the Western and Atlantic Railroad between Chattanooga and Atlanta. Mitchel commanded the Third Division in the Army of the Ohio from December 1861 to July 1862 and was placed in charge of the defense of Nashville. He died of yellow fever in Beaufort, South Carolina, in October 1862.

On April 11, Gen. Ormsby Mitchel and his 8,000 men of the Third Division in Buell's Army of the Ohio arrived at Huntsville from Shiloh, seized the town without a shot being fired and captured a large number of engines and cars. Mitchel assigned Captain Yates to be superintendent of the railroad and ordered him to prepare two trains for expeditions, one to Decatur and the other to Stevenson, to secure his right and left flanks. Mitchel led the expedition to Stevenson and Col. John B. Turchin, commander of the Eighth Brigade in the newly organized Third Division, led the one to Decatur. Also on the eleventh, Buell ordered Gen. Negley at Columbia to begin fortifying the N&D, presumably meaning that troops would be placed in encampments at the key points along the tracks.

> John B. Turchin (1822–1901) had been born Ivan V. Turchaninov in the Russian Empire. He was a Colonel of Staff in the Russian Guards and fought in several regional conflicts. Turchin and his wife immigrated to the U.S. in 1856, eventually settling in Chicago. He worked for the Illinois Central Railroad, joined the Union Army in 1861 and became colonel of the 19th Illinois Volunteer Infantry Regiment. Turchin's wife followed him on the field during some of his campaigns to witness his battles and wrote the only known woman's diary of the military campaigns. He resigned his commission on October 4, 1864, after contributing to Sherman's "scorched earth" policy in his march from Atlanta to the sea. Following the war, he returned to Chicago. Turchin suffered from dementia and in 1901 was moved to the Southern Illinois Hospital for the Insane in Anna, Illinois, where he died.

Being situated on the Tennessee River and at the intersection of the N&D and the M&C, Decatur was a critical location for transportation of supplies during the war. Both armies realized this and knew that control of this hub was important to victory not just in the battles in the west but in the war. This made the town subject to periodic attacks.

On the next day, April 12, Turchin, the 24th Illinois Infantry and two companies of the 19th Illinois set out for Decatur on a train with a gun mounted on a flat car in front of the locomotive. Upon the Federals' arrival on the 13th at the north side of the river across from Decatur, the small Confederate garrison at the town set fire to the railroad bridge but the Federals were able to extinguish it. Turchin crossed and secured the town. On about the fifteenth, Confederate Col. Scott and his cavalry arrived in Moulton, Alabama, 20 miles southwest of Decatur. His mission was to cross the Tennessee River and destroy all of the Union-controlled railroad and telegraph that he could. On that day, Turchin's command, except for a guard for his baggage train, was ordered west to Tuscumbia, arriving there late the next day. He left men in Tuscumbia, Leighton and Town Creek to block Scott's intended northward route. Near Tuscumbia, Scott's cavalry captured a Black man who was known for providing information to the Union Army. They put the man in fear for his life. After considerable pleading from the man, Scott agreed to release him if he promised not to tell the Union soldiers that Gen. Sterling Price and 15,000 troops were advancing on Tuscumbia—which was a lie. After his release, the man rushed off to report this in Tuscumbia, which was just what Scott had intended. Turchin believed him and informed Gen. Mitchel that Price and his large force had threatened Tuscumbia, fallen back to Town Creek and would probably head for Decatur. Mitchel ordered Turchin to retreat to Decatur and for the garrison there to prepare to burn the M&C railroad bridge over the Tennessee River. About a week later, on the twenty-fourth, the 3rd Ohio Infantry filled the bridge with combustible material and had it ready to burn in case the Federals had to move to the north side. Turchin seems to have skirmished with Price's advance guard near Tuscumbia, then arrived at Decatur at 8 p.m. on the twenty-sixth, crossed the river and set up camp near Decatur Junction. The next day, the 18th Ohio Infantry, under Col. Timothy R. Stanley, arrived in Athens and encamped in and around the town, most of them at the Niphonia Fairgrounds just northwest of town.

Federal pontoon bridge and piers of the burned M&C Railroad Bridge on the Tennessee River at Decatur, Alabama (Library of Congress).

3. Innes and the 1st Michigan Build Their Reputation 39

On April 27 or 28, the Federals on the north side of the river set fire to the Decatur railroad bridge. Within a few minutes, it was ablaze along its entire length. The Federals built a pontoon bridge there, just downstream of and anchored to the remaining piers of the railroad bridge. The pontoons seem to have been the primary means of crossing there until the Federals removed them in November 1864. Because of its importance to the Federals, the bridge would have been well protected on both ends, by the garrison at Decatur and troops stationed on the north side of the river. The railroad bridge was rebuilt after the war.[15]

Pontoon boats and bridges played a crucial role in getting armies across waterways where there was no adequate regular bridge. The boats could be any of a number of types and sizes. Many were wooden and heavy. A common type in use at the time was 21 to 22 feet long, made up of two matching side rib cages covered with canvas. The two halves were transported on standard wagons to the crossing site where the halves were connected by hinges and pins. Pioneers and pontoniers gathered in Nashville in late 1863 to

Wooden pontoon boats (Library of Congress).

Pontoon train (Library of Congress).

fabricate a large number of the boats so that by the following spring every army corps would have such a bridge for its own use.

The month of April also saw the third T&A locomotive taken by the Federals. On the nineteenth, the *Franklin* was captured on the T&A tracks. It was driven to Nashville and became USMRR locomotive No. 224, still called the *Franklin*. At some time in 1862, the T&AC's *Luke Pryor* was captured by Union forces and became USMRR locomotive No. 229, the fourth N&D locomotive to be captured.

At 2 a.m. on May 1, there was gunfire west of Athens, followed by cannonading. Scott and the 1st Louisiana Cavalry were attacking Stanley's men of the 18th Ohio at one or two of the bridges and then skirmishing on the outskirts of Athens with three small brass field pieces mounted in country wagons. Stanley ordered his wagon train to leave Athens immediately for Huntsville, followed by the remainder of his forces. They departed so hastily that most of their tents, supplies and equipment were left at their camp at the fairgrounds. Some of the local citizens joined the Confederates in pursuit of the 18th Ohio. Men shouted and hooted. Women jeered at the fleeing soldiers and waved handkerchiefs in derision. Then Scott and about 200 Confederates rode into Athens from the west, greeted with jubilation. Some of the local ladies presented Scott with a Confederate flag. He quickly dispatched 30 men to burn the railroad bridge over Limestone Creek, between Decatur and Huntsville, where a firefight erupted. A southbound Union supply train wrecked, yielding the Confederates 1,000 bags of coffee. Before Scott's cavalry departed, he cleared and torched the 18th Ohio's camp. The actions of the citizens angered the Union troops and some of their commanders.[16]

Mitchel's superior was Buell, who had issued a general order for all soldiers of the Army of the Ohio not to threaten, harm, damage or interfere with civilians or their property. Mitchel took a harder approach to secessionists than did Buell and was furious. Mitchel sent word to Stanley that he and Athens would be immediately reinforced. He ran his train back to a telegraph station and ordered Turchin to return from Huntsville by rail with his 19th Illinois Volunteers, the 37th Indiana Infantry and the 24th Illinois to retake Athens. Turchin had recently heard a rumor that some citizens of Athens had helped Confederate guerrillas derail the federal supply train, so his anger with Athens was growing.

The men under Turchin's command went by rail to the point on the M&C nearest Athens and marched from there. At daylight on May 2, they met the 18th Ohio slowly falling back in response to Scott's superior numbers. The combined Union presence forced the Confederates to retreat, driving them several miles past Athens. Upon returning to Athens that day, Turchin ordered the 37th Indiana and the 24th Illinois to take positions outside the town while the 18th Ohio and 19th Illinois remained in town. Turchin apparently told the men of those two regiments, "For two hours, I see nothing," meaning that they could do whatever they wanted in the town. It seems that some men from the 37th Indiana and 24th Illinois came to join in the revelry.[17]

The men executed what became known as "The Sack of Athens," in which they broke into, ransacked and stole from stores, businesses and homes, burned most of the buildings and raped at least one enslaved woman. Athens' business district was the primary target, though the more intrusive acts were directed toward the homes of the town's wealthiest citizens. On May 3, a group of citizens submitted a formal complaint to Mitchel regarding the actions of Turchin's men, reporting the loss of an amount exceeding $54,000 to 54 individuals. Mitchel's response was unsympathetic.[18]

In late June, Buell moved his headquarters from Corinth to Huntsville and launched his own investigation of the actions of Turchin and his troops. On July 2, Buell formally relieved Turchin of command of the Eighth Brigade and ordered him to report to his regiment, the 19th Illinois Volunteers. Buell notified Sec. Stanton of his action and, learning that Turchin had been recommended for a promotion, suggested to Stanton that Turchin was not fit for duty. On July 5, Buell's headquarters called for a general court-martial at Athens on the seventh at 10 a.m. or soon thereafter, for the trial of Turchin and any others deemed appropriate. Charges would include neglect of duty, conduct unbecoming an officer and a gentleman and disobedience of orders. That same day, Turchin submitted a written statement in which he resigned and expressed dismay that he was being punished rather than rewarded for all the good he and his men had done. Lt. Col. Joseph R. Scott, who had commanded the 19th Illinois, also resigned, stating that he knew of no justification for the insults his unit was now receiving.[19]

The court-martial proceedings started as appointed on July 7 and were initially overseen by Brig. Gen. (and future president) James Garfield, but he had to resign from the panel due to health reasons. Col. John Beatty of the 3rd Ohio Infantry sat on that court. Many of the witnesses in the trial were bystanders who observed only the destruction. Others had suffered violence and damages at the hands of the Union. However, no one would testify that Turchin had given the order to punish Athens. The trial ended on July 30. Turchin was found guilty of most of the charges made against him, including not restraining his men, but was given some leniency on the grounds that his offenses were committed under "exciting circumstances, and errors of omission rather than commission." He was ordered from the service. Perhaps his previous abuse of residents in Bowling Green, Kentucky was a factor in the ruling. However, by now the Union Army was gaining large areas of the South to occupy and protect. President Lincoln and some of the Union commanders were beginning to favor Turchin's toughness toward troublesome secessionists, regarding it as supportive of active Unionists in federally occupied areas. They also saw this toughness as a way of waging the war to bring it to an earlier conclusion. On August 5, the decision to order Turchin from the service was overruled and he was, instead, promoted to Brigadier General. Turchin's actions against the citizens can be seen as a precursor of the "total war" approach to the Civil War that would later be taken by Sherman and others.[20]

Buell's army of 48,000 was supplied largely by the N&D until about the middle of May. The 12,000 men under Gen. Mitchel were being supplied mainly by the N&C. In late May, Buell swung more towards Chattanooga, after which time the two railroads were supplying about equal amounts. This would continue until about August 8, 1862, when Confederate Gen. Braxton Bragg's army marched north, and the Federals fell back to Nashville. By September 8, the Federals had withdrawn and the last Union train south of Nashville had gone north to the safety of the city. After abandonment of the lines on that date, the Federals did not return until late that fall. When they did, they found the bridges and trestles generally gone. The tracks were little used until February of the following year.

> John H. McPherson (1840–1926) was born in Xenia, Ohio. In October 1861, he enlisted as a private in Company C of the 74th Regiment, Ohio Volunteer Infantry. His diary furnishes wonderful documentation of some of his experiences. In April 1862, his company and others in the 74th arrived at Nashville by boat from Cincinnati. Most of his time in Tennessee would be spent on guard duty. McPherson had a sense of humor and a fascination with heights. He remarked that one day the rain fell so hard that they felt like getting into the Cumberland River to keep from getting wet. He spent some of his free time in May exploring local high spots. One was the state Capital, the peak of which he claimed was 200 feet and nine inches above the ground. Another was the 120-foot-tall water tower on the property of Col. Joseph A.S. and Adelicia Acklen that contained their summer home, the Belmont Mansion. Unfortunately, years later, Mr. McPherson would climb one time too many. His obituary of August 1926 indicates that he had died at age 85 in Xenia "of shock following a fall from a fruit tree."

On Monday, June 2, 25 men from Company C of the 74th Ohio Volunteer Infantry, including John H. McPherson, left Nashville for Franklin guarding a train of 50 wagons. Because the wagons had no brakes, there were two mules in the rear to slow them and protect the four mules in front. They arrived at Franklin early the next day and entered town on the north end of the two-track wagon bridge over the Harpeth River. While crossing, one of the mules found itself on the other track, got tangled up and broke its neck. The men dragged him out and rolled him onto the side of the road. With the wagons delivered, all 25 men got into a wagon and returned to Nashville. Later, on the twelfth, he witnessed a total eclipse of the moon. Yes, events in the heavens continued like clockwork without regard for whatever the humans down below had gotten themselves into.[21]

In the spring of 1862, food and forage were in short supply for the federal troops in Athens and Huntsville and had to be sometimes rationed one day at a time. There were several reasons for this. The area north of the Duck River could provide almost nothing to eat because the forces in Nashville and along the N&D had thoroughly foraged it. Also, until that spring farmers between the Duck and Tennessee Rivers and between the N&D and the N&C had put out less cotton and more corn. However, all of the ripe corn had been eaten, so the animals had to eat green corn as did the troops as part of their rations. Because of guerrillas, it was not safe to go far with wagon trains to find subsistence and it was not practical to send enough troops to secure the foragers. Sacks of corn and bales of hay for the animals had to be brought in from Louisville or Nashville on the N&D.

Rebels had raided Murfreesboro on the same day that the N&C repairs were completed, and the road re-opened to Stevenson, thus making Mitchel increasingly reliant upon the N&D for supplies. Reynolds' Station became a Union supply depot at about that time and supplies had already been sent southward on the N&D and stockpiled there. The Federals would normally have run trains on the N&D south of Reynolds' Station to transport supplies to Athens and Huntsville, but several large bridges and trestles below Reynolds, including the bridge over the Elk, had still not been rebuilt.

All of this created a logistical nightmare regarding the delivery of food and forage to northern Alabama. Without a railroad bridge at the Elk, the Federals had to ferry, pontoon or ford across the river. However, passage of the heavy wagons over the Elk with ferries or pontoons was not dependable because the river often ran high and fast. Therefore, heavily secured wagon trains had to be sent from Reynolds and run around Madry's Ridge and the break in the rails, a detour of 40 miles each way. Those trains had to ford the Elk River at Elkton, upstream of the burned railroad bridge. This was the best they could do but terribly slow due, in part, to the muddy terrain. It was imperative that the bridge at the Elk and the remainder of the N&D south of Reynolds' Station be repaired and protected as soon as possible. The Union never had enough troops to secure the entire line, so it was ordered that swift punishment come to those who destroyed track, bridges or trestles.[22]

Rebuilding of the Elk River bridge started in early June when Capt. Crittendon and Companies A and K of the 1st Michigan arrived. That would be the largest job the 1st Michigan would have over the next couple of months. The bridge was at the southernmost point on the 23-mile break in the railroad. It had 700 feet of trestle, was 58 feet high and was in as much as 20 feet of water. At the same time, John Anderson, who was in charge of repairs on the N&D, and his civilians were repairing the N&D from Nashville to the Elk and Gen. Mitchell and other companies of the 1st Michigan were working on the railroad from the Elk to Decatur Junction.

Construction at the Elk did not, however, progress as quickly as desired. There was too much work for the available workers, and it was common practice for the men to be shuttled back and forth between the N&C and N&D, depending on the work priorities. This happened a lot that summer and delayed work on the N&D. For example, on June 12 Buell ordered 1st Michigan Companies A and K to the N&C to repair small bridges and several of Mitchell's companies to the N&C for the more important track repair.[23]

To reduce the wagon trip from Reynolds' Station to Athens by 23 miles, on June 18 Buell ordered that the Madry's Ridge tunnel be planked and made passable by the wagons. The next day, he ordered Col. E.M. McCook, Col. 2nd Indiana Cavalry, commanding 1st Cavalry Brigade, to take charge of a wagon train to Reynolds' Station to pick up rations and forage and deliver them to Athens, presumably using the newly planked tunnel. To ascend to or descend from the north entrance to the tunnel would still require quite an effort. The trestle could have been planked over for use by the wagon trains, but it had not yet been rebuilt. Because of the risk of being attacked, McCook was to take two battalions of cavalry to help him get the 200 wagons safely to their destination. On the twentieth, the wagon train, apparently under the command of quartermaster Capt. C.H. Gaubert, had started from Florence toward Reynolds' Station. After delivery to Athens, he was to return the empty wagons to Reynolds' Station and continue making round trips until further notice. This seemed to be the answer to the food and forage crisis until the bridges and trestles at the Elk and elsewhere were completed and the tunnel unplanked.[24]

On June 29, McCook, who was in command of the post at Reynolds, was also charged with general superintendence of the wagon transportation of army supplies between Reynolds' Station and the Elk River. He was to do all within his power to push the supplies to the Elk rather than have them accumulate at the station. At that time, it was hoped that the N&D would be ready in another 10 days, thus eliminating the need for wagons.

The same day, Maj. James B. Fry, Chief of Staff under Buell, ordered Col. Thomas Swords, Assistant Quartermaster at Louisville, to ensure that the L&N was prepared at all times to transport forage and rations to Union forces to the south at a rate of 200 tons per day and at a ratio of three-and-a-half of forage to one of rations. Those supplies were to come through Nashville and along the N&D to Reynolds' Station. Then, hopefully in about 10 days, they were to be taken along the N&C which also was still being repaired. On the thirtieth, Col. Swords reported that a lack of rolling stock from Louisville was one of the causes of the shortage of supplies through Nashville. He ordered that trains were to come down from Louisville through Nashville to Reynolds without changing cars in Nashville.

On July 2, Buell ordered Hunton, who was with the 1st Michigan and stationed at Huntsville, to send two companies and an officer to help repair the 23-mile break in the N&D. The men were to replace Companies A and K which had left on June 12 for the N&C. A train was to come on the third to take the men to the Elk. On the fourth, Pvt. Stearns and Companies G and H of the 1st Michigan left camp at daylight and took the rail from Huntsville to Decatur Junction and then north on the N&D to the Elk. On the fifth, they went by foot through the Madry's Ridge tunnel to Pulaski. Stearns wrote, "and the following day we took the road and marched to where we are at present and passed through a tunnell on the railroad that I forgot to speak about before where our men have torn up the track and ties for the purpose of making a wagon road of it as there is no other road that they can pass. The tunnel is about 80 rods in length and as dark as a dungeon in the center." The men groped their way through, some of them falling. Because Buell had recently ordered that the track in the tunnel be planked, it seems that the Federals had planked the tracks in mid–June and then removed the planks and track in early July. A rod is 16.5 feet, which makes the tunnel about a quarter mile long.[25]

On the sixth or seventh, three companies of the 1st Michigan were at work on Richland Creek Bridge No. 1, others at Richland Creek Bridge No. 2 and more at another bridge over Richland Creek, all of which Scott had burned on his way south. Later, two companies would be working at the heavy trestle at the north end of the tunnel. At one of the Richland Creek bridges, the men were raising bents. A bent is a frame shaped like the Greek letter Pi. It is a common component of trestles and is set perpendicular to the track, giving the structure vertical and lateral support. While raising a bent at this site, the coupling of a train above them broke and the train came down the steep slope at a high rate of speed. The men were able to get out of harm's way but two flat cars and a truck (the framework under the cars that has bearings and holds the wheel axles) jumped over an abutment, crushing their work and damaging the cars. On the ninth, Hunton asked Gen. Nelson about the arrival of additional men he had requested to help repair the railroad. He was told that the 31st Indiana Regiment had marched out that morning toward the Elk River.

At the Elk, the Confederates had left the stone abutments and the three stone river piers. The 1st Michigan was making good progress there and had raised seven bents for each of the four spans. Fry emphasized that the very existence of the troops in Huntsville depended on the repairs because they were running short on food. Rations had become scarce to the point that they were being issued one day at a time. On July 10, McCook reported that the bridge over Richland Creek near Reynolds' Station would be completed by the fourteenth, that three companies of the 1st Michigan Engineers were working on the Elk River Bridge and three more would soon be working on the trestle at the north end of the tunnel. Eventually, four companies and a large infantry detail were working on the Elk River Bridge. That project lasted from July 7 to August 3, much longer than the Federals had hoped. It seems that, in addition to the upper surface that supported the track, they built a second surface at the tops of the piers that was used as a footbridge.[26]

On July 8, Brig. Gen. James S. Negley, commander of the Seventh Brigade in the Department of the Ohio, reported, "There is constant danger of the bridges being destroyed; several attempts, one nearly successful, have been made. There are numerous straggling parties of returned cavalry and guerrillas infesting the lower counties, who are constantly committing depredations. As they are aided in a measure by the disloyal citizens it is hardly possible to drive them away." Because of this, Negley assigned companies of the 78th Pennsylvania to Reynolds' Station, Lynnville and Culleoka. On the twenty-ninth, Culleoka suffered its first damage of the war when guerrillas burned the train depot and robbed some local residents. To deal with the attacks, Negley stated that protection of the railroad would require mounted infantry if cavalry could not be distributed along the line. Col. Cummins was commander of the garrison of Union soldiers stationed at Culleoka's Fort Palmer. He ordered all males between the ages of 16 and 60 living within three miles of Culleoka to help build the fortifications and entrenchments that were at each end of the long trestle there.[27]

James S. Negley (1826–1901) was born in Pittsburgh, Pennsylvania. He was brigadier general in the Pennsylvania Militia and raised a brigade of Pennsylvania Volunteers. In November 1862, Negley was appointed Major General of Volunteers and took command of the 8th Division, Army of the Ohio. He played a key role in the Union victory in the Battle of Stones River. Negley was relieved of his division after his apparent ineffective leadership during the Union defeat at Chickamauga but was acquitted of any wrongdoing. Fort Negley, the largest stone inlaid fort built during the war, constructed in Nashville in 1862, was named for him. He was elected to Congress from Pennsylvania and served from 1869 to 1875, then was reelected and served again from 1885 to 1887. After retiring from politics, he was engaged in the railroad industry.

From early June through early August, the 1st Michigan completed the three bridges over Richland Creek, the Tunnel Trestle and the Elk River railroad bridge, built several small bridges, laid three miles of track, and "cleared" the Madry's Ridge tunnel, perhaps meaning that they were assigned the task of removing the planking from the tracks. This allowed trains to once again run from Reynolds' Station with food and forage for Athens and Huntsville.[28]

4

Raids and Stockades

Union commanders were frustrated with the amount of damage and disruption of service the Confederates were causing to the N&D. The encampments they had placed at the crossings were not providing a sufficient level of protection for the troops. Some other form of fortification was needed to protect the men so they could protect the railroad. Wooden stockades were chosen as the next deterrent. On July 12, 1862, federal leaders ordered that a stockade be built as soon as possible at each of the important crossings between Athens and Reynolds' Station. It is reasonable to assume that this stretch of the N&D was selected to receive the first stockades because it had proven critical to supplying the federal forces in northern Alabama and had recently been rebuilt.

Stockades constructed on the N&D and N&C were of at least two types. One was a square wooden fort with four corner bastions large enough to hold a Sibley tent. The bastions could be covered by the tents and used as both guard posts and quarters. One of the locations of this type of stockade would be in Franklin, Tennessee, just west of the railroad bridge over the Harpeth River. This site needed one because Fort Granger had not yet been built to protect the town, the railroad and the railroad bridge. The stockade had a trench around it, with the excavated soil placed against the outer walls of the structure. This was probably the standard design of the square stockades. Another type was a wooden fort in the shape of a cross with arms of equal length. In the first half of 1863, seven railroad bridges along the N&C would be protected by stockades of this type. Work on the stockades below Reynolds' Station began quickly, with several being completed in the next few days. After building them from there to Athens, the troops were to work on additional stockades north of Reynolds.[1]

Revisions to the stockade plan were sometimes necessary. On July 20, it was ordered that, because the guard at the Sulphur Creek Trestle was too small, the existing stockade be replaced with a larger one nearer the trestle. Also, because the stockade at the Mill Creek bridge (three miles south of the Elk River) was too far from its bridge, another one was needed. On the twenty-fifth, Capt. Charles C. Gilbert, acting Inspector-General of the Department of the Cumberland and the Army of the Ohio, traveled from Nashville to Athens on a special train to inspect the defenses at each bridge. Many of the stockades along the N&D had been built before the inspection, though construction continued into August. A few days later, apparently as a result of this inspection and perhaps others, Gen. Buell ordered that stockades be quickly constructed at the other railroad bridges in Tennessee. Gilbert was to select the sites and develop the designs of the stockades. Construction was to be performed by the men in the command of Maj. J.M. Wright, Assistant Adjutant General in Buell's headquarters in Huntsville. The 74th Ohio was in Franklin and headquartered there from early August through early September. It

4. Raids and Stockades

Stockade at N&D Bridge at the Harpeth River, Franklin, Tennessee, 1862–63 (sketch by Henry Mosler, courtesy Williamson County Historical Society).

was under the command of Col. Granville Moody. Companies C and H were on provost guard at Franklin and for some time they were quartered quite comfortably in a hotel. It is likely that this was when the stockade at the Harpeth River railroad bridge was built. The 74th also guarded the railroad between Franklin and Columbia.[2]

While the N&D's stockades were being built, there was plenty of activity along the tracks, especially north of Reynolds where stockades had not yet been constructed. On July 13, a large force of Confederate cavalry was reportedly threatening the bridges between Franklin and Columbia. At this time, the Federals needed to keep the N&D open because they had just suffered significant losses at Murfreesboro and Buell had ordered Gen. Nelson and his division in Athens to travel up the N&D to Nashville and down the N&C to Murfreesboro to guard the rails. On the night of the seventeenth, Confederates again raided the bridges between Franklin and Columbia but did little damage. The next day, Mother Nature inflicted her own destruction when heavy rains washed away the N&D bridges over the Harpeth and Duck Rivers and damaged one of the bridges over Richland Creek. All available bridge workers, including two companies of the 1st Michigan, were sent to work at the Duck. According to Innes, the crew at the Duck often had help from "citizen bridge builders."[3]

On July 20, a train ran off the N&D track 10 miles north of Reynolds' Station. Capt. Ezekiel H. Tatem of the 6th Ohio Infantry died and a woman and several Union soldiers were badly hurt, though the First Engineer was not injured. The train was traveling at 45 miles per hour, which was much too fast, so it was believed that the engineer had intentionally wrecked it. The next day, Gen. William Negley at Columbia reported to Maj. Fry that the telegraph had been cut between Columbia and Franklin and that a large number of men, probably a concentration of the guerrilla band from the lower counties of Tennessee, were threatening Columbia. The guerrillas damaged some bridges or trestles between Reynolds' Station and Columbia, including the one at the Duck River, and attacked several forage trains. Negley asked Fry to send two companies of the 78th Pennsylvania by rail from Nashville to Franklin to deal with the attackers and repair the damage. On the morning of July 22, John Anderson told Buell that he had safely sent a train from Nashville to Franklin. He warned of a party coming to damage the N&D on that day and instructed trains at Columbia to start back north as soon as the bridge over the Duck was rebuilt. There were four trains in Columbia that were stranded there until the bridge was ready and the track to the north safe for travel. Also, in late July, Buell ordered Anderson in Nashville to procure five small engines to carry about 12 men each at high speed to patrol the various railroads, including the N&D.[4]

The garrisons at the stockades were generally replaced about every 30 to 60 days, with a train usually bringing the replacements from Nashville and the old guard taken back there to receive their next assignment. Guards at the stockades were given specific, strict rules to follow. The following were among the guidelines sent out by Maj. Fry in Huntsville on behalf of Gen. Buell on July 20:

> The guard's camp shall be near but not habitually within the stockade. Must keep a barrel of water in the stockade. One or more guard must at all times be on watch. The entire guard shall remain at their posts at all times except when absent for a necessary purpose. When a train approaches, the entire guard shall turn out under arms and remain in line until the train has passed "as this is the time when an attack may be expected." They shall also turn out under arms at daylight. No member of the guard shall ever sleep or spend the night outside the stockade except the sentinels on post.
>
> The commander of the guard shall acquaint himself with the approaches to his position and the country immediately around it and will at all times be on the alert.
>
> The bridges or other points under guard must be defended to the last extremity, and no excuse can be regarded as satisfactory for a surprise, a weak defense or a surrender.
>
> The guards will be visited twice a week at irregular intervals by special inspectors. One of these visits will be to remind them of their duties and to correct irregularities regarding either their duties or the inhabitants of the country, and the other by passing along on rail cars to see if the guards are attentive and vigilant. If the commander of a stockade is deemed to be negligent, he shall be arrested and taken in for trial.
>
> Regimental commanders will visit the posts to inspect all aspects of the operation of the stockade.[5]

By late July, the track between Nashville and Columbia had reopened and many of the stockades on the N&D had been built, seemingly mostly those below Columbia. However, the Confederates didn't care what kind of protection the Federals were putting up. They continued to harass the enemy and slow the procession of federal supply trains, so the railroad did not stay fully open for long.

On August 7, Captain Phillip Roddey and his cavalrymen burned two trestles and cut the telegraph at two points near Decatur. Two-and-a-half miles from Decatur, he captured a train, 123 Federals and 56 small arms, a federal officer was killed, and several federal soldiers wounded.

On the nineteenth, the T&A's *Columbia* was captured on its tracks and taken to Nashville, becoming USMRR engine No. 20, still named the *Columbia*. At about the same time, some of the Union forces in northern Alabama and Middle Tennessee began withdrawing by rail into newly fortified Nashville. Though it is not clear who or what caused it, one of those northbound trains wrecked five miles north of Columbia on August 23. Several Union soldiers were badly hurt and a number of others injured when

4. Raids and Stockades

they jumped from cars that were leaving the track. Another train carrying soldiers of the 19th Illinois Infantry, one of Turchin's regiments, was running north from Decatur Junction. It stopped in Athens on the night of the twenty-seventh. The men set fire to the Niphonia fairgrounds and the east side of the square, perhaps as more punishment for the residents of Athens. The next day, that train was attacked by Confederates six miles north of Pulaski, with at least three Union soldiers killed.[6]

Gen. Gordon Granger (1821–1876) was born in New York state and graduated from the U.S. Military Academy. He worked his way up and was promoted to major general and made commander of the Army of Kentucky. He is probably best known as commander of the Reserve Corps at the Battle of Chickamauga where, without orders, he sensed Maj. Gen. Thomas' dangerous situation and ordered two brigades under Steedman's command to help Thomas retreat to safety. That action helped him get his promotion in late 1863 to commander of the newly formed Fourth Corps in Thomas' Army of the Cumberland. Fort Granger in Franklin, Tennessee, had been under his command and was named for him. Granger remained in the Army in a variety of roles until his death. One was as commander of the District of Texas. On June 19, 1865, he read in Galveston his General Order No. 3 that freed all enslaved people. This established the first Juneteenth celebration.

In early September, attacks on the railroad continued. General Gordon Granger put troops aboard a train in Decatur and sent them north to find Confederate cavalry who were reportedly attacking the railroad. They surprised the culprits at Lynnville while they were burning a freight train and drove them off.[7]

At about that time, Gen. "Bull" Nelson, considered by many of his own men to be a loud-mouth and bully, departed his post in Pulaski on a northbound train loaded with federal troops. He had orders to travel through Nashville and on to Kentucky to help stop Gen. Bragg who was leading his Army of Tennessee into Kentucky. North of Lynnville, with the train starting its way down the slope toward Campbell's Station, the engineer and fireman opened the throttle to the maximum, jumped off the train and disappeared into the woods. The train accelerated until the locomotive and all the cars finally left the tracks and crashed, killing dozens of soldiers, mostly those in the forward cars that struck the engine. Nelson survived because he was at the rear of the train. As it turned out, the engineer and fireman were Confederate sympathizers who wanted to get the better of the general. Nelson was livid and demanded justice. He rounded up the growing crowd of locals at the site and threatened to shoot, hang or dismember all of them. However, he had his orders, caught a passing train and continued northward. Later that month in Louisville, Nelson's temper would be his undoing. He dismissed fellow officer Brig. Gen. Jefferson C. Davis for his lackadaisical behavior in the recent defense of Louisville and insulted him in front of witnesses. Davis shot and killed him.

That fall, bridges along the Nashville-to-Decatur corridor continued to take their hits. By order of Gen. Bragg, the railroad, wagon and Murfreesboro Road bridges in Franklin and numerous other bridges in Middle Tennessee were burned on about November 10. In early December the Confederates blew up the piers of the N&D railroad bridges crossing the Harpeth and Duck Rivers, and perhaps others, that had previously been burned and removed all the rails and destroyed the cross ties between Franklin and Columbia and a little beyond. It seems they damaged so many of the N&D bridges and trestles that much of the railroad was not operating from October 1862 through February 1863. Evidence of this, and that the Federals did not rebuild the structures until late winter, is that there are no references in Appendix D to federal guards being on the railroad during that period. Though not related to the N&D, it is interesting to note that in late 1862 travel along the M&C through Huntsville to Decatur Junction and up to Athens on the N&D was aided by the loan of a locomotive and cars from the Western and Atlantic Railroad. The engine was brought by steamboat from Bridgeport down the Tennessee River.[8]

Nashville was a key transportation and supply center and needed better fortification than it had. The Federals started construction of Fort Negley on St. Cloud Hill, just south of the center of town, on August 6, 1862. The fort was named for Gen. James Scott Negley who was commander of the 7th Brigade in the Department of the Ohio. It was occupied in October and completed on December 7 of that year. When finished, it was the largest inland masonry fort built during the Civil War, covering more than four acres. After its completion, two lesser forts and a heavy blockhouse were constructed on hilltops not far from the fort. Nashville was then the most heavily defended city except for Washington, D.C.[9]

For some time, Forrest had been threatening to again burn the recently rebuilt Franklin bridges that led to Nashville. He did just that on January 24. As they did numerous times during the war, the Confederates again took temporary control of Franklin, but Gen. Davis—probably the same Jefferson Davis who killed Nelson—took the town back for the Federals on February 2. Later that month, John Anderson organized a force and was repairing the bridges between Nashville and Franklin. He also repaired the N&D's Duck River bridge which had two spans of 100 feet and two of 200 feet. Anderson then repaired the track and culvert at Hurricane Creek, five miles below Columbia, and the long trestle at Culleoka and rebuilt the bridge over Robertson Fork Creek, one over Richland Creek and perhaps others. The Federals were finally able to reopen the road in March.[10]

On February 12, a detachment of the 1st Michigan and some infantrymen were ordered to work on several of the N&D's bridges. They were sent to a camp on the Rains property two miles south of Nashville. This would be their base of operation for rebuilding bridges to the south. Each morning the builders would take their construction train to wherever their job site was, work all day and ride back to camp at night. Some of the men would remain at camp during the day to get out timber and frame the bents that were then sent by rail to the crossing where the builders were working. Wood for the bridges first came from trees near the camp and then from trees near the track, progressively farther down the line. Once the men were working a significant distance from camp, the felled trees had to be hauled back to camp on cars. On the thirteenth, 13 men from each of five companies of the 1st Michigan were sent to their first site. They rode cars to two miles south of Brentwood to rebuild the small bridge across the Little Harpeth River and replace about 330 feet of track that had been torn up. That bridge was completed the next day.[11]

On the sixteenth, the men started work on the bridge over the Harpeth River at Franklin. Their experiences with that structure provide insight into the types of difficulties they could have in building bridges and trestles. This project became quite a challenge, primarily because the water was high and fast. They cut and made up the timber for the bridge, waiting for the track to be repaired to Franklin so a train could deliver the timber to the site. On the nineteenth, with trains coming through, the men loaded trusses onto the rail cars at the camp. Kimball wrote in his diary, "Co's D, C, & H went to Franklin on the cars but did not work much. Fired at dogs, rabbits, etc., from the train. Very windy at night." They intended to raise the trusses into place, but it was difficult because the water was so high. One man almost drowned trying to swim his horse across the river. The next day, the same companies returned to the site and were able to do some work on the foundation at the bank but could not lift any trusses into position. Per Kimball's diary, "The same Cos went again. Capt Fox (ordered) no guns to be fired but by some means mine went off at the sight of a rabbit when Fox said he would arrest the man that fired the next gun." On Saturday, February 21, they got only one truss up before heavy rains stopped their work. The cars went back for more timber and did not return until the twenty-fourth when the rain had stopped, and the water was down. They found that the truss they had raised on Saturday had fallen and spent the day raising that piece plus three more from the water. Work continued on the twenty-fifth, but another rain soaked the ropes they were hoisting with, making it hard to put the trusses up. Heavy rains on the twenty-sixth kept them in camp. The next day, they found several trusses knocked down by the current. On the twenty-eighth, rain again kept them in camp. Upon returning on March 2, they found three more bents down, one having been destroyed. The following day, they got the third bent up and put on stringers. On the fourth, they got up the second tier of bents and put on some stringers. The next day, they finished the bridge structure and planked it over so that troops and cavalry that had been waiting could pass. With the weather and river finally cooperating, they removed the planking on March 6, laid the rails and ran a train over it that afternoon. On Sunday, March 8, they went to the Episcopal Church as they often did, then planked the bridge again so infantry and cavalry could use it. After duties elsewhere in Middle Tennessee, the men broke down camp on March 18.[12]

Down the track in southern Tennessee and northern Alabama, more work on the bridges and trestles was underway. During March, Sulphur Creek Trestle was being rebuilt and two spans were being put in at Richland Creek Bridge No. 4, below Pulaski. Once those projects were completed, it appeared that the N&D would be open once again.[13]

Earl Van Dorn (1820–1863) was born in Mississippi. A great-nephew of Andrew Jackson, he graduated from West Point near the bottom of his class. He replaced Jefferson Davis as major general and commander of the Mississippi State forces when Davis was elected president of the Confederacy. Van Dorn entered the Confederate Army as Colonel of infantry and held several positions before being ordered to join the Army of Tennessee. He set up headquarters at White Hall near Spring Hill, Tennessee, and then at the home of Martin Cheairs. On May 7, 1863, Van Dorn, who was known as a womanizer, was shot dead by Dr. James B. Peters, the husband of Jessie McKissack Peters with whom Van Dorn had been "spending too much time." Peters caught them together and at gunpoint made Van Dorn promise he would write a full confession. When the doctor came back and received the paper, he saw that there were numerous omissions that Van Dorn said he could not write because they would ruin his career. After Van Dorn ordered Peters out of his office, Peters shot him in the head. Peters escaped and was arrested in Mississippi by Confederate authorities for the murder of a Confederate officer but was never brought to trial. Van Dorn's body was buried in Alabama at the graveyard of his wife's family. However, at the request of his sister, his remains were returned to Mississippi and buried next to their father at Wintergreen Cemetery in Port Gibson.

Maj. Gen. Earl Van Dorn and his cavalry were at Tupelo, Mississippi, when he was ordered to join the Army of Tennessee in Middle Tennessee. On February 22, he had arrived at Columbia with his command, which included Forrest with Capt. Samuel L. Freeman's battery of six guns. Van Dorn soon moved his men to a new headquarters at Spring Hill. This advance by the Confederates allowed them to gain control of the N&D through Maury County and gave them access to abundant sources of food and forage. Confederate Commissary-General Lucius B. Northrop had ordered that the N&D be repaired from Athens to Columbia, including a rebuilt Elk River Bridge. Northrop maintained his push to keep the railroad operating from Decatur to Columbia so he could have continued access to the crops in Maury County. The Confederates kept the road open for their use until at least July and had also taken part of the N&C. These combined actions supported the movement of troops for Gen. Bragg and helped transport to him the food and other supplies that he needed. When control of the N&D in that region was lost to the Federals that summer, the retreating Confederates burned the bridges they had recently built. The Confederate presence that spring is reflected in Appendix D by the absence of federal troops guarding the railroad south of Columbia during those months.[14]

The near disaster at Perryville and the lethargic pursuit of Bragg's retreating forces convinced the Lincoln administration that Buell needed to be replaced. Maj. Gen. William S. Rosecrans was chosen, partly because of his engineering background. Rosecrans thought the failure of his predecessor was linked to his inability to establish and maintain transportation infrastructure to support the army. He was not going to make the same mistake. Rosecrans faced a severe shortage of men capable of maintaining his supply lines in the rugged back country of Tennessee. His was going to be an army on the move and to move he needed engineers. The 1st Michigan was the only dedicated engineer asset on hand but was not enough. Rebuffed in his calls for engineer reinforcements because it would literally take an act of Congress to raise them, he formulated his own plan. On November 3, 1862, he issued General Order No. 3 calling for the formation of an "engineer corps" from the assets already on hand. He ordered 3,000 skilled craftsmen and artisans be hand-picked from his army's infantry regiments to spend the next 18 months in the new Pioneer Brigade. Each company of every regiment of infantry in his army was to detail two men. The men were to be selected specifically for their ability as craftsmen and were to be well equipped, and the most promising lieutenants and non-commissioned officers were assigned to lead them.

The regimental commanders did not like to lose some of their best men and many of the soldiers did not want to leave their units. The commanders sometimes considered assigning their malcontents to the Pioneers but were warned not to do so. Eventually, most of the assignees quickly adapted to their new role, favoring it over infantry duty, and were soon proud of the distinct crossed hatchet sleeve insignia of the brigade. The men trained in Nashville for a month and James St. Clair Morton was commissioned to lead them.

The Pioneer Brigade started their new duty on December 7. Their job, like the 1st Michigan, was to perform the tasks of military engineering. Typically, they were armed soldiers who went ahead of a marching force to prepare the route and the battle ground, improve the rail lines and construct bridges and hasty breastworks. They did not usually travel with a pontoon train. As with the 1st Michigan, there were problems from the start. Division quartermasters were to make immediate requisitions to fill the needs of the men in the Brigade. However, it didn't work that way. They were slow to get what they needed. Originally, smaller groups of the men were to be brought together only when needed but this proved impractical. Instead, three battalions, each with 1,000 tradesmen, supported Rosecrans' three corps. Formation of the Pioneers was an innovative solution to his problem, a command decision that would pay off handsomely.

> James St. Clair Morton (1829–1864) was born in Philadelphia and was an assistant engineer on construction of forts near Charleston, South Carolina, including Fort Sumter. He was appointed by the Department of the Interior as chief engineer of the Washington Monument, then in May 1862 was appointed chief engineer of the Department of the Ohio. In August 1862, he began construction of Fort Negley in Nashville. It was built by more than 2,700 impressed runaway enslaved people and free Blacks. Six to eight hundred of them died during the project and only about 300 were paid for their work. In October 1862, Morton became Chief of Engineers of the Army of the Cumberland and was put in command of the Pioneer Brigade under Rosecrans. He fought at Tullahoma and Chickamauga in 1863, made tactical errors at both places and was relieved of his commands. Morton was denied a transfer. He requested and, in November 1863, received a reduction in rank to the Regular Army rank of major, the only known incident of a general volunteering to reduce his rank. Morton was supervising engineer on the construction of defenses at Nashville until January 1864 and chief engineer in the Ninth Corps under Gen. Burnside. He was shot and killed at the Second Battle of Petersburg in June 1864.

The Pioneers would make a name for themselves at Murfreesboro. Adding to their reputation as valuable engineers, they made a bold stand there against the assault of Brig. Gen. McCown's Confederate division. The success came at a high price, however, with the casualty list reporting 12 Pioneers dead and another 23 wounded. The unit would continue its valuable service until recognized as an independent unit. Oddly, the status they had sought spelled the end of the brigade. Being officially recognized as engineers came with three stipulations: a new regiment would be formed of Veteran Volunteer Engineers, only the three-year men were allowed to reenlist in the new status for the duration of the war and duty would be confined to fort construction in Tennessee. The options gradually drained away the strength of the brigade until they were disbanded on September 10, 1864.

Fort Granger would be the primary fortification at Franklin. It was built between March and May of 1863 on Figuer's Bluff overlooking the N&D and the north bank of the Harpeth River. White soldiers and former enslaved people provided the manual labor. As of March 11, Sergeant Silas Jones, Company C, 125th Ohio Volunteer Infantry, had on his roll 250 able African Americans equipped with pick, ax and shovel. A Contraband Camp for these men was a few hundred yards north of the fort. Capt. Merrill designed the fort and the other defenses at Franklin and the Pioneer Brigade oversaw their construction. Among the features of the fort were two tree trunks used as spy trees. Roper's Knob and several small artillery positions supported the fort. The fort allowed the Union to command the critical railroad bridge, Franklin itself and the northern and southern approaches to the town. It was part of a large military site, reaching from the fields just west of Franklin Pike to present-day Highway 96 East, the site of the bridge that Bragg had burned. The area extended back from the river about two-thirds of a mile. The site contained camps, drill fields, sentry posts, corrals, stables and warehouses. Another feature of the area was the N&D underpass that still stands near present-day Liberty Pike. By the end of April, about 8,000 Federals, including approximately 2,700 cavalry, were stationed there. The Federals had a pontoon bridge nearby and several fords along the river, to the east and west, could be crossed easily when the river was not high. Presumably, the stockade at the railroad bridge was taken down after completion of the fort.[15]

In mid–March, while Fort Granger was being constructed, the 1st Michigan started work on Fortress Rosecrans in Murfreesboro where Morton was supervising the work of the Pioneers. When completed in late June, the earthworks fort covered 200 acres and was the largest earthen fort built during the war.

There was competition, sometimes healthy and sometimes not, between the 1st Michigan and the Pioneers. Morton fought in vain to have the 1st Michigan merged into his command. It did not help that he and Innes had a dislike for each other. The competition became serious during construction of Fort Rosecrans and surfaced again in July 1863 at the 470-foot-long Elk River Bridge on the N&C that the retreating Confederates had destroyed. Innes promised Rosecrans that he and his men could rebuild it in seven to 10 days, while Morton said it would take six to eight weeks if the groups merged under his command. On July 9, Rosecrans took Innes up on his bold "promise" and let him do the work. To the chagrin of Morton, Innes completed the bridge on July 18 after only eight days of work. What made the outcome even more upsetting for Morton was that Rosecrans had created several new flags, one for an engineer group. Morton had it before the bridge at the Elk was built but Innes got it afterward as a reward. On August 11, Rosecrans appointed Innes to replace John Anderson in taking control of the railroads in the Department of the Cumberland, while retaining command of the 1st Michigan. Innes was superintendent of the railroads until at least late October.[16]

Though the Federals had taken control of the N&D in early 1862, they did not maintain control of the entire road all of the time. In addition to the times when the Confederates had damaged and shut down portions of the N&D, there were periods when they controlled large sections of the railroad. As previously stated, one of these times was from early 1863 until early July when Van Dorn and Forrest took over a portion of south-central Tennessee and that part of the N&D. The months of March through June 1863 witnessed several significant engagements involving these Confederates and the Federals.

On the afternoon of March 4, Col. John Coburn, commander of the 1st Brigade, Department of the Ohio, and his 3,000 troops left Franklin to do a reconnaissance of the countryside around Spring Hill. He had five regiments of infantry, 600 cavalry and six guns. The following day, they encountered Van Dorn who was moving southward about midway between Franklin and Spring Hill and had captured Thompson's Station. Where the N&D ran near Columbia Pike, Van Dorn and two regiments totaling about 1,000 dismounted Confederate cavalrymen, including the 11th (Holman's) Tennessee Cavalry, drove most of the Federals northward. Brig. Gen. William "Red" Jackson's cavalry made a frontal assault while Forrest swept around the Federals' rear to cut off Coburn's potential retreat on the road to the north. Three-and-a-half regiments of Federals were left on a hill just west of Thompson's Station. During the conflict, Lt. Col. Edward Bloodgood and part of 22nd Wisconsin Infantry which he commanded broke off from the engagement and moved to the Union rear. It is not clear whether he was ordered to do so. Forrest attacked the hill, got a surrender and took prisoners. He also captured Coburn's wagon train. Fierce fighting went on for about five hours before Coburn surrendered.

During the fight, the 92nd Illinois Infantry was near Nashville and the 96th Illinois Infantry was at Nashville. Learning of the engagement at Thompson's Station, the 92nd Illinois and 84th and 115th Indiana were piled into and onto cattle cars headed south to support Coburn. Later that day, the 96th Illinois and 40th Ohio Infantries were railed southward, as well. Because the second train was being pulled by a worn engine and struggling to climb the grades, it took four to five hours for it to travel the 17 miles. Both trains apparently arrived too late to make a difference. Van Dorn lost about 350 killed, wounded or missing. About 1,200 to 1,300 Federals were captured and 300 to 500 killed or wounded. Two famous stories related to the engagement are that 17-year-old Alice Thompson ran into the open waving a Confederate flag, encouraging the men in gray to protect the town, and Roderick, one of Forrest's favorite mounts, was killed when it broke free and ran onto the battlefield.[17]

Brentwood was a source of food and livestock for the Union Army. It is interesting to note that, by now, the road from Nashville, through Brentwood to Franklin had been macadamized. This means that several layers of same-size crushed stone had been laid and compacted to form a relatively durable road surface. The Federals had two positions near the town, both under the command of Lt. Col. Edward Bloodgood of the 22nd Wisconsin Infantry. There was a post atop the hill just west of the town center. Also, a stockade known as Camp Brentwood was just south of Brentwood at the railroad bridge over the Little Harpeth River. Brentwood Station was on the railroad in town. In mid–March, Van Dorn considered the garrison at Brentwood to be vulnerable and gave Forrest permission to attack. On the twenty-fourth, Forrest captured a federal courier who had a dispatch for the commander in Franklin asking for help at the Little Harpeth. That day, Col. James Starnes, a doctor in command of the Second Tennessee Cavalry Brigade, cut the telegraph, tore up track near Mallory Station, just south of Brentwood, and cut off any retreat. The next morning of the twenty-fifth, a message from the stockade warned the post that Starnes and some of the 10th Tennessee were about to attack. Bloodgood held the post with about 500 men. He knew he needed help from Franklin but could not request it because the telegraph had been cut. Forrest came and demanded surrender but was refused, so he surrounded the post, prepared to attack and then got a surrender from Bloodgood, who was later court-martialed for cowardice, convicted and reinstated. For some time, the 22nd would be relegated to garrison duty.[18]

The large stockade at Camp Brentwood was under the command of Capt. Elisha Bassett of Company B, 19th Michigan Infantry. Forrest, with General Frank Armstrong, Starnes and their 5,000 men and artillery, moved to the south and surrounded the camp. A few weeks earlier, Bassett had lost his nerve under fire at Thompson's Station and deserted. This was not properly reported, however, and he was given command of the stockade. With him were 70 men of his company and about 160 men who were left there after the March 5 battle at Thompson's Station, of whom about 100 were sick and feeble. The Confederates fired a few rifle rounds, then Capt. Freeman fired a shell into the stockade and quickly got a white flag of surrender. Per Forrest's report of April 1, 1863, "With the Fourth Mississippi Cavalry and the Tenth Tennessee and the pieces of artillery, I moved on the stockade at the bridge across Harpeth River, about two miles south of Brentwood. After getting position and firing one gun, they surrendered. We captured 275 prisoners, 11 wagons, 3 ambulances, with all their arms and equipments." Forrest then destroyed the bridge over the Little Harpeth and all the tents and supplies that could not quickly be moved, then headed south and crossed the Harpeth near Franklin. On March 27, Granger ordered infantry, cavalry and artillery to the stockade to secure it. He also remarked that additional forces would be made available in the future if needed. Bassett was among those captured. He was imprisoned at Libby Prison and exchanged later that year. When he was released, he was immediately arrested and later dishonorably discharged. Interestingly, he had been one of the most prominent citizens in his hometown of Allegan, Michigan. Even after his discharge, he was respected enough to be elected mayor back home. Bassett was apparently a better politician than soldier. He died in 1865 from consumption—the deadly stage of tuberculosis—which he had apparently contracted while in prison.[19]

Soon after the victory at Brentwood, Van Dorn learned from his intelligence that Franklin should be vulnerable because most of the Union forces had withdrawn from Fort Granger. At this time, there seem to have been at least three depots at Franklin. The T&A had passenger and freight depots there and the Federals still had their supply depot on the north side of the Harpeth. Because the wagon bridge was not in-place, the Federals also had a pontoon bridge over the Harpeth near the fort, as they typically did while occupying Franklin. Early on April 10, Van Dorn, Forrest and about 9,000 Confederate cavalry and mounted infantry plus two regiments of infantry moved toward Franklin. Forrest came up Lewisburg Pike while Van Dorn and Jackson's divisions entered the town on Columbia Pike. Gen. Granger knew about the Confederates, however, and was ready for them with 2,700 cavalry and 5,000 infantry. At that time, the main works of Fort Granger had not been completed and the outworks had not yet been started. The Confederates attacked the fort but were repulsed. At about noon, Maj. Gen. David S. Stanley engaged in combat with Van Dorn's cavalry and infantry just south of Franklin on Columbia Highway in what can fittingly be referred to as "The First Battle of Franklin." Stanley and a brigade from the Fourth U.S. Cavalry Regiment crossed the Harpeth River behind Van Dorn at Hughes Ford at about 2:30 and captured Captain Freeman's Tennessee Battery on Lewisburg Pike but lost the guns when Forrest counterattacked. Van Dorn ordered a withdrawal after losing 19 dead, including Freeman, and several wounded.[20]

> David S. Stanley (1828–1902) was born in Cedar Valley, Ohio. He graduated from West Point, was engaged in several Civil War battles and quickly rose to brigadier general, then to major general. Stanley led the Union cavalry in the Tullahoma Campaign. He was commander under Sherman of the Fourth Corps in the Army of the Cumberland during the Atlanta Campaign, then took command of that Corps. Sherman sent him and his Fourth Corps to Tennessee to deal with Hood. Stanley was wounded in the neck at Franklin and, because he led one of his brigades in a critical counterattack there, President Grover Cleveland later presented him with the Medal of Honor. After the war, Stanley stayed in the military. He commanded the Yellowstone Expedition of 1873, exploring several unmapped areas which led to settlement of the region. He retired in 1892.

On June 3, Forrest realized that Gen. Granger had moved his headquarters and a large part of his garrison from Franklin to Triune. Col. John P. Baird, in command at

Fort Granger, and his 85th Indiana regiment were left at the fort. The next day, Forrest came up from Spring Hill with Gen. Armstrong's and Stearn's brigades and two batteries to determine the federal strength at Franklin. Starnes came up Columbia Pike and Armstrong up Lewisburg Pike. At 3 p.m., they entered town on Carter's Creek Pike. Fighting broke out with some resistance coming from Fort Granger. Forrest drove the outnumbered Federals back, scattering them through town and pushing them across the river into the fort. He sent a flag of truce demanding surrender. Seeing at the fort a signal flag that he mistakenly thought was one of surrender, Forrest approached the fort but a Union officer warned him off. Forrest and a detachment of two companies responded by taking control of the town for several hours. They broke into the jail and released several Confederate prisoners, burned a depot—seemingly the temporary federal depot on the north side of the river—and raided some of the sutler's stores. Gould and his three pieces of light artillery on Carter's Creek Pike drew fire from the fort away from Forrest. That worked for some time, but the artillery at Fort Granger, federal cavalry and Col. Ferdinand Van Derveer with his 35th Ohio Infantry drove Forrest from town. Forrest's wounded and the stolen supplies were taken to Columbia.[21]

On June 7, 12 Confederates returned to Brentwood, cutting the telegraph and partially burning the railroad bridge over the Little Harpeth. The bridge was repaired the next day when, just before sunset, another memorable, morbid event began to unfold. Two strangers who had left Columbia the day before rode up to the gate at Fort Granger and were escorted to the headquarters. They introduced themselves to Col. Baird as Col. Lawrence W. Auton, Acting Inspector-General, and Major George Dunlop, Assistant Inspector of the Western troops. The two men produced a pass and a War Department order supposedly from Gen. Garfield, Chief of Staff. They said they were on an inspection tour of the western army and had come from Rosecrans at Murfreesboro. They claimed to have been surprised by a Confederate party near Murfreesboro and barely escaped. The two were allowed to give the fort a thorough inspection, dined with some officers and stated that they needed to go to Nashville for the night but needed money. Col. Baird prepared their passes to the city and gave them some money. However, the Federals were becoming suspicious, so Baird reviewed their papers. The documents were very well written and detailed. Auton and Dunlop departed with the cash, the pass, the password and the countersign. As they were leaving the fort, Col. Lewis Watkins of the 6th Kentucky Cavalry arrived and recognized Auton. He asked Baird who they were. When Baird replied that they were Union inspectors, Watkins stated that he recognized one as a former army officer who was now in the Confederate service. Baird ordered Watkins and his orderly to pursue the two "inspectors." Upon catching up with them near the picket line, Watkins told them that Baird wanted to see them before they got to Nashville; no reason was given. The two agreed to return and did not resist. They all returned to the fort and went to Watkin's tent on the grounds where they were guarded. Watkins went to the fort where Baird asked him to bring in the two men. A signal was sent to Granger at Triune but with the foggy air the telescope man at the signal station at Triune could not fully understand what was being transmitted. He was able to signal back that Lt. Wharton would come from Triune, about 15 miles away, to investigate.[22]

In the meantime, Gen. Rosecrans at Murfreesboro was informed of the situation. Then word was telegraphed to Gen. Garfield who replied at about 11 p.m. that no such men were in the Union Army. Baird replied to Garfield that a hanging would be appropriate. At midnight, Garfield sent a dispatch ordering Col. Baird to convene a court-martial at once and to hang them if they were found to be spies. Upon further examination of Auton and Dunlop, it was found that their swords and caps had their names on them, followed by "C.S.A." The men had no federal information or maps on them. Auton turned out to be Lt. Col. William Orton Williams, Chief of Artillery, about 32 years old, and Dunlop was Lt. Walter Gibson Peters, about 26 years of age. Both were on the staff of Gen. Bragg, commanding the Confederate forces in Tennessee. It turned out that the two were cousins and that Williams was a first cousin of Gen. Robert E. Lee. At dawn, they were found guilty of spying but denied being spies. Baird was now beginning to regret asking for a hanging. He asked Garfield to change his mind but that did not happen because of concern that they may know something important that they could later tell the Confederates. A cherry tree, about 40 yards up Liberty Creek from the river and 20 yards east of the creek, was prepared for the hanging. The men's request to be shot, instead, was denied. They were given paper and pen to write a few letters. One was to the lady to whom Williams was engaged. After the hanging and being pronounced dead, their bodies were placed in two plain coffins with the ropes still around their necks and buried in a Franklin cemetery. Col. Watkins ordered, however, that the bodies be exhumed so that the ropes could be removed. Their remains were later taken by friends to their respective homes in Virginia and the tree was cut down after the war. The specific mission of the two spies is still not clear.

A discussion of the N&D would not be complete without some detailed information about what the railroad transported. Some of the available records regarding transportation from Nashville via the T&A for the period of March through June 1863 still exist. Quartermaster Simon Perkins was at Nashville at this time. Several different types of documents were created under his direction. They included orders that particular items be transported, receipts for materials and supplies that were left with the Quartermaster's Office to be subsequently transported and travel stubs for people and horses. Those records indicate that the destination along the T&A for that time period was almost always Franklin and occasionally Brentwood. Nearly every day, at least 10 soldiers were transported on the railroad to Franklin. In April and May, the average number of troops traveling per day was about 20, with five days of 50 to 80 troops each. The busiest days were June 12 and 13, when 210 and 393 men were transported, respectively. Occasionally, guards would travel with their prisoners. There is reference to one female nurse traveling to Franklin. During these months in early and mid–1863, train travel must not have been allowed past Franklin because of the presence of Van Dorn and Forrest in the Spring Hill area.

On many days, oats, hay and corn were sent to Franklin, as well as food for the troops. The food items included hams, pork, bacon, potatoes, beans, peas, rice, mixed vegetables, onions, grits, peaches, pickles, hominy, bread, flour, meal, sugar, coffee, tea, molasses, vinegar, salt, pepper and whiskey. Nearly every day, a train delivered to Franklin some of the following: sanitary or medical supplies, stationery, soap, candles, blankets, tents, chests, desks, tables, stools, kettles, mess pans, buckets, coal, oil, lime, tools, pulley blocks, rope, litters, boxes and shooks (disassembled boxes), horses, carts, ambulances, horse and mule shoes, jockey sticks, ordnance, ammunition and siege guns. On three days in April, shipments totaling over 12,000 feet of lumber were made to Franklin. Interestingly, the records show no reference to shipment of clothing or shoes. The U.S. Sanitary Commission was responsible for sending the sanitary supplies. It was a private relief agency for the Union Army that had thousands of volunteers.

The commission operated about 30 soldiers' homes, lodges or rests and raised money to support the soldiers.[23]

> Simon F. Perkins, Jr. (1838–1911), received his commission as Captain and Assistant Quartermaster of Volunteers at age 23. Quartermaster Meigs ordered him to Nashville where he was in charge of forage and fuel. Perkins was later depot quartermaster at Stevenson, Alabama, and then Quartermaster for the Headquarters of Maj. Gen. Rosecrans in the Army of the Cumberland. In 1863, he was quartermaster and then disbursing officer at the Nashville depot. Gen. Simon Perkins, Capt. Perkins' grandfather, was one of Akron, Ohio's founders. In 1815, he had purchased 1,300 acres of land for $2.08 per acre that would become most of downtown Akron. In 1825, he and another man donated 100 lots of land to the state, thus founding the City of Akron and making their land much more valuable.

Large quantities of the supplies sent to Franklin were stored, at least temporarily, in the federal depot there that had been built in early 1862. The records of Quartermaster Perkins provide some insights. They show that there were no deliveries to Franklin on March 26–28. This seems to be due to Forrest's burning of the bridge over the Little Harpeth on the twenty-fifth. The papers also show that there were trains to Franklin most days in June, with an absence on back-to-back days only twice. However, there was no rail activity during the seven consecutive days of June 4–10. It is a near certainty that this pause in deliveries was related to Forrest's burning of a depot in Franklin on June 4. Because Forrest would have been more motivated to burn the Union depot than the T&A freight depot, it is likely that the depot he burned was, indeed, the Union supply depot. It appears that this depot was rebuilt by June 10 because deliveries resumed on the eleventh. Also, Confederates had again burned the bridge over the Little Harpeth River on June 7, but it was rebuilt the same day or the next.[24]

One might wonder if the period of March through June 1863 was typical. Relative to other times during the Civil War, the period does not appear to have experienced an exceptional amount of activity on the T&A between Nashville and Franklin, except perhaps related to the construction of Fort Granger. Ignoring any major troop transport for Fort Granger and except for the first half of December 1864 when Gen. John Bell Hood's presence prevented federal trains from coming south of Nashville and times when a bridge was out between Nashville and Franklin, the T&A might have been about as busy during the other months between April 1862 and the end of the war as it was during those four.

Other records for the T&A from September 13 through October 10, 1863, indicate that a number of different locomotives were running up and down the line. Engines departing Nashville usually pulled one baggage car, one to three flat cars, one to two box cars and sometimes a passenger car, an average of about five cars, not including the tender car. The *Franklin, Springfield, Carrol, Rosecrans, Williamson, N. Alabama, Nashville, Union* and others did the pulling, as well as steam dummies. Steam dummies looked like passenger cars but were equipped with steam engines for propulsion. They were normally used in cities because it was thought that the look of a passenger car would not frighten horses as much as a typical locomotive. They were seldom taken long distances but were useful for track inspection or transport of officers. The October 10 record shows 10 box cars going from Carter's Creek Station to Nashville. On most days, there was a morning train that ran from Nashville to Franklin and sometimes to Smith's or Carter's Creek Station, and an afternoon train to Nashville from Franklin and sometimes from Smith's or Carter's Creek Station. Trains did not travel south of Carter's Creek at that time because of the nearly perpetual damage to track at and below the Duck River.[25]

On May 29, 1863, a request had been made to remove the 12 miles of T&A track between Columbia and Mount Pleasant for use on the N&C between Chattanooga and Tullahoma and in Naval Construction. Approval was given on June 25 and, presumably, the track was removed soon thereafter. It was not replaced until 1865.

The months of July through October saw continued significant damage to the track and bridges along the N&D. In late August, Union Maj. Gen. Alexander McCook's First Corps of the Army of the Ohio was rebuilding bridges between Franklin and the Duck River, including the one at the Duck. It is not clear how or when those bridges were damaged. In September, Companies A, B, F and L of the 1st Michigan were working on the Harpeth River bridge and several other companies were at the Elk. By October, probably primarily as a result of attacks by the Confederates, all or almost all of the bridges between the Tennessee River and the Duck River, including the Elk, were again in ruins.

In late August, Col. Daniel McCook, Jr., at Columbia was looking to Gen. Granger for help with some of the local residents who were actively engaged on behalf of the Confederacy. Apparently, Granger had dealt with similar folks in Franklin and Pulaski. A Mrs. Hunter on Carter's Creek Pike had stated that she helped burn some of the bridges before and would do it again. McCook was suggesting that she and her daughter be "Grangerized" and sent south of the Tennessee River. With three McCooks having now been discussed, it is fitting to reflect on two Ohio brothers, Daniel and Dr. John J. McCook. Those men and a combined 13 of their sons were involved in the war, becoming one of the most prolific families in American military history. Six of the 15 attained the rank of brigadier general or higher.[26]

On November 15, it was reported that guerrillas were active between Lynnville and Columbia. The next day, the telegraph wire from Decatur to Columbia was broken in a number of places. It was expected to be repaired in a few days if the required materials were readily available. The seemingly constant damage to the railroad and telegraph was causing great inconvenience and accumulating great expense for the Federals. Keeping the telegraph in operation was virtually impossible but they were ready to provide better protection for their expensive, new bridges and trestles.

5

Dodge and Boomer Rebuild Trestles and Bridges

Gen. Grenville M. Dodge, the second highlighted builder, commanded the Left Wing of the Sixteenth Corps. His division had been at Corinth, Mississippi, and moved north to be attached to Gen. William Tecumseh Sherman's army which was marching from West Tennessee into Middle Tennessee on their way to join Gen. Grant in Chattanooga. On October 23, 1863, Sherman had taken over for Grant as Commander of the Army of the Tennessee. The N&D was to carry some of the supplies in support of the federal troops there but was open only from Nashville to the confluence of Rutherford and Carter's Creeks. It needed a large number of new bridges and trestles and some track repaired all the way to Decatur Junction as soon as possible.

> Dodge (1831–1916) was born in Danvers (now called Peabody), Massachusetts. At age 14, in the early years of American railroad development, he worked in railroad surveying and construction. He would have a lifelong passion for the railroad and the nation's westward growth. Dodge attended Norwich University to focus on civil engineering and military service, then worked as a surveyor and assistant engineer for railroads and was in charge of the first railroad surveys across Iowa. In 1854, he settled in Council Bluffs, Iowa, across the Missouri River from Omaha, Nebraska. He performed surveys to the Rocky Mountains, this leading him to become a national expert in terrain and railroad routing. In 1859, Dodge met young lawyer Abraham Lincoln whom he would influence to later sign the Pacific Railroad Act of 1864 which called for Council Bluffs to be the eastern terminus of the Transcontinental Railroad. He joined the Union Army, and, in July 1863, Sherman made him commander of the Left Wing of his Sixteenth Army Corps in the Army of the Tennessee. Dodge was promoted to major general in June 1864 and commanded the Corps during Sherman's Atlanta Campaign against Gen. Hood. He finished the war by replacing Rosecrans as commander of the Department of the Missouri. By that time, Dodge had become an effective lobbyist, especially for railroad interests. He resigned from the military in May 1866.[1]

On November 4, John Anderson in Nashville reported to General Grant: "Nashville and Decatur Railroad is in working order to a point within six miles of Columbia. It will be next to impossible to make trestle stand during the winter in the streams this side of Duck River. In Richland Creek, which the road crosses five times between Columbia and Athens, trestles will not stand the freshets of winter. There are 18 bridges between this point and Athens, all of which I understand have been destroyed. Would it not be better to contract with reliable parties to make and erect permanent bridges at the earliest day on the line?" The Federals wanted the N&D in top working order, which meant having trestles and high-quality bridges where they needed to be.[2]

The next day, Gen. Grant was planning to have Dodge repair the railroad and ordered his command to report to Athens. On about November 8, Dodge was crossing the Tennessee River at Eastport, Mississippi. Grant wanted better bridges built on the N&D and preferred that they be framed in the North and sent south.

On the sixth, John Anderson sent to Lucius B. Boomer in Chicago and two other contractors a list of bridges that needed work, asking for bids. On November 15, Anderson reported to Grant that only Boomer, who is the third highlighted builder, had bid on the job because he was the only one who could procure the needed lumber in the required time. His bid averaged $63 per linear foot, and he proposed that, if not impeded by the government, the enemy or weather, he would pay $75 for every day over 100 that it took him to complete the work or be paid $200 per day for every day under 90. It is not clear what the terms of the approved contract were.[3]

On November 10, Dodge was ordered to stop at Pulaski to evaluate the bridges and trestles along the N&D and start making the necessary repairs. He was to be supplied from Columbia. In addition to the railroad work, Dodge was to hold Gen. Grant's right, picketing the Tennessee River on the north side with Confederates on the south. The 81st Ohio Infantry with about 10,000 men and 8,000 animals had come with Dodge from Corinth to be stationed with him, but had not brought most of their tents. With winter approaching

Gen. Grenville M. Dodge (Library of Congress).

Lucius B. Boomer (Lake Forest College, Chicago, Illinois).

and needing good shelter, many of the men constructed wooden huts from any available planking. When their tents finally arrived, they used them as roofing for the huts.[4]

> Boomer (July 4, 1826–1881) was born in Massachusetts. He got his first taste of railroads at age 16. In 1846, he started work for Boody, Stone and Co., a premier bridge builder. Three years later, he saw opportunity in the West and moved to Cleveland, Ohio. There, he was a part of the new firm of Thatcher, Stone and Company, who built railroad bridges throughout the West. In 1851, Boomer and Stone left that firm and went to Chicago to form the firm of Stone and Boomer. They did the same business as before and held rights to the Howe truss. In the following years, they built virtually every railroad bridge in the West. One of their more notable jobs was supplying trusses for the Rock Island Bridge, the first one across the Mississippi River. In 1852, Boomer and Stone added the manufacture of rail cars as the Union Car and Bridge Works. After a fire destroyed his business, he started again on his own five years later as the Boomer Bridge Works, still in Chicago. Boomer was most productive during the Civil War and into the 1870s when his company designed and supplied trusses and built a large number of bridges. All of the bridges used Howe trusses transported from Chicago. Much of Boomer's work was by government contract, sometimes building as much as 2,000 feet of bridge in a month. One of those contracts was to construct numerous bridges along the N&D.
>
> William Tecumseh Sherman (1820–1891) was born in Lancaster, Ohio. He graduated from West Point and was a captain in the army but resigned in 1853. From then until 1859, Sherman tried his hand at various professions. One was as the first superintendent of the Louisiana State Seminary of Learning and Military Academy, later named Louisiana State University. In early 1861, he resigned from the school and returned north, becoming president of a streetcar company. In May of that year, Sherman got a commission in the regular army and was promoted to Brigadier General of Volunteers in the Department of the Cumberland in Louisville. However, he felt the strain of duty, struggled emotionally and was put on leave, even contemplating suicide. By December, he had recovered enough to serve in what was to become the Department of the Mississippi. Sherman's success at Shiloh and Vicksburg led to his promotion to brigadier general in the regular army in addition to his rank as Major General of Volunteers. When General Grant was given control of the Union Armies in March 1864, he appointed Sherman to succeed him as head of the Military Division of the Mississippi, which meant command in the Western Theater. In September 1864, Sherman forced Hood to abandon Atlanta. He and 62,000 men set off on their "March to the Sea" in November. They lived off the land and employed Sherman's "hard war" strategy, capturing Savannah in December. They then marched through South Carolina and captured Charleston in February 1865. After his army disbanded, he spent most of the remainder of his life in New York City, where he died of pneumonia.

Another service performed by Dodge during the war was in military intelligence. He had tested aspects of it in Arkansas and refined his techniques in Mississippi and West Tennessee. Dodge formed a group from the 24th and 25th Missouri Regiments called the Corps of Scouts who gathered information to help plan military actions. As time went on, his network expanded to over 100 agents funded by the sale of captured Confederate cotton. The organization was the first secret service and eventually merged into the Bureau of Military Information. One organization that Dodge was eager to destroy was the Confederate Coleman's Scouts. They had been formed in the late summer of 1862 and consist of between 50 and 100 men. Their purpose was to travel into federal territory to obtain information about enemy resources and furnish it to Gen. Bragg. Capt. Henry B. Shaw, a.k.a. E.C. Coleman, was their commander.

That November, Bragg sent Shaw and several of his Scouts into Middle Tennessee to gather information on the federal forces there. On the twentieth, 20-year-old Sam Davis, one of the Scouts, was captured by the 7th Kansas Cavalry inside the federal lines near Minor Hill, Tennessee, about 15 miles south of Pulaski. Others of the Coleman's Scouts were captured at about the same time. Davis was a courier and was dressed as one, wearing the clothing of a Confederate. A spy would have normally been dressed as a civilian. He and the other Scouts were jailed at Pulaski. The Federals found hidden in Davis' saddle detailed plans of several federal fortifications in Middle Tennessee and an in-depth report about the Union Army in Tennessee that he was carrying to Gen. Bragg. More troubling was a letter found in his boot from Coleman to Bragg's command. To the Federals these items identified Davis as a spy. Davis was brought before Gen. Dodge, who interrogated him. Dodge was most interested in determining who Coleman was and what federal officer was providing the information to the Confederacy. However, Davis did not divulge any information. A Military Commission met at Pulaski under Col. Madison Miller for his trial, and he was found guilty of spying. Two-thirds of the commission concurred that his sentence would be death by hanging. Davis was offered his freedom and safe travel to the Confederate lines if he would say where he got the plans, but he still refused. He told Dodge he would die a thousand deaths rather than betray a friend. At 10:00 a.m. on November 27, his twenty-first birthday, young Davis was taken about a mile from the jail and hanged in a public manner. His execution was an unpleasant necessity for Dodge who, after the war, contributed to a monument erected to Davis in Nashville.

One of the other men brought in was Capt. Shaw. He was captured a few miles north of Pulaski and put into the same jail at Pulaski as Davis after Davis had been sentenced to death. Dodge did not know that the infamous Coleman, the man that Davis refused to betray, was right there as Shaw and available for trial and execution. Shaw had been traveling under the guise of an itinerant herb doctor whose appearance was that of an unkempt, grizzled old man. He remained incognito in jail because, though some of the other men in the jail knew his true identity, none revealed it. So he was able to avoid the sentence of execution that spies typically met. Shaw was sent to Johnson's Island, Ohio, in Lake Erie where he was imprisoned until his release in 1865.[5]

> Sam Davis (1842–1863) was born in Rutherford County, Tennessee. In 1860–1861, he was a cadet at Western Military Institute (WMI) in Nashville. The school closed during the war. In April 1861, he signed up as a private in Company I in the 1st Tennessee Infantry Regiment. He joined Henry B. Shaw's famous Coleman's scouts in late 1862 or early 1863. Later, in 1867, when Montgomery Bell Academy was founded, the classes that had been offered at WMI were offered there, instead.

Among Dodge's spies were men, women, teenagers, older people, runaway enslaved people and Unionists living in Confederate territory. He identified them by

5. Dodge and Boomer Rebuild Trestles and Bridges

a letter or number, had the only list of their names on him at all times and kept information about them in his head. It seems that only the spies and four officers directly under him knew of the operation. When they went into Confederate territory, they carried mail addressed to actual southern people, giving them an excuse if stopped and questioned. They often wore Confederate uniforms and were loaded down with convincing contraband. When they went through a Confederate line, they were usually sent to a commanding officer or provost marshal to obtain a pass. On the way, they would observe the type of unit and its strength. Sometimes, the mail they carried had hidden messages in the form of pinpricks or the Route Cipher, which was in common use by the Union. They were to communicate their findings to Dodge, often via a network of supporters. The spy would typically remain in Confederate territory as much as possible and transfer his or her reports to an Alabama family member of a soldier in the 1st Alabama Colored Infantry, 1st Alabama Cavalry or 1st Tennessee Cavalry Regiments. The family member would, in turn, come to Dodge's camp ostensibly to visit the relative. They would have to come to Dodge's tent to be given permission to visit, at which time they handed him the spy's report. Dodge normally had two spies working the same area so he could confirm the intelligence he received and have sufficient confidence to act upon it.[6]

Gen. Dodge soon reported to Sherman, "There are in this section of country some one thousand rebel cavalry, guerrillas, robbers, &c., and the moment they see we intend to repair this railroad they will begin to burn." To protect his men and the construction that his men were about to do, Dodge planned to put guards at all of the important structures between Lynnville and Athens. He put his largest brigade of Col. J.W. Fuller, commander of the 27th Ohio infantry, at Prospect where he was to guard the railroad from the Elk River to Athens and repair the track and structures in that stretch. A regiment of mounted infantry was sent to Athens and Companies C, D, H and I of the 81st Ohio and two brigades remained at Pulaski. Dodge ordered Col. M.M. Bane, commander of the Third Brigade, Second Division, to take his brigade on November 12 to near Reynolds or Buford Station to repair the track and protect the structures that would be repaired between Lynnville and Wales. The 39th Iowa Infantry was posted at Reynolds' Station and two of its companies were ordered to protect railroad bridges and to work at two local grist mills grinding flour and meal. Company A of the 81st Ohio was sent to Wales Station to guard the railroad bridge at Pigeon Roost Creek and Companies B, E, F, G and K were tasked with running grist and sawmills to provide meal and lumber for Dodge's command. The primary goal was to repair the N&D and get it open again as soon as possible.[7]

On November 10, Maj. Gen. Lovell Rousseau of the 5th Kentucky Infantry became the military authority over the District of Nashville which included the N&D as far as Columbia and the N&C to the Duck River. The following day, Dodge ordered Bane to have an inspection performed of the railroad immediately and to send in the results. On the fifteenth and sixteenth, Dodge reported on the recent examination of the N&D. Col. Mizner, commander of the 14th Michigan Mounted Infantry, had informed him that there were seven bridges north of Columbia, not including the Duck, that needed work. Another report stated that there were seven, including the Duck. Mizner also said that there were 150 men working on the small trestles between Columbia and Lynnville, probably meaning Harris and Gracey's but not Culleoka because it was very large.

> Henry R. Mizner (1827–1915) was born in Geneva, New York. Practicing law in Detroit, he enlisted in May 1861 with the 18th U.S. Infantry. Mizner rose to colonel and commander of the 14th Michigan on November 11, 1862. He made brevetted lieutenant colonel in September 1864 for his service in the Atlanta Campaign, then brevetted brigadier general of the U.S. Volunteers in March 1865. Fort Mizner, where he had his command in Columbia, Tennessee, was named for him.

In addition to the seven bridges north of Columbia, Dodge reported the following in mid–November to Maj. R.M. Sawyer, Asst. Adjt. Gen. Dept. and Army of the Tennessee. There were six bridges, averaging 100 feet in length, between Columbia and Pulaski which he planned to rebuild in the next 10 days. The bridge at Lynnville Station over Robertson Fork Creek (see Appendix C, Tables 1, 2 and 3; Dodge No. 15, Wright No. 23) was partially destroyed as was another bridge over Richland Creek three-and-a-half miles south of Lynnville Station (Dodge No. 16, Wright No. 24). At Reynolds' Station, the bridge over Richland Creek (Dodge No. 17, Wright No. 25) was badly damaged and another three miles south of Reynolds (probably actually at Richland Creek; Dodge No. 18, Wright No. 26) was partially out. About two miles south of Richland Station (Dodge No. 19, Wright No. 28), the 200-foot by 36-six-foot-high bridge was gone. The Tunnel Hill Trestle (Dodge No. 20, Wright No. 29) was gone and the 600-foot by 40-foot-high bridge at the Elk River (Dodge No. 21, Wright No. 30) was nearly gone. Two-and-a-half miles south of the Elk, the 300-foot trestle bridge over a small creek (Mill Creek; Dodge No. 22, Wright No. 32) was gone. The trestle over Sulphur Creek (Dodge No. 23, Wright No. 33) had been destroyed as well as a small trestle in Athens (Town Creek; Dodge No. 25, Wright No. 36) and the bridge over Swan Creek 10 miles south of Athens (Dodge No. 28, Wright No. 39) was gone. Spring Creek (probably Pryor Creek; Dodge No. 29, Wright No. 40), five miles north of Decatur, and the structure over the bottom near Decatur (at Decatur Junction; Dodge No. 30, Wright No. 41) were out.[8]

The reports raise several questions. They indicate that there were seven bridges north of Columbia, including or not including the Duck, that needed work. However, Dodge's list of constructed trestles contains only five. The system at the Duck consisted of two spans of trusses and two trestles. The different tabulations seem to arise from the way in which the trusses and trestles were counted. Dodge also stated that there were six short bridges between Columbia and Pulaski. If that is correct, those structures would have probably been Harris, Robertson, three at Richland Creek and probably Pigeon Roost near Wales. Pigeon Roost is a mystery. It is interesting that the bridge there, about three miles northwest of Pulaski, is not included in the list of damaged structures. The 81st Ohio was sent to Wales in late 1863, implying that the bridge was still there. Therefore, it seems not to have been damaged and not included in Dodge's February 23 list of rebuilt structures. So it may be that there were actually five between Columbia and Pulaski. After February 1864, the Pigeon Roost bridge was rebuilt only once, as opposed to an average of twice for the other bridges in that area. It is possible that it was not damaged in October 1863 because it was a bit out of the way. Also, when compared to the Dodge list of February 23, it is apparent that four of the trestles he constructed were not addressed on November 15 and 16. Wright Nos. 21, 35, 37 and 38 (Dodge Nos. 13, 24, 26 and 27), all of which Dodge rebuilt, were not implied or specifically referenced in the inventory. Dodge had said that every bridge had been destroyed, but that seems to have been an exaggeration.[9]

Four bridges, Robertson Fork (Dodge No. 15) through Richland Creek No. 3 (Dodge No. 18), had been truss type bridges. Dodge planned to build trestles there although they would need to be replaced by bridge trusses before the rainy season. He also intended to rebuild the Tunnel Trestle (Dodge No. 20) and the Elk River Bridge (Dodge No. 21) with trestles, though he said they would need to be replaced by 150-foot trusses before Christmas. It is not clear why he wanted to replace the Tunnel Trestle with bridge spans. Dodge stated that other than for the damaged crossings, the railroad was in fine running order, had a good road bed, good quality rail, plenty of spare rail along the track and good cedar ties its entire length, but it needed new water tanks. He reported that there were good stockades at nearly every bridge.

On the nineteenth, Dodge's main force was encamped from their headquarters in Pulaski all the way up to Lynnville and had a detachment at the Elk River and two regiments in Athens but by this time had not made much progress north of Pulaski. Sherman and Grant were discussing whether to have Dodge focus on the smaller bridges and Anderson work on the larger ones, or if Dodge should be put in charge of the entire N&D. On the twenty-third, Grant relieved Anderson of work on the railroad because he was too slow and gave all of the work to Dodge. Col. George G. Pride was to direct the work. By that time, Dodge had a large number of men working on 10 damaged bridges from Columbia to the Elk River, including the Duck and the Elk. Because the troops were building with trees near each bridge site, it did not matter that the bridges were out and trains were not available to them. Dodge planned to finish the Duck River Bridge and work southward. A week later, work was to soon start on the Tunnel Trestle. On December 2, Grant ordered that the trestle at the Duck be built as soon as possible. The next day, Dodge requested that Gen. Rousseau supply men to put up five small trestles (Dodge Nos. 6–10) north of the Duck so he could get wood in by rail to the Duck to finish it. Rousseau replied that he did not have men to spare and Mizner said he had only 300 men and could spare only 50 soldiers and 100 Blacks.[10]

Soon, Boomer Bridge Works would be busy replacing the temporary trestles on the railroad with bridges that incorporated Howe trusses. Trusses were the primary structural components of bridges; they were not used in trestles. William Howe was a Massachusetts farmer who had invented and patented the truss in 1840. He married the sister of A.B. Stone, a bridge builder. Stone, in turn, wed Boomer's sister. These three men would develop business relationships that helped expand America's railroads. Though there were several trusses available at the time, the Howe trusses were typically 100 to 200 feet long and considered best for long spans like those needed for railroad bridges. In fact, it was the most popular truss used in railroad bridges in the second half of the nineteenth century when the railroad industry was growing rapidly. The L&N bridge at Nashville, which was burned in February 1862, used the trusses. They had a combination design, meaning that they were made of both wood and steel. The vertical structural members were steel. With steel being much more efficient in tension than wood, the Howe trusses were less costly than most other trusses. They were also easier to fabricate than most.

Boomer worked on the railroads in Tennessee and Georgia for at least a year. As early as October 1863, he was preparing to build the Running Water Bridge at Bridgeport. That November, he was doing bridge work on the N&C at Whiteside, Tennessee.

He would work on the N&D from December through at least May 1864 and as late as October 8, 1864, was apparently preparing to replace several bridges in north Georgia that had washed out, pending McCallum's approval.[11]

On November 22, Maj. Gen. Grant informed John Anderson that Boomer had contracted to build permanent bridges between Nashville and Decatur Junction. On December 4, Boomer wrote Dodge that he had the contract for all the bridges on the N&D and would be installing Howe trusses. Grant had told Boomer that Dodge was instructed to put in bridges and trestles so that the road could be opened as soon as possible. For the sake of expediency, other than the two trusses at the Duck, Dodge was commanded to construct only trestles, including the approach trestles at the Duck and several that would not stand up well to the flooding of the upcoming rainy season. Boomer was to come behind Dodge as soon as possible and, hopefully within 90 days, remove the "temporary" trestles at a number of sites and put in permanent bridges with Howe trusses.[12]

On December 8, Dodge reported to Rousseau on the status of the five bridges north of the Duck. A 350-foot by 50-foot-high bridge (probably at Rutherford Creek No. 4, Dodge No. 10) was to be delivered to Mizner to be put in by his command. There were three other bridges over Rutherford Creek 200 to 400 feet long and 25 to 35 feet high (Dodge Nos. 7, 8 and 9). The fifth bridge was over Carter's Creek and 200 feet by 20 feet (probably Dodge No. 6); it was framed and ready to put up. Dodge requested that about 50 mechanics be put at each bridge. As of December 15, those five bridges were nearing completion. Also, as of the fifteenth, the crossings and track south of the Elk River, except for the Sulphur Creek trestle, were expected to be open by the end of the first week in January and Dodge had nearly completed the structures from Columbia to Elkmont. On the sixteenth, Dodge reported that he had finished all seven structures between the Elk and Duck Rivers. That is less than the nine between Columbia and the Elk. It could be that he did not include some of the trestles in his count.

By January 6, all but one bridge between Smith's Station, near Carter's Creek Bridge No. 2, and the Duck had been completed except for a few bolts. The next day, a depot at Pulaski—probably the supply depot—was destroyed by fire because of the "criminal" negligence of some of the troops.[13]

On the twelfth, Maj. Parks, Superintendent of Repairs, reported to Dodge by telegraph that the Mill Creek trestle (also called Holt's Trestle, Dodge No. 22) was nearly done and the Blacks who were not cutting wood for the trestle were building a stockade there. On the sixteenth, Dodge reported that work on all of the structures between Pulaski and Decatur would be completed by February 1 if the weather cooperated.

Dodge specifically mentioned several trestles which he planned to build as "temporary," all soon to be replaced with trusses by Boomer. These trestles were said to be at the north approach to the Duck (not the ones on the steeper south side), the four crossings at Richland Creek, the tunnel and the Elk. Dodge's report indicates that he built trestles at Carter's Creek No. 5 (Dodge No. 6) and the four crossings over Richland Creek; all of those were badly in need of bridges.

Even before Dodge had finished, Boomer was coming behind him replacing trestles with bridges. Boomer seems to have started at the north end and worked south. Because Dodge had worked from north to south, the railroad was generally open for Boomer to bring his trusses, men and supplies to the trestle sites where he needed to work, without interference from Dodge. On February 8, 1864, Boomer was reported to be replacing the seven trestles north of the Duck. He was also at the Duck and would be there for probably a couple of months. While Boomer was there, Dodge ordered forces be sent to the site to prevent materials from being washed away by flooding or stolen by the enemy. On March 5 Boomer also seemed to be working on one or more of the trestles at or below the northernmost bridge over Richland Creek, perhaps at Swan Creek, because a train carrying lumber for them wrecked north of Richland Creek on that day. Also, they were at the Elk on May 19 and the Swan, north of Athens, on May 25.[14]

The temporary trestles that were built were not in use for long, probably from one to three months. It might seem wasteful to invest the labor and expense of building temporary structures only to have them demolished so quickly, but that indicates how urgent it was for the Federals to have the N&D open as soon as possible. Boomer had produced prefabricated trusses not only for the trestles that Dodge was working on, but also for all of the other bridges along the N&D. The photos of Rutherford Creek and the Duck show a great deal of woody debris on the banks. Much of this is likely to be timber from the removed trestles.

George N. Barnard, who worked for Matthew Brady before the war, took the photos of Boomer's bridges. In 1863, Barnard was appointed official photographer of the Military Division of the Mississippi, documenting camps, fortifications and rail lines. He accompanied Sherman on his "March to the Sea." Under the direction of Captain of Engineers Orlando M. Poe, Barnard ran the military's photographic operations. The photos included here and those of the other bridges along the N&D show that the bridges had Howe trusses, which would have been installed by Boomer in early to mid–1864. Barnard probably took the pictures in about March of 1864 when Sherman was touring the N&D. The Howe trusses are easily identified because they had iron rods that served as the vertical tension members whereas the trusses built by the federal troops did not.[15]

It would have made sense for Boomer to replace all of the N&D's bridges, thus having all of the structures in good condition. Evidence of this having been done is that Barnard's photos include one of the Harpeth River Bridge with Howe trusses, implying that

Boomer's N&D Bridge at the Harpeth River, Franklin, Tennessee, 1864 (National Archives and Records Administration).

Boomer's N&D Bridge at Rutherford Creek Crossing No. 4, 1864 (National Archives and Records Administration).

Boomer's N&D Bridge at the Duck River, 1864 (National Archives and Records Administration).

Boomer constructed Howe trusses north of Carter's Creek. Other photos by Barnard show all five of the Carter's Creek and all four of the Rutherford Creek crossings having Howe trusses. However, at the Duck the Howe trusses are shown but the approach trestles had not yet been replaced by trusses. That confirms that Boomer, who was working north of the Duck on February 8, had not yet completed the Duck. It is not clear how many trestles Boomer was contracted to replace and had made trusses for or how many were stored for potential future use. He seems to have replaced trestles with bridges at

5. Dodge and Boomer Rebuild Trestles and Bridges

anywhere from 22 to 29 of the crossings along the N&D. The crossings in doubt are those north of Franklin, at the West Harpeth and several over Carter's Creek. Regardless, most of Boomer's bridges were destroyed the following fall by the Confederates. Forrest, Gen. Joseph Wheeler, commander of cavalry in the Army of Tennessee, and Col. Hylan Lyon probably destroyed most of the Howe trusses. After those bridges were rebuilt by the Federals, presumably with their own designs, Hood destroyed some of the remaining Howe trusses along Rutherford Creek and at the Harpeth River.

> Joseph Wheeler (1836–1906) was born in Georgia and was appointed to the U.S. Military Academy, attending the U.S. Army Cavalry School. He took command of the 19th Alabama Infantry Regiment and was promoted to colonel in September 1861. Wheeler fought at Shiloh and Corinth, then transferred to the cavalry branch and was promoted to brigadier general in October 1862. By December he was commanding the cavalry of the Army of Tennessee. He was promoted to major general in January 1863, then fought at Chickamauga, Chattanooga and Atlanta. In late 1864, rather than accompany Hood to Middle Tennessee, he became the only effective Confederate force to oppose Sherman on his "March to the Sea." While covering Jefferson Davis' flight in May 1865, Wheeler was captured, imprisoned for two months, then paroled. He served in the U.S. House of Representatives from Alabama from 1881 to 1883 and 1885 to 1899. In 1898, he volunteered to serve in the Spanish-American War and commanded a cavalry division that included Theodore Roosevelt's Rough Riders. He died in Brooklyn and is one of the few former Confederate officers buried at Arlington National Cemetery.

Boomer probably replaced the in-stream trestles with trusses at the crossings below Pulaski, along Richland Creek north of Pulaski, at Pigeon Roost and along Carter's Creek. He built some between Spring Hill and Franklin. It is not clear what Dodge built at the four crossings of Rutherford Creek—bridges or trestles. There is evidence for both. For instance, Dodge reported that he was putting in bridges there. However, Barnard's photographs show Howe trusses at those four crossings, probably meaning that either Boomer replaced Dodge's bridges with his own or Boomer's trusses were installed while Dodge was working there. Also, Dodge's list identifies the vast majority of his 25 crossings as trestles but does not specify the type of crossings over Rutherford Creek. This implies that they were bridges.

The bridge at the Elk River was initially rebuilt as a trestle but a freshet washed it out in December, so it was replaced with a bridge having 50-foot spans resting on 18-foot-high cribs. On February 2, it was decided that the pier at the Elk River Bridge needed to be lowered one or two courses to fit the new trusses. It appeared that the bridge would be completed in two weeks. On the third, work at Sulphur Creek was still ongoing. The next day, the railroad was not open below Dark's Mill, at the southernmost crossing of the N&D over Carter's Creek, meaning that there was still trouble with one or more of the structures at Rutherford Creek. On February 12, Capt. Longstreet at Pulaski was scheduled to depart on the eighteenth for Swan Creek Trestle (probably Dodge No. 28), get out the wood there and frame the trestle at Decatur Junction. As of the sixteenth, track had been laid on Mill Creek Trestle which made travel possible from Athens to Sulphur Creek Trestle. This indicates that Sulphur Creek Trestle was still not open. The CS lost a locomotive, the *Maury*, on February 8 when federal troops captured it on CS tracks. It seems to have been prevented from returning southward because of damaged bridges. The Federals took it to Memphis where it became USMRR Engine No. 69, the *Gen. Logan*. The lack of bridges and trestles probably also contributed to the capture of the CS locomotive *Thomas Buford* on February 24. It, too, was taken to Memphis where it became USMRR Engine No. 99, the *Gen. McPherson*.[16]

Dodge was busy with more than just rebuilding the N&D. On December 15, he reported the capture of a party of Confederates under the command of Major Jo Fontaine who was subordinate to Phillip Roddey, now a general. They had been scouting the N&C and N&D and tapping the telegraphs. Their mission was to examine the railroad thoroughly between Columbia and Nashville and attempt to capture a trainload of prisoners coming from Chattanooga. And on about February 16, Dodge's men captured at Columbia a man named Worthum who was a member of a band of robbers from Culleoka. He had promised to disclose all he knew about the operations of the group. That same day, the railroad between Nashville and Pulaski had been completed and trains were running there safely, meaning that the Duck had been completed and track laid on it. On the seventeenth, about 21 miles west of Columbia, the famed guerrilla Duncan B. Cooper and 10 members of his band were captured. It is likely that they were on their way to burn railroad bridges. At that time, the railroad was in good running order as far south as Prospect which tells us that the Tunnel trestle had just been completed.

On the twenty-third, Col. Henry Sweeney and the 111th Illinois Infantry Volunteers were ordered to report to Col. Swayne of the 43rd Ohio Infantry at Decatur Junction. Sweeney was to put up an earthwork there in the most commanding position and examine and repair the railroad approaches to Decatur. Also, a party was to be sent to build a trestle and a 30-foot by 100-foot warehouse at the Junction.[17]

The Duck River railroad trestle bridge was large and a priority to get open. It had an approach trestle on each end and two long bridge spans. During its construction, until a pontoon bridge could be put in, the Federals needed a way to get troops and supplies over the river. On November 30, Dodge ordered that a 100-foot by 10-foot ferry boat be built and sent down to the Duck on the N&D for that purpose. He also ordered that a boom be placed upstream of the trestle bridge to protect it from driftwood.

On December 2, Grant commanded Mizner to start building the trestles. Mizner and his 14th Michigan Infantry would help build that trestle work and other railroad bridges north of Columbia. Boomer was contracted to supply and construct the bridge spans and would soon be on-site. At this time, Mizner's force was down to 300 men because he had relieved the Pioneers at Smith's Station and sent two companies to Franklin, and Thomas had called the Pioneers away for other duty. Dodge needed help badly and convinced Gen. Grant that former enslaved people were the solution. He was given authority to arrest any other federal who was trying to recruit Black workers away from him for the U.S. Colored Troops (USCTs).

On the third, the wooden components of the bridge spans, which were contracted for in November, had arrived in Nashville on cars from Louisville. These sections were probably fabricated by Boomer in Chicago. As was the case here, bridges pieces were sometimes prefabricated in Chicago or elsewhere and shipped to the site for quicker assembly. On the ninth, Dodge told Boomer that the previous bridge at the Duck had been a deck type and he wanted it replaced by the same design. One hundred of

5. Dodge and Boomer Rebuild Trestles and Bridges

Boomer's bridge builders were to soon be on their way from Chicago to the Duck and Dodge had asked Boomer to be sure to send a superintendent to oversee the work.

On December 15, Dodge reported that the bridge should be open by the end of the first week in January. However, there were delays. On the twentieth, Boomer was having trouble getting his bridges railed to the South. Gen. Grant had to urge the Michigan Central Railroad to give priority to his cars. There was also a delay in the masonry work at the Duck. Dodge's men finished the two trestles and on January 16 the bridge was primarily in the hands of Boomer. On February 16, work was finished, and trains were able to cross the structure.

The Federals were concerned that the Duck River Bridge was not properly guarded. The nearest force was one of Dodge's companies at the Duck River Station, about half a mile north of the bridge. The station had a sidetrack and storehouse, so Dodge's men were guarding supplies arriving there by train. With the bridge vulnerable to attack by the Confederates, we can assume that troops were sent there in February.[18]

Gen. Dodge was important to the Union in a number of ways. As previously mentioned, to support military intelligence, he had formed the Corps of Scouts from two Missouri regiments. Their capture and execution of Sam Davis and others was intended to discourage other potential Confederate spies. Another of his contributions was that, while rebuilding the trestles, he raised and organized two regiments of troops in North Alabama and had a third regiment on the way. The first two were the 2nd and 3rd Alabama Colored Infantry Volunteers who would later become the 110th and 111th USCTs. The other was the 4th Alabama which would become the 106th. Some of the USCTs were guarding the railroad as early as January 1864 and did so as late as that October. Dodge seemed to have no trouble raising colored troops wherever they stopped on their marches.[19]

February 23 was a big day for Gen. Dodge. Sulphur Creek Trestle, the last structure being worked on, was complete and ready for trains. That day, he reported to Gen. Sherman and Maj. Sawyer, "I have the honor to report the duty performed by this command in repairing the railroad from Nashville to Decatur. The command arrived at Pulaski on November 11, 1863 and was soon scattered along the railroad from Columbia to Athens, and details of work parties placed to work on all the bridges, every bridge on the road being out. I soon after received orders to take charge of the work north of Duck River, and placed parties to work on seven bridges north of that place and also a heavy detail on Duck River; the piers to that bridge were destroyed." The list of the trestles and bridges he had constructed is shown in Table 1 of Appendix C. The structures were identified as northernmost No. 6 at the southern end of Carter's Creek through No. 30 at Decatur Junction. Of the 25, it seems that 20 were trestles and only one, at the Duck, had both a bridge and trestle. It is not clear whether the four at Rutherford Creek were bridges or trestles. At the Duck, Boomer had installed two of the four spans. That bridge was rebuilt as a deck truss because the Confederates had destroyed the piers, making it impractical to rebuild it as a through-truss. Dodge stated that he had also built two pontoon bridges. One was put over the Duck, 340 feet long consisting of 12 bateaux (flat-bottomed riverboats) made from plank and timber found at a sawmill. That bridge was in place from about February through November 1864. Dodge's other pontoon bridge was at the Elk, 300 feet long and made of flat boats so they could be run in the Tennessee River as ferry boats if needed. Except for the Duck River pontoon bridge, the timber for all the bridges came from standing trees. At Prospect, Dodge built a large warehouse and a steam sawmill capable of sawing 3,000 feet of lumber per day. At each bridge that was not adequately protected, he constructed substantial earthworks or stockades to protect the troops guarding it. He put the water tanks, switches, track and other railroad features in good working order and cut and put on the road about 3,000 cords of wood. His men had lived entirely off the country except for sugar, coffee and salt which they got from the government.[20]

Twenty one of the 25 bridges and trestles in Dodge's "completed" list are specifically or indirectly included in the November 1863 inventory. For some reason, Culleoka and three structures between Sulphur Creek Trestle and Decatur (Dodge Nos. 24, 26 and 27) were not specifically mentioned in the inventory but were rebuilt and included in his February 23 report.[21]

Wright Nos. 18 and 19 had not been built yet, so they were not in Dodge's list. Wright Nos. 27, 31 and 34 were not damaged at the time of Dodge's inventory in November 1864 and did not need to be repaired. Compared to the six between Columbia and Pulaski that he said needed work, it seems that Dodge rebuilt or repaired seven, Dodge Nos. 12 through 18.

The men in Dodge's command performed work on most of the repaired and rebuilt trestles, track, water towers and other features but they got a lot of help. Col. Mizner and the 14th worked on the Duck and the structures to the north of the Duck. The Pioneers and impressed Black workers assisted, as did Boomer who worked on the bridge spans at the Duck from December 1863 through February 1864. The 1st Michigan did not seem to be involved; they had worked on the N&D in 1862 and part of 1863. And of course, as previously mentioned, Boomer came behind Dodge and replaced the temporary trestles with permanent truss bridges.

In summary, it seems that before the war the N&D built 37 bridges and trestles (probably 23 bridges and 14 trestles) and their part of the Junction Trestle, Dodge rebuilt

Dodge's N&D Trestle at Culleoka, 1864 (National Archives and Records Administration).

25 of them and Boomer constructed Howe trusses at between 22 and 29 of the trestles that either he helped Dodge build or that Dodge had built himself. The four in Wright's list of 41 that the N&D did not build are Wright Nos. 6, 7, 18 and 19. Although bridges and trestles had been rebuilt numerous times, including in the great effort of the spring of 1862, Dodge's work is emphasized because it came at a very busy time on the N&D and his work is fairly well documented.

On February 26, Dodge told Grant that he was pleased with the sturdiness of the new structures, even though not all, including two over Richland Creek and the one at the Elk, were not yet changed out to Howe trusses. Because Boomer had already fabricated trusses for all the bridges on the N&D, Dodge said he would have the completed structures inspected and for those that were adequate but had Howe trusses ready, the trusses would be stored for potential future use. It is not known how many spare trusses were put into storage. The first through-train along the repaired track ran south to Decatur Junction on February 27. It could not have come all the way from Nashville, however, because the Franklin bridge was not repaired until March 6. Thomas estimated that 2,000 infantry and 2,000 cavalry should be able to protect the rebuilt N&D. After completing work on the N&D, Dodge and his division remained in the Decatur area, holding the town for the Federals.[22]

Dodge's rebuilding of the trestles took about three months. The Federals had invested a great deal of labor and expense and were keen on protecting their new structures. In January, while the crossings were being rebuilt, Gen. George H. Thomas had ordered Merrill to construct railroad defenses on the N&D all the way back to Nashville. On about January 25, Dodge's headquarters and some of his companies from the 39th Iowa Infantry moved north from Reynolds' Station to join their regiment at Culleoka. Two companies were to protect the railroad bridges while others picketed, garrisoned or worked on fortifications. Culleoka had a large stockade and rifle pits which protected the 1,000-foot-long trestle. That month, the 39th Iowa was continuing to put up stockades or earthworks at all the bridges and trestles that were not adequately fortified. On March 11, it was ordered that if there were not already stockades near the bridges and trestles, they were to be built immediately to protect the railroad.[23]

In late January, the Confederates were especially active on the lower N&D. On the twenty-fifth, Lt. Bailey reported that he had heard from Mizner that 1,400 Confederates were dividing into squads to attack the various bridges on the Duck. With Mizner's permission, he had started building a stockade at the Duck. He asked Dodge if he could complete it. Though the record about this is uncertain, the stockade was probably finished. At sunset the same day, Lt. Col. Moses W. Hannon of the 53rd Alabama Cavalry accompanied Capt. McCall and 300 men to meet Gen. Roddey at Brown's Ferry on the Tennessee River about 10 miles below Decatur. Roddey told him he intended to attack Union-held Athens with Patterson's regiments of Moreland's cavalry brigade, two pieces of artillery and McCall's 300 men. The town was held by the 75 to 100 men of the 9th Illinois Mounted Infantry Regiment under Captain Emil Adams. At about 3 a.m. on the twenty-sixth, the combined Confederate force of 600 men, one squadron on horseback and the remainder on foot, crossed the river at Brown's Ferry with their artillery and attacked the town. Although the Federals were heavily outnumbered and did not have a good fort to protect them, they forced the Confederates to retreat after a two-hour battle. The Union lost 21 men and the Confederates 30, and the railroad was not damaged. Dodge warned Mizner that Confederates had been at Athens and were moving north approaching the Elk River and sent all his trains north of Pulaski in case of an attack.[24]

By early 1864, Giles County had been foraged clear. The county had lost most of its horses, cattle and grain to foraging and troops. The county's supplies had been drained in November 1863 when Sherman's 100,000 men came through on their way from Memphis to Chattanooga. Dodge and his men took more during their six months in the area, from November 1863 through April 1864. Dodge had demanded that Giles Countians provide food for his 8,000 troops. If the residents brought food to the mills, he gave them vouchers they could exchange for cash. However, the vouchers were valid only if the resident took an oath of allegiance to the Union. It was common for those with grain who did not offer it to have it taken by the troops.[25]

In March, with Dodge's work complete and the rebuilt N&D operating again, the railroad published a schedule which shows that a passenger/freight train ran daily departing Nashville at 9:15 a.m., stopping at 25 stations before arriving at Athens at 6:16 p.m., then going to Decatur Junction. Another train ran daily from Decatur Junction, stopping at Athens at 8:10 a.m., then making the same 25 stops before arriving in Nashville at 5:30 p.m. Yes, it took about nine hours to travel the 107 miles between Nashville and Athens, an average of 12 miles per hour. Those two trains crossed in Columbia at about 1:20 p.m. One can imagine the number of delays and cancellations there must have been due to a variety of factors. In addition to the scheduled trains, there was other traffic on the tracks. Because Boomer was still replacing temporary trestles with bridges and swapping out old bridges with new trusses, his work would have created a number of lengthy shutdowns of the track at various locations. Also, that spring a hospital train made three trips weekly from Bridgeport to Nashville on the M&C and N&D. That train had a passenger car, a mail car, three box cars and three hospital cars. And wrecking trains made frequent runs along the railroad, as well. On March 8, a train was to report to the Nashville to pick up all valuable railroad property along the N&D and return it to Nashville.[26]

For some time that spring, the Union was sending twice as much over the N&D as it was over the N&C. The impressed Union leaders asked Dodge about it. He told them he had been very efficient by running the N&D in sections, having ample sidings at the necessary passing points, keeping the trains on schedule and not letting them get overloaded. Overloading would slow the trains and increase the risk of derailment. Dodge probably deserved some credit. However, the N&D was in better condition than the N&C and Dodge certainly had some help from McCallum who had made the USMRR an efficient organization and from W.J. Stevens, superintendent of the railroads in and out of Nashville in 1864. By that June, the N&C would be improved so the Federals could take advantage of the shorter, direct route to Stevenson. The N&C then took over as the busier of the two, handling virtually all of the trains to Stevenson and seeing a high volume of traffic to furnish Sherman's great needs.[27]

Though the N&D was in good condition, upkeep of the railroad still required almost constant effort. There was no stopping the wrecks and attacks. The weather and the Confederates continued to knock out bridges and trestles. On March 5, a train carrying timber for a bridge that Boomer was building wrecked two miles north of one of the Richland Creek crossings. On the twenty-second, the detachments at the bridges at Wales and Reynolds' Stations were warned that Forrest had pontoons and was thought to be crossing the Tennessee River to attack the N&D above Athens. Also, on March

UNITED STATES MILITARY RAILROADS.
NASHVILLE AND DECATUR LINE.
TIME TABLE, NO. 1.
TO TAKE EFFECT TUESDAY, MARCH 1ST, 1864,
AT 9:15 O'CLOCK, A. M.

TRAINS SOUTH.		STATIONS.	TRAINS NORTH.	
No. 1 Pass. & Fr't. A. M.	Distances from Nashville.		Distances between Stations.	No. 2 Pass. & Fr't. P. M.
9.15		Le ....NASHVILLE........ Ar	9,5	5.30
10.02	9,5	" ....BRENTWOOD........ Le	3,0	4.40
10.16	12,5	" ....OWENS........ "	6,2	4.22
10.47	18,7	" ....FRANKLIN........ "	6,3	3.47
11.18	25,0	" ....WEST HARPETH........ "	3,5	3.14
11.35	28,5	" ....THOMPSON'S........ "	3,2	2.55
11.52 M.	31,7	" ....SPRING HILL........ "	4,3	2.36
12.12 PM.	36,0	" ....CARTER'S CREEK........ "	6,0	2.14
12.40	42,0	" ....DUCK RIVER........ "	8,7	1.41
1.00 } 1.20 }	45,7	Ar ....COLUMBIA........ Le Le ....COLUMBIA........ Ar	5,8	1.20 } 1.00 }
1.50	51,5	" ....HURRICANE........ Le	4,0	12.32
2.08	53,5	" ....PLEASANT GROVE........ "	2,8	12.13 P.M.
2.22	58,3	" ....CAMPBELL'S........ "	5,2	12.00 M.
2.47	63,5	" ....LYNNVILLE........ "	3,2	11.35
3.03	66,7	" ....BUFORD'S........ "	2,0	11.20
3.12	68,7	" ....REYNOLD'S........ "	5,6	11.10
3.39	74,3	" ....WALES........ "	4,4	10.45
4.00	78,7	" ....PULASKI........ "	6,0	10.24
4.30	84,7	" ....RICHLAND........ "	6,0	9.55
4.59	90,7	" ....PROSPECT........ "	2,8	9.27
5.11	93,5	" ....STATE LINE........ "	5,0	9.15
5.36	98,5	" ....ELKMONT........ "	8,5	8.50
6.16	107,0	" ....ATHENS........ "	5,0	8.10
	112,0	" ....McDONALD'S........ "	2,0	
	114,0	" ....FOOTES........ "	3,0	
	117,0	" ....HOBB'S........ "	2,0	
	119,0	Ar ....JUNCTION........ Le		
P. M.				A. M.

GENERAL RULES.

1. Trains going South are entitled to the track ONE HOUR beyond Sched'le time. But when more than one hour behind time they become Irregular, and must be kept off the time of all Regular Trains.

2. Trains going North will not leave a siding unless THEY CAN WITHOUT DOUBT reach the meeting point before the time marked in the Schedule for the departure of the approaching Train.

3. Trains going North will wait at the meeting point ONE HOUR AND FIVE minutes beyond the time marked for the approaching Train.

4. A Train going South, and failing to make a meeting point within the hour allowed, must wait at the siding where it expects to meet the Train running North, thirty-five minutes behind the Schedule time for the approaching Train to be there after which the Train running North also becomes Irregular, and NEITHER TRAIN can proceed, where there are curves in the Road, or the weather so foggy as to prevent an uninterrupted view of the track ahead for more than one-half mile, except by keeping a man at least 600 yards ahead with a RED FLAG by day or a RED LIGHT at night.

March 1, 1864, N&D (USMRR) Schedule (Tennessee and Alabama Railroad Co. Records, 1864–1865, AC. No. 92–056, Box S-1, Tennessee State Library & Archives).

25, Major Frank Evans and the 81st Ohio Infantry Volunteers at Nance's Mills, near Cornersville, Tennessee, were informed that small parties of well-armed, mounted rebels were at the track at Culleoka. Evans was to send his mounted men there and Capt. DeHews of the secret service and 10 men also went to determine the size of the rebel force.[28]

Decatur had been taken and retaken by the Federals several times. The Confederates had it during this period, but the Federals wanted to reclaim control of the town as a base of operations in northern Alabama. Dodge had been assembling pontoons for an amphibious assault from the north bank. Seventy-six pontoons were linked together to form a walkway most of the way across the river. They were anchored to the piers of the burned-out M&C railroad. In the early morning fog on March 8, Dodge and Company B, 27th Ohio Infantry made their way most of the way across the river on the bridge, then completed the journey in individual pontoons. They attacked and removed the small force of Confederates. Once he had control of Decatur, Dodge authorized agents to begin recruiting freed local Blacks for service in the Union Army. He also wasted no time in building substantial fortifications there to guard the river and protect the pontoon bridge. On the eleventh Dodge reported that Col. Fuller was showing progress on the western fort (Number 1) and that Mr. Hurd had arrived and started work on the eastern fort (Number 2). The forts would be connected by a one-mile-long line of breastworks that tied into the riverbank.

Also on the eleventh, Dodge was planning to move his headquarters to Athens in the next few days and to use the MacLand and Hobbs houses for his offices. On March 19, he issued orders requiring all citizens within one mile of the Decatur town limits to leave by the twenty-fifth so the entire town could be used for Union purposes. Residents could go wherever they chose. Except for a few key buildings, Decatur was cleared to provide a good view of the surroundings. Even the three churches had been burned or torn down. The few remaining buildings included the Dancy Polk House, the McCartney Hotel, the McEntire House, which was used as a headquarters by both sides alternately, and the Old State Bank Building, which was used as a headquarters and hospital. On April 4, a large number of residents of Decatur were at Decatur Junction with their belongings, ready to relocate from the town but unable to because of a shortage of rail cars. Many had been waiting there for several days without shelter. Some of the luckier people were in four cars and had been stranded there for two days. On April 20, Dodge reported to Huntsville that there were significant problems with the new fortifications at Decatur, including improperly placed rifle pits, which he intended to remedy. By the thirtieth, virtually every family had left Decatur except that of Mrs. McCartney, and Decatur was an armed Union camp. In spite of a recommendation to abandon the town because of fears that they would have trouble holding it once the garrison moved out, Sherman insisted that control be maintained so the Confederate cavalry would stay out of the area.[29]

In Washington, D. C., Secretary of War Stanton was working to support McCallum and the USMRR. McCallum later stated, "In my report of January 19, 1864, I had estimated the rolling-stock necessary for the business anticipated on the lines that would probably be operated out of Nashville at 200 locomotives and 3,000 cars, while only 47 locomotives and 427 cars were on hand." The city was critical as a foothold in the South from which supplies could be sent on the network of rails extending from it. On March 23, Stanton told the nation's locomotive manufacturers that they must produce more engines and cars to meet McCallum's demand. The companies responded energetically. While the new stock was being manufactured, however, the Union needed to find additional stock elsewhere. Because the railway gauge in both Tennessee and Kentucky was five feet, additional rolling stock from Kentucky was temporarily impressed into government service and sent south to Nashville. As of June 1864, 21 engines and 195 cars were taken, mostly from the L&N.

By late spring, Nashville was receiving an average of one new locomotive and 15 new cars daily; these were especially needed at this time to support Sherman's campaign in Georgia. By September 14, the influx of new rolling stock had brought the number of locomotives to 144 and cars to 1,305. By December, there were 187 engines and 2,596 cars; those numbers do not include what had been impressed. In January through May of 1865, an additional 414 cars were delivered, so in May there were an estimated 208 engines and 3,205 cars, including those taken from Kentucky. Those numbers included a few locomotives and cars that were not serviceable or had been captured. McCallum's goal of 200 and 3,000 had been met.[30]

An effect of the anticipated increase in rail traffic and rising number of required repairs to locomotives and rolling stock was that the Nashville yard expanded its facilities in about March of 1864. Because Nashville was the main terminal station of 500 miles of track running from it to the west, south and east, the facilities had to be very large. A massive machine shop and an extensive car shop were built. Occasionally, 100 engines and 1,000 cars would be at this expanded facility. There were also large storehouses at Nashville and Chattanooga with all the materials necessary to rebuild or repair track, bridges, buildings, engines and cars. In case the rail was cut to the north of either city, supplies of all sorts were available in both cities to last a significant length

N&C Railroad Depot at Nashville (Library of Congress).

of time. Those two cities were the centers through which rail operations converged, and they were protected accordingly.[31]

Statistics for the railroads in the Department of the Cumberland, which included the N&D and N&C, are impressive. Between September 1, 1863, and about November 14, 1864, during which time Sherman marched to Atlanta, the department brought 40,000 sick and wounded back to Nashville, returned 50,000 veteran volunteers from the front in Georgia and moved 10,000 prisoners north. As of November 1, 1863, the department had 123 miles of military railroad with 30 locomotives, 350 cars, 187 men in the Transportation Corps and 4,000 men in the railroad service. The average dispatch was 40 cars per day. By September 14, 1864, the department had expanded to manage 956 miles of track, and had 165 locomotives, 1,500 cars, 150 men in the Transportation Corps, 10,805 in the railroad service and 150 cars dispatched daily. Troops generally loved being transported by rail, but because the N&C and N&D were used primarily for hauling supplies, most of the troops had to march out of Nashville.[32]

The term "impressment" had several meanings during the Civil War, one being to force another into labor. That labor was often not fully paid or not paid at all. By early December, Dodge had impressed every available Black man to cut timbers and place ballast for the railroad. U.S. law allowed this but not the forcing of former enslaved people to serve in the military. This issue arose again on February 23, 1864, when J.M. Nash, Superintendent of Repairs in the Military Division of the Mississippi, reported to Adna Anderson that a "negro conscripting party" had taken nearly all of the Black laborers working on the railroad between Columbia and the Duck River. The 50 were returned per Thomas' order.

The manners in which the Civil War impacted the lives of Black Americans, particularly in the South, is a fascinating aspect of the war that could fill volumes. The author has devoted a chapter to discussion of a small part of the local story.

6

U.S. Colored Troops, Contraband Camps and Tunnel Hill

Especially after the Federals occupied Athens in April 1862, Black men in North Alabama were deciding whether to remain enslaved on their plantations or flee northward and enlist in the Federal Army, gaining a degree of freedom. President Lincoln issued the Emancipation Proclamation on January 1, 1863. It gave freedom to the 600,000 to 700,000 enslaved Blacks in states that were not under federal control. This applied to Alabama but not Tennessee, so even greater numbers of Blacks in Alabama fled northward. Black soldiers had already been working for both armies in unskilled jobs such as construction labor. The Proclamation provided enslaved people additional incentive to leave their homes and cross into Union-held territory. It also made some landowners start paying freed enslaved people. On May 22, 1863, the U.S. War Department established the Bureau of Colored Troops to help the Union Army recruit Black soldiers to fight. The Bureau opened a Nashville office on September 10, 1863.

By the war's end, 178,000 men would have served in 170 USCT regiments. Over 20,000 would be from Tennessee and 7,300 from Alabama. About 75 percent of the Black men who joined the USCTs were enslaved people, either runaways from the South or people from border states who volunteered to serve in exchange for their freedom. In northern Alabama, mostly runaway enslaved people and freedmen volunteered for the USCTs. The troops were commanded by White officers. The soldiers' duties included infantry, cavalry and artillery. Many of the Black soldiers guarded supply lines, served as prison guards, hunted Confederate guerrillas or were garrison troops. Some rode aboard and guarded supply trains. There were several regiments of colored infantry active along the N&D, including the 12th, 13th, 14th, 40th, 106th, 110th and 111th USCTs. The names of the regiments had been changed from state designations to the USCTs.

The 12th USCT, formed as the 3rd Tennessee Volunteers of African Descent, was recruited in Tennessee from July through August 1863. It garrisoned the Elk River Bridge in the fall of 1863, fought Hood at the Battle of Nashville and chased him during his retreat. The regiment mustered out in January 1866.

The 13th USCT was formed as the 2nd Tennessee Volunteers of African Descent. It was organized in Nashville in November 1863. It, too, garrisoned the Elk River Bridge at some time during the war and fought Hood at the Battle of Nashville. They mustered out in January 1866.[1]

The 14th USCT was organized at Camp Stanton at Gallatin, Tennessee, on November 16, 1863. It was organized and commanded by Col. Thomas J. Morgan. During 1864 the regiment was attached to the post in Chattanooga, Department of the Cumberland.

U.S. Colored Troops (Library of Congress).

They fought in the Battle of Decatur in October 1864 and, along with several other USCT regiments, fought in the Battle of Nashville that December and chased Hood over the Tennessee River. They mustered out in March 1866.

The 40th USCT was organized at Nashville in late February 1864. Their main function locally was protection of the railroads out of Nashville, but not the N&D or N&C. In September 1864, they were supporting other USCTs at Fort Henderson in Athens when they were captured by Forrest.

The 4th Alabama Colored Infantry was organized at Decatur on March 31, 1864. The majority of these soldiers were former enslaved people from Morgan and Lawrence Counties, Alabama. Many of the men had been building the two forts at Decatur just weeks before. They garrisoned at Pulaski and served primarily as railroad guards. On May 16, 1864, the regiment changed its name to the 106th USCT. They were attached to the District of North Alabama, Department of the Cumberland until February 1865 and saw action against Forrest at Athens on September 23–24, 1864 but were not at Sulphur Creek Trestle.

The 2nd Alabama Colored Infantry was organized in November 1863. Most of the men had been enslaved field hands in northern Alabama and Mississippi. The majority of them made their way to contraband camps behind Union lines, bringing their families with them. A large number of the men were impressed or recruited at the camps, mustered in at Pulaski and eventually assigned to guard the railroads in North Alabama. On June 25, 1864, its name was changed to the 110th USCT. It was attached to the District of North Alabama, Department of the Cumberland until February 1865. The various companies of the 110th saw duty over the next few months between Pulaski and Decatur Junction. Many of the troops were placed at Athens or as guards along the N&D. Some of the companies were at Sulphur Creek Trestle when Forrest attacked in September 1864. Company A was stationed at Athens in January and February 1864,

6. U.S. Colored Troops, Contraband Camps and Tunnel Hill

then in March and April was attached to the Pioneers, Sixteenth Army Corps at Decatur Junction. Company B was at Decatur Junction from December 11, 1863, through February 1864, then at Decatur through April. Companies D and K were at Athens from March through August 1864. Company E was at Pulaski from December 12–31, 1863. Company F started working on fortifications at Athens on April 10, 1864, and was there through August. Company G was at Athens in March and April 1864. Company H was at Pulaski in March and April 1864 and at Athens from May through August. Company I was at Decatur in March and April 1864, then Athens from May through August. After the 110th was replenished with new troops, some of the men served as riflemen or guards at the Battle of Nashville. The 110th mustered out on February 6, 1866.[2]

The 3rd Alabama Colored Infantry was also established in Pulaski in November 1863. On June 25, 1864, its name was changed to the 111th USCT. Like the 110th, most had come from northern Alabama and Mississippi to contraband camps where many were recruited or impressed. The majority were stationed at Pulaski and Athens guarding the railroads. Some of the companies were at Sulphur Creek and the Low Trestle (Wright No. 34) in September 1864 when Forrest attacked. Company A was at Sulphur Creek Trestle from January 13, 1864, through June. Company B was at Mill Creek Trestle from January 30, 1864, through April, then moved four miles to Sulphur Creek during May and June. Company C was at Sulphur Creek in late June 1864 and at Tunnel Trestle in July and much of August. Company D was at Sulphur Creek from February through April 1864, at Athens in June and July, and Richland Creek in August. Company E was at Sulphur Creek in late February 1864, then at Swan Creek from March through October. Company F was at Sulphur Creek from February 8, 1864, through June. Company G was at Sulphur Creek doing garrison duty from February 20, 1864, through April, at Athens from May through July, then at Richland Station for garrison duty in August. Company H was at Sulphur Creek in June and part of July 1864, then at Prospect from July 23

Contraband Camp near Helena, Arkansas, ca. 1865 (RG 3323–06–12, Nebraska State Historical Society).

through much of August. Company I was at Sulphur Creek from March through June 1864. Company K was at Sulphur Creek from March 15, 1864, through about the end of April, then moved five miles south to Mill Creek Trestle where they did garrison duty from May through August. In October, the 111th was stationed at Pulaski. From there they went to Nashville, arriving on November 28. After they were replenished with new troops, some of the companies served at the Battle of Nashville. The 111th mustered out on April 30, 1866.[3]

One story of an enslaved man-to-soldier story is that of Andrew Ewing. He was born in 1831 in Williamson County and was owned by local landowner Alexander C. Ewing and then his son William. In 1862, Andrew left the Ewing home and went to Nashville where he joined many other former enslaved people working on the fortifications there, including Fort Negley. In August of the following year, he enlisted in the 12th Pennsylvania Volunteer Infantry, Company B. He and his company were soon sent to the Elk River Bridge. In December of that year, he was promoted to Sgt. Maj. of the 12th. For much of the remainder of the war, his regiment was based at Johnsonville on the Tennessee River. They were guarding the Nashville and Northwestern Railroad which the Federals had extended to that point after capturing Nashville. At the Battle of Nashville, a cannon ball broke a tree limb that injured one of his legs. Andrew remained with the 12th as they chased Hood until he was left at Franklin as "sick." He was discharged in October 1865. By January of the next year, he was working under contract in a blacksmith's shop in Williamson County. Sgt. Maj. Ewing died in 1901 at age 70.[4]

On August 10, 1863, in General Order No. 51, Major Theodore S. Bowers ordered that "at all military posts within the Department of the Tennessee where slavery has been abolished per Proclamation of the President, camps will be established for such freed people of color as are out of employment. Military Superintendents will see that rations are provided. All such persons supported by the Government will be employed in every practicable way so as to avoid them becoming a burden on the Government." These would be called contraband camps. Though the term "contraband" generally refers to property or other items brought in illegally, in this book it refers to former enslaved people—considered to be property of Southerners—who came into Union-controlled territory. The term was in common use during the war, though a less harsh term in use at the time was "Freedman."

Camps had been set up as early as 1862 in other parts of the country, mostly for Blacks but some for Whites. They were established where the Federals had a strong presence and could protect the inhabitants. The Federals helped the residents but also benefited themselves because the camps were great sources of laborers, cooks, laundresses and more. In about September 1863, the Freedmen's Department of the Army was formed and started managing the nation's contraband and refugee camps. Establishment, management and protection of the contraband camps became another major mission for the Federals.

There were several contraband camps in Middle Tennessee and northern Alabama. The first of these was in Pulaski on the Jonathan Phillips plantation two-and-a-half miles northwest of the town at the present site of the industrial park. It was established on December 1, 1863. By the end of May 1864, there would be local camps at Huntsville, Decatur Junction, Tunnel Hill (the second of the local camps to be opened), Pulaski, Franklin, Nashville, Clarksville, Gallatin and Hendersonville, Tennessee. There seem to have been at least three camps at Nashville, the main one being at Edgefield.

6. U.S. Colored Troops, Contraband Camps and Tunnel Hill

On February 4, 1864, Adjutant General Lorenzo Thomas issued Orders No. 2 establishing a camp near Nashville to receive contrabands. It was to be controlled and supervised by Captain Ralph Hunt, 1st Regiment Kentucky Volunteers. The Quartermaster's Department would provide all of the necessary materials and supplies. An effort was to be made to house the people in log structures that the Blacks would build themselves. Tents would be furnished in the interim. All male Blacks coming within the federal lines who, upon examination, were found to be capable of bearing arms would be mustered into companies and regiments of the USCTs. All others, instead of remaining idle in the camp, were to perform whatever work on plantations or farms was suited to their condition. All loyal civilians who had plantations, farms, wood yards or similar, could apply to the Commandant of the camp to hire Blacks, including some children, for service. The employers would enter into a written agreement to pay, feed and humanely treat the people. The term of hire was to be for not less than one year, commencing on January 1, 1864. The cost of any clothing provided by the employer could be deducted from pay. If there were not enough of this sort of work available, the remainder of the Blacks were to be put to work on abandoned or confiscated plantations or farms. In such cases, they were to be self-sufficient so as not to become a burden on the government. The wages to be paid for labor were to be not less than seven dollars per month for able-bodied males over fifteen years of age, not less than five dollars per month for able-bodied women over the age of fifteen, and half of those amounts for children between the ages of twelve and fifteen. Children under the age of fourteen were not to be field hands and families were to be kept together whenever they desired. Also, the employer was to provide any required medical advice at his expense. To better carry out the order, abandoned plantations could be leased to loyal citizens on terms that were equitable. Eight men from regiments of African descent would support Captain Hunt. It would be their duty to visit the places where the people worked to ensure that their working conditions were adequate and the relationships with their employers were satisfactory. Any abuse by an employer was to be immediately reported to the nearest Military District.[5]

Smaller, temporary camps seem to have been established at some of the federal construction sites like Fort Negley at Nashville and Fort Granger at Franklin. The camp at Franklin was a few hundred yards north of the fort and was occupied mostly by Blacks who had deserted the services of their Williamson County owners. The camp near Decatur Junction was set up on March 14, 1864, on the Hobbs property with about 2,000 acres. In the spring of 1864, the camp at Pulaski had about 1,700 residents, "tidy log cabins" and a school with 100 students. Teachers for the schools were often paid for by the camp inhabitants. On August 1 of that year, the Pulaski camp had 1,000 inhabitants and Decatur Junction about 600. The Huntsville camp was on the Calhoun plantation, about a mile from town. Several of these camps were under the oversight of Lt. Joseph W. Harris of the 57th Illinois Infantry. At the end of May 1865, there were about 5,500 refugees in the eight or more local camps.[6]

At the local contraband camps, whatever work that could be found was given to the inhabitants. That included gathering cotton that had been abandoned. During the first winter of 1863–64, the cotton that was collected sold for about $9,000. Those funds were deposited into a treasury and drawn by Lt. Harris as needed. Subsequently, about 1,000 acres of cotton and 400 acres of corn were planted. The draft animals used at the camps were typically beasts that had been worn out by their military service. In March and April 1864, many of the planters requested the army to allow their former enslaved people to return to their plantations to work for wages. Most of the Blacks seemed not to trust their former masters, so only a few went.

In June 1864, the camps in Middle Tennessee and North Alabama were determined to be poorly run. There was little shelter, no good plan for the refugees' future and the people were still primarily dependent upon the government. When the Union Army retreated north toward Nashville that November, the Blacks were encouraged to stay behind and scatter among the people, which many did quite successfully. However, about 1,500 followed the army north.

In March 1865, Congress created the Bureau of Refugees, Freedmen and Abandoned Property, commonly known as the Freedmen's Bureau, to better meet the temporary needs of destitute and suffering refugees, former enslaved people and their families. It was the first national welfare agency and would eventually help about four million former enslaved people adjust to freedom. The bureau provided food and built schools and hospitals and managed abandoned lands within former Confederate territory. By that June, operation of the camps was much improved. At that time, there were only about 4,000–5,000 local refugees, many of whom had been put to work at farming, milling or mechanical labors. They were working approximately 2,500 acres of cotton, corn and tobacco and operated two gristmills, a sawmill and a shoe factory. The government's cost of operating the camps had been drastically reduced because of sales of what was being grown or made and the people were generally making a living. The bureau also encouraged Blacks to go back to work for Union-sympathetic Southern planters under fair terms. Col. R.W. Barnard had become Superintendent of Freedmen, Department of the Cumberland in June 1864. On July 1, 1865, he reported that he had seized 1,000 additional acres for Pulaski (making it about 2,000 acres total), 2,500 additional acres for Decatur Junction (bringing it to about 4,000 acres), and 2,400 acres for Huntsville. He planned to soon be seizing more land for the other camps.[7]

The government had always intended the camps to be temporary and wanted them closed as soon as practicable. By the end of the war, there were a great number of camps in operation, including about 100 in the South. Shortly after Gen. Clinton B. Fisk became assistant commissioner of the Bureau in Tennessee in June 1865, he ordered the Tennessee camps closed as soon as duty to the weak or sick allowed. The Tunnel Hill camp remained open until the spring of 1866. Some of the others seem to have been closed before that. It is estimated that by early 1866 more than 500,000 people had resided in the contraband camps across the country since the beginning of the war.

The land north and south of the Tunnel Hill camp, near the nine or so miles of railroad between Richland Station and the Elk River, is one of the most interesting and overlooked sections of the N&D. There was the bridge or trestle and its blockhouse—a sturdy wooden house with loopholes—to the north of Tunnel Hill at Richland Creek crossing No. 4. But they were just a small part of the federal military complex near Tunnel Hill.

William L. and Thomas J. Brown had abandoned their plantations during the war and were descendants of ex-Governor Aaron V. Brown, Jr., of Tennessee. Aaron Brown was a democrat with great political influence who had died in 1859 while postmaster under President Buchanan. Thomas Brown's Tunnel Hill property was taken by the army and Lincoln's Republican administration as punishment. His 63 enslaved people stayed on to help transform the property into a camp. The community of Midbridge was about five-and-a-half miles northwest of Elkton on the Pulaski turnpike and about three miles east of the railroad. William Brown's plantation was on the Pulaski turnpike and about three-quarters of a mile southeast of Midbridge. It must have suffered a similar fate.[8]

The Freedmen's Department of the Army took over William Brown's plantation not for a contraband camp but as a place for poor White people, whom the Blacks called "white trash." They were among the many Whites in the Confederacy who would become refugees, going to wherever the Federals were willing to let them stay. They came to the camp primarily from Pea Ridge and other nearly barren regions of North Alabama where, like Giles County, food was scarce, and many people simply could not survive.

The large Tunnel Hill contraband camp was on the plantation of Thomas Brown on the west side of Richland Creek, about two miles southwest of Midbridge and near where Sanders Road is today. The camp itself was probably on the higher ground less than a mile east of Tunnel Hill, putting it out of the floodplain. Gen. Dodge built a sturdy bridge across Richland Creek to connect the Black and White camps. This bridge was at the eastern extremity of the Sanders Road bend. The two camps could probably signal between each other and, because the general and his officers were frequently seen at the White camp, were probably used by Dodge for agent debriefing.[9]

In late 1863 and early 1864, Gen. Dodge was recruiting colored troops in the area. Men of all ages and physical states were coming into southern Tennessee to be enrolled, potentially, in the army. To appease them, every effort was made to allow them to bring their families as well. The inhabitants of the camps ended up being primarily women, children, old men and other men who were rejected by the army. A large number of the men were recruited at the camps, many of whom mustered at Pulaski and served in the 110th and 111th USCTs. In August 1864, some of those troops were assigned to Richland Station, Prospect and blockhouses at Tunnel Hill, perhaps placing some of them near their families at Tunnel Hill.

The Tunnel Hill camp would probably have been predominately to the north and east of the tunnel. The drawing of the north side of Madry's Ridge is viewed obliquely from the north. It is not exactly to scale, and south is up. It is a conjectural, yet very interesting and thoughtful, depiction of the camp's features in 1864. The trestle is shown as starting just north of Petty Branch and extending southward toward the tunnel. However, the two blockhouses, one near each end of the trestle, are not shown. On August 1, 1864, the camp had 1,400 people and about 240 small log houses, each 14 by 6 feet, and the camp was working about 100 acres of cotton. The houses had taken about six months to build. By August 1865, its inhabitants numbered below 500. The size of the plantation varied, as well. In its early days, it contained 1,400 acres of which 600 were tillable. Lt. L.B. Barnes was put in charge of the camp on February 28, 1865. That June, the camp was expanded to about 2,000 acres. The Federals had a commissary near the tunnel that also served the Blacks. There were school buildings, a gin house, a gin and a stable.[10]

During the war, Forrest twice raided the camp. In late September 1864, he had the inhabitants remove the bedding and clothing from their homes, burned most of the structures and then went north to raid, but not destroy, the Pulaski camp. About 2,500 people from those two camps moved north toward Nashville just before Forrest's arrival. Many of those who were still there when Forrest rode in ended up scattering and finding shelter elsewhere. The other event was that November when Hood came through. Residents at the local camps were told to abandon their shelters. Approximately 1,500 made

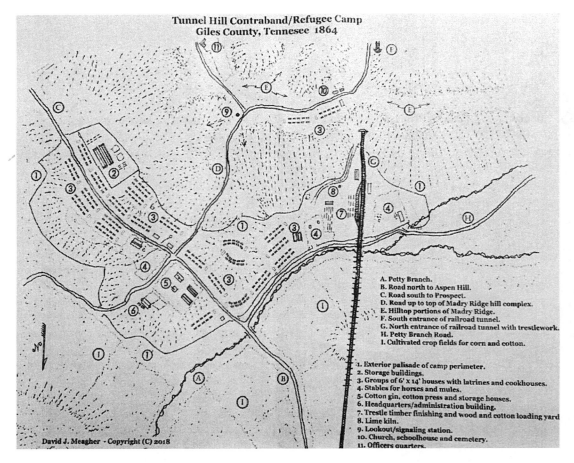

North End of Madry's Ridge and Tunnel Hill, 1864 (Tunnel Hill Contraband/Refugee Camp, Giles County, Tennessee) (© 2021, David J. Meagher, used by permission).

their way to Nashville. In August 1865, Thomas Brown was pardoned, and it was ordered that his property be restored.[11]

Another key feature of this stretch of track is, of course, the quarter-mile long tunnel. It is still open on both ends but is dangerous to enter and located on private land. A trestle was constructed on the north side of the ridge to allow the railroad track to climb to the entrance of the tunnel. The trestle was protected by two blockhouses that were garrisoned by USCTs in July and much of August 1864. Near the north end of the tunnel there was at least one lime kiln, which is still there. Another kiln was south of the tunnel; it is no longer present. About 16,000 cubic yards of limestone were blasted and removed from the tunnel. It was crushed into smaller pieces which were burned, with wood as the fuel, to make quicklime. The quicklime would have been railed from the site to be used in making cement, mortar, whitewash and other products.

There were other features south of the tunnel, as well. The drawing of that side of Madry's Ridge is not to scale and north is up. It is a conjectural depiction of the area in 1864 and is based on artifact concentrations and local history. When combined with the drawing of the north side, the great extent of development and activity at Madry's Ridge become apparent. The heavily wooded hills made the stretch of track between Prospect

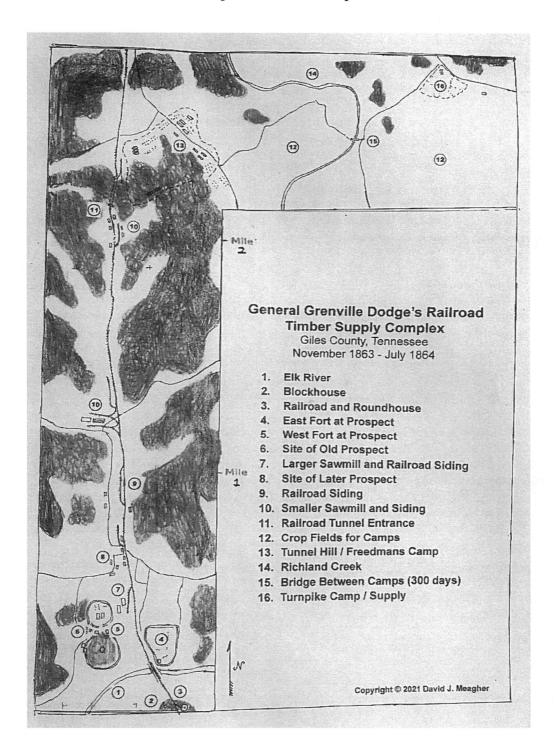

South End of Madry's Ridge and Tunnel Hill, 1864 (Gen. Grenville Dodge's Railroad Timber Supply Complex) (© 2021, David J. Meagher, used by permission).

and Lester's Hollow a great place for sawmills. Dodge built one at Prospect soon after he arrived in November 1863 and assigned companies of his 81st Ohio Infantry to operate it. The mill would have been used to prepare timbers for the trestles and bridges that he was constructing and to cut cordwood for the locomotives. Near both ends of the tunnel were shipping points from which timbers were taken by rail to repair bridges and trestles up and down the railroad. It is likely that some of the inhabitants of the Tunnel Hill camp worked at the mill and shipping points. There seem to have also been at least two smaller sawmills on the south side. They were probably portable, being built on a rail car and rolled onto the sidings. The blades would have been powered by steam generated by a boiler on the car.[12]

At the start of the war, there had been a water tank at the south end of the tunnel which was fed by a spring. It is likely that the Federals used this tank or a replacement. It and the lime kiln south of the tunnel are not shown on the drawing. At some time during the war an artillery site appears to have been constructed on the hill about 2,000 feet to the west of the Elk River railroad bridge. That "fort," another one on the east side of the track and the blockhouse south of the Elk are shown. The "white trash" camp is shown to the east of Richland Creek as well as the bridge that connected the two camps.[13]

With all those features, one can imagine how busy the area was in February through June 1864. Dodge was creating the USCT regiments, and the Tunnel Hill contraband camp and "white trash" camp were in operation. Troops were busy sawing cordwood and timber, sending out by rail the timbers for Dodge's construction of trestles, including the one at the tunnel. Once the trestles were completed, the 1st Michigan was building blockhouses and Boomer was constructing railroad bridges north and south of the tunnel. Boomer's and the 1st Michigan's construction trains and the passenger/freight trains running back and forth between Nashville and Decatur Junction were frequently running through the tunnel, as were Sherman's 16 daily trains. This was not only one of the most interesting sections of the N&D, but also one of the most active.

By March 1864, the N&D was again in good operating order. Gen. Sherman had taken command of the Military Division of the Mississippi on March 18. He was planning his campaign into Georgia and Atlanta and needed the N&D, N&C and M&C to handle the dramatic increase in traffic required to support him.

7

Relying on Merrill's and Innes' Blockhouses

Sherman was preparing for Georgia and Atlanta. By the end of March, he had planned his campaign and assembled a force of about 110,000 men at Chattanooga consisting of three armies: Gen. Thomas' Army of the Cumberland with 73,000 men, Gen. James Birdseye McPherson's Army of the Tennessee with 24,500 men and Gen. John M. Schofield's Army of the Ohio with 13,500.

On about March 23, Sherman performed an inspection tour of the rail lines to support his mission. He rode a train down the rebuilt N&D, through Decatur Junction, then on the M&C through Huntsville to Chattanooga, on to Knoxville and, later, on the N&C. The N&D and M&C seemed to Sherman to be in good operating order. However, the N&C, the preferred and more direct route to supply him at Stevenson, needed work. While inspecting the N&C, Sherman found the track to be laid in a poor manner on an unballasted dirt bed, with light U-rails on wooden stringers (not cross ties) that had decayed badly. There were accidents nearly every day because the rails would spread, allowing the engines and cars to drop between them. The long track lay in enemy territory and was vulnerable to attack, and subsequent closure, by Confederate troops, guerrilla bands and South-sympathetic citizens. The bridges, trestles and depots were especially important. For Sherman to be able to rely on the N&C, the track would need to be repaired and the line operated more efficiently and better protected than it was. One necessary step was assuring that there were plenty of sidings to allow timely passage of trains.

By about June, the Federals had put the N&C back in good operating order, but the N&D had again suffered major damage at the hands of the Confederates, this time below Rutherford Creek. The Federals were still counting on the N&D to supply the Army of the Tennessee; however, only the 39 miles from Nashville to Dark's Mill, at the southernmost crossing over Carter's Creek, were open. The N&D would soon be repaired and fully open as evidenced by Adna Anderson's October 25, 1864, report to Gen. McCallum for the year ending June 30, 1864. That report stated that all 200 miles from Nashville through Decatur to Stevenson were in operation.

To make the N&D, M&C and N&C more efficient, the Federals issued several orders. On April 6, Major Sawyer circulated Sherman's General Orders No. 6 limiting use of the railroad. The document stated that troops were not to be transported by rail when it was possible for them to march, except when permitted by the division. Private citizens and private freight were to be allowed only by permission of a high-ranking officer. Express companies were to be allowed one car per day each way to carry small parcels for soldiers and officers. One additional car per day would be allowed for sutlers' goods and officers' stores if permitted by the quartermaster in Nashville. Horses, cattle and other stock would be allowed only with permission of the Commanding General. Trains on their return trip would be allowed to bring private freight when doing so did not interfere with the military effort, with permission given by the Quartermaster. Until the burden on the railroad was relieved, all military posts within 35 miles of Nashville must haul their stores by wagon. Later, on July 13, Lt. Col. James L. Donaldson, Chief Quartermaster for the Department of the Cumberland, ordered that until October 31 there would be no transport on the N&D of the deceased picked up south of Nashville unless the bodies had been properly embalmed. That same month, Donaldson ordered that no citizens, goods or periodicals were to be transported on the N&D except authorized carriers with regular mail.

> George H. Thomas (1816–1870) was born in Newsom's Depot, Virginia, into an upper-class, plantation lifestyle. His parents owned 685 acres and 24 enslaved people. Thomas determined early in life that slavery was a terrible institution. He was appointed to the U.S. Military Academy where he connected with John Schofield. On Thomas' recommendation, Schofield had been expelled for disciplinary reasons. Thomas later commanded him in several significant battles in the Civil War, including at Franklin. In December 1861, Thomas was given command of the First Division of Buell's Army of the Ohio. He was promoted to major general in April 1862 and given command of the Right Wing of the Department of the Mississippi. Thomas resumed service under Buell as commander of the Center Wing of the new Army of the Cumberland, commanded the Fourteenth Corps and then, in November 1863, succeeded Rosecrans as commander of the Army of the Cumberland. After the war, he continued in command positions. None of his blood relatives attended his funeral because they had not forgiven him, a Virginian, for his loyalty to the Union.
>
> John Schofield (1831–1906) was born in Gerry, New York, and graduated from the U.S. Military Academy. In April 1863, Schofield took command of the Third Division in the Fourteenth Corps of the Army of the Cumberland. His Army of the Ohio fought with Sherman in the Atlanta Campaign. After the Battle of Franklin, Schofield was made brigadier general and then brevet major general in March 1865. During reconstruction, President Johnson named him military governor of Virginia. He served as Secretary of War from June 1868 to March 1869. Schofield served as head of the Department of Missouri and, following Thomas' death, as head of the Military Division of the Pacific. From 1876 to 1881, he was superintendent of the U.S. Military Academy, but was removed from that position because of a scandal at the school. He then served in several other military divisions until 1888 and was the first president of the Army and Navy Club. In 1891, he became the Commanding General of the United States Army.

Sherman was promoting another idea to make the railroads more efficient. In late March and early April, with the N&D repairs nearing completion and the N&C still in need of work, he had been trying to convince McCallum that there would be a great advantage in running the trains counter-clockwise along the three-railroad loop. They would travel from Nashville through Decatur Junction and unload at Stevenson, thus sending the lightened cars along the N&C. The one-way flow of trains would reduce the likelihood of collisions and running the emptied cars along the poorly maintained N&C

would reduce the number of derailments. By April 9, Sherman had permission to do so and amended the General Orders to direct that the trains run counterclockwise.[1]

Supplying what Sherman needed created quite a logistical problem that could be solved by having an adequate number of engines and cars and running them to Chattanooga often enough. At a planning conference in April, the Federals estimated that supplying the armies would require that 130 railroad cars, each with 10 tons of supplies, be sent between Nashville and Chattanooga each day. A report of June 30 stated that, after receiving all the engines for which there were contracts, there would be 209 on the various rails from Nashville. So, they would have the locomotives they needed and, presumably, enough cars as well. Sherman's trains would run in groups of four trains of 10 cars each. Daily, he sent four groups of trains. That means on an average day he sent a total of 16 trains and 160 cars, which exceeded the 130 cars he thought would be required. Sherman later reported that his trains from Nashville had run at 10 mph to reduce the risk of derailment of the heavily loaded cars. This is not surprising because it was not uncommon for a railroad company to run their passenger trains at no greater than 15 miles per hour and freight trains at no more than 10.[2]

William E. Merrill (1837–1891) was born in Wisconsin. He graduated first in his class and was class president at West Point. Merrill was conscientious, modest and devoted to his country. He was assistant engineer on several forts, then assistant professor of engineering at West Point. Merrill started service in the Civil War in July 1861 and worked on a number of fortifications. During the war, he received the successive brevets of captain, major, lieutenant colonel and colonel for gallant service. He was temporarily in charge of construction of the defenses of Washington, D.C., chief engineer of the Army of Kentucky and then the Army of the Cumberland when the Army of Kentucky merged with it. In that role, he constructed defenses at Franklin, Tennessee. He was engaged in a number of major battles and was in charge of the Topographical Department of Gen. Thomas' Army of the Cumberland and chief engineer in the Army of the Cumberland. Merrill was an expert mapper with his own complete establishment for map production—printing presses, lithographic presses, cameras, photographers, lithographers and draftsmen. He supplied some of the best maps produced during the war. In July 1864, he was appointed Colonel of the First Regiment of U.S. Veteran Volunteer Engineers, which he commanded until he was mustered out. Merrill and the regiment designed and constructed 160 blockhouses and defensive works along the military railroads in Tennessee, northern Alabama and Georgia. He mustered out of volunteer service in September 1865.

The Federals did not want more damage like that which the railroad had sustained in the fall of 1863 when guerrillas, Confederate cavalry and storms took turns shutting down sections of the road. The bridges and trestles were hardest to rebuild, and the Federals needed to provide better protection than the stockades offered. The stockades had proven effective against infantry but not against artillery or plunging fire. Dodge and other federal authorities thought that properly designed blockhouses with heavy walls and sturdy roofs would address the weaknesses of the stockades. Merrill, the fourth highlighted builder, was to design and the 1st Michigan was to build effective blockhouses on the railroads operated by the Army of the Cumberland, including the N&D. Merrill was also to oversee construction of the houses. Lt. Col. Kinsman A. Hunton of the 1st Michigan was Merrill's and Innes' right-hand man. Merrill and Hunton toured the N&D in February, stopping at every bridge to select the blockhouse sites.[3]

Dodge believed that a company, about 25 to 30 men, in a blockhouse was equal to a regiment, about 1,000 men, in attack power. This indicates the confidence that he had in a properly located, built, manned and operated blockhouse. The Federals would design a structure that could typically house and protect a garrison of 20 to 30 men. They assumed that the enemy would have dismounted cavalry and light artillery rather than heavy field pieces. And they figured that the attackers would not engage in a lengthy battle because word of the attack would probably quickly get to another Union stronghold, and reinforcements were likely to arrive soon. Sturdy roofs were needed because the railroad bridges and trestles and their fortifications were naturally located at low points and were often vulnerable to plunging fire from higher points on nearby hills. Also, the structure needed to be near enough to the structure it was protecting to allow the troops to fire effectively from that distance. The longer bridges and trestles were to have two houses, one near each end.

Starting in January of 1864, Merrill and Hunton oversaw a series of experiments on a spare blockhouse at La Vergne, Tennessee, near the N&C. They used different styles and thicknesses of wooden defenses against various types of firearms and artillery pieces. After trial and error, they settled on square or rectangular wooden blockhouses that would be built from the usually abundant standing timber near the construction site. Although details of the structure built at a particular site would vary with the specific needs and resources, the houses were intended to have two stories, with the second story set diagonally relative to the ground floor. The walls of the lower floor were to be double-thickness timber, at least 40 inches of total thickness, with 20-inch-thick timbers set vertically and sunk into the ground as an inner wall and the outer 20-inch-thick wall laid horizontally. Because discarded train rails were often available near the blockhouse sites, they would be attached horizontally to the walls if available, making the structure much stronger. The smaller second story turned at an angle would give a better vantage point for seeing the enemy. Its walls would be single-log thickness because this area would be

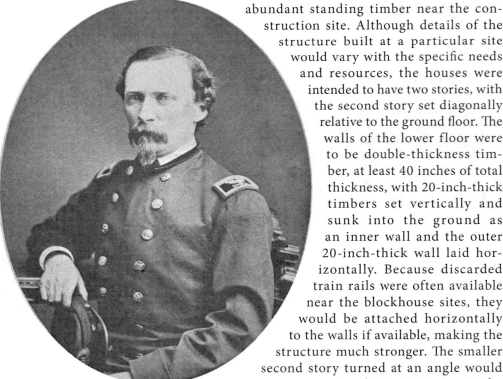

Col. William E. Merrill (Box 6, Folder 4 from the American Geographical Society Library, University of Wisconsin–Milwaukee Libraries).

evacuated during an attack. The houses were to have earth fill placed outside up to the loopholes.[4]

The blockhouse roof was to consist of one or two layers of logs with earth placed atop. Shingles of board or batten would provide water tightness. Ventilators, cellars, water tanks and bunks were to be added for a garrison of 20 or more. The doorway was the weakest point in the house. To prevent the enemy from gaining direct access to it or firing into it, the typical entrance seems to have been through a narrow gallery, only about three feet wide. Entry to the gallery from the interior was cut through the blockhouse wall, with the gallery making a quick turn to one side and then turning again perpendicular to the house and through the earthen fill.

Framing and erecting were to be done by the 1st Michigan but, because they had a large number of blockhouses to build as quickly as possible, they were not expected to be available to build the second exterior ground floor wall or the second story. The outer layer of timber, placement of dirt fill and the finishing touches, including the second story if there was to be one, would be left to the garrison. It seems that few, if any, of the houses on the N&D would get second stories.[5]

The Federals planned to build houses at the bridges and trestles on the N&D, M&C and N&C. In spite of the fact that octagonal houses were thought to provide a

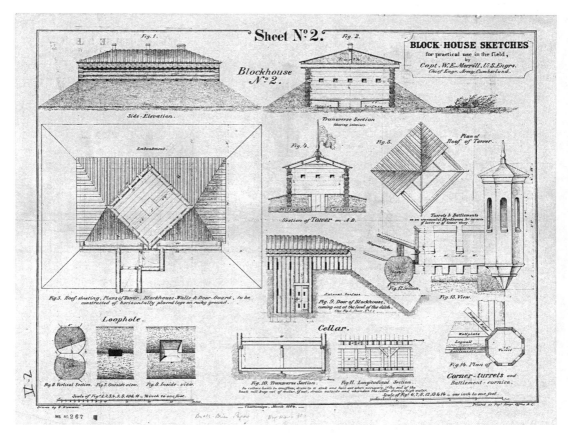

Merrill's block-house sketches (Generic Design); Buell-Brien Papers, 1806–1943 (Tennessee State Library & Archives).

A Blockhouse on the N&C Railroad (Library of Congress).

better defense, square or rectangular houses were built initially. Octagonal structures would be built in late 1864 and 1865, especially as replacements for the houses that had been burned by Hood, Forrest and others. The number of octagonal houses built is not known.[6]

Merrill and the 1st Michigan quickly got about the business of building the houses. On March 1, when Dodge was nearing completion of his work on the trestles, Col. Innes, eight companies of the 1st Michigan and two regiments of USCTs were ordered to start constructing blockhouses and other defenses along the N&C. On about the thirteenth, Major John B. Yates and the 600 men of Companies A, F, G and H of the 1st Michigan were sent to the N&D to work on some of the 36 houses that were to be built between Nashville and Decatur Junction. Yates' troops were divided into squads of about 20 to 30 men and scattered along the N&D, each being assigned a house to build. They started on the northern end and generally worked toward the south. The northernmost house seems to have been five miles north of Columbia at Carter's Creek. Once the 1st Michigan had finished work on a house and was ready to depart, the garrison would prepare it for occupancy, work on the exterior and probably dismantle the stockade. On the twentieth, James M. Sligh, Quartermaster Sergeant and Captain in Company G, wrote home saying he thought the houses would be complete by about the end of April.[7]

In his diary, William Kimball, of 1st Michigan Company H, working under Yates, described some of the work his squad performed at one of the several houses being built at the bridges over Carter's Creek. It was 53 by 21 feet inside and was estimated to require 2,400 cubic feet of timber. On March 15, his group prepared the timber for the 12 × 18 sills, posts and plates and 12 × 12's for the roof. However, they slacked and were reprimanded. The men continued on April 2, framing the sills and plates and starting to put up the vertical posts. Two days later, they laid the foundation and on the sixth they nearly completed one wall. By the ninth, they had finished the walls, making them 18 inches thick with portholes. On the thirteenth, they put on the plates, then put some railroad T rails on for additional strength. The roof pieces were so heavy that they needed help getting them on and finished that on the eighteenth. On April 23, Kimball and some men remained to finish the house, while others went to work on the house to the north of them, probably another on Carter's Creek or possibly the one at the West Harpeth. Though this house was larger than most, it seemed to be slow in completing. Two days later, Kimball was working to get the timber out for a bridge. By the end of April, Yates, his companies and Kimball were sent to the N&C to construct blockhouses.

While houses were being built in Tennessee and probably in northern Alabama, there was activity in Alabama where houses had not yet been constructed. On March 14, guards were being sent to a trestle (Dodge No. 24) between Athens and the Low Trestle where a blockhouse was to be located. In spite of their presence, at dawn on the twenty-fifth the trestle was attacked by guerrillas causing some of the Union troops to flee. Also, on the twenty-fourth, Dodge ordered Lt. Col. Joey A. Dewey at Athens to patrol the N&D once each day and once each night, at varying hours. He was to do this as far north as midway between the Elk River and the trestle at Mill Creek just south of the state line.[8]

On April 12, Major J.R. Willett of the 38th Illinois Infantry, Inspector of Fortifications for the District of Nashville, rode on the N&D to check on progress of the blockhouses and other fortifications. Regarding the blockhouses being built on the N&D, he reported, "They were in an unfinished condition, and I should judge that they were three-fourths done; the most of the work remaining to be done is to put on the roofs." Willett's report on Fort Granger stated, "I visited Franklin and found the principle work, Fort Granger, in a dilapidated condition; no attempt appears to have been made to keep it in proper order or repair. The magazines are very damp and entirely unfit to store ammunition. I noticed green mold on the ceiling. All the heavy guns are being remounted, and I understand it is the intention to keep two field pieces at the fort."[9]

On May 14, Kimball and others from the 1st Michigan were back at work on the N&D at Mud Creek. It appears that Swan Creek, about four miles north of Athens, was called Mud Creek at that time. There were two low trestles over that reach of Swan Creek not far from each other. The men seem to have been at the site where guards had been sent on March 14. On May 16, they started getting the timber out for a 21-foot by 21-foot blockhouse. Two days later, they finished preparing the timber. Early on the morning of the nineteenth, they heard gunfire and the stoppage of a train that had been coming up from the south. They went down the track and saw that the engine and two cars had made it over some damaged track, but the rest of the train was wrecked. Confederates had torn up the track then gone down the line toward the train to fire at the engineer, knowing he would open the throttle to speed the train so more of it would pass over the bad section of track. Union infantry arrived soon after, running the Confederates off. The engineer, who was a brother of Gen. George A. Custer, was injured in the hand and a brakeman was nearly killed. On May 25, the 1st Michigan put the sills in place and a large number of bridge builders arrived to put up a bridge. It seems that Boomer's men had arrived to replace Dodge's temporary trestle with Howe trusses. By the twenty-eighth, Kimball and the others had finished the blockhouse walls.

Swan Creek would not have been the only site where Boomer and the 1st Michigan worked side by side late that spring. Both started at the north and worked generally southward. Boomer's group began the work before the 1st Michigan and seems to have made quicker progress along the N&D. This concurrent work would have required that the movement of the various trains—those with Boomer's men and supplies, those for Innes' work and the passenger/freight trains that had started running again in March—be well coordinated.

On June 29, George Burroughs, Lt. Engineer and Acting Chief Engineer, Department of the Cumberland, reported to Brig. Gen. William D. Whipple, Chief of Staff in the Department, that there were 36 "block-houses," all with single-thickness walls and a water tank (one-half of which were inside the house), along the N&D. Twelve still needed the exterior timber casing built and the roof covered with earth. This work would continue at some blockhouses for several months. It seems that most houses eventually got the second layer of timber on the lower level. Even as late as August 20, Jacob Sigmund, First Lieutenant, Company E, 7th Pennsylvania Cavalry, wrote that his company was getting out the timber for the double casings of several blockhouses on the N&D, following up on the work that had been started by the 1st Michigan.[10]

In summary, the timeline for the work done by Dodge, Boomer and the 1st Michigan on the N&D was:

Dodge built trestles—November 1863 through February 1864.
Boomer replaced the temporary trestles with bridges—December 1863 through May 1864.
1st Michigan Engineers and Mechanics built block houses—March through about June 1864.

And status of the railroads:

N&D was back in good working order—March 1864.
Trains were running on the loop—April–June 1864.
N&C was repaired, improved and protected and trains running on it—June 1864.

Table 3 in Appendix C lists the crossings where blockhouses and other fortifications are thought to have been located in mid–1864. It appears that one or more blockhouse was built at each of the bridges and trestles that did not already have a fort or other adequate form of protection. Several sites, including Culleoka and Lynnville, seem to have ended up with both blockhouses and a stockade. Those stockades, however, were larger and not the type that had been built near the crossings and subsequently replaced by blockhouses. Although blockhouses replaced the stockades, a small number of the small stockades might have remained and been used when the site warranted more troops than the blockhouse could hold. Literature provides evidence that, once the blockhouse at a site was ready for occupancy, the existing stockade was emptied, the men moved into the house and the stockade was dismantled as soon as possible. Because a blockhouse offered better protection if the area around it were cleared of trees and other obstructions, it makes sense that the stockades would probably have been removed if they were not to be used. Forrest stated that he captured and burned blockhouses in September and October 1864 but did not make much reference to stockades. When he did mention a stockade, it could well have been in reference to the few that remained, like those at Culleoka and Lynnville.

From June 1864 through about June 1865, blockhouses were the dominant form of fortification for the bridges and trestles on the N&D. The square or rectangular houses proved to be successful against small attacks. Usually, the garrison of 20 or 30 men could hold out long enough for reinforcements to arrive or for the enemy to give up and depart. However, they did not fare well against an enemy that had heavy artillery, a strong force or a stern determination to take the house. Such was the case in the fall of 1864 when Forrest and then Hood came in large numbers and destroyed many of them. Forrest often took a house by threatening the occupants with annihilation by artillery, causing the commander to give in to the temptation to surrender.

The garrisons at the blockhouses were probably ordered to follow guidelines very similar or identical to those for the stockades.

In spite of this, the blockhouse garrisons did not always follow the guidelines, which could put the positions at jeopardy. It was not uncommon for the inspector to arrive to find only two or three men at a house, with the remainder away on some unrelated activity. On at least one occasion, the few men at the house explained that the majority were out cutting wood.

Construction of the houses was successful, but not without drama. There was ill will between Merrill and Innes which seems to have stemmed from the competition between the 1st Michigan on one hand and the regular engineer office and Pioneer Brigade on the other. Merrill was suspicious of wood-contracting activities involving the 1st Michigan that had been going on for some time and was eager to have the matter investigated. In August 1864, Captain Henry Cist investigated and learned that civilian contractor Benham & Company had hired three subcontractors with close ties to the 1st Michigan. One of the duties of the 1st Michigan was to cut and haul wood. They had procured 100 wagons from Nashville, supposedly to be used for blockhouse construction only, but also used them for a wood-selling business. In the questionable contract, they sold cut wood to the contractor for $4.50 per cord, dividing $1.00 among the principal men, $0.50 going to 1st Michigan company officers and the remaining $3.00 going to the contractor. On September 4, Merrill wrote in a private letter that Col. Innes and several other men were swindlers. Merrill stated that Innes, whom he called an "accomplished, smooth-tongued" individual, seemed the guiltiest and asked for further investigation. That investigation ended with the contractor being assessed $47,000 for the wood that had been contracted in an unethical manner and the contract with Benham & Company being annulled. There was no action, however, against Innes or the 1st Michigan.[11]

While the blockhouses were being constructed, Confederate attacks had, of course, continued. On April 17, Dodge received word in Athens that about 3,000 Confederate infantry, with artillery and cavalry, were approaching Decatur. He and the 9th Illinois rushed south and found a sharp fight underway. Dodge led the 9th Illinois in a mounted charge, supported by infantry, and forced the Confederates to retreat to the southwest of Decatur. On May 4, guerrillas placed a stone on the track between Franklin and Spring Hill. Between the fourth and tenth, guerrillas fired into two trains, killing the engineer and fireman on the tenth, and attempted to destroy the Sulphur Creek Trestle. Also, a quantity of cut wood was set afire on the track at several places between Nashville and Franklin. On May 13, Dodge told Sherman that the railroad was in great danger and that his troops were along the railroad holding it from Lynnville to Athens.[12]

Jacob Sigmund's letters give additional insight into some of his activities and the locations of some of the blockhouses on Rutherford Creek. In a letter of June 10, 1864, to his brother from Lynnville Station, he wrote, "I have left Buford Bridge. I left there on the first of this month to take charge of Co. E, 7th Pa. V.V. Cavalry & a great company it is. Company E is composed of 139 men of all grades & sizes of every co. in the Reg't. Well in fact it is the shisers (?) of the Regt. True I have a good many good men but the majority of them are cripples, convalescence & c." "23 of them are mounted & some isn't, I will try to classify them as well as I can. 23 of them are mounted & armed with Spencer Carbines. They are used for scouts & c. 34 of them are at Gracys Trestle guarding the trestle work." Sigmund went to Gracey's for some time then departed there on about August 1, taking rail cars to Columbia. He then received orders to take 48 men up the rail to Blockhouse Numbers 9 and 10 on Rutherford Creek to relieve the 2nd Michigan Cavalry, who were to report to Franklin. Sigmund's headquarters was at house Number 10. Sgt. S.B. Darrah and House Number 13 were about three-fourths of a mile away. Corp. Wasson was at house Number 11, only about 150 yards away on the opposite side of Rutherford Creek. Also, about a quarter mile away was house Number 12. As of August 28, Sigmund was still at Number 10, expecting an attack on the railroad the past several days. His men were busy getting out the timber to double-case a blockhouse.[13]

As important as the system of trains, tracks, bridges, trestles and blockhouses was, it was now there primarily to support something bigger—Sherman in Georgia. The Federals found a way to further increase the efficiency of this railroad system. Although the distance from Nashville to Stevenson and back to Nashville via Decatur along the counter-clockwise loop was about 85 miles longer than on the 120-miles of the N&C alone, using that longer route had been necessary to keep troops and supplies moving until mid-1864 because the N&C track was not in a condition to handle too much traffic. The shorter, direct route along the N&C always had the potential to be the most efficient path for getting supplies to Stevenson. That potential became a reality in June 1864 when the N&C and its operation were improved to efficiently handle a large volume of two-way traffic on a single track with sidings. Sherman then used the road, rather than the loop, to supply him. With so much two-way traffic on one main track, and many trains having to wait on sidings for trains going the other way to pass, the Federals would obviously have to operate the N&C with extreme care. Even after the counter-clockwise circuit was no longer the primary route, the M&C and N&D provided a secondary route, and the N&D was still important for local supply purposes until early fall when Forrest destroyed much of it. After those attacks, the N&D would not be whole again until February of the following year.

Sherman and the 100,000 or so men of the Armies of the Cumberland, the Ohio and the Tennessee had been in Chattanooga in the late spring of 1864, preparing for their drive into north Georgia and Atlanta. They were receiving virtually all of their needs from Nashville, mostly along the loop. In May, Gen. Sherman moved his army into north Georgia, calling in most of his forces that had been in North Alabama. By early June, his forces were driving deeper into Georgia and extending their supply lines. The N&C had become the main supply route for Sherman before the Battle of Atlanta in July and his November and December "March to the Sea." It was now the line over which most of the provisions, clothing, camp gear, forage for the animals, arms, ammunition and all the other necessities of war were being sent to the front. The sick, wounded, disabled, discharged soldiers, refugees, freed men, prisoners and materials needed at the rear were sent back by it. Sherman needed the N&C to remain open, so he had built blockhouses on the N&C and provided plenty of troops, especially at the bridges, trestles and storehouses. The Federals could repair damaged track fairly quickly, but that was not the case for the structures. In case the railroads were shut down for a significant length of time, he had extra supplies stored in Chattanooga. A report for that next

November indicated that more than twice as many troops were sent along the N&C than via Decatur, showing that, though both routes were important, the N&C was dominant.

Though the N&D did not play a major role in the Civil War or in bringing freedom to enslaved people, it can be argued that the N&C did. The railroad helped Sherman defeat the Confederates and seize Atlanta on September 2, 1864. The victory provided President Lincoln a political boost that helped him to be reelected that November 8. With Lincoln remaining in office, he was able to continue his push for the 13th Amendment, which was approved by Congress on January 31, 1865, and enacted on December 6, 1865, well after his assassination. The amendment freed the remaining 3.3 to 3.4 million Blacks who had not been freed by the Emancipation Proclamation.[14]

The blockhouses along all the railroads seemed to be making a difference. For the next few months after they were put in place and manned, there were activities and incidents along the N&D but not much related to Confederate attacks. The Elk River Bridge was an active site. On May 19, construction of two spans of that bridge was well under way. The bridge was ready for ties and iron and was expected to be open that night. This work on the Elk was probably done by Boomer when they were replacing Dodge's temporary trestles with Howe trusses. On Sunday afternoon, May 24, there was a strange accident at the Duck River Bridge. A horse was alarmed by an approaching train and, rather than distancing itself from the track, ran onto the bridge, fell between the timbers and got stuck. The train could not stop in time. The engine and tender passed over the horse, but the first car hit him, knocking him into the river. The car left the track, but the coupling held, and the engine continued on for some distance, dragging along the track a number of additional cars that had jumped the track. It is fortunate that no one was killed and that the bridge was apparently not damaged. On July 19, it was reported that heavy flows on the Harpeth damaged four bents of the railroad bridge in Franklin, rendering it unusable. The bents were probably on the short approaches at each end of the bridge. Sigmund wrote on August 20 that the Duck River pontoon bridge at Columbia was washed away, and the Federals were having to cross the river on the nearby railroad bridge instead.[15]

Though the blockhouses were reasonably effective in protecting the bridges and trestles, Forrest and others were still able to slow traffic to Stevenson by damaging the N&D track and a few of its bridges. On the morning of September 2, Company E, 102nd Ohio Infantry took train cars southward to Athens. They found that Wheeler had destroyed the track six miles north of town, so they were ordered to remain at Athens to repair and guard the railroad. That same day, Pvt. Stephen A. Jordan and Company G of the 9th Tennessee cavalry tore up and burned track from three miles south of Franklin to Spring Hill. On the fourth, Forrest attacked Athens. Company F of the 102nd Ohio was at Fort Henderson when it surrendered after three hours of fierce fighting. That same day, Wheeler attacked the rail just south of Lynnville Station where the 9th Indiana Cavalry was guarding the crossing at Robertson Fork Creek. He surrounded the Lynnville stockade where Company F of the 9th Indiana had been garrisoned since August 12. They refused to surrender and eventually got reinforcements from the 9th and 10th Indiana Cavalries, driving Wheeler off. On September 10, Wheeler reported that he had destroyed bridges and several miles of track between Nashville and Columbia. That portion of the track was repaired immediately.[16]

Chaucla Bickford and his Co. E of 4th Michigan Cavalry were at Blockhouse Number 19, the exact location of which is unknown, on Monday, September 19 when the house was attacked by Wheeler. They refused to surrender and survived numerous attacks from Wheeler's artillery which had been placed at a number of different locations. Wheeler left after suffering heavy losses. This seems to be one of the earlier specific reports of a Confederate attack on a blockhouse.[17]

Blockhouse Number 19 fared well in this attack. However, it would probably be one of the many to be destroyed in the attacks on the bridges, trestles and blockhouses along much of the N&D that Gens. Forrest, Wheeler and Abraham Buford initiated later that week.

8

Forrest Comes Calling

Battles had been raging in Georgia and Sherman captured Atlanta on September 2. The railroads, primarily the N&C, supplied him on his way through Georgia and would continue to do so as he was preparing for his "March to the Sea."

The Confederates were compelled to do what they could to disrupt the flow of supplies to Sherman, which meant attacking the supplying railroads. The situation called for the best they had. They needed the speed of cavalry, boldness, logistical skills, the appropriate artillery, a lot of men and the determination to succeed. Who better than Generals Forrest, Buford and Wheeler? Lt. Gen. Richard Taylor, commander of the Department of Alabama, Mississippi and East Louisiana, ordered Forrest to attack the N&D and N&C, and in late September and early October the three would make the Confederates' grandest raids on the railroads. Their primary goals were to slow rail traffic, especially the N&C, and to draw federal troops away from Sherman to protect the railroads, thus reducing the pressure he was applying to Georgia and South Carolina. In the end, they would be very successful in disrupting traffic on the N&D, but unable to do anything to the more important N&C or to deter Sherman.

> Abraham Buford (1820–1884) was born in Kentucky. He attended the U.S. Military Academy and was a successful breeder of thoroughbred horses at his farm Bosque Bonita in Woodford County. Like his home state, he tried to stay out of the Civil War, but he joined the Confederate Army in September 1862 under the rank of brigadier general. He served as a cavalry general in the Western Theater and led a cavalry division under Forrest. Buford fought in several battles including Vicksburg and Brice's Crossroads and was wounded on December 24, 1864, at Richland Creek while a part of the rearguard helping Hood retreat. After the war, he returned to Kentucky to breed horses. A series of family tragedies drove Buford to take his own life in 1884. He is buried in Lexington, Kentucky.

Cherokee, Alabama, lay on the M&C about 60 miles west of Athens and was the point where Forrest brought in and collected everything he needed to start his next campaign. With 10 days rations, he, Buford and the rest of his men left Cherokee at daylight on September 21 with the intention of attacking and damaging both the N&D and N&C. Artillery, ordnance and wagons were ferried across the Tennessee River at Newport, which at that time was about mid-way between Mussel Shoals and the Alabama-Mississippi state line. A bit downstream at Newport's Ross's Ford (Colbert Shoals), Forrest and his cavalry forded the river and camped that night near Florence.

The next morning, they moved toward Athens and were joined east of Florence by Gen. Roddey's cavalry. Forrest's force now consisted of about 3,500 of his own men, about 900 from Roddey and about 600 with Wheeler, a total of approximately 5,000. About 400 were dismounted, but they expected to soon be mounted on horses that would be captured from the enemy. They also had 10 cannons.[1]

The defense of the N&D was managed at this time by Maj. Gen. Rousseau who had brigades under Brig. Gen. Robert Granger at Decatur, Brig. Gen. John C. Starkweather at Pulaski and Col. William B. Sipes at Columbia.[2]

At about 10 p.m. on the twenty-second, with most of the men near Rogersville, Alabama, Forrest started a move on Athens. Single-cased Blockhouse Number 1 sat nearest Decatur Junction. It had 44 dismounted men from the 4th Tennessee Cavalry under the command of Lt. Hunter. Forrest did not attack this house or its trestle, perhaps because doing so would have brought federal reinforcements sooner than Forrest wanted.

In 1864, the Tennessee River was an uncontrolled whitewater river and Decatur Junction was located northeast of the present-day railroad junction. Wheeler Dam, which is just downstream of Decatur, was completed in 1936. Its impoundment flooded the land to several thousand feet north of the previous north bank of the Tennessee River, but not as far north as Decatur Junction.

Moving up the railroad on the morning of the twenty-third, Forrest found that double-cased Blockhouses Number 2 at Pryor Creek (Dodge No. 29), Number 3 at Swan Creek (Dodge No. 28) and Number 4 at a tributary of Old Schoolhouse Branch near McDonald's Station (Dodge No. 27) had been evacuated. They had been garrisoned by a total of about 100 men from the 111th USCT under the command of Capt. James Henry. The Federals must have known the guards at those houses would be killed or taken prisoner, so ordered that they dessert the sites. Forrest burned the three houses and the first two bridges and continued northward. The trestle at the Old Schoolhouse Branch was fired later in the day. Lt. Henry C. March, Asst. Inspector of Railroad Defenses, had responsibility for the blockhouses as far north in Alabama as the state line. He later provided a report on the fate of the 11 houses on the N&D.[3]

Forrest ordered some of his horsemen to capture a federal corral near McDonald's Station, destroy the telegraph line and track and block Federals who might come up from Decatur or Huntsville to reinforce Athens. Continuing northward and approaching Athens late in the evening, he heard the whistle of a locomotive at the Athens railway station. Forrest ordered some men to ride north of the town to cut the railroad and the telegraph wires, so there could be no communication or trains to the north out of Athens. Then he surrounded the town.[4]

The main defense in Athens was a 180-foot by 450-foot earthwork fort atop Coleman Hill, later named Fort Henderson. It was a little more than half a mile southwest of the town square and about the same distance west of the N&D. The fort had been completed in early 1863 and protected the town and railroad. Part of the fortification was made with 20-foot lengths of tree trunks lashed together with honeysuckle vines. The trunks were placed in a circle large enough to enclose the area. A line of abatis was added, and a 12-foot-deep moat was dug around the outside, with the dirt from the moat piled onto the trunks to form a rampart. In 1862, before the fort was built, troops and impressed Blacks under Turchin had cut down the forest on the west and south sides of Athens to prevent a surprise attack by the Confederates. It seems that the fort was reconstructed later in the war, perhaps in 1864, because its description was much different in a June 1865 report.[5]

8. Forrest Comes Calling

In late April, Col. Wallace Campbell of the 2nd Alabama Volunteers had been put in charge of the U.S. troops guarding the N&D from the Elk River to Decatur Junction, and Maj. Gen. John D. Stevenson put in command of all U.S. forces on the N&D from Lynnville to and including the junction.[6]

At 4 p.m. on the twenty-third, Col. Campbell, commander of Fort Henderson, was notified that a body of Confederates, about 200 to 300 strong, was tearing up track four or five miles to the south. He sent Major Samuel W. Pickens and 100 to 150 men, including some of the 3rd Tennessee Cavalry, down by rail on the evening train that had just arrived from Nashville. Another 100 men went down the Decatur Road. The Confederates were driven off and a burning trestle, probably the trestle at the Old Schoolhouse Branch (Dodge No. 27), was saved. The train crossed to the south side of the trestle, then about a mile farther down the track rebels appeared at its rear. The train was reversed north toward Athens and drove the attackers off the track. Upon reaching the outskirts of town, it was attacked by about 1,000 Confederates, so the train was ordered to be taken to the protection of a blockhouse, either Number 5 or Number 6 just to the north at Town Creek. After more than an hour of fighting at that blockhouse, the Union fell back to the fort. Forrest did not take the house at that time.[7]

By now, Confederates had surrounded and entered all sides of Athens and tried several times to take control of the town but were pushed back. However, their numbers and determination were too great to be driven away. The quartermaster's building was set afire, and the T&AC's combination passenger/freight depot was taken and set on fire as were the commissary building and probably several other buildings around the square. Part of the Confederate 14th Tennessee Cavalry had stayed south of Athens to watch for troops coming up from Decatur. Gen. Robert Granger at Decatur had sent Lt. Col. William F. Prosser and about 300 to 500 men from the 2nd Tennessee Cavalry to Athens. The two forces engaged, and the Federals slowly pushed the Confederates back toward Athens.[8]

About 9 p.m., the 2nd Tennessee reached Athens. Campbell ordered Prosser to charge his cavalry to the public square to drive the Confederates from the burning depot, but he refused because he did not want to sacrifice his horses. Campbell dismounted about 30 of the cavalry, took 20 Black infantry and ran to the depot, drove the Confederates away, extinguished the fire and captured a surgeon and a soldier. The soldier told him that Forrest had 10–12,000 men and nine pieces of artillery. Sometime very early on the twenty-fourth, all of the Union troops, including some men from the 3rd Tennessee, were moved to the fort except those who remained in the two blockhouses. At that point, the garrison consisted of about 571 men: 105 men and four officers of the 106th USCT, 233 men and 17 officers of the 110th, 80 men and eight officers of the 111th, and 120 men and four officers of the 3rd Tennessee Cavalry.[9]

Campbell ordered Prosser and the 2nd Tennessee to remain at or near the fort, but he again refused to obey, saying that even with his force the fort could not be held. Then Lt. Samuel M. Kneeland of Granger's staff ordered Prosser and his men to return to Decatur. Campbell told Prosser to report at Decatur what was occurring at Athens. He also sent two couriers with dispatches to Gen. Starkweather at Pulaski. However, one of the couriers was killed on the edge of town and the other was wounded and returned to the fort.

Forrest had the town, fort and two blockhouses surrounded, and his artillery in place to shell the fort. At 7 a.m. on September 24, he advanced and fired his artillery.

The cannon fire lasted about two hours, with about 60 Confederate shells coming into and around the fort but little damage done. At about 9 a.m., Forrest sent a written demand for immediate surrender. Among his terms were that all White soldiers would be treated as prisoners and all Blacks would be returned to their masters. Campbell declined. A bit later, a parlay was conducted during which Maj. J.P. Strange, Forrest's Adjutant-General through the entire war, told the Federals that Forrest was determined to take the fort, and if he stormed no lives would be spared. Campbell refused again. Forrest then asked for a personal interview with Campbell outside the fort. Campbell agreed and rode out to meet him with Capt. B.M. Callender of the 1st Missouri Light Artillery. Forrest told them that he would take the fort, he had 10–12,000 men, as opposed to the actual 5,000, and wished to avoid the imminent bloodshed within the fort. Campbell surveyed the troops and thought he saw troops in the numbers stated by Forrest. He went back to consult some of the other officers, telling them that to defend the fort would be worse than murder. Campbell took another soldier out again to inspect the forces and seemed once again satisfied that there were at least 10,000 men and probably more than a dozen pieces of artillery. At about 10:45 that morning, he agreed to surrender the fort and the entire garrison.

Two different strategies had been at play during the negotiations. While conducting the interviews with Campbell, to make it appear that he had more troops than he really did, Forrest had numerous campfires lit in the distance and commanded his men to dismount and march as if they were infantry, then remount and change positions to appear as cavalry. Forrest also had his artillery moved around so it would seem that he had more than the actual eight or nine. On the Union side, Campbell was stalling in the hopes that reinforcements from Decatur would arrive, but he saw no sign of them and finally felt compelled to surrender after delaying for about two hours.

The Union soldiers, especially the USCTs, were not happy about surrendering. This was probably because they had heard about the unnecessary carnage when Forrest took Fort Pillow and did not want to meet that same fate. Many within the fort thought they could defend their position effectively, even without reinforcements. Some of the White officers later wrote from prison that, once the surrender was announced, they had to threaten shooting their own men to get them to comply.

About the time of the surrender, heavy fighting was heard down the road toward Decatur. About 378 men from the 18th Michigan Infantry and 102nd Ohio Infantry sent that morning from Decatur by Gen. Granger had arrived at the breach in the track made the night before by Forrest and were being attacked by Confederates. The Federals pressed through the woods toward the fort, fighting all the way with heavy losses. The engagement culminated with the 18th Michigan and 102nd Ohio within 300 yards of the fort, finding that Lt. Gen. Jesse Forrest, one of Bedford's brothers, and the 21st Tennessee Cavalry stood between them and the fort. The Federals advanced toward the fort and fought for three hours before surrendering. During the fight, Lt. Gen. Forrest was seriously injured in the thigh. The surrendered Union soldiers were marched up to the fort no more than 30 minutes after the defeated garrison in the fort had exited and stacked their arms. Before the surrender, Col. William H. Lathrop, Union commander of the 111th USCT at Sulphur Creek, had sent his mounted force toward Athens but found the town already heavily surrounded.[10]

The wooden features of the fort, two engines and two trains of cars from Athens, probably the one at the blockhouse plus one more, were burned. Earlier on the twenty-fourth, all but three men of Company E, 111th had been captured by Forrest. Capt. McTaggart subsequently escaped and took command of the company. The 111th USCT's regimental headquarters was there. All of their records were burned. Nearly all of the 571 or so men from the 106th, 110th and 111th USCT Regiments and the 3rd Tennessee were captured that day, as well as two howitzers, 30 wagons, 300 horses, many small arms and a large amount of supplies. Company F, 110th USCT and Company G and a detachment from Company D, 111th USCT, were taken prisoner by Forrest. Col. Campbell and 58 men from Company H and some men from Company K of the 111th surrendered, as well. The sergeant major and commissary sergeant escaped, but the surgeon and hospital steward stayed behind to care for the wounded.[11]

Blockhouse Number 5, a mile south of Athens at a tributary of Town Creek (Dodge No. 26), was double-cased and garrisoned by 40 to 50 men of the 106th USCT under First Sgt. H.C. Weaver. Forrest surrounded it with dismounted cavalry and got a surrender at about noon on the twenty-fourth. Blockhouse Number 6 sat on the west side of the trestle across Town Creek (Dodge No. 25). It was double cased up to the loopholes and garrisoned by Capt. A. Poe and 40 men of the 106th USCT. After the fort surrendered, the Confederates demanded surrender of the house, but Poe refused. Forrest brought in his cannons, but they still refused so he had his battery fire several shots that penetrated the walls. This killed and wounded several, after which the house was surrendered at about "12 m" (noon). Forrest burned those two houses and their bridges. During all this, word had gotten out that Athens was taken, so the Federals ordered that all trains on the track north of Athens be run farther north.[12]

Later, on October 17, 1864, numerous officers who had been at Athens signed a statement explaining that they felt the surrender by Col. Campbell was unwarranted. They declared that Campbell had seen Forrest's forces and consulted some of the other federal officers and all but two voted to surrender, but the officers of the largest commands were not consulted. They said that the vast majority of the troops were eager to fight and thought that even though Forrest had greater numbers, he could not take the fort. The men, especially the USCTs, did not want to be Forrest's prisoners because they feared how they would be treated. Also, the 18th Michigan and 102nd Ohio Infantries were on their way to the fort and were within musket range at the time of surrender. They stated that Campbell could hear them firing in the distance but surrendered anyway. A third of those infantrymen were killed or wounded in three hours of hard fighting. The signing officers requested a thorough investigation. The statement was sent to Maj. Gen. Thomas and then Sherman. Col. Campbell was subsequently released in a prisoner exchange but not formally court-martialed and apparently did not even go to trial. Later, on January 21, 1865, the Union had the names of about 869 soldiers from the 106th, 110th and 111th USCTs who had been taken prisoner by Forrest at Athens and Sulphur Creek Trestle and put to work for the Confederates in Mobile.[13]

With Forrest heading north of Athens, it is appropriate to discuss the difficulty in locating and numbering the next blockhouse he encountered and, just as importantly, the location of "Low Trestle." There were only two trestles between Athens and Sulphur Creek, both of which were very low, meaning that they were almost at ground level and located in a wet area. In March 1864 a blockhouse was reportedly to be built at a bridge (or trestle) between Athens and Low Trestle. If that is true, Low Trestle must be the more northern of the two, which is Wright No. 34. Wright showed No. 34 and No. 35 to be five and nine feet high, respectively, which supports the idea that No. 34 would have had the distinction of being Low Trestle. Contradicting this is Forrest's report of his raid on the blockhouses in September 1864 which states that Blockhouse Number 7 was at Low Trestle, four miles north of Athens. The crossing at that distance from Athens was Wright No. 35, about three-quarters of a mile south of Wright No. 34. It is possible that Forrest confused the two trestles and likely that the house really was four miles from Athens. It is also interesting that neither Forrest nor Lt. March reported a crossing or house between the crossing four miles north of Athens and Sulphur Creek. What is most significant is the apparent absence of a blockhouse. If "Low Trestle" Wright No. 34 did not have one, the reason is not apparent. The trestle needed protection. The Federals reported that troops were at Low Trestle when Forrest made his raid, so it appears that they were stationed at Wright No. 34 without a blockhouse. The blockhouse at Dodge No. 24/Wright No. 35 has been referred to as both Number 6 and Number 7. It was more likely Number 7. In the following discussion, the next encounter with the Federals is assumed to occur at the trestle at Dodge No. 24 and its blockhouse Number 7.

At 5 p.m. on the twenty-fourth, the last of Forrest's men had headed north from Athens along the railroad. That evening, they captured Blockhouse 7 at the trestle on Swan Creek about four miles north of Athens (Wright No. 35), which was in a heavily forested area. The house was double-cased and garrisoned by 25 men from Company K of the 111th USCT under Lt. J.J. Phifer. It was surrendered without a fight, perhaps without justification because Forrest had no artillery there. It was probably still at Athens. The house and trestle were burned within 20 minutes and the garrison taken prisoner. Forrest camped that night at Hays Mill, two miles north of the blockhouse.[14]

The very large Sulphur Creek Trestle lay about two miles north of Hays Mill. It was 72 feet high and 570 feet long. Its defenses consisted of a 300-foot by 300-foot earthwork fort on a prominence, two howitzers in the fort, an expansive redoubt and two double-walled blockhouses, Numbers 8 and 9. The fort there was not yet completed and was considered to be poorly sited. The fort, redoubt and blockhouses were defended by about 1,000 to 1,200 men. Of these, about 470 were from the 110th and 111th USCT (who also manned the blockhouses), 196 men were with Lilly and the 9th Indiana Cavalry that arrived that day, 300 were from the 3rd Tennessee Cavalry who also arrived on the twenty-fourth and there seem to have been some troops from other regiments.[15]

At 4 a.m. on the twenty-fifth, Col. George Spalding, 12th Tennessee Cavalry Regiment, dispatched Starkweather that he planned to take his men from the Elk River Bridge into the fort at Sulphur Creek to resist a likely attack by Forrest. However, they would not make it into the fort. The men from several companies of the 9th Indiana Cavalry who had been stationed at Pulaski under the command of Major Lilly and the 3rd Tennessee Cavalrymen under Col. John Minnis were also ordered into the fort and made it.

That morning, Forrest rode to Sulphur Creek. He had Captain John W. Morton's artillery battalion place their guns at four locations north, east and southwest of and apparently above the fort on some of the higher nearby hills. They initiated the attack at about 7 a.m., pouring 800 shells into the fort and doing great damage. At the same time, the infantry approached the fort from the south. At 10 a.m., a sergeant under Lilly reported at Pulaski that when he left Sulphur Creek at 9 a.m., the Confederates had about six pieces of artillery firing on the fort from three sides. He estimated 800 men to be within the fort. After several hours of fierce fighting, the federal soldiers had run low on ammunition and their cavalry was completely out. They could offer no further

Sulphur Creek Trestle, 1864 (Limestone County Archives Collection. Courtesy of Limestone County Archives, Athens, Alabama).

resistance. At about noon, Forrest sent in a flag of truce. Commanding Col. Lathrop had been killed, so Col. Minnis took command. However, Minnis had been wounded, so Maj. Lilly came out on his behalf to speak with Forrest. After a short parlay, Lilly consulted with Minnis and surrendered the fort and both blockhouses, thus ending North Alabama's bloodiest Civil War battle.[16]

Forrest reported on October 17: "The Sulphur Springs Trestle was only two miles off, and on the morning of the twenty-fifth I move upon that place, said to be the strongest on the road. The enemy's pickets were driven in with but little difficulty and the place was soon invested. His defenses consisted of two block-houses and a large fort situated upon an eminence, but fortunately for us surrounded by hills still more elevated. I ordered the artillery to be placed at once in position." "The necessary disposition of troops being made, a general advance was ordered upon the fort. General Buford's division moved with alacrity and great promptitude. Colonel Kelley dashed across the field, followed by his brigade, and after reaching his desired position the enemy dared not raise his head above his own works. Colonel Johnson and his brave troops on this occasion acted with conspicuous gallantry in marching up and assaulting the enemy's works. Mean time the eight pieces of artillery from four different points poured a concentrated storm of shell into the fort. After two hours' bombardment the enemy's guns were silenced and he exhibited no show of resistance. I deemed this an appropriate occasion to demand a surrender and sent a flag of truce for that purpose. After a short parlay with Col. J.B. Minnis, the commanding officer, who had expressed a desire for an interview, the fort surrendered. The colonel commanding was killed early in the fight. Almost every house was perforated with shell, and the dead lay thick along the works of the fort. The fruits of the victory consist, besides the prisoners, of 700 stand of small-arms, 2 pieces artillery, 3 ambulances, 16 wagons, 300 cavalry horses and equipments, medical, quartermaster's and commissary stores. The trestle-work at this fort was 72 feet high and 300 feet long, and defended by two large block-houses, all of which were consumed by fire, and the prisoners turned over to Colonel Logwood, who started with them to the Tennessee River."[17]

The Union had lost 100 to 200 men plus 973 taken prisoner. Of Lt. Dunlavy and the 30 men from Company H, 9th Indiana Cavalry who had come with Lilly the day before, all but four were either killed or captured. The surviving Federals were taken prisoner except the surgeons, the wounded and a few who escaped.[18]

A large number of the prisoners were from the 110th and 111th USCTs. Among them were James Moore and Alford (MacKey) McKay, both of Company I, 111th USCT. They were born in Maury County, Tennessee, enlisted in Columbia on February 1, 1864, and mustered in at Pulaski. Both had been farmers. Moore was 36 years old, and McKay was 21. Both lived after the war on Carter's Creek Pike in Williamson County. Another member of the 111th who was taken prisoner at Sulphur Creek was Sgt. William Holland. He was assigned as personal servant to Forrest's chief surgeon, Dr. James B. Cowan, and rode with Forrest for about three months until he was able to escape near Pulaski in December when Forrest was rear guard for Hood's retreat from Nashville. Lyle G. Adair of Vigo County, Indiana, was a young White farmer who enlisted as a sergeant in the 81st Ohio Volunteer Infantry but was demoted to private and sought to regain his rank. He had an opportunity to re-enlist with the 3rd Alabama Colored Infantry (later named the 111th USCT), something that only 3 of the 75 in his company were willing to do. He did so in January 1864 at the rank of sergeant and served as a recruiter. Adair was at Sulphur Creek as well, was taken prisoner, held at five different Confederate prisons and finally released in April 1865.[19]

As the Confederates moved northward, Spalding and his men were repulsed at Elkmont and fell back with their cavalry toward the Elk. He seems to have advised the 45 men of the 111th under Capt. S.B. Akins at Blockhouse Number 10 at Mill Creek (Holt's Trestle, Wright No. 32) to fall back as well. He then ordered Blockhouse Number 11, south of the Elk (Wright No. 31), evacuated to reinforce the fortifications at the Elk, probably a blockhouse and a fort. Later that day, the garrisons from Mill Creek Trestle (a detachment of Company K, 111th USCT) and Tunnel Hill (Company C, 111th USCT), fell back toward Pulaski. They skirmished with the enemy along the way. Forty-eight men from Company K were captured.

Forrest and Buford continued northward early Monday morning, September 26, but took different paths. Forrest went to Elkmont, then toward Elkton and forded the Elk River headed for Pulaski. Buford and Lyon's brigade went along the dirt road that paralleled the railroad, destroying culverts as they went. After four miles they arrived at the 315-foot-long trestle at Mill Creek. They burned the trestle and its abandoned double-cased Blockhouse Number 10, then moved on and burned the evacuated, double-cased house Number 11. That morning, Spalding was holding on at the Elk River fortifications, which included a blockhouse. However, sensing that he was about to be surrounded, he abandoned the bridge and the two fortifications at 5 a.m. At 8 a.m., Buford's men seized the deserted bridge and burned it, the extensive approach trestle on the south side of the river and the two fortifications. Spalding took the road toward Elkton, hoping to slow Buford's progress. Forrest later reported that they had also taken the fort at the Elk. This was probably the artillery site on the hill just west of the railroad. At this time, the blockhouse at Richland Creek Bridge No. 4 was being evacuated as well, but Spalding ordered its garrison to stay.[20]

Buford came up the railroad to Prospect and destroyed several thousand cords of wood. That day, Company H of the 111th USCT marched from Prospect to Tunnel Hill where the Federals put up resistance from 8 a.m. until almost noon against part of Buford's command. The Federals were nearly surrounded, so they evacuated and lost the site to the Confederates. In the meantime, Forrest had come up to the east side of the tunnel and Madry's Ridge where Buford rejoined them. The contraband camp on the plantation of Thomas J. Brown was there. When the Confederates were only six or seven miles away, Federals warned the inhabitants, giving them time to grab what they could and quickly head north toward Nashville. Most of them would never return. Forrest's report of October 17 states, "From Elkton I directed my course toward a government corral at Brown's plantation, toward Pulaski. At this place I found about 2,000 negroes, consisting mostly of old men, women and children, besides a large amount of commissary stores and medical supplies. General Buford having completed his work at Elk River joined me at this place, where I issued to command several days rations, distributing among the troops as much sugar and coffee as they needed. The negroes were all ragged and dirty, and many seemed in absolute want. I ordered them to remove their clothing and bed clothes from the miserable hovels in which they lived and then burnt up this den of wretchedness. Near 200 houses were consumed."[21]

The 7th Cavalry burned the trestle at the north entrance of the tunnel and the two blockhouses. Spalding and the 111th were marching to the 360-foot-long Richland Creek Bridge No. 4 (also known as Rockland Station; Wright No. 28), six miles south of Pulaski. He ordered the garrison to make a stubborn stand to protect the bridge. The Confederates attacked and shelled the blockhouse there. After furiously defending it for two hours, Col. Hillery J. Walker and his 45 men of the 111th surrendered the house and it was burned. Spalding drove the Confederate skirmish line back and held the bridge for three-and-a-half hours but was finally defeated and retreated toward Pulaski while the Confederates burned the bridge. Forrest and Buford stayed the night of the twenty-sixth along Richland Creek and the Elkton-Pulaski Road.

Between Decatur and Pulaski, the Confederates had cut the railroad and destroyed 14 blockhouses, a fort, six small railroad bridges, five railroad bridges longer than 300 feet each and part of the Elk River Bridge. The fighting and destruction had gotten the attention of Union commanders, so they sent reinforcements. On the morning of the twenty-sixth, dismounted members of the 9th Indiana Cavalry, guarding blockhouses north of Pulaski, had counted 14 trains loaded with troops headed south into Pulaski. Many of those troops had been sent up the N&C to Nashville and then down the N&D. The next morning, numerous troop-filled trains were going the other way, headed north again through Pulaski as the Confederates were pushing them back. About this time, Sherman was so perturbed by Forrest that he ordered Gen. Thomas and his forces in Tennessee to do all they could to kill him.[22]

Early on the twenty-seventh, Forrest was heading north to Pulaski by the railroad and a parallel pike. Just north of Tarpley's Shop, the 10th and 12th Tennessee and parts of the 9th and 10th Indiana under Spalding ambushed Lyon's 7th Kentucky and drove them back. Forrest helped repel the Federals toward Pulaski with pressure from Kelley, Johnson and Lyon and the Federals took to their fortifications at Pulaski. Forrest wanted to attack the fort but learned that it was occupied by 5,000 Federals and decided it would not be wise to do so.[23]

Late on the twenty-seventh, Forrest left Pulaski intending to attack the N&C at

Tullahoma. He reached Fayetteville on the twenty-eighth, stayed the night five miles east of the town and sent two detachments to cut the telegraph lines on the railroad on both sides of Tullahoma. Forrest heard that the town and railroad near Tullahoma were well defended by two infantry units that Sherman had sent up plus some men whom Rousseau had railed in from Pulaski via Nashville. Given that he was a bit short on troops and ammunition, he chose not to engage. On September 29, being in a vulnerable position, he decided to subdivide his command and depart. Forrest headed one part that was to strike the N&D at Spring Hill, breaking its connection with Columbia. Buford was in charge of the other part consisting of between 1,500 and 2,000 men and was ordered back to Florence to cross the river. He was to burn the M&C bridge over the Flint River at Brownsboro, Alabama, capture Huntsville, then destroy as much rail on the M&C as he could between Huntsville and Decatur. Buford did make it to Huntsville on the thirtieth but did not engage the Union there. He went four miles to the west to tear up track, then on to Athens to try to capture it.[24]

The Union had re-occupied Fort Henderson at Athens on the twenty-eighth, only four days after losing it on the twenty-fourth. Lt. Col. A.B. Wade had it defended by the 73rd Indiana Infantry, 10th Indiana Cavalry (dismounted) and Battery A, 1st Tennessee Artillery. Being vulnerable to artillery, the Union built a temporary bomb-proof shelter outside the fort. They did so by covering their 15-foot-wide, six-foot-deep ditch with logs and some earth and made an entrance to it through a covered passageway under the gate to the fort. It served them well and Wade subsequently recommended that the bomb-proof shelter be made standard in all stockades.

At 6 a.m. on October 2, Buford attacked Fort Henderson. Once the fort started receiving cannon fire from opposite sides to which everyone in the fort was susceptible, the entire garrison except for the sentinels was ordered into the bomb-proof shelter. At 8 a.m., Buford asked for a surrender but was refused. There was additional skirmishing and two hours of cannon fire; then Buford thought he could not take the fort by force. He withdrew and moved on to Florence where he arrived on the third. The bomb-proof had served the Federals well.[25]

Meanwhile, on September 29, Forrest had headed toward the N&D. He passed through Lewisburg, crossed the Duck River at Hardison's Mill and camped on the north side of the Duck near his hometown of Chapel Hill. At this time, he had a force of about 10,000 men and 15 pieces of artillery. That evening, he sent Wheeler north of Pulaski to destroy the railroad and telegraph between Pulaski and Columbia. Wheeler apparently accomplished this with particular success at Campbell's Station. On his way north, he burned a large woodyard along the railroad.[26]

At dawn on Saturday, October 1, Forrest and his men were moving toward Franklin but turned west to Spring Hill and captured a stagecoach running from Columbia to Nashville along with two wagons. That day, he arrived at Spring Hill, captured it and seized its telegraph office, which was operating from Pulaski to Nashville. Forrest intercepted several official Union dispatches about the location of federal troops and sent back a number of misleading telegraphs to Rousseau, one stating that "Forrest" was still to the south destroying track and blockhouses. He burned the Spring Hill depot and cut the telegraph lines, then headed south toward Columbia and sent out a small force to destroy the short bridges on the N&D between Spring Hill and Franklin. After traveling south a few miles, he turned west to the N&D at Carter's Creek where there were several bridges and blockhouses. Forrest started his assault on the structures along the creek.[27]

8. Forrest Comes Calling

On Monday, October 3, A. Kramer, First Lt., 68th New York Regiment, Assistant Inspector of Block-Houses, reported, "On Saturday, 1 p.m., came General Forrest and staff with flag of truce to Block-house No. 5, which was in command of Second Lieut. E. Nixon, Seventh Pennsylvania Infantry, and demanded a surrender of the block-house with garrison, which demand Second Lieut. E.F. Nixon complied with without firing a gun. Lieutenant Nixon, who was in command of Block-house Nos. 3, 4 and 5, ordered the sergeants in command to surrender. Sergt. A Frohn, Company L, Seventh Pennsylvania Cavalry, in command of Block-house No. 4, bridge No. 4, and Sergt. W. Rhinemiller, Company M, Seventh Pennsylvania Cavalry, was in command of Block-house No. 3, Bridge No. 3. Sergt. W. Rhinemiller refused three times to comply. Lieut. E.F. Nixon then threatened to place him in arrest; he also fired on the flag. Lieut. E.F. Nixon rode with Forrest's adjutant to First Lieut. J.F. Long, Company B, Seventh Pennsylvania Cavalry, commanding Block-house No. 6, Bridge No. 5 and tried to induce him to surrender, which (he) refused to do, and ordered Lieutenant Nixon, with the adjutant of General Forrest, away from his block-house. First Lieutenant Long fought him from 2 p.m. until 12 m.; killed 10 rebels and wounded several; but they succeeded in destroying his bridge; his command and block-house were uninjured. During the truce, the rebels under cover of the railroad bank, succeeded in firing the bridge with turpentine; one end was burned, and the whole fell in. Block-houses 3, 4 and 5 are burned to the ground; also, Bridges Nos. 3 and 4. It is learned Carter's Creek Station, the water-tank, and saw-mill, and the railroad destroyed from there to Spring Hill. Rumor says Lieutenant Nixon surrendered for a bribe of $10,000. The rebels had no artillery, and his three block-houses were double-cased up to the top log of the loopholes. The garrisons of the three block-houses and water tanks and saw-mill were taken prisoner, except 1 man escaped. Block-house No. 3 was garrisoned by thirty-two men, Block-house No. 4 with 22 men, Block-house No. 5 with thirty-one men. Thirty men garrisoned the water-tank and saw-mill. Altogether 115 men captured. Rumor says they have all been paroled, and arrived this day at Franklin."[28]

Nixon was captured, dismissed from the service on December 7 for disgraceful conduct in surrendering to Forrest and dishonorably discharged on January 7, 1865. Federal Lt. Albert Kramer said he needed to rebuild three houses at Carter's Creek. Forrest reported that he had burned three bridges and four blockhouses in the Carter's Creek area, one more blockhouse than reported by the two Federals. It is not clear whether Carter's Creek Bridges Nos. 1 (Dodge bridge No. 2) and 2 (Dodge bridge No. 3) were affected.

Gen. Forrest marched until 10 p.m. on the night of October 1 and camped eight miles south of Spring Hill on the south side of Rutherford Creek. The next day, he attacked several blockhouses along Rutherford Creek but without inflicting significant damage. He crossed the Duck River, went to Columbia and started positioning his troops around the town. However, he determined that he had too little artillery to attack and headed toward Mount Pleasant for the night.

Forrest had not gone north of Pulaski on the twenty-eighth, so he did not have the opportunity to damage the bridges and trestles between Columbia and Pulaski. On the first, he sent Brig. Gen. Lyon's brigade to burn the bridges and trestles between the two towns, with emphasis on Culleoka. As previously stated, it is not clear what success Lyon had. Culleoka, Robertson Fork and Richland Creek Bridges Nos. 1, 2 and 3 were probably destroyed by Wheeler or Lyon in October or by Forrest during the December 1864 retreat. It is not known, however, whether Lyon or Wheeler had the artillery necessary to capture the blockhouses and burn the bridges and trestles. Regardless, it is likely that Wheeler did significant damage to the track. The Richland Creek Bridges were rebuilt in the next month or so. As evidenced by the presence of square earthworks at the remains of the blockhouse there, it seems that Gracey's trestle escaped destruction at this time. If the house had been burned, it should have been replaced with an octagonal structure.[29]

Forrest went west to Westport where he again crossed the Duck. With the Tennessee River rising, he decided to end his raid, cross the river and return to Cherokee. On October 3, he was near Lawrenceburg, heading for Florence. The Federals did not want Forrest to get away easily. They were chasing him with 3,000 federal cavalry and Thomas had ordered two gunboats up the Tennessee River to Florence, in hopes of cutting off and destroying him. Forrest had the strong rear defense of Col. Francis M. Windes, commander of one of Forrest's regiments. On the fifth, with the Union closing in, Forrest reached Shoal Creek, Alabama, and rested for the evening. The next day, he moved his main body to Cypress Creek, just downstream of Florence, to cross. Forrest brought boats down to the mouth of the creek and ferried some of his men over. Union forces appeared in Florence, so the boats were sent farther down river and the ferrying continued around the clock. The Union was now pressing, so Forrest ordered all the troops that had not crossed, except one regiment, to go to the north bank of the river, mount their horses and swim them across a slough 70 yards wide to Koger's Island. From there they were able to be ferried across at a more leisurely pace. Col. A.N. Wilson's 21st Tennessee Cavalry Regiment was left behind to skirmish until all the troops had reached the island. Wilson was successful and held 15,000 Federals back until the eighth. He crossed at the island on October 12. Except for the rear guard, Forrest and his forces reached Cherokee on the sixth.[30]

The damage done to the N&D by the Confederates was not repaired until late November. Carpenters and laborers from the USCTs were among those who worked nearly six weeks to rebuild the bridges and trestles between Athens and Pulaski, including the Elk River Bridge and Sulphur Creek Trestle.[31]

Orlando M. Poe (1832–1895) was born in Ohio and graduated from West Point. Early in the war, he was chief topographical engineer for Gen. McClellan's Department of the Ohio. In 1862, he was named colonel and commander of the 2nd Michigan Volunteer Infantry Regiment. He transferred to the Western Theater, where he oversaw the 1st Michigan Engineers and Mechanics while they built blockhouses on the N&C. As chief engineer in the Twenty-third Corps, he was primarily responsible for the design and construction of defenses at Knoxville. In 1864, Sherman named him chief engineer of the Military Division of the Mississippi. Many maps were created under his direction. Poe collected and later donated numerous maps that had been produced during the war, especially related to defenses. Two of the maps in his collection were those referenced in this book showing defenses at and below Carter's Creek on the N&D. He oversaw the burning of Atlanta and the dismantling of all buildings that would have been of use to the Confederates. Following the war, he was chief engineer and then District Engineer of the Great Lakes 11th Lighthouse District.

8. Forrest Comes Calling

Civil War terminology can be confusing. For instance, it is frequently found on maps and in literature that a blockhouse is called a stockade, though they are very different structures. Some of Poe's maps, probably produced in about October 1864, show several "stockades" or "Block House Stockade" Numbered 1–13 at the numerous crossings along Carter's and Rutherford Creeks. The maps also show "block houses" at the Harris, Culleoka and Gracey's trestles. The presence of a blockhouse at Gracey's was also reported in a survey conducted by the Tennessee Division of Archaeology. Because the replacement of stockades by blockhouses started generally at the northernmost crossings and proceeded to the south, the structures north of the Duck in the fall of 1864 would almost certainly have been blockhouses rather than stockades awaiting replacement. Evidence that the maps were created in about October is that they show blockhouses in place along Carter's and Rutherford Creeks. This was after Forrest's raids of early October, so they had apparently been replaced. Also, the maps show a burned Rutherford Creek Bridge on Columbia Pike; it had probably been burned by Forrest in early October and not yet rebuilt. Hood burned it again on December 18, but it was rebuilt in the next couple of days.[32]

It seems that on this expedition Forrest captured 2,360 and killed or wounded 300 to 400. He

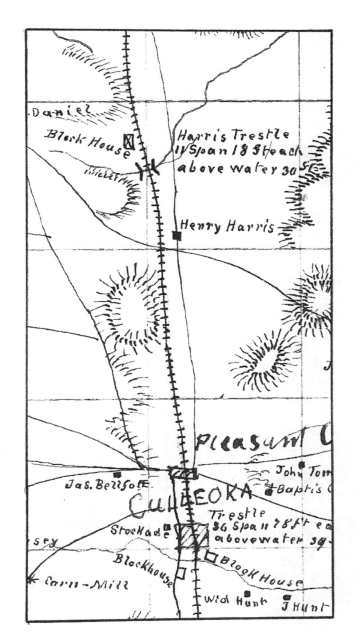

Map 8—Harris Trestle (Map segment, Stack 330, Record Group 77, Records of the Office of the Chief of Engineers Series: Civil Works Map File, National Archives and Records Administration).

recorded that this total was equivalent to one for each man he had at these engagements. Also, he destroyed four locomotives and 100 cars, captured 800 horses, seven pieces of artillery, 2,000 stand of small arms, 50 wagons and ambulances, a large volume of supplies, rations and more. Forrest estimated that his losses were 47 killed and 293 wounded. He, Wheeler and Buford had destroyed 17 or 18 blockhouses: Alabama House Numbers 2 through 11, one at the Elk, the two at the tunnel, the house at Richland Creek Bridge No. 4 and three or four on Carter's Creek. They also destroyed about 16 railroad bridges and trestles (nine in Alabama, at the Elk and tunnel, one on Richland Creek and four at Carter's Creek) and about 30 miles of track. It is worthy of note that there do not seem to have been raids on the camps or stockades to rival the magnitude of what Forrest and the others did to the blockhouses. However, because the N&C was not impacted, Forrest had done little or nothing to interfere with Sherman's plans and his mission cannot be seen as a significant strategic success.[33]

On October 13, 1864, McCallum reported on Forrest's attacks of September and early October. In addition to much that has already been stated, he indicated that an engine and 12 cars were burned on a trestle near Decatur Junction, that all of the

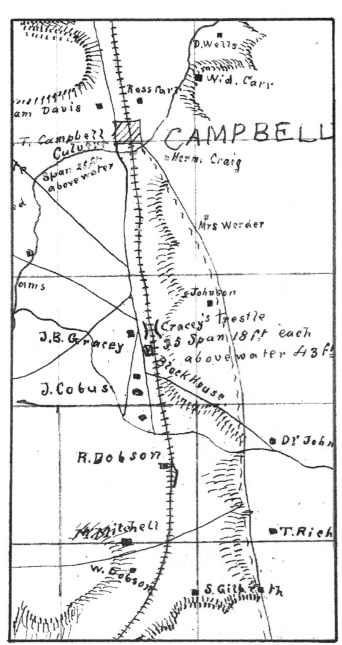

Map 9—Gracey's Trestle (Map segment, Stack 330, Record Group 77, Records of the Office of the Chief of Engineers Series: Civil Works Map File; National Archives and Records Administration).

8. Forrest Comes Calling

bridges and trestles between Pulaski and Athens were destroyed, including the bridge over the Elk, and two-and-a-half miles of track had been partially destroyed. Also, between Spring Hill and Columbia, three bridges had been destroyed along with two to three miles of track.[34]

Forrest had captured most of the federal troops that he encountered at Athens, Sulphur Creek Trestle and the blockhouses. These men, about 2,000, did not have an easy future. Most of the approximately 1,200 USCT soldiers captured were marched to Cherokee, Alabama. They were then sent to Mobile to work on fortifications. Approximately 569 were taken there by train, with the rest making the 12-day journey on foot. Many of those troops died while at Mobile. On January 21, 1865, federal Lieutenant and Acting Adjutant, 111th U.S. Colored Infantry O.O. Poppleton reported, "I have ... the names of 569 soldiers belonging to the One hundred and sixth, One hundred and tenth, and One hundred and eleventh Regiments of the U.S. Colored Infantry, who were taken prisoners by a force of the enemy under Maj. Gen. N.B. Forrest, at Athens and Sulphur Branch Trestle, Ala., on September 24 and 25, 1864, and placed at work on the defenses of Mobile, Ala., by the order of rebel authorities. Lieut. William T. Lewis, adjutant One hundred and tenth U.S. Colored Infantry, has a paper of later date than this, containing the names of nearly 300 more soldiers of the same command, also at work on the defenses of Mobile." Most of the approximately 800 captured White troops were sent to Castle Morgan Prison in Alabama, also known as Cahaba.

After the war ended the following April, federal prisoners held in the South were being returned to their homes in the North. Vicksburg, Mississippi, was the city the Confederate Office of Exchange had designated for sending northward the prisoners who had been held east of the Mississippi River. A large number of Union soldiers sent to Vicksburg had been released from Andersonville prison in Georgia and Cahaba. Many of them were emaciated from the terrible conditions at the prisons and died on the way to Vicksburg.

Several ships had been contracted to transport troops on the Mississippi River. One was the U.S.S. *Sultana*, a side wheeler which belonged to the Merchants' and People's Line. It had left Cairo, Illinois, on April 15, 1865, the day that President Lincoln died, on its way to New Orleans. The vessel returned northward and had docked at Vicksburg on the night of the twenty-third. While there, its boilers were inspected. A bulge was found in one boiler, and there was evidence that all of the boilers had been burned and somewhat damaged due to an insufficient supply of water. A local boiler repairman said that two steel boiler sheets needed to be replaced, but the authorities were in a hurry and ordered that the bulging boiler be patched. The repairman placed an 11 by 26-inch steel patch over the defective area.[35]

The *Sultana* took on its passengers. It was certified to carry 376 but was crowded with approximately 2,100. The 260-foot wooden-hull steamboat was carrying about as many people as the 882-foot-long *Titanic* would 47 years later. The passengers included about 2,000 troops, the vast majority being from the states of Tennessee, Indiana, Michigan and Ohio. Many of the approximately 800 White men from the four regiments that had been along the N&D in September were among them. In addition to troops, there were about 100 civilians, including 22 women, some Confederate prisoners with their guards on their way to northern prisons and a crew of 85. It also carried a great deal of freight, including 70 to 100 mules and horses. Passengers were everywhere on the boat, in any place where they could sit down, stand or hold on.

The *Sultana* (Library of Congress).

Local federal authorities were influenced by bribes from the ship line and ordered that excessive numbers of soldiers be placed on the boat, even though other steamboats were departing Vicksburg on about the same day with few or no soldiers. The number of troops that boarded was even greater than the authorities intended because rolls had not been fully prepared before boarding. The *Sultana* was not, however, the only side wheeler that left Vicksburg overcrowded with people after the war.

The vessel departed Vicksburg at 9 p.m. on the twenty-fourth, arrived at Memphis at 6:30 p.m. on the twenty-sixth and departed at 11 p.m. that night. It was on its way to Jefferson Barracks at St. Louis from which the troops would be sent to Camp Chase, Ohio. At 2 a.m. on the next morning of the twenty-seventh, with the *Sultana* a few miles north of Memphis, there was an explosion. One of its four boilers had ruptured, leading to immediate explosions of at least two of the others. The vessel was ablaze.

The *Sultana* had three levels and was a very open structure with a great deal of fancy woodwork. The upper decks were coated with a paint that contained turpentine, benzene and other flammables. The four coal-burning boilers were 18 feet long, working at capacity, very hot and at a pressure of about 135 pounds per square inch at the time of the disaster. Those factors and a breezy night made for an inferno that spread quickly. The vessel was ill-prepared for an evacuation in that it had only 76 life preservers, one yawl (a small sailboat) and one metal lifeboat.

Many were killed aboard from the explosion or fire. Many others jumped or were thrown into the river and fought for flotsam to help them stay afloat, hoping to reach land or to be rescued before their bodies turned numb in the frigid water and they sank to their deaths. The river was flooded and about four miles wide at the site of the explosion. Because of the darkness, the distant riverbanks were invisible and those in the water did not know which way to go. Weeks later, bodies were still being found in the river several miles downstream.

About 1,200 people perished, nearly as many as the 1,500 who died on the *Titanic*.

8. Forrest Comes Calling

The *Sultana* is still the worst maritime disaster in U.S. history. About 300 of the 1,200 died in hospitals after the disaster. Many of the dead were buried at Memphis.

One of the survivors was Corporal Robert M. Elza of Company E, 3rd Tennessee Cavalry. His story was told in a newspaper years later. Elza was 23 years old when captured by Forrest at Sulphur Creek and imprisoned a few miles south of Selma, Alabama, in a cotton warehouse that was missing part of its roof. He was eventually ordered to Vicksburg to be exchanged but Lee surrendered, and he was ordered to Camp Chase, Ohio, to be mustered out. The *Sultana* was to be his vessel north. It was the largest boat on the river. Elza knew its boilers were being repaired. Maj. A.S. Prosser of the 2nd Tennessee Cavalry protested about the excessive number of passengers, but his concern was ignored. Once the boiler work was completed, the *Sultana* left Vicksburg for Memphis. When they departed Memphis, the ship's captain reported that 2,336 were aboard. The vessel took on coal at about midnight and continued northward. Elza recorded that the *Sultana* was so crowded that not everyone could lie down. Word was soon going around that the boilers had too much water, which was dangerous. A boiler finally blew. Some men were thrown into the river senseless. Others were hit by flying debris. The boat was ablaze, and hundreds ended up in the water fighting for survival and looking for something to hang onto. The story Mr. Elza told in a newspaper years later is tragic but enlightening: "The men in the river fought for planks and pieces of timber as hard as they had fought in the army. Some were praying and others swearing. I never saw a sight like it before or after. It was dark, the only light being from the burning boat. Finally two men came floating along on the gang plank. I tried to get them to turn it over and it would have held seventy men, but they refused. I got on, making twenty-one men on the gangway. The river was out of banks, and we would hit the swirls and the gangway would whirl around. Finally we drifted into a tree and I was knocked off and sank twice but the boys pulled me out. In a short time five more men came along clinging to a bale of hay. In this crowd was W.J. Barley of Blue Grass, Tennessee. Barley yelled that he had touched bottom and we sighted a cabin and made for it."[36]

They went out and brought more men to the cabin, making about 30. A boat came by to pick them up. Its captain called Elza into his cabin and gave him brandy to warm him up. Elza was taken to a Memphis hospital to recover.

The ensuing investigation never determined the cause of the boiler explosions. There was little evidence to examine. It is likely that the first boiler probably failed because it had been low on water and the steel plate used at Vicksburg to repair the damaged, bulging boiler was of insufficient thickness. Another likely factor is that the boilers were a new, experimental type that was difficult to clean. The investigative report estimated that 1,238 had perished. It is possible that the loss was greater than that because the count may not have included those who later died in hospitals. Several men were found primarily responsible for overloading the vessel, but the army absolved itself of any wrongdoing. One was Capt. Frederick Speed, officer-in-charge of managing the transportation of former prisoners of war. He was court-martialed for negligence and scheduled for dismissal but, instead, was mustered out without a stain on his record. It was concluded that to meet the military needs of war, vessels were often harmlessly overcrowded without being overloaded. That statement does not seem reasonable, however, because the war was over, and the priority was supposed to be getting the troops safely to their homes rather than potentially exposing them to dangers as great as those they had experienced in the field and in prison.

Eight hundred or so White troops had been captured in northern Alabama in September after very lively fighting with Gen. Forrest. They were imprisoned under terrible conditions at Cahaba. Upon their release, many were put happily aboard the *Sultana* to go home after the war. Then, after all they had been through, about 200 to 300 of them perished because of greed and the *Sultana*'s poorly maintained boilers. Because passenger rolls and other records are incomplete, the numbers presented here regarding troops captured by Forrest and passengers on the *Sultana* are approximate, though conceptually accurate.

At the time of its occurrence, the story of the *Sultana* did not get the attention it deserved and still does not today. When the disaster took place, the Civil War had ended just a few weeks before, President Lincoln had been assassinated less than two weeks before and John Wilkes Booth had been killed on the previous day. The incident occurred in the Western Theater and most of the men were from the Midwest. If the incident had occurred in the East and involved easterners, the big papers there would have printed the story and given it greater exposure.

Because the Mississippi River has shifted position over time, the main channel in the area of the disaster is now about two miles east of its location in 1865. In 1982, archeologists found some remnants of the boat at a depth of 32 feet beneath a soybean field on the Arkansas side of the river. The *Sultana* Disaster Museum in Marion, Arkansas, tells the story of the disaster and contains artifacts from the boat and survivors.

The loss of humanity related to the 1865 *Sultana* disaster is staggering. But, returning to the fall of 1864, the Federals' focus along the N&D was about to shift from Forrest to Hood and an even larger number of casualties that his march into Middle Tennessee would create.

9

Hood Looks for a Fight

In July, Gen. Hood had been elevated to take command of the Army of Tennessee with Gen. Benjamin F. Cheatham taking charge of Hood's corps. At age 33, Hood was the youngest man on either side to command an army. In mid–October, after losing Atlanta to Sherman, Hood and his troops departed Georgia on their way to Alabama, planning to cross the Tennessee River at Decatur and move into Tennessee. Forrest left Paris, Tennessee, to meet Hood in Middle Tennessee. A primary goal was to make Sherman feel that he needed to come defend Middle Tennessee, thus drawing him out of Georgia behind them and into a battle in which Hood would cripple his army. Whereas Forrest, Buford and Wheeler had been unable to distract Sherman in September, Hood would prove at least able to compel Sherman to send Gen. Thomas to deal with him. Thomas was assigned to Middle Tennessee on October 28 and Sherman gave him full responsibility for defending Tennessee and destroying Hood's army. This allowed Sherman to remain focused on his "March to the Sea."

Hood's nine-day march from Florence, Alabama, to Franklin, Tennessee, covering about 90 miles, would see the burning of rail cars, wagons, the Duck River Bridge and numerous blockhouses and the destruction of government supplies at Columbia. As Schofield rushed north with Hood on his heels, the Federals, who had been bringing troops and supplies down to confront Hood, found themselves running their engines and rolling stock toward the safety of Nashville the best they could and, of course, abandoning the track. It is interesting that a month later, the roles would be reversed, and the Union would be pushing Hood southward toward the Tennessee River over much of the same ground after the Battle of Nashville.

John Bell Hood (1831–1879) was born in Owingsville, Kentucky. At West Point, his classmates gave him the name "Sam" which he would carry for the rest of his life. Hood was a junior officer in both the infantry and artillery in the antebellum U.S. Army. Early in the war, he commanded the 4th Texas Infantry. At Gettysburg, he was wounded and lost the use of his left arm. At Chickamauga, he was again wounded and lost his right leg to amputation, requiring that he be strapped to his horse. On July 18, 1864, on the outskirts of Atlanta, he was promoted to temporary full general and command of the Army of Tennessee. After his defeats at Franklin and Nashville, he was relieved of his command. He moved to Louisiana after the war and worked as a cotton broker and president of an insurance business. Hood married in 1868 and, in 10 years, fathered 11 children including three sets of twins. A yellow fever epidemic in New Orleans in the winter of 1878–79 ruined his life. Just days after his wife and oldest child had died of the disease in 1879, he did as well.

> Benjamin F. Cheatham (1820–1886) was born in Nashville, Tennessee, on a plantation called Westover. He joined the CSA as a brigadier general in May 1861 and served under Maj. Gen. Leonidas Polk. In March 1862, he was promoted to major general and given command of a division in the Army of Mississippi. He led his division at Shiloh and fought under Bragg at Chickamauga and under Johnston and Hood in the Atlanta Campaign. He served under Hood at Franklin and Nashville but was blamed for allowing Schofield's army to slip by at Spring Hill, leading to Hood's defeat at Franklin. After Nashville, he joined Johnston's command for the Carolinas Campaign as a division commander and surrendered to Sherman in North Carolina in April 1865. After the war, he served for four years as superintendent of a Tennessee State Prison and was postmaster of Nashville from 1885 to 1886. Cheatham died in Nashville and is buried there at Mt. Olivet Cemetery.

It made sense for Hood to attempt to cross at Decatur because the pontoon bridge was there and the river was relatively shallow. Also, on the north side lay the N&D and a well-maintained national road, now U.S. Hwy 31, which would help him advance quickly to Nashville. The M&C bridge had not yet been rebuilt. By this time, Decatur was essentially depopulated and most of the houses had been burned or demolished. The Union had two strong forts on the southern bank of the river that were connected by a line of breastworks about a mile long. Fort 1 was on the western end and Fort 2 on the eastern. Fort 3 on the western end would be constructed later. The pontoon bridge and the right of way of the M&C hit the south bank within the earthworks.

At this time, Col. Charles C. Doolittle at Decatur commanded the approximately 1,800 men contributed by a number of regiments. They included the 73rd Indiana Infantry, 13th Wisconsin Veteran Volunteer Infantry and parts of the 11th, 12th and 13th Indiana Cavalries which were on the railroad from Athens to Stevenson. Brig. Gen. Robert Granger was in charge of the District of Northern Alabama. He had felt certain that Decatur would be attacked by Hood and his force of about 35,000 men, so he sent every available man from Huntsville plus the 29th Michigan Infantry.

At 1:30 on the morning of October 26, Hood's force arrived at Decatur. He found the Union troops defending an entrenched line that included the two forts. Hood had expected the

Gen. John Bell Hood (Library of Congress).

9. Hood Looks for a Fight

town to be lightly defended and would witness the federal defense strengthen even more over the next three days. That night, Capt. Naylor and the Union gunboat *Stone River* arrived at Decatur with 200 men from the 102nd Ohio and 18th Michigan Infantries. Also, detachments of the 73rd Indiana Infantry arrived by train from Athens. On the twenty-seventh, the 14th USCT Infantry was brought in on the M&C and the 68th Indiana Infantry and 13th Indiana Cavalry came as reinforcements as well. The Illinois 2nd Artillery, Battery D was also part of the federal defense. That gave Granger a total of 3,000 to 5,000 men.[1]

At about 3 a.m. on the twenty-eighth, Hood initiated engagements in what he would later refer to as a "demonstration" and would generally be known as the Battle of Decatur. Granger's 4,000 or so men would prevent the 35,000 men of the Confederate Army of Tennessee under Hood from crossing the Tennessee River at Decatur. Hood advanced and took positions nearer Granger's main defenses but was driven back later in the day by shelling from the guns at Fort 2. During the night, Hood established rifle pits and a battery of eight guns on the south bank of the river. However, under the cover of darkness Granger had sent a section of Battery A, 1st Tennessee Artillery to the north side of the river. As the 1st Tennessee was harassing Hood's battery, Granger ordered Col. Doolittle to send the 14th USCT to charge the battery and a detachment of 500 men to support them. With the *Stone River* gunboat engaged as well, the crossfire was more than the Confederates in the battery could stand and their position was taken, but only temporarily as Hood sent in superior numbers. Later that day, Captain Gilbert Morton and the U.S. steamer *General Thomas* arrived and joined the *Stone River*. Granger ordered both of the ships and Captain Beach's battery to shell the Confederates' riverside battery across the river which they had just reoccupied. Shielded by the crossfire of Beach's shells and the rifles on the Union left, both vessels dropped down the river until immediately across from the Confederate works and opened with their broadside guns. The Confederates could not withstand this assault and vacated their position again. Some retreated to their main line while others rushed down the bank to the protection of the trees along the riverbank. However, the guns of the boats, double-shotted with canister, were turned on the men along the water and poured in a devastating fire. Many bodies were later found in the river. Though this engagement lasted only 30 minutes, the Confederates suffered great losses, while the Union losses on the gunboats were only two killed and 11 wounded. On the morning of October 29, the Confederates were withdrawing and by late afternoon the Union's original picket line was reestablished. Overall loss to the Union was 113 killed, wounded or taken prisoner, compared to much greater numbers, perhaps 1,000 to 1,500, for the Confederates.[2]

Hood moved 45 miles west to cross at Florence, arriving on October 31. It was to the Confederates' advantage to get into Middle Tennessee as soon as possible because the Federals were outmanned but could bring in reinforcements if given the time. Hood had hoped to be across the Tennessee River and leave Florence on November 8 or 9 and got to work on his pontoon bridge. He had trouble building it, and on November 4 federal cavalry cut loose a section of it. Hood's work on the pontoons may have been premature because he wasn't ready. He could not cross until rations arrived, and he needed Forrest there to secure the wagon trains as they crossed. Hood would end up waiting two-and-a-half weeks because the rains came and the river overflowed there. This delay gave the Union forces more time to take positions south of Nashville. Forrest arrived at Florence on November 14. Generals Alexander P. Stewart (commander, Third Corps),

Cheatham (3rd Tennessee), Stephen D. Lee (Second Corps, Army of Tennessee) and Forrest and his 9,200 cavalry were all there on the fifteenth. Hood put Forrest in command of all the cavalry.[3]

> Alexander P. Stewart (1821–1908) was born in Tennessee, graduated from the U.S. Military Academy and entered the Confederate Army in August 1861 as a major of artillery. He was promoted to brigadier general in the Army of Tennessee in November and to major general in June 1863. Stewart fought at Tullahoma, Chickamauga and the Atlanta Campaign, where he replaced Maj. Gen. Leonidas Polk in command of the Army's Third Corps after Polk was killed. He led the Third Corps at Franklin and Nashville, surrendering in April 1865. After the war, he was an insurance executive in Missouri and Chancellor of the University of Mississippi from 1874 to 1886. From 1890 to 1908, Stewart was a commissioner of the Chickamauga and Chattanooga National Military Park, the first of its kind in the country.
>
> Stephen D. Lee (1833–1908), no relation to Robert E. Lee, was born in South Carolina. He graduated from the U.S. Military Academy and joined the Confederate Army as a captain in the South Carolina Militia. As aide-de-camp to Gen. P.G.T. Beauregard, on April 11, 1861, Lee was in the group that delivered the ultimatum to Union Major Robert Anderson at Fort Sumter, demanding its evacuation. He fought in a number of engagements and was promoted to brigadier general, then major general. Lee commanded several artillery departments, then in June 1864 went to fight with Forrest, threatening Sherman's supply lines to Georgia. That June, he was promoted to lieutenant general, making him, at age 30, the youngest at that grade in the Confederate Army. Lee led the Second Corps, Army of Tennessee and fought in the Atlanta Campaign. After the Battle of Nashville, he and his men were the fighting rear guard for Hood's retreat for three days. Following the war, he was a state senator from Mississippi and, from 1880 to 1899, the first president of the Agricultural and Mechanical College of Mississippi, now known as Mississippi State University.

Lt. Thomas J. Stokes was a young man with the 10th Texas Infantry of Gen. Patrick Cleburne's division. He had been writing letters to his half-sister Miss Mary A.H. Gay in Decatur, Georgia. He told her that he had been at Decatur, Alabama, on October 28 engaged in the fighting and then at Tuscumbia from October 31 until November 10. Stokes thought the delay in crossing the river into Tennessee was due to the river being too high and fast. He wrote that one corps had managed to cross the river to Florence and that, on the twelfth, the river had risen further but they planned to cross soon because it was expected to fall by the following Monday the fourteenth.[4]

At Mussel Shoals, Hood prepared for his move northward. He had a mighty infantry consisting of the corps under Generals Stewart, Cheatham and Lee. This totaled about 30,000 to 35,000 men, plus Forrest's cavalry corps of 10,000 to 15,000. At this time, Wheeler was not available, being in Georgia to combat Sherman.[5]

Seeing that Hood had passed Decatur and was apparently preparing for an offensive into Middle Tennessee, the Federals had stiffened their defenses along the N&D. By November 7, some of Gen. Thomas' Fourth Army Corps, Schofield's Twenty-third Corps and Gen. Smith traveled by rail to Nashville, then south on the N&D to Spring Hill, Columbia and Pulaski. Because the bridges and trestles below Pulaski were still out, that was as far as they could go by rail. Among the other resources that Thomas had were the men of Col. Sipes' 7th Pennsylvania Cavalry in Columbia. He and about 1,300 cavalrymen garrisoned at Columbia and occupied numerous blockhouses along the railroad. Gen. Grant had said on October 13 that he wanted Thomas to abandon the N&D between Columbia and Decatur to free up additional forces to put against Hood, assuming he came into Middle Tennessee. Lower down on the railroad Gen. Stanley, now commander of the Fourth Corps, was becoming increasingly annoyed with the citizens at Lynnville. He was having trouble keeping the telegraph wires up in that area and stated on the sixth that he might burn the country around Lynnville if they continued to cut the lines. At about that time, the federal 10th Tennessee Cavalry burned most of the town's 30 houses in revenge for being fired upon by some guerrillas near there. On the tenth, Stanley gathered the Lynnville citizens and told them he would burn the rest of the town if the telegraph did not remain intact there. The threat of burning was not uncommon. At times, it was deemed necessary to torch houses that guerrillas occupied at night or a house or two belonging to a local secessionist if nearby track was damaged and the residents did not furnish information about the perpetrators.[6]

Union Col. Silas A. Strickland's 50th Ohio Infantry was based in Columbia. On November 8, two of their brigades went by rail from Franklin to Spring Hill but had bridge problems at Carter's Creek and disembarked the train. The bridges had probably been rebuilt since early October and subsequently been washed away by heavy rains. On the ninth, Capt. Williams reported that all but two of their pontoons on the Duck River had been sunk and swept away by the same storm. He requested 12 more pontoons to allow repair of the bridge. It was important to complete that bridge because troops and 1,500 beef cattle for Gen. Stanley were stranded on the north side and needed to cross. Schofield had instructed Strickland to keep the Duck River railroad bridge planked, as needed, for the passage of troops and wagons.[7]

Jacob D. Cox (1828–1900) was born in Montreal, Canada. A lawyer, he was elected to the Ohio State Senate in 1858. While in the legislature, he accepted a commission with the Ohio Militia as a brigadier general and studied military science. In April 1861, he entered the Union Army as Brigadier General of the Ohio Volunteers. Cox was commander of the Third Division of the Twenty-third Corps. He became major general in December 1864 following his success at the Battle of Franklin and mustered out in January 1866. Cox was Governor of Ohio from 1866 to 1868, President Grant's Secretary of the Interior from 1869 to 1870, President of the Toledo and Wabash Railroad from 1873 to 1878, a U.S. Congressman from the State of Ohio from 1877 to 1879, Dean at the Cincinnati Law School from 1871 to 1897 and President of the University of Cincinnati from 1885 to 1889.

On November 9, General Jacob D. Cox reported that some of his men had reached Nashville at 9 a.m. and were on a train to Franklin at 5 p.m., mobilizing to take on Hood. At Franklin, they were delayed because of a wreck that had closed the track near Spring Hill. They traveled as far south as Thompson's Station and stayed there overnight. The next day, they made it to the site of the wreck, a mile south of Thompson's Station, where they unloaded from the train. Cox reported on the eleventh that his wagons were crossing the Harpeth River in Franklin. With the track also damaged seven miles north of Columbia at Carter's Creek, he planned to march to Columbia. While that damage was being repaired, any supplies from the south that were needed in Thompson's Station were to be railed to the break and then taken beyond on baggage wagons. The construction train was there, and it was estimated that the repairs would be completed the next day. All of this is a reminder that sections of the railroads were often shut down and that the armies had to be flexible and sometimes revert to pre-railroad technology to meet their military objectives.

On November 11, when Sherman started his "March to the Sea," Maj. Gen. Schofield, commander of the Army of the Ohio, was detached from Sherman and sent to Pulaski. He and his Twenty-third Corps would serve under Thomas to engage Hood. Schofield arrived on the thirteenth. That corps was joined by part of Stanley's Fourth Corps to form a force of about 23,000 infantrymen. When combined with about 4,000 from Gen. James H. Wilson's Cavalry Corps, the Federals had amassing approximately 27,000 who would soon be going against Hood at Franklin.[8]

> James H. Wilson (1837–1925) was born in Illinois, graduated from the U.S. Military Academy and received a commission in the Topographical Engineers. In the Western Theater, he served Maj. Gen. Grant's Army of the Tennessee as a lieutenant colonel and topographic engineer. In 1864, he switched from engineering to cavalry and that May was promoted to brevet major general. Though an excellent administrator and organizer, he was best as a combat engineer and commanded the Western Cavalry Corps. Wilson and 17,000 troopers were attached to Thomas' Army of the Cumberland for the November–December 1864 Franklin and Nashville Campaign. He and his men captured Confederate President Jefferson Davis and Andersonville Prison Commander Henry Wirz in May 1865 as they fled through Georgia. Wilson resigned from the army in 1870 and worked as a railroad construction engineer and executive and in numerous other activities.

The Confederates did not have enough pontoons to cross at Mussel Shoals, so they built a trestle bridge part way across the Tennessee, with pontoons going the rest of the way. Forrest started putting his men across the Tennessee River on November 17 and headed north on the nineteenth. Hood was eager to cross the river but needed the M&C and Mobile & Ohio railroads in Mississippi and northern Alabama repaired so he could get supplies. On the nineteenth, those roads were open, and supplies were rolling in. The army crossed and was on the north bank of the river on the twentieth. On the morning of the twenty-first, Hood marched out of Florence toward Nashville. He wanted to beat Schofield to the Duck River or at least get between him and Nashville and rout the Federals. Ominously, the weather was becoming unpleasant. There had been a lot of rain since the fourteenth that continued through the twentieth. That would be followed by snow and cold weather on November 21 and 22 and, seemingly, rain and freezing rain until about the twenty-eighth.[9]

In response to Hood's advance, on the twenty-first Schofield was preparing to fall back to Columbia. He telegraphed Stanley ordering him to have his quartermaster send all supplies from Pulaski to Columbia by the morning of the twenty-third. All trains were to be loaded and started to the rear as soon as possible. At 3 a.m. on the twenty-fourth, the trains were ready and ordered to move out. All were at Columbia by midnight. Thomas later stated that, had Hood been delayed another 10 days, the Federals would probably have been prepared to engage him at Pulaski.[10]

> Thomas J. Wood (1823–1906) was born in Munfordville, Kentucky, attended the U.S. Military Academy and was commissioned as a second lieutenant in the U.S. Army Corps of Engineers. He was Brigadier General of Indiana Volunteers and commanded a division in the Army of the Ohio, and then one in the Army of the Cumberland. Wood fought at Shiloh, Murfreesboro and Chickamauga, commanded the Fourth Corps at the Battle of Nashville and pursued Hood toward the Tennessee River. Lincoln appointed him Major General of Volunteers in 1865. Wood mustered out in 1866 and retired in 1868. He settled in Dayton, Ohio, where he died, the last remaining member of his West Point class.

On November 22, Cox and Stanley were moving northward as well. Cox departed Lynnville and marched 10 miles northward toward Columbia while Stanley, with Wood's Fourth Corps and Gen. Nathan Kimball's division, reached Lynnville. Both Schofield and Cox arrived at Columbia just ahead of Hood before noon on the twenty-fourth, thus preventing him from taking control of the bridges over the Duck. Schofield made his headquarters at the Athenaeum, the beautiful rectory for two girls' schools, and Cox at the Martin Place (later owned by A.N. Akin). They, with the help of contrabands, threw up heavy defenses in front of the town. One of their tricks was to cut nearby trees down to the stump and spike telegraph wire between them to trip the advancing Confederates. Wilson's cavalry was watching up and down the Duck River for Hood to make moves to cross it. Buford and Gen. Red Jackson came over from Lawrenceburg, chasing Gen. Edward Hatch's division of Wilson's cavalry toward Pulaski. Hatch was able to delay the Confederates' advance, then fell back to Columbia on the twenty-fifth.[11]

The Union troops in blockhouses along the N&D had to deal with many hours of quiet which were sometimes interrupted by short bursts of great activity. Things had certainly been tough at the houses when Forrest came through. Many had been burned and rebuilt. Now, here came Hood and an even more overwhelming force. Hood seems to have burned most of the houses he or his men passed. Buford and Cheatham may have destroyed those at Culleoka on their way north. Also, it is likely that Hood's army destroyed the two houses at the Duck, the five at Carter's Creek, the house at the West Harpeth, the one at Spencer Creek, assuming there was one, and perhaps others at minor crossings. Hood did not have the opportunity to destroy the four houses at Rutherford Creek because the Federals had already burned them when they were evacuated in late November. It is not clear why the Harris trestle or its blockhouse were apparently not destroyed in November or December 1864.

On the twenty-fourth, Company D of the 175th Ohio Volunteer Regiment was stationed at Blockhouse Number 16 south of Pulaski at Richland Creek Bridge No. 4. They may have been the first captured in Hood's march northward as they found themselves in his path and were taken prisoner. That same day, troops of Companies B and E at Blockhouse Number 15 just north of Pulaski were captured. On the twenty-fifth, Company G at Blockhouse Number 14 on Richland Creek, near Reynolds' Station, was captured but Company E at Blockhouse Number 13 was able to evacuate and escape.

Hood's infantry approached Columbia from Mount Pleasant and Lynnville, with

Forrest's cavalry in front of both. They appeared before federal-held Columbia on the twenty-fourth but did not attack. That day and the next, Schofield and the Confederates, mostly dismounted Confederate cavalry, skirmished. Gen. Stephen Lee got to Columbia on the twenty-sixth and relieved Forrest's cavalry. Most of the Army of Tennessee arrived at the outskirts of Columbia by that night. Rather than attack the entrenched Federals, Hood chose to make a demonstration intended to convince Schofield that they would attack the town. He hoped the Federals would remain there while most of the Confederate forces crossed the Duck, cut off the Federals' retreat and captured or killed the enemy.

On the twenty-fifth, the Federals prepared good approaches for a pontoon bridge on the Duck at Santa Fe Pike and moved troops to the north side of the river to protect it. They also planked the railroad bridge to allow passage of troops and wagons. The next morning, Thomas ordered Schofield to hold the north bank of the Duck until Gen. Andrew Jackson Smith and the Sixteenth Corps could arrive from Nashville to reinforce him. Schofield planned to move his trains across that afternoon and infantry that night. They started crossing at the N&D bridge, but heavy rains and overwhelming darkness postponed the move. On the twenty-seventh, Cox reported that the pontoons had been moved down to where the crossing would be made near the Columbia railroad bridge and Schofield put troops at both bridges to protect them. Gen. Thomas H. Ruger, commander of a division of the Twenty-third Corps, held the railroad bridge. At 2:30 that afternoon, the artillery and trains were ordered over the Duck, with more infantry to follow that night. They had trouble getting the wagons down the bank to the pontoon bridge and up the other side. By midnight, two of the pontoons had sunk but been quickly repaired. In the meantime, Cox's men had been preparing the pontoon and railroad bridges for burning. That day, to slow the Confederates, they destroyed one span of the railroad bridge. The Federals set fire to the fort and magazine at Columbia that night but only a portion burned. Schofield and Cox left the town by 5 a.m. on the twenty-eighth, crossed the Duck on the pontoon bridge, burned it and entrenched themselves on the north side.[12]

On November 27, Col. George W. Hoge's 183rd Ohio National Guard Infantry had been sent by rail from Nashville to Columbia to engage Hood, as had Companies B and D of the 44th Missouri Infantry. Early the next morning, the 183rd arrived by rail at the Franklin depot, followed soon by the 44th, and continued southward. Later that day, Company D and other companies of the 183rd arrived at Carter's Creek but, with the Confederates approaching, per orders from Gen. Stanley sent their baggage back to Spring Hill before the train and baggage could be captured by the enemy. That same day, the 44th Missouri arrived at Rutherford Creek "Block House No. 12" and moved to the Duck River Station. Though many of the 175th were being pulled back to the north on the twenty-seventh, those who had been manning the four blockhouses at Rutherford Creek remained there. Hood had been temporarily headquartered at Ashwood Hall, the home of Col. Andrew J. Polk between Mount Pleasant and Columbia. He moved his headquarters to Beechlawn, the home of Amos and Cornelia Warfield, just south of Columbia.[13]

On the morning of the twenty-eighth, with the Federals no longer at Columbia, the Confederates started entering the town. Maj. Gen. Carter L. Stevenson's division of Lee's Corps was among them. Though these were "their own people," some of Stevenson's troops looted stores and many homes in Columbia. When Hood heard about the looting, he ordered it stopped.

While the Union soldiers were shuttling in and out of the various blockhouses, the Confederates continued streaming northward. Their pontoon train that entered Columbia had been drawn by long-horn Texas steers, the first ever seen there, and rather than ropes or leather, the wagons were drawn using grapevines. There were enough pontoons to make three bridges across the Duck.[14]

On the twenty-seventh, Lt. Col. Stephen Presstman, Chief Engineer for the Army of Tennessee, and others were laying pontoons several miles above Columbia. In the early afternoon of the next day, Forrest's 4,500 troopers were the first Confederates across the Duck. They crossed on the pontoon bridge at Huey's Mill, about seven miles east of Columbia, and at nearby fords and were running interference for Hood, pushing back Wilson's cavalry. This put less than half a day between Schofield and the Confederates. That afternoon and into the early hours of the twenty-ninth, Hood's infantry was pouring across the pontoon bridge at Huey's Mill and probably fording at other points between Columbia and Lewisburg Pike. By the morning of the twenty-ninth, the pontoon bridge at Davis' Ford, three or four miles above Columbia near Sowell's Mill, had been laid but the approaches were not ready. After finishing cutting the banks, components of Cleburne and then Cheatham, Bate, Brown, Stewart and others crossed that bridge. The Confederate infantry rushed to try to get north of Schofield, attempting to cut off his path of retreat. Until about midnight, Lee and some of his men were working to get Hood's artillery and trains over the Duck.[15]

Federal trains were still busily running on the N&D as far south as they could. On November 28, federal troops were being loaded from an ambulance train into a railroad train at Spring Hill and Confederate prisoners were being put onto a train at Thompson's Station. Both were headed for Nashville.

Early on the twenty-ninth, seeing that the Confederates intended to sweep to his left, Schofield sent about half of his army and the large wagon train with Stanley quickly northward toward Spring Hill to get ahead of the Confederates and secure the town. A large number of Black and White refugees accompanied the train. With most of the small federal cavalry picketing at the fords east of Columbia, infantry had to be the advance guard. The movement started about 8:30 a.m. with the train towards the rear. The race for Spring Hill was on. The ground had thawed and was very muddy. Already, many of the Confederate infantrymen were without shoes.[16]

Cox, the 111th Ohio Infantry and others had been left at Columbia to protect the crossing until all the other Federals had departed. Other federal troops covered the ford near the railroad bridge at Rutherford Creek. Hood, too, kept a significant presence at the Duck. He had ordered two of Lee's divisions and most of his artillery to remain there to slow Schofield and follow him if he headed north. Lee demonstrated with artillery fire against the Federals on the north side of the Duck.

At about 10 a.m., the 73rd Illinois, 120th Indiana and the rest of the federal advance guard were first to arrive at Spring Hill. Troops and the wagon train were entering the town at mid-day, with the wagons parking just to the northwest. At about noon, Forrest's cavalry was arriving in great numbers. Federal artillery arrived about then, as well. With only about 700 Federals in the town, they were critical in warding off Forrest who made several charges. Stanley's infantry arrived just in time to stop the Confederate assault of federal trains on the N&D and the Federals were holding the crossroads at Spring Hill. That afternoon, the Battle of Spring Hill was in full swing. The Federals withstood several Confederate attacks from the south and east. Hood was not able to remove the wagon train and army from the pike.

That day, Schofield was planning his move to the north of Franklin. He sent his engineer officer Capt. William J. Twining and a small cavalry escort to sneak around the Confederates and go into Franklin to determine how to best cross the Harpeth River. Twining telegraphed Thomas who, in turn, telegraphed Schofield about the absence of the wagon bridge over the river just downstream of present-day Franklin Pike. The river was high and difficult to ford. It seems that Cox had crossed the river on the wagon bridge on November 11 and that it was then washed out by the persistent rain that fell from about November 14 to 28. The lack of an adequate method of crossing highlights the disadvantage of having to hastily retreat across a river. The situation would not have been so dire if the Federals in Franklin had notified Schofield earlier about the loss of the wagon bridge, but that didn't happen. So, Schofield had to find another way to cross. He telegraphed Thomas to immediately send pontoons from Nashville by rail. However, it seems the telegraph wires were down and Thomas either never received the message or received it late. At about noon, not having heard back from Thomas, Schofield repeated his request. Schofield then assumed, and certainly hoped, that the pontoons would be waiting for him when he arrived in Franklin. He heard from Twining that Thomas had finally answered by suggesting that some of the excess pontoons at the Duck River be used. Thomas probably did not want to send the pontoons down from Nashville because he assumed those at the Duck would suffice. Schofield ordered that those pontoons be sent up to Franklin by wagon. However, they were not true pontoons but, rather, heavy wooden boats that were not easily transportable to Franklin because there were no wagons suitable for doing so. While trying to bring the boats across the Duck on the night of the twenty-sixth after there had been heavy rain, the northern riverbank became so unmanageable that the troops struggled to cross any artillery and just a few wagons and caissons but could not get the heavy boats up the bank. Later, on the twenty-ninth, the Union Pioneers abandoned and sank the pontoon boats at the Duck. Word of this reached Schofield, which meant that he would once again be depending on the pontoons from Nashville.[17]

In mid-afternoon on the twenty-ninth, with the Confederates streaming northward, the Federals better understood the Confederate plan to surround them and the danger that both the huge supply train and the men at the Duck and on their way to Spring Hill were in. Schofield was ordered to send most of the remainder of his forces at the Duck, including some of the 111th Ohio, northward to protect the train and hold the crossroads at Spring Hill to allow federal passage to Franklin. They started departing the Duck at about 4:00. The remainder, including much of the 111th Ohio, stayed on the north bank of the river to guard the nearby fords and the railroad bridge.[18]

Pvt. Joseph T. Garner, with Company A of the 175th Ohio Infantry, had enlisted with the 60th Ohio Volunteer Infantry, Company B in August 1862. With that regiment, he had fought at Harper's Ferry and surrendered in September 1862, mustering out that November. Not being finished serving the Union, he reenlisted with the 175th on September 1, 1864, and was sent to Columbia on October 17. His diary and some letters record a few of his experiences. At Columbia, he performed post and garrison duty in the town and guarded bridges along the N&D north and south of Columbia. He was detailed to Pulaski to work on blockhouses, presumably adding the outer second layer of the walls, and had been at the blockhouses at Harris trestle and Culleoka.

9. Hood Looks for a Fight

At 5:30 a.m. on November 24, his group was ordered to leave their blockhouse and burn all they could not take with them. They marched to Columbia that night, arriving before 10 p.m. The next day, he saw trains going through Columbia all day moving troops. On the twenty-sixth, he was guarding the pontoon bridge and helping to move it down the Duck. The next day, Columbia was evacuated but he stayed to destroy government supplies, then seems to have crossed over a pontoon bridge at the Duck on the twenty-eighth heading for Spring Hill. At dawn on the thirtieth, his unit was attacked as they were rushing to Franklin.[19]

It wasn't just troops, horses and wagons that were in motion between Columbia and Franklin. Trains were on the move, too. A.P. Cutting was a First Lieutenant in the 82nd Ohio Infantry who had been wounded outside Atlanta and transferred to non-field duties. On the morning of the twenty-ninth, he was ordered to run his two trains south from Nashville to deliver ammunition and help move troops and supplies northward ahead of Hood. He took one of the trains to Franklin and was to report there for orders. Upon arriving, he was told to move a carload of ammunition to Thompson's Station. He did that and was then ordered to take his train down to the Duck. When he arrived there, however, Schofield had already started his retreat, so Cutting was told to reverse the train and take it north to Rutherford Creek. He was to pick up some baggage of the 44th Missouri and 183rd Ohio which had been accidentally left there. The carload of ammunition at Thompson's Station was later burned by Lt. Col. Daniel McCoy and his 175th Ohio after they saw some Confederate troops approaching.

From Rutherford Creek, Cutting was ordered north to the Spring Hill Station where he arrived at 4 p.m. There he met one of his engineers with the other locomotive, but not its cars. Cutting was told to leave his train there until further notice and met with Gen. Stanley. Stanley told him that the other train had been fired into south of Thompson's Station, so the engineer panicked and cut his locomotive lose from the train and ran it to the south. Being on an incline, the cars rolled down the track to the north. The Confederates could not stop the cars which ended up near the blockhouse at the West Harpeth River that was manned by troops of the 75th Pennsylvania Infantry. Because the Confederates had no artillery there, the blockhouse was not captured. The cars were saved but everyone on them had jumped off and been captured. Confederates then damaged a small culvert just south of Thompson's Station to trap the engines and cars. Stanley thought Cutting would have to destroy the two engines and burn the train. To save them, however, Cutting asked for 50 to 100 men to guard the train while the railroad men put in a temporary culvert. Stanley told him that he could not spare a single man and that Cutting could ask Schofield later that night. At 11 p.m., Schofield asked Cutting how he intended to destroy the engines if needed. Cutting replied that it could be done by putting some musketry ammunition into their fireboxes. Cutting's engineers, however, claimed that they could disable them by simply removing some parts, which would be much safer. Schofield said he was going to move rapidly northward and would inspect the culvert and inform Cutting whether he was to run the train and engines up or destroy them. At 5 a.m. on the thirtieth, with Hood threatening Spring Hill, Schofield sent an orderly with a command to burn the cars and disable the engines. The cars were set afire but the engineers, who had been given permission to remove some parts, failed to disable the locomotives. The two engines were captured by Hood and used against the Federals at Nashville. In hindsight, Schofield and Cutting must have regretted not blowing up the locomotive's fireboxes. The last thing they wanted to do was to aid the Confederates.[20]

On the afternoon of November 29, Capt. W.S. Thurstin of Company D, 111th Ohio was still at the Duck. The company had orders from Stanley to hold the railroad bridge and burn it if it had to be abandoned. By 3 p.m., the troops remaining at the Duck were the only force between Hood and Blockhouse Numbers 9 through 12 at Rutherford Creek. Those houses were under the command of Capt. William P. Wolf, Company G, 175th Ohio Infantry who was set up at Blockhouse Number 11. Wolf was to head north with his 100 men once the 111th Ohio and some men from the 24th Missouri Infantry came by. However, by nightfall the 111th had not yet arrived. A courier from Gen. Johnson, in charge of railroad defenses, ordered Wolf to burn the four houses and march to Spring Hill to join his regiment. Wolf immediately set them afire with ammunition and supplies inside. After doing so, he and his company marched that night along the railroad track toward Spring Hill. About two miles south of Spring Hill, he veered right to the turnpike that paralleled the railroad, presumably to get better footing. He saw a row of campfires about 200 yards long on the east side of the road, which a local Black man said were Confederates who had just come up after dark. Wolf and his men safely passed the fires. One of the Company G soldiers remarked that they must not have been Confederate fires, probably expressing disbelief that Confederates would not have seen them and attacked. Later that night, Wolf was marching alongside Schofield's wagon train, perhaps not aware that Schofield's troops and the train had somehow passed the Confederate camp unscathed. At 4 a.m. on November 30, Confederates attacked the wagon train, firing into it and burning six wagons. Wolf arrived at Franklin at about 10 a.m. and joined his regiment.[21]

During the day, Lee was working to cross the Duck. His task was to push the Federals toward Spring Hill and cover the south in case of a federal retreat that way. With federal fire coming from the north bank, he sent a pontoon boat loaded with men across and back numerous times. At 4:00, men were still crossing to the north side. By 5:00, about 2,000 men were across, enough to attack the Federals. They drove the Federals back and halted, having cleared enough area north of the river for the Confederates to take a foot hold. Then they laid pontoons and crossed more troops after dark. These federal troops found the pike from Columbia at 10 p.m. and hurried toward Spring Hill. Lee moved up quickly from Columbia and caught up with Hood.

At dark, about when the blockhouses at Rutherford Creek were being burned and Lee was attacking at the Duck east of town, Cox burned the town bridge. He had been ordered to remain at the Duck after Schofield's departure until dark and then proceed to Spring Hill. They moved out at about 8:00 and were still marching at midnight, often harassed by the enemy.

To the north, the Confederate infantry had arrived in great numbers at Spring Hill at about 4:00 and did not wait long to attack from the southeast. They pushed the Federals back into town at which time the federal artillery again became very active. Confederate troops continued arriving on the outskirts of Spring Hill past 5:00. There was significant fighting until dark but the Confederate command, thinking they could take Spring Hill, had not organized themselves and did not make an effective attack. Schofield and a large number of troops were still not far from Columbia, harassed by and often within rifle range of the Confederates.

That day, several companies of the 44th Missouri Infantry took the N&D from Nashville to Columbia but would find themselves marching back to Franklin. While marching northward, Companies B and D engaged Hood at Spring Hill. Many other units were making their way to Franklin as well. The 65th Indiana, for example, had left Columbia at 8 p.m. on the twenty-ninth and walked the 22 miles from Columbia to Franklin without halt, arriving at 4:30 a.m. on the thirtieth.[22]

Hood later reported that at about dark on the twenty-ninth he ordered Cheatham, and then Stewart, to block the pike north of Spring Hill. As it turned out, neither did. To add to the Confederate troubles, Forrest's men had run low on ammunition. They and some of the other Confederate troops would not be supplied with more until the next morning.[23]

Schofield arrived at Spring Hill at about 7:00. The wagon train was still extending three miles to the south and continuing to roll into town. He felt that his army might be trapped there by the Confederates and, an hour later, decided to start towards Franklin. He forced his way through some Confederate resistance on the pike, thus allowing the train and troops to pass to the north. Between about 9:00 and 11:00, while Schofield was on the move, much of the Confederate Army was still positioning at Spring Hill and settling in for the night. The Federals were headed to Franklin, being periodically attacked, while most of the Confederates were still at Spring Hill.

As the last of the Federals were marching into Spring Hill at about midnight, most of the Confederates were within a third of a mile and within rifle range of them. Because of this, many of Schofield's men moved west of the pike to march at a safer distance. The Federals were slipping by the huge Confederate Army who were in camps that were dotted with countless campfires that the Federals could see and that extended perhaps four miles parallel to the pike.

That night, Hood dined and spent the night at Oaklawn, the home of Absalom Thompson, about two miles south of Spring Hill. For several hours during the late night and into the early morning hours of the thirtieth, Hood's troops could see and hear the Federals passing, less than half a mile away. Hood's orders to attack were seemingly not given or at least not followed. And some Confederate commanders did not know the land well enough to make a confident attack in the dark, anyway.

It was the middle of the night when Hood learned that Schofield was getting away. He ordered again that the pike be blocked but those orders were apparently not followed. The pike remained open for the enemy to use. At about 3:00 a.m., the wagon train was again attacked at Thompson's Station. About 30 wagons were taken or destroyed. Before dawn, the 111th Ohio reached Spring Hill from Columbia and the last of the Federals were soon leaving the town as quietly as possible. At this time, the road from Spring Hill to Franklin had been macadamized, presumably making travel easier. The federal train passed slowly, single file over the bridge at the West Harpeth River. By 5 a.m., the last wagon had crossed, and all of the Federals were well north of Spring Hill. Light of day would expose them, so they hurried on.[24]

Hood was livid that morning when he learned that the road had not been blocked. He was irate at the inaction of his officers. In spite of the popular story, it does not appear that he had breakfast at Rippavilla, the home of Nathaniel and Susan Cheairs, about one-and-a-half miles west of Oaklawn or met with his officers there. He would probably not have taken the time to do that because the enemy was escaping to the north. Hood had ordered Cheatham to put skirmishers in front to confuse and delay the Federals, so he could attack that morning, but nothing was done. It is likely that Cheatham never received the order. To compound the dysfunction, Hood's men were running low or had run out of ammunition, so an attack may not have been successful.[25]

Forrest was outraged as well; he didn't like to lose. Hood ordered his commanders to attack the federal wagon train as it moved north of Spring Hill, but the attacks were weak. His plan of surround-and-defeat had been poised for implementation but was not accomplished. Hood decided that his next strategy would be to catch Schofield and drive him into the Harpeth.[26]

At about 6:30 a.m., Confederate cavalry and infantry were ordered to follow the Federals toward Franklin and do what damage they could. They chased on Columbia Pike as far as Winstead Hill but with little effect.

Early that day, Thomas ordered Schofield to relieve all of the garrisons from the blockhouses and to send them back to Nashville on the N&D, probably from Franklin. In spite of that, 20 men of Co. E, 75th Pennsylvania were captured by the advancing Confederates at the house at the West Harpeth River. Back at the Duck, there were federal troops who were never informed of the move north. Probably 100 men, including about 40 men of the 112th Illinois, were captured.

The Battle of Spring Hill was over. The Confederate dead and wounded numbered about 500, as opposed to about 350 for the Federals. The railroad lay to the west of most of the action and was little affected. The Confederates had not beaten Schofield to Columbia, nor cut him off north of Columbia, nor stopped him at Spring Hill. Now, they were chasing him again. On the morning of the thirtieth, Hood had a staff meeting at the home of William Harrison just south of Winstead Hill. In the meantime, the last of the Federals were entering Franklin—infantry, wagon train and all—and starting to take their defensive positions.[27]

10

The Battles of Franklin and Nashville

Several hundred miles to the southeast, the Federals had already decimated Atlanta. Desperate survivors, soldiers and civilians alike, attempted to carry on. Miss Mary A.H. Gay was one. She did not yet know that she would earn a place in the history of the small town of Franklin, Tennessee. Miss Gay lived outside Atlanta in Decatur, Georgia. She had land, a house, enslaved people and Confederate money, none of which could buy anything. The scarcity of food required that she and her enslaved people do something to keep from starving. She heard about a store in Atlanta that bartered provisions for war munitions. Minie balls were particularly valuable, so she and a maid went to the battlefields around Atlanta to search for them. On one of the days there, November 30, they found a bonanza of minie balls at a Confederate magazine and dug them from the frozen ground with old case knives. Trading them helped provide sustenance to get them through the hardest of times. She was not aware that on that same day her half-brother Thomas J. Stokes, with the 10th Texas Infantry under Gen. Cleburne, would be killed at Franklin. Miss Gay would survive, but not her kinsman. Ultimately, she honored her beloved relative and his fellow soldiers. After the Battle of Franklin, she collected $7,000 and contributed it to help pay to rebury in the nearby McGavock Cemetery the soldiers who had fallen at Franklin. An engraved silver plate bearing the name of Mary A.H. Gay is affixed to the entrance gate to the cemetery today.[1]

November 30 was a long, horrible day at Franklin, the worst that the N&D would witness.

Schofield was at the head of the Union column. Upon arriving at Franklin before dawn, he was upset to learn that there were still no pontoons waiting for him. He and Capt. Twining would have to develop other plans for crossing the Harpeth in case the pontoons were still on their way from Nashville but did not arrive in time. Schofield put Cox in temporary command of the Twenty-third Army Corps in the Carter House just south of town. Cox was to hold Hood back at least until the supply train was safely across the Harpeth, escaping capture by Hood.[2]

Twining reported that there were four potential ways of crossing, each of which would require some work.

The first involved rebuilding the wagon bridge which had been washed away. It connected Franklin Pike to present-day First Avenue North, between Main and Bridge Streets. The structure was originally built in 1819 as a large, two-span covered bridge with a massive central pillar, resting on high stone abutments. It had two lanes with a partition down the middle and two open windows on each side. Confederates had crossed the

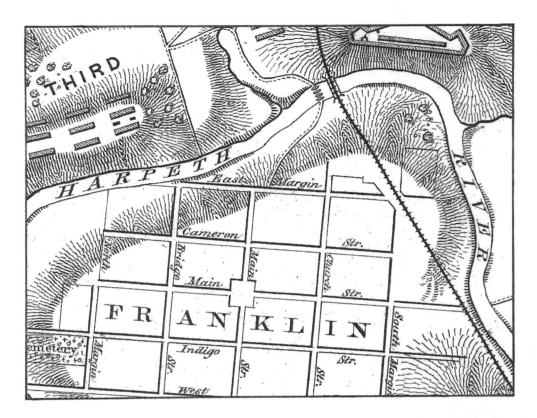

Map 10—Franklin, Tennessee and River Crossings on November 30, 1864 (Library of Congress).

bridge on their way south from Nashville after its occupation by Federals in February 1862. It seems to have been destroyed twice since then. The first was by Col. Scott in early 1862 after the Confederates had abandoned Nashville and the other per order of Gen. Bragg on November 13, 1862. Bragg burned this bridge, the wagon bridge at present-day Murfreesboro Road and many other bridges in the area to keep the Federals from surrounding him. About three miles northwest of town, Capt. Thomas Perkins burned another bridge over the Harpeth in October 1862. It is on present-day Cotton Lane.[3]

They could plank and prepare approaches to the railroad bridge which was otherwise ready to use. This would allow passage of wagons. It is not clear how long this bridge had been there. Boomer's Howe truss bridge had been completed on March 6 and there is no indication that it had been replaced, though it may have. The mid–July damage to the bents probably did not affect the trusses.[4]

A third option was reconstruction of what was known as the County Bridge. It was located just downstream of the railroad bridge and had been burned in a skirmish earlier in the year. The bridge had been cheaply built on trestles and posts with little clearance over the river. The northern bank was quite high, making for a fairly steep approach on that side. A road connected it to town on the south side and to the Franklin Pike on the north.[5]

The fourth, and least effective, of the options was improving the ford located between the railroad bridge and the County Bridge. It was in very bad condition.[6]

10. The Battles of Franklin and Nashville

There had been another bridge over the river at Franklin on Murfreesboro Pike (present-day Highway 96 East) on the east side of town. It, too, had been washed out in a rainstorm. There was no reason for the Federals to rebuild it because Schofield's retreat needed to be to the north.

Schofield's goal was to get his everybody and everything across the river before Hood attacked. While he was preparing his crossings and getting the wagon train and other assets across, he would need to keep a large number of troops ready for an attack. Though Thomas wanted him to hold Hood at Franklin for three days, Schofield thought that one day was more realistic.

He was under immense pressure to build the crossings to get everybody to the safer north side of the Harpeth. Schofield ordered that the wagon bridge be rebuilt and the railroad bridge modified to allow passage of wagons. The County Bridge was to be rebuilt by sawing off the burnt tops of the posts close to the water level, then placing new beams and planking on top. Also, the ford was to be improved. This would give the Federals multiple means of crossing. It was not intended or expected that all four would be ready for use at the same time. The preferred means of crossing would be the wagon and railroad bridges, which could pass the army more quickly than the other two. However, those two large bridges would require more time to prepare. While they were being finished, the Federals would have to use the ford and the County Bridge.[7]

Though Schofield could not be sure of it, Hood was preparing to attack, determined to drive him into the river. Hood's infantry and Forrest got into position, with Forrest on the Confederates' right. Hood ordered what little artillery he had not to fire because they would harm the people in the town. It seems that Hood had kept much of his artillery and Stephen Lee's infantry too long at Columbia, trying to keep Schofield focused on Columbia while the Confederates were crossing the Duck. Lee and the bulk of the artillery didn't arrive at Franklin until about 4 p.m. They would be held in reserve.

Given the circumstances, it seems that Hood's decision to attack the Union at Franklin was a strategically poor, though perhaps necessary, one. It has been suggested that he was under the influence of the pain medicine he had been taking for his wounds and amputations. Even if so, he was certainly motivated to either attack Schofield fairly quickly at Franklin or make a flank movement similar to that at Columbia and try to cut off his retreat to Nashville. When he attacked, Hood knew that Schofield already had most of his train and some troops across the Harpeth and could probably cross the remainder in time to foil an attempted Confederate flank move. Hood must have thought that even if the battle had to be fought at night, so be it. If he were to defeat Schofield, it would need to be done that afternoon and night. To delay would allow Schofield to be over the Harpeth that evening and on to the safety of Nashville with the bridges burned behind him. Gen. Thomas later stated that if Hood had delayed his advance into Tennessee until late November, he would have been ready to engage him somewhere south of the Duck River. Instead, Hood headed out from Florence on the nineteenth and Thomas did not have sufficient forces to confront him there. So, here they were at Franklin at the end of November with bridges again playing a key role in the war.[8]

It was going to take several hours for Schofield to have the crossings ready and move his army to the north side of the river. At about 8 a.m., the Federals started building their defenses to deal with Hood if he attacked. At about the same time, they would have started work on the ford and the three crossing structures. The eastern end of their works tied into the Harpeth River above Franklin. On the western end, Schofield placed another division between Carter's Creek Pike and the Harpeth River below the town.

Schofield set up his headquarters in Dr. Daniel McPhail's building on East Main Street and, later, the Alpheus Truett house across the river on what is now Franklin Pike. When the battle started, he relocated to Fort Granger where he spent most of his time during the fight. Cox set up his headquarters in the Carter House on Columbia Pike.

Gen. Schofield's supply train of at least 800 wagons would have been about five miles long in single file. On the outskirts of Franklin, the Federals had left Columbia Highway open so the doubled lines of the main wagon train, artillery and other trains, including those with the wounded, could pass into town. On the morning of the thirtieth, the wagon train rolled into Franklin. It was broken up and parked in the side streets of town. The wagons clogged the little town, but they were parked so that the main roads remained open to the river crossings. From their fortifications on Columbia Pike through town all the way to the bridges, the side streets were overflowing with wagons and troops from house front to house front.[9]

During the day, the Federals labored to get as much as they could across the Harpeth. While construction was taking place on the three bridges, the artillery and a large portion of the wagon train crossed the swollen river via the ford. Because the water was above axle height and the riverbed was soft, anywhere from six to 24 horses were needed to pull a cannon or a wagon across. Among those struggling to cross the ford early in the day were the 15th and 23rd Indiana Light Artillery and the 1st Ohio Volunteer Light Artillery. Battery D of the 1st Ohio was placed at the fort while the other two were parked in reserve. Later, the banks at the ford were shoveled into the river to make them flatter and firmer and the crossing less difficult.[10]

By about 10 a.m., Union hospital and ambulance wagon trains had arrived in Franklin from around Columbia and Spring Hill. Federal Surgeon Maj. Charles S. Frink, Medical Director of Brig. Gen. James W. Reilly's Third Division, Twenty-third Corps, found a railway train of box cars on the north side of the river that was loaded with fodder and ready to depart for Nashville. He persuaded the conductor to wait a few minutes while he galloped to Schofield's headquarters to procure from the general an order to unload the cars enough to accommodate the sick and wounded. At that time, crossing the river was still limited to the ford, which was not a viable option for the ambulances considering the rough flow and depth of the water. They were forced to wait for one of the bridges—it would be the County Bridge—to be completed and would have to take another train.

Later that morning, the large wagon train was still crossing at the ford. At about noon, the Pioneers and pontoniers had completed the County Bridge so the ford was no longer as important. The County Bridge was intended for troops but was found useful for crossing wagons, as well, if done carefully. The ambulances, Wood's infantry and the remainder of the wagon train crossed over it. In using it, however, the distance traveled along its road to the Franklin Pike was about a quarter mile longer than via the wagon bridge. Because of this and its steep slope, the County Bridge was not the best way across. After crossing the County Bridge, the wounded were loaded onto rail cars and sent to Nashville in the early afternoon.

As some of the materials for the wagon bridge and railroad bridge came in by rail, the men wasted no time unloading them. The soldiers used wood delivered that day by train but also relied on wood they had stripped from fences and nearby houses and other

10. The Battles of Franklin and Nashville

buildings. At the railroad bridge, troops had been preparing the two approaches to the track and placing wood across the cross ties and rails to form a wide, sturdy surface for the passage of troops, cannon and wagons. Not long after the County Bridge was completed, the railroad bridge was ready for use. We can assume that the Federals started crossing it at once.

Throughout the day, a steady stream of troops crossed the Harpeth. Early that afternoon, Capt. Thurstin of the 111th Ohio had to go north across either the County Bridge or wagon bridge to resupply his men with ammunition. Upon returning, he labored to make his way in the direction opposite to that of the flood of infantry, wagons, pack horses and more.

It seems that the wagon bridge was completed by early afternoon, thus becoming the fourth and preferred method of crossing both troops and the heavy wagons. By about 3:30, many other ambulance teams had crossed the river and were headed to Nashville. A small ammunition train was yet to cross.

At about 2 p.m., Stanley had met with Schofield at the McPhail house. Because at that time it did not seem likely that Hood would attack, Schofield planned to lead all his troops over the river at dark. He then moved his headquarters across the Harpeth to the Truett house, not knowing that after dark his men would still be in Franklin and engaged in a horrific battle.

By about 8 p.m., the wagon train was on its way toward Nashville. That night, two railroad trains loaded with the wounded who had fought south of Franklin arrived in Nashville. There must have been others. In the meantime, Surgeon Sparks selected a place for the general field hospital on the Nashville Turnpike some distance north of the Harpeth.[11]

After about seven hours of crossing the ford, preparing the other three crossings and then crossing them, the Federals seem to have had everything over the Harpeth except what they needed to deal with Hood. Animals in the wagon train were taken at least a half mile north of the Harpeth where they were fed and watered in preparation for the drive to Brentwood.[12]

Some maps of Franklin and its battlefield show a pontoon bridge at the site of the County Bridge. Also, some literary accounts of the battle state that the Federals relied upon a pontoon bridge during their retreat from Franklin. These do not appear to be correct because there is no evidence that pontoons were used at Franklin on November 30. The pontoons at Columbia never arrived and the pontoons that had been requested from Nashville arrived by rail at about noon on the thirtieth when construction of the other bridges for the crossing was well underway. No longer needing them, Schofield ordered the pontoons returned to Nashville. Although the Federals seem to have installed a pontoon bridge at Franklin and routinely used it and the County Bridge during their occupation of Franklin, there is no indication that one was constructed, removed or burned on or about the thirtieth. It is not known what happened to that earlier pontoon bridge. It seems that the troops who crossed the rebuilt County Bridge in darkness that night thought it was a pontoon bridge. After the war, Cox explained the misconception about the bridge as follows: "Its floor was so near the water that many who crossed it thought it was a pontoon bridge, and it was so spoken by several officers in reports and printed statements. They had heard that a pontoon bridge was expected, and naturally assumed that it had been laid."[13]

At about noon, when the Federals were about halfway through building their structures and crossing, Hood and the advance Confederate columns had arrived at Winstead Hill, just south of Franklin, and pushed the federal skirmishers back to their works. From about 1 p.m. to 3 p.m., Hood formed his line, even though most of his artillery had not yet come up from Columbia. At 3:30, his men advanced northward across the open fields toward the entrenched Federals. This happened to be about when the Federals had finished moving their trains across the river. The swift work of the men tasked with rebuilding the Harpeth crossings had allowed the Federals to put their trains, animals, artillery and many of their troops across the river in a much safer place. The remainder of their troops would have joined them by midnight, but Hood did not allow that to happen.[14]

When the fighting commenced at 4:00, Schofield moved his headquarters to Fort Granger. During the battle, there was constant traffic and communication between Schofield at the fort and Cox at the Carter house. That evening, the 19th Ohio Volunteer Infantry took up position on the east side of Fort Granger, throwing up temporary breastworks. They occupied the fort with the 79th Indiana Volunteers. From that location, they would later provide cover as the Union troops crossed the river. Their duties included preventing the Confederates from damaging or destroying the rebuilt bridges before the Federals had crossed them.

The fighting raged into the night. Though horrible to imagine, the fiercest combat was in the dark from about 5 p.m. to about 9 p.m. Forrest tried to push back the Federals' left, crossing the Harpeth at Hughes' ford. Wilson sent Hatch's cavalry and some infantry who succeeded in driving Forrest back across the river. The intensity of the battle slowed a bit at 10 p.m. During the short but intense fight, the Confederates were repulsed many times. At one point, Schofield had ordered Wood to be ready to cover the bridges and other river crossings in case the Confederates broke through the Union defenses, requiring a hasty retreat. That would not be necessary.[15]

There were huge losses on both sides, mostly suffered by the Confederates. The Union had prevailed in a devastating defeat of the Confederate Army. Six of their generals were killed—John Adams, John C. Carter, Cleburne, States Rights Gist, Hiram B. Granbury and Otho F. Strahl. On January 20, 1865, Gen. Thomas reported to Lt. Col. R.M. Sawyer, Asst. Adjutant Gen., Military Division of the Mississippi, on the Confederate losses at Franklin, "At the time of the battle the enemy's loss was known to be severe and was estimated at 5,000. The exact figures were only obtained, however, on the reoccupation of Franklin by our forces, after the battles of December 15 and 16, at Brentwood Hills, near Nashville, and are given as follows: Buried in the field, 1,750; disabled and placed in hospital at Franklin, 3,800, which with the 702 prisoners already reported, makes an aggregate loss to Hood's army of 6,252, among whom were 6 general officers killed 6 wounded and 1 captured." In contrast, Schofield later estimated the Union loss at Franklin to be 2,326, including 189 killed, 1,033 wounded and 1,104 missing.[16]

Schofield had to decide what he would do next. He could stay and continue the battle from one side of the river or the other. However, he did not have enough ammunition and could not receive reinforcements quickly enough to assure that he would hold Hood. The day had seen his men build defenses at Franklin, construct crossings over the river, transfer everything they could to the north side and then engage in an excruciating battle. But there was more to do. Schofield had made his decision and, as the battle was at its height, released orders sometime between 6 p.m. and 7 p.m. calling for a midnight retreat. Though the orders were not clear about when the artillery was to be taken across the river, much of it was the first to be moved, commencing late that night. At about midnight, the last of the guns was heading toward the river. The Union flanks were to withdraw simultaneously at midnight, with the pickets coming afterward. As ordered, troops on the Union's left, essentially everything on the east side of Columbia Pike, were to cross the Harpeth via the planked-over railroad bridge. Troops on their right, everything on the west side of Columbia Pike, were to pass through town and cross via the rebuilt wagon bridge. To accelerate the crossing, some of the army used the County Bridge and perhaps the ford. To reduce the chance that their movement would be detected by the Confederates, the army was ordered to withdraw in silence and with no fires. The 19th Ohio and 79th Indiana Infantries covered the crossing and protected the retreat to Brentwood. The Federals had to leave many of their wounded and dying on the battlefield. And a large number of their sick and wounded had to stay behind to receive care in makeshift emergency hospitals set up in homes, buildings and churches near the battle scene.[17]

To the consternation of the Union Army, Confederate sympathizers had set a fire in the town at about midnight or 1 a.m. Federal soldiers found an old fire engine and, with the help of citizens, subdued the flames. Gens. Wood and Stanley sent some of their staff to oversee the effort. To prevent their withdrawal from being seen by the Confederates, the Union troops were forced to delay their move for about an hour until the fire was extinguished. As it turned out, the residual smoke from the fire was a mixed blessing for the withdrawing troops. It provided additional cover for them but, because of the darkness and thick smoke, the retreat through town was confusing for some of the Union troops coming in from their right flank. Many struggled to find their way to the wagon bridge. Some said the burning buildings were a livery stable or a house. Others said it was the Odd Fellows Hall on the east side of the square where the City Hall is today. It is likely that the flames spread, leaving as many as eight buildings totally or partially consumed. Before the fire, it had been rumored in Franklin that the Federals would burn the town when departing. The fire made that appear to be the case, but it was not.[18]

When the Confederates saw this fire in the town, they thought it was the railroad bridge being burned by the Federals. From their position in darkness a mile away, they fired shells just to the right of the fire, hoping to do damage to the Union forces in the area of Fort Granger. Their shells fell, however, just to the right of the center of town in the residential area on the east side, crashing into homes and yards. The panicked citizens were the victims as no harm was done to the Federals. About 150 rounds were fired before the Confederates realized that they were shelling the town and ceased their fire.[19]

Once across the river, the troops were halted by Schofield until all but Wood's division and the skirmishers were over. Some, upon reaching the north side of the river, had become separated from their regiment. Once reunited with their units, the men started their march toward Brentwood. General Smith had brought reinforcements to Brentwood to support the battle fatigued soldiers.

Lt. Fusselman and 20 men of the 19th Ohio were initially detailed to burn the railroad bridge but were given an alternative plan to slow Hood in the event he decided to chase the Federals. They were ordered to remove the planks from the bridge and did so. Wood watched the crossing until 3 a.m. Then, with the withdrawal nearly complete and the majority of Schofield's army on its way to Brentwood, his troops placed and lit bundles of kindling on the wagon and County bridges. They guarded the two structures until they knew the blazes could not be extinguished by the enemy. By 4 a.m., the wagon bridge was crumbling into the river and the County Bridge was fully engulfed. Wood was the last to leave embattled little Franklin. He came up as rear guard and had Wilson on his flanks as they moved north along Franklin Pike to Brentwood.[20]

At about 3 a.m., seeing the two blazes and assuming they were an indication that the Union was withdrawing, one of Hood's battalions opened up heavy cannon fire on them but received no return fire. The lack of a response was proof enough that their adversary had departed. The Federals were gone and separated from the Confederates by a river that was once again difficult to cross. This battle, the primary and "Second" Battle of Franklin, was over.

On the night of the thirtieth, Hood had ordered that his attack be renewed on the following morning. At 7 a.m., his artillery that had come up from Columbia was to start firing 100 rounds per gun. At 9 a.m., a general charge was to be made by the entire army. Confederate Maj. General E.C. Walthall, commander of a division in Stewart's Corps, delivered the news to Hood that the Union had withdrawn during the night. Hood would need another plan.[21]

The federal forces had now abandoned Fort Granger and Schofield had some distance between himself and Hood. They reached Brentwood by 9 a.m. on the first day of December and Nashville later that day. Their exit from Franklin was not without a swift reaction from Forrest, however, who pursued them for a few miles only to harass them. There were some sharp fights four or five miles north of Franklin, with Buford and Jackson making some charges and taking about 100 prisoners.[22]

The defenses awaiting at Nashville were significant and would be even more so with Schofield's men present. Fort Negley was there, as well as two lesser forts and a blockhouse on hilltops just south of the city. From December 1–4, the 4th U.S. Artillery, Battery M, was positioned at the blockhouse on the west side of Franklin Pike atop the hill where the City Reservoir is currently located. This house was much more substantial than the wooden houses along the railroad.

On December 2, Gen. Grant telegraphed Thomas, ordering him to dispose of Hood quickly and telling him that if Hood was to retreat, Thomas was to "give him no peace." Grant was frustrated that Thomas had not been more aggressive and, rather than retreat to Nashville, engaged Hood between Franklin and Nashville. Thomas argued, however, that he retreated because he did not have the men to be victorious, especially being so outnumbered in cavalry. Grant's frustration grew over the next few days. He ordered Thomas to attack on December 7 after his troops were safely back at Nashville, but that did not occur, partly because Thomas wanted to increase his force of mounted men. This led to talk between Halleck and Grant of replacing Thomas with Schofield, whom they thought would take immediate action.[23]

It was up to Hood to make the next move. His original plan had been to go to Kentucky to recruit more troops, then to the aid of Robert E. Lee at Petersburg, Virginia. Instead of implementing that plan or taking some other strategy, the Confederate general chose to go on to Nashville and await Thomas' attack. By 3 p.m. on December 1, some of Hood's troops had passed through Franklin and forded the river there, while others had crossed the Harpeth just east of town, probably via a ford but perhaps aided by a pontoon bridge. They headed for Nashville along Franklin Pike which straddled the N&D. The railroad would prove critical to supplying Hood in his fight at Nashville. Hood spent that first night in Brentwood. The next morning of December 2 he set out for Nashville where he established headquarters at the house aptly named Travellers Rest, the home of

10. The Battles of Franklin and Nashville

Judge John Overton. It was on the pike, about six miles south of Nashville and only 100 yards east of the railroad. He set up camp and formed his lines a couple of miles south of the city. Travellers Rest, which is today a well-preserved museum house, would be Hood's place of refuge and preparation for his next confrontation with the Union forces and occupiers of Nashville. The city's strategic importance to the Union cannot be overstated. Transportation assets, including rail and water, were a valued component of the Union's overall strength in waging war against the Confederacy. Hood resolved to defy that powerful occupation. Forrest joined Hood at Nashville, then went to Murfreesboro on the fifth where he was able to destroy blockhouses on the N&C.[24]

Even though Hood was mostly focused on a victory at Nashville, he had to make improvements to the crossings at Franklin, now at his rear. This would help him prepare for the battle at Nashville. He may have rebuilt the wagon and County Bridges which would assist him in crossing the Harpeth in the event of a retreat. Hood seems to have laid at least one pontoon bridge there to use while at Nashville.

He brought trains up from south of Franklin to supply him. On December 6, Hood was running trains on the N&D from his camp to as far south as Pulaski and, with the railroad still under repair, would be able to run them to Decatur in another day or two. At the same time, the Confederates were repairing the railroad from Corinth to Decatur because Hood would soon be running trains north from Decatur loaded with supplies needed by his army. These were critical items, especially clothing and shoes, not available to him locally. In a telegram to Gen. Beauregard in Montgomery on the thirteenth, Hood requested for his army 10,000 suits of clothing and all available blankets. With no railroad bridge or pontoon bridge at Decatur, they would have had to ferry supplies across the Tennessee River. Since wagon transportation was so difficult in the winter, rail transport was critical to supplying the needed supplies. Hood thought he had enough rolling stock captured from the Federals to meet his purposes. That included at least four engines and their trains that were already running on the N&D and a train and engine in Decatur ready to go. And there were other trains that could be put to use, among which were two locomotives and several cars that he had captured, perhaps at Spring Hill. Also, before the fighting started at Nashville, Hood had ordered that two rail cars be pulled by oxen across country from the N&C to the N&D and was preparing to pull a locomotive across. When the fighting commenced, he called an end to the deliveries.[25]

Grant remained eager to see Thomas take immediate action against Hood. He was becoming increasingly impatient with Thomas for delaying the attack. Grant did not want Hood to somehow get away, cross the Cumberland and wreak havoc in Kentucky, Ohio or elsewhere. Grant sent reinforcements to Louisville and ordered Thomas to follow Hood if he tried to go north, but not try to cut him off. On December 9, Halleck ordered that Thomas be replaced by Schofield. Thomas explained that a storm of freezing rain and frost that would last two or three days had hit on the day before, making attack impractical. Without protest, Thomas told Grant he would step down peacefully if told to do so. Late that afternoon, Grant gave Thomas the benefit of the doubt and suspended the replacement. On the eleventh, Grant again ordered Thomas to take the offensive. Thomas explained that he would have attacked on the tenth except for the sheet of ice covering the ground, making the surface hard, slippery and not conducive to attack. Grant waited again. Per a later report from Thomas, both armies were, indeed, ice-bound from about December 8 to 14. On the fourteenth, the ice had melted but the land was a sea of mud. Having had ample time to develop his plan, Thomas called a meeting of his corps commanders that afternoon to discuss his strategy. With the weather having moderated, the army was in position by 6 a.m. on December 15. Thomas had already told Grant that he would attack on that morning and he did. In the meantime, Gen. Logan had been ordered to Nashville to take the place of Thomas, but the Federals attacked before Logan arrived.[26]

The two armies engaged in the Battle of Nashville on Thursday and Friday, December 15 and 16. Hood's 30,000 men, which included about 22,000 infantrymen, were outnumbered nearly two to one by the 55,000 in the combined forces of Thomas' Army of the Cumberland, already in place protecting Nashville, and Schofield's Army of the Ohio.[27]

At about 6 a.m. on the fifteenth, Thomas' men moved out with a heavy fog helping somewhat to conceal their advance. They made a demonstration on their left, east of Nolensville Pike, drawing some of Hood's attention to that area and were repulsed by Hood. In the early afternoon, Thomas made his main assault on the federal's right along Harding and Hillsborough Pikes. Wilson's cavalry and two corps of infantry engaged in fierce close-range fighting and took several earthen redoubts and eight guns. This forced the Confederates to retreat about two miles to the south that night, digging in and protecting their potential retreat route via Franklin Pike.[28]

Sometime after noon of the sixteenth, the Federals attacked both Confederate flanks. They were repulsed on their left but later in the day Brig. Gen. John McArthur captured Compton's Hill, now known as Shy's Hill, turning the Confederate left flank and sending most of them into retreat. By sundown, the Confederates had left the field. That night, what remained of Hood's army started its retreat southward towards Franklin. At daybreak on the seventeenth, the Federals pursued along Granny White Pike and then Franklin Pike.

On December 16, Gen. Roddey had received orders from Hood to leave Decatur and join the army near Nashville as soon as possible. On the way, he was to destroy the railroad between Huntsville and Stevenson, Alabama, and then head to Murfreesboro. Roddey left a regiment to garrison Decatur and protect his battery there. He reported that a company of engineers had arrived from Hood's army to place a pontoon bridge at Decatur and assist in getting some captured engines across the river there and then onto the N&D. Neither Roddey's presence nor the additional engines would have altered the outcome of the battle.

When Gen. Hood took on Thomas's stout defenses at Nashville, he had not foreseen a repeat of the defeat and suffering his men experienced at Franklin. However, his army was beaten again, with 1,500 Confederates killed or wounded and 4,500 captured or missing. In contrast, the Union suffered 400 killed, 2,600 wounded and 110 captured or missing. But the fighting and hardships were not over. Hood's defeat at Nashville was followed by an arduous and frantic retreat to the south side of the Tennessee River.

11

Chasing Hood

The Battle of Bridge Builders

The conveyance of troops over waterways, or the inability to do so, had played a major role in military maneuvers in November. The same would be the case in late December as the Federals chased Hood in miserable weather across terrible terrain. Even without a battle, per se, the outcome of this chase would have ramifications similar to one. Should the Federals capture Hood before he crossed the Tennessee River, the glory to the Federals of a victory and gloom to the Confederates of a loss would be huge. It did not seem that Hood could win; at best, he could avoid another defeat. This would largely be a battle of bridge builders because there were several waterways to cross and not many structures already there to be used. Railroad bridges would not play a significant role. The Union would be moving and laying pontoon bridges and building temporary wooden bridges. Hood would be transporting, laying and removing his pontoon bridges. Whichever side was more efficient would likely be the victor. Hood had suffered two recent defeats and would need a successful retreat to avoid a third.

The Federals engaged the Confederates in what would become a running battle over nine-and-a-half days and about 100 miles to the Tennessee River. Not including the two additional days required for Hood to cross his pontoons on the Tennessee, progress averaged ten-and-a-half miles per day. A typical march could cover 10–15 miles in a day. The chase would be characterized by bad weather, the armies' push to make the maximum amount of progress each day and the death, waste and destruction along the way. Men and animals would become ill or die, and bridges, wagons, arms and ammunition would be burned.

Both armies left Nashville on the night of December 16. Lt. Gen. Stephen Lee's infantry and some of Walthall's infantry were in the Confederate fighting rear guard while they rushed southward toward Franklin. That night, Lee camped seven miles north of Franklin. They started out again at dawn on the seventeenth. On their way, they briefly encountered a portion of Wilson's cavalry near Hollow Tree Gap, about five miles from Franklin. Around 9:00 a.m., in a second encounter, two mounted federal regiments attempted a frontal assault on the Confederates. That morning, Lee and Walthall were joined just north of Franklin by Buford's and Gen. James R. Chalmers' divisions of Forrest's Cavalry Corps.[1]

When Hood reached the Harpeth, his reinforced rear guard was just to the north, Wilson's cavalry on their heels and Wood's infantry not far behind Wilson. With the Confederates slowing to cross, Wilson and the rear guard engaged for several hours in a battle of 6,000 to 10,000 cavalrymen in the vicinity of present-day Harlinsdale Farm and the railroad underpass north of Fort Granger. This brief yet massive event can appropriately be called "The Third Battle of Franklin."[2]

Most times, the Harpeth would not have been stressful to cross, but not now. The lives and freedom of Hood's men depended on a quick and safe transit. It seems that Hood had a pontoon bridge there and the railroad bridge was still intact, though perhaps not planked over. Fords were still available, though difficult to use. And it is not clear whether the wagon and County Bridges were ready to cross. With such a large force, an organized crossing would have taken many hours. Under these circumstances, with a massive and determined enemy upon him, Hood did not have the luxury of time, so the army's crossing created a frantic scene.[3]

As their rear guard held the Federals back the best they could, the Southerners crossed the river any way they could, preferring the pontoon and railroad bridges. Additional Confederate cavalry moved in to cover Lee's flanks as the men made their way into Franklin. Confederate artillery was set up. It and the cavalry fired from the riverbank, allowing most of the remaining troops to get into the war-torn town by 10 a.m. Captain Coleman, engineer officer under Lee, and a party of Pioneers sank the pontoons and burned the railroad bridge while under heavy fire from Union sharpshooters. Hood would also have ordered Lee to burn the wagon and County Bridges if they had been intact. Some Southerners were still on the north side and had to either swim to safety or be captured or shot. The Federals captured about 1,000 prisoners. Knowing that the town was full of the wounded, an estimated 1,500 Confederates and 150–200 Federals, and probably wishing not to subject them and the residents to too much gun fire, Lee and the rear guard left Franklin quickly rather than putting up significant resistance there.[4]

As was usually the case, the Confederates wanted to destroy anything of value to the enemy. On their way out of town at about 10:30, Lee's men set fire to a commercial building, probably the N&D freight depot at the site of the current one. The building contained seven wagonloads of ammunition. The burned structure would not have been the Union depot because that structure was located on the north side of the river. As soon as the Confederates departed, a brave older citizen who lived nearby, Robert Rainey, climbed a ladder onto the roof and extinguished the flames using several buckets of water. His heroism prevented a potential massive explosion.[5]

Once some of the Federals had made their way across the river, they were again in control of Franklin, capturing the hospitals and all of the Confederate wounded. The town was garrisoned for several months by Company C of the 75th Indiana Infantry. They were under the command of Lt. Col. Alvin Von Matzdorff and almost entirely German mercenary troops, very few of whom could speak English.[6]

To help get his army across the river, Thomas had planned ahead and, on the afternoon of December 16, ordered that troops bring a pontoon train by wagon from Nashville to Franklin. It seems that the Federals wanted it to arrive at the Harpeth about mid-day on the seventeenth. Unfortunately for them, but fortuitously for the Confederates, the train was sent out the Murfreesboro Pike, which ran to the southeast, rather than Franklin Pike to the south. It is not clear whether Capt. Ramsey, Assistant Adjutant General, miswrote the order after awakening from a deep sleep or Thomas misspoke; probably the former. Regardless, it was a mistake that went unnoticed until late on the morning of the seventeenth when the pontoon train had already traveled 15 to 20 miles to La Vergne. At that point, the Federals at Nashville ordered that the train stop

11. Chasing Hood

and be brought westward cross country to any desirable point between Brentwood and Columbia. This would be a difficult task because the muddy fields and roads were almost impassable.[7]

Wilson's cavalry was the first to chase Hood south of the Harpeth. Early on the afternoon of December 17, his men forded the river west of Franklin and rode out Carter's Creek Pike and Columbia Pike. They engaged the Confederate rear guard several times. One was about two miles below Franklin at Winstead Hill and another near the West Harpeth River at about 1 p.m. where Gen. Lee sustained a foot wound. That evening, while camped near Spring Hill, Hood was thinking about the logistics of crossing the Tennessee River, if that should become necessary. He ordered that all available pontoons at Corinth be prepared for delivery to a location yet to be determined. It is not clear how many pontoons Hood had with him or if he ever used the pontoons at Corinth. Wilson caught up with Hood's rear guard again about two miles below Spring Hill and skirmished.[8]

At about 1:20, the head of Wood's infantry column arrived at the Harpeth. Gen. James B. Steedman's 14th Ohio Infantry and others in his "provisional" division that also accompanied Wood's column found the bridges destroyed and that high water made the fords uncrossable by infantry. They were among the many who camped on the north side of the river, waiting for a bridge.[9]

At 2 p.m., the Federals got busy putting a bridge across the Harpeth. Col. Isaac C.B. Suman and his 9th Indiana Voluntary Infantry were directed to construct a new wagon bridge, not to be confused with the one that had just been burned. It is not clear where it was to be located. Because the water was high and rising, it would be a difficult task. Thomas ordered Wood to cross the Harpeth as soon as Suman had completed his bridge or the pontoons had arrived and been laid, whichever happened first. Early that night, Suman reported that he was struggling with the rising water but would continue trying. It appeared that the wayward pontoons would not be at Franklin until the next morning. Early on the 18th, Suman announced that, although the water had risen so fast that they could hardly work and the bridge had been washed out once, the men had labored through the night and finished it. At 8:00 a.m., Wood started crossing and strained to catch up with their cavalry. On the following January 13, Gen. Thomas reported to Brig. Gen. W.D. Whipple, Asst. Adjutant Gen., Department of the Cumberland, that on December 18, "7:30 a. m., Colonel Suman reports that he has been working all night, and has just finished the bridge; the river rose so fast that he could scarcely work, and his bridge was once washed out. 7:30 a. m., orders at once sent to division commanders to move at once—Nathan Kimball to lead, followed by General Elliott, then Beatty; battery of artillery to follow each division, and the rest of artillery to follow the corps; then ammunition trains, then hospital train, and then headquarters trains and regimental baggage; the troops will march down the Franklin pike. 8 a. m., leave Franklin; head of our column just starting."[10]

Because of the poor conditions between Murfreesboro Road and Franklin, the pontoons did not arrive at Franklin until late on the morning of the eighteenth, after Wood had already started crossing Suman's bridge. Some of the pontoons would be laid at Franklin and others taken southward to support the army chasing the Confederates.[11]

Thomas was planning ahead and intended to use the Union Navy on the Tennessee River to destroy the Confederate pontoon bridge when and if Hood tried to cross. On about the eighteenth, he ordered Admiral Samuel Philips Lee, Acting Rear Admiral in the Mississippi River Squadron, to send as many gun boats as possible up the Tennessee River to Florence near where Hood was likely to cross. This gave Thomas a back-up plan in case Wilson and Wood couldn't catch Hood, which didn't seem likely because Hood was slowed by his very large wagon and pontoon trains. Thomas thought it impossible that Hood would escape. Admiral Lee arrived at Chickasaw, Mississippi, on December 24, destroyed the Confederate battery there and captured two guns with caissons at Florence Landing. He was positioning to fire on Hood's pontoon bridge if needed.[12]

The effort to build crossings over the Harpeth was reminiscent of November 30. It was only two-and-a-half weeks earlier that the Federals were building multiple bridges over the river to escape. This time, it was the Confederates who were in retreat. To accelerate the crossing of troops, some of Wood's troops started laying a pontoon bridge while others worked to rebuild the railroad bridge and old wagon bridge. The swift current and driftwood made it very difficult to assemble the pontoons. Work continued into December 19 when it was finally completed, allowing more of Wood's men to cross. The misdirection of the pontoons toward La Vergne had delayed delivery of the pontoon bridge by about a day. This was the Federals' first significant delay related to pontoons during Hood's retreat but would not be the last. Union pontoons would also arrive late at Rutherford Creek after another crossing had already been built and would arrive late and be slow to install at the Duck. Each of these delays helped Hood stay ahead of the Federals. That same day, the nineteenth, the wagon bridge was completed but the trestle that was being built to temporarily replace the railroad bridge was still under construction. It would not be finished until about the twenty-second.

Travel was very difficult for both armies. There had been prolonged rains and the muddy fields and crossroads were not passable by wagons and artillery. Reliable footing was available only on the pikes. The rain was followed by snow and sleet. On the nineteenth, intense cold set in that left the saturated, muddy ground covered by a layer of ice. The infantrymen and horses struggled to traverse the terrain and wagon wheels were breaking. The fords and approaches to the pontoon bridges were still deep in mud. Earlier in the month, Thomas had opted not to attack Hood in similar conditions. This time, just like Hood, he did not have a choice and had to bear down and push through whatever Mother Nature threw at him. The conditions were worse for the Federals, however. Hood had left in his wake deep, muddy, unsteady terrain from the wear that their boots, hooves and wheels had created.

Hood must have left a large number of his pontoons south of the Harpeth before going to Nashville. On the eighteenth, though Rutherford Creek was a torrent, his trains crossed it apparently using some of those pontoons. His rear guard crossed later that day and burned the Rutherford Creek turnpike bridge and the nearby railroad bridge behind him. Hood took up the pontoons and kept pushing southward.[13]

That same day, some riders with Gen. Hatch's cavalry, one of Wilson's divisions, arrived at Rutherford Creek. They found that the pike bridge and two spans of the railroad bridge over Carter's Creek, about a mile west of the pike, had been burned. The next morning, Hatch arrived at Rutherford Creek, finding the infantry engaged, presumably with Hood's rear guard. He moved to his right and, just above where Carter's Creek meets Rutherford Creek, pushed some of the Confederates across Carter's Creek which he thought was Rutherford. He ordered some of his dismounted troopers to go across on the charred remains of the Carter's Creek railroad bridge to chase the enemy, but this did not go on for long because much of the bridge soon floated downstream.

11. Chasing Hood

Wilson and his 4th U.S. Cavalry continued pursuit and also reached Rutherford Creek that day. It was impassable, running high and fast, with no good way to cross. As soon as the Confederate artillery withdrew from the south side of the creek, Wilson began building a trestle bridge at the piers of the Rutherford Creek turnpike bridge while trying with moderate success to get some of his men across. Still trying to catch up with Wilson, at mid-afternoon that day the head of Wood's infantry column reached Spring Hill. It had been raining hard all morning. That night, Wood met up with Wilson at Rutherford Creek where they all stayed for the night, not yet having a pontoon bridge or other bridge to cross.[14]

Forrest, most of his cavalry and some other detachments had earlier been sent off from Hood's main army to Murfreesboro. Forrest had left Murfreesboro on the night of December 16 to meet Hood and part of his command had joined Hood between Franklin and Spring Hill. Forrest and some of his cavalry, infantry and wagons were taking a different route, planning to ford the Duck at Lillard's Mill to get to Columbia. Because that was difficult, those who did not cross there went to Columbia another way. Hood was near the Duck on the afternoon of the eighteenth and started crossing on two pontoon bridges placed about half a mile east of Columbia. Both Hood and Forrest were in the town that evening while the infantry continued to cross the river. Hood had considered making a stand against the Federals at Columbia and the Duck but considered his army not to be in a condition to do so. He ordered Forrest to hold Columbia as long as possible after the infantry had moved out. Then, Forrest was to proceed to Pulaski and on to Florence, Alabama, protecting Hood's rear. The new powerful rear guard now consisted of Forrest's cavalry and Gen. Walthall's 3,000 infantry, many of whom were having to march shoeless in the frigid mud. On the night of the nineteenth, Thomas told Wood he thought Forrest's cavalry, considered to be about 7,000 strong, might be vulnerable between Rutherford Creek and the Duck. He wanted Wood to cross Rutherford Creek and engage them the next day. That did not seem to happen.[15]

For nearly two days, some of Forrest's cavalry protected Hood's troops as they passed over the bridges at the Duck. The last of the Confederate infantry to cross was the 48th Tennessee with Col. Henry G. Evans in command. As the 48th was making its way over early on the morning of December 20, the pontoon bridge broke from the pressure of some heavy drift and several soldiers took a cold bath. Three Confederate cannons that could not be hauled across the Duck were spiked and dumped into the river, later to be retrieved by the Federals. Since leaving Nashville the night of the sixteenth, the Federals had collected more than 60 pieces of Confederate artillery. Repair of the broken bridge created a significant delay in getting the rest of the 48th across. Evans eventually finished crossing the two pontoon bridges and took them up. Once everything that could be transported was across the Duck, Hood ordered Forrest to withdraw at 3 p.m. and went into camp at Columbia.

A cold rain set in as the Federals worked day and that night to rebuild the turnpike bridge at Rutherford Creek. Wilson's cavalry was able to start crossing on December 20. Meanwhile, Gens. Kimball and W.L. Elliott built two footbridges per Wood's order half a mile apart over the same creek. Though exceedingly difficult to build and under great pressure to do so, the weary men completed them, allowing Wood's infantry and one or two of his batteries to cross on the afternoon of the twentieth, putting them closer to the Duck.[16]

On the day before, the nineteenth, Cox led his men across the Harpeth and set up headquarters at Franklin. The railroad bridge at the Harpeth was still being repaired. Smith had gone ahead to Spring Hill, making camp there the same day. Schofield had arrived and camped at Franklin. So, the Federals had thousands of infantrymen moving south, ready to attack Hood again in the event he elected to make a prolonged stand. Bridge sites were again being garrisoned along the N&D where a number of bridges were about to be rebuilt. Also on the nineteenth, "the block house" between Nashville and Franklin—perhaps the one at Spencer Creek—was occupied as was the one at the West Harpeth.[17]

By 6 p.m. on December 20, Willett and the federal 60-boat pontoon train, more than enough for Rutherford and the Duck, arrived at Spring Hill after the trek from Franklin. Five hundred mules and horses had been required to accomplish the task. The head of the train arrived at Rutherford Creek at 1 p.m. on the twenty-first. As with the Harpeth, the pontoons arrived after another crossing had been built. The train was given the right of way over the completed trestle bridge at the pike and most of it crossed, headed for the Duck. Wilson's men put a pontoon bridge in at Rutherford, finishing at about dark. Then, Smith's infantry crossed as did some wagons loaded down with materials to build the pontoon bridges at the Duck.

In the words of Gen. Thomas in his report of January 20, 1865, "The pontoon train coming up to Rutherford's Creek about noon of the twenty-first, a bridge was laid during the afternoon and General Smith's troops were enabled to cross. The weather had changed from dismal rain to bitter cold, very materially retarding the work in laying the bridge, as the regiment of colored troops to whom that duty was intrusted seemed to become unmanned by the cold and totally unequal to the occasion. On the completion of the bridge at Rutherford's Creek sufficient material for a bridge over Duck River was hastily pushed forward to that point, and the bridge constructed in time to enable Wood to cross late in the afternoon of the 22d and get into position on the Pulaski road, about two miles south of Columbia. The water in the river fell rapidly during the construction of the bridge, necessitating frequent alterations and causing much delay." The Rutherford Creek pontoon bridge was left in place so the remainder of Wood's men could pass. Schofield detailed a commissioned officer and at least 30 men to guard that bridge.[18]

On the twentieth, Hood decided to make his Tennessee River crossing at Bainbridge, Alabama, just east of Florence. The majority of the Confederates departed Columbia that day. Hood's men were generally disorganized, disheartened and half-armed as they headed for Pulaski. And, as noted earlier, many were barefoot. A blessing to them, however, was that their rear guard was stout and determined. Because they had not been a part of the defeats at Franklin and Nashville, members of the guard were rested compared to the men they were protecting. Hood's main force arrived at Pulaski on December 21 while the rear guard was still being formed by Forrest and Walthall at Columbia.[19]

The last of Hood's men were crossing the Duck on the twentieth. Kimball's division of Wood's infantry and Hatch's cavalry were the first Federals to reach the Duck, doing so at 2 p.m. that afternoon, less than a day behind Hood. They were unable to cross because the Duck was high and impassable without a bridge. Hood had destroyed all the bridges around Columbia and the Federals needed pontoons. Hatch commenced heavy shelling of Columbia. Forrest was still in the town and rode to the bridge abutment with an escort carrying a flag of truce. Hatch came with an escort to the north side. Forrest told him from across the river that Hood had left Columbia, at which time the shelling was ceased. The night of the twentieth, Wood's infantry camped on the north bank of the Duck, to the east of the turnpike, and Hatch's cavalry to the west.[20]

During the day of the twentieth, Gen. Lee, leading the Confederates, crossed Richland Creek seven miles north of Pulaski and stayed the night two miles north of the town. Hood rode into Pulaski on the night of the twenty-first and took inventory of his firepower. He had only about 59 cannons, many fewer than the 124 he had brought into Tennessee. The next day, Lee and his corps went through Pulaski and crossed Richland Creek south of town. On the twenty-second, Forrest evacuated Columbia.[21]

The weather had been miserable for most of the trek southward. Rain, then bitter cold. Ice, then more rain. George E. Cooper, surgeon and Medical Director of the Department of the Cumberland, said the horrible conditions had made so many of the men ill that hospitals in the area were at capacity. The suffering was not limited to the fighting men. The much-needed animals also felt the severe conditions and hungered for sustenance as the shortage of fodder persisted.

It was not until the evening of December 21 that the pontoon train, less those that were used at Rutherford Creek, began arriving at the Duck River, one or two miles east of Columbia. By dawn of the next day, all of the boats had arrived. Gen. Abel D. Streight launched a few of the canvas pontoons above Ashton's Mill, a mile northeast of Columbia, and sent a detachment across to secure the south side of the ford where the bridge was to be constructed. Unfortunately for the Federals, the construction corps of skilled pontoniers was in Georgia with Sherman. So, Streight's entire brigade was instructed to lay the bridge. It was quite a task. The river was running full and with a lot of drift, and the bridge broke two or three times. There was a cold wind and the ropes froze. During construction, the water fell so much that frequent alterations were required, creating delays. The bridge, referred to as No. 1, was completed by about 7 p.m. on the night of the twenty-second at which time Wood's Fourth Corps crossed into Columbia.

The Federals had spent about two days on the north side of the Duck waiting for a pontoon bridge to be built, days that put Hood farther in the lead. This delay was the first of five key factors that would have to go in the Confederates' favor for them to escape.

Wood's men occupied the town, bivouacking a mile to the south. Meanwhile, laying of a second bridge, No. 2, started on the night of the twenty-first and was completed the next day. Both bridges continued to break from the drift or falling water and had to be repaired. Wilson was delayed even more than Wood because of frequent breaks in his bridge. Wood, who had crossed with his artillery before sunrise on December 23, continued without him.[22]

To the rear of the retreat action, there was a great deal of activity. On the twenty-first, Grant moved his headquarters to Nashville, making it the Union command center for the Western Theater of the war. Back in Franklin, at noon of the same day, William G. LeDuc, quartermaster under Thomas, reported that he had 15 long, whale boat-type pontoons, pointed at both ends, there and was sending them down toward Columbia. It is not clear whether these were ever used, perhaps replacing pontoons that had been broken or lost. Also, it looked like the railroad bridge would be finished by 10 a.m. on December 23. The Federals performed an inspection of the railroad bridges south of Franklin. The first and second bridges over Carter's Creek were not badly damaged, but the third, fourth and fifth were gone. There was damage to bridges over Rutherford Creek. The Duck River Bridge was gone but the trestle on the south side was complete to the bank. It had been destroyed by Hood after he rebuilt the one that Schofield burned. Thomas hoped the construction corps would have the bridges rebuilt to Columbia in four or five days. On the twenty-third, crews were working on the five railroad bridges along Carter's Creek.[23]

With the delays he had experienced, Thomas now found himself wondering if his troops could stop Hood. Despite the Federals' best effort to pursue, Hood had managed to stay well ahead of their army. On the twenty-first, Thomas decided to keep Wood and Wilson after him. The bad weather was relentless, with rain, sleet or snow from December 17 through at least the twenty-second. The trip between Columbia and Pulaski would have been especially difficult for everyone, given the hilly terrain.

Hood, in Pulaski on the morning of December 22, ordered his Pioneers to go out and prepare Lamb's Ferry Road, which is present-day Highway 11, the best they could for the coming heavy use by his army. The weather had not been kind to the road, and its condition had deteriorated even further because Lt. Col. Presstman and the heavy pontoon train had started down the road that morning. Mules were taken from abandoned Confederate wagons for the critical work of pulling the pontoon wagons. That day, most of the main Confederate Army moved out on Lamb's Ferry Road while Cheatham took his infantry west on present-day Highway 64 toward Lawrenceburg and the wagon train took Powell's Ferry Road. On the south side of Pulaski, Hood's Army of Tennessee crossed the N&D and Richland Creek for the last time, leaving only the rear guard on the other side of the tracks. Hood had told Stewart to send all his Pioneer troops to help Presstman. They were to load some empty wagons with planking for the pontoon decking that had been gathered from buildings on Lamb's Ferry Road. The planking was to be delivered, of course, to the crossing site.[24]

Wilson's cavalry spent the entire day of the twenty-third crossing the Duck to rejoin Wood. Thomas was in Columbia by that evening. The next day, Wilson's men and the rest of Wood's Fourth Corps infantry finished crossing the pontoon bridges at the Duck. As the infantry continued down the Pulaski road, the cavalry marched on both flanks across the fields. Gens. A.J. Smith's and Schofield's men were nearby in case they were needed.[25]

By nightfall that same day much of the Confederate Army was in Alabama. Forrest was still protecting his army's rear. That night, he camped at Lynnville to hold the Union and give Hood's livestock and wagon train a chance to stay ahead. Forrest had 3,000 cavalry and 1,600 effective infantry to stave off the Union's pursuing 10,000 cavalry and 30,000 infantry, but he was up to the task and maneuvered skillfully. His effectiveness and boldness seemed to encourage the disheartened Confederate infantry to continue their difficult journey.

By December 24, the N&D's bridges had been repaired to allow trains to run as far as Spring Hill. Although the reconstruction of bridges was progressing, those below Spring Hill still needed work. It was expected that the bridges over Carter's Creek would be completed on the twenty-sixth and Columbia would regain rail service in about 10 days. To help construct the Duck River bridge as quickly as possible, about 300 bridge builders were on their way to the site. With trains running again and bridges and trestles needing protection, the Federals mobilized more troops to guard the N&D. On the twenty-fourth, 400 men of the 175th Ohio were ordered from their camp at Fort Negley back to Columbia to retake the town and occupy the blockhouses, or the former sites of any burned houses, between Franklin and Columbia. They continued this duty until

11. Chasing Hood

June 1865 and were the only unit still in the area that had earlier manned the N&D's blockhouses.

On the twenty-fourth, rain fell again and froze over the mud. Many of the shoeless Confederates had covered their feet with rawhide from cattle they had killed. That morning, Forrest took a position in a delaying action at Richland Creek where the railroad crossed it. This was adjacent to the present-day Milky Way Farm at Richland Creek Bridge No. 1. For two hours, Wilson encountered Forrest there in a severe engagement. Six thousand Union cavalrymen and 12 federal guns faced the 3,000 Confederate cavalrymen with eight pieces of artillery. Forrest held and gave Hood and his trains more time and distance. During the fight, Buford suffered a foot wound near Buford Station. Captain Morton, commanding Hood's artillery, helped check Wilson's cavalry before crossing Richland Creek and setting fire to the bridge. As expected, the Confederates were eventually overwhelmed so Forrest ordered a retreat. The federal advance was so rapid now that Forrest, who had been destroying wagon bridges on his way south, was unable to destroy the bridges over Richland Creek. Wilson continued his pursuit of Forrest but could not catch up with him. Late that day, Forrest and the rear guard arrived and rested at Pulaski. The weather and Forrest were slowing the Federals and Hood now had a big lead on them, but Forrest did not. Forrest dined that night at the home of Thomas Martin in Pulaski but had to leave quickly when he was informed that Wilson was approaching.[26]

On Christmas Day, Gen. Smith and his Sixteenth Corps were crossing the Duck. Also, per Forrest's orders, 1,000 cavalrymen under Gen. Red Jackson had remained in Pulaski to remove all the ammunition they could and hold the town as long as possible. They apparently destroyed 20 wagons of ammunition, burned a locomotive and a train of five cars loaded with arms and ammunition and threw two cannons into Richland Creek. They burned 10,000 stand of small arms and a large amount of military supplies abandoned by Hood that couldn't go on two southbound trains. After crossing with everything over Richland Creek just south of town, they were to destroy the covered bridge there. Later that day, Wilson entered Pulaski with Wood right behind him. Jackson departed and fired the bridge. The Confederates were trying to hold the bridge with a heavy force until it was destroyed, but the federal 8th Indiana Cavalry ordered two guns in position to fire across the creek and forced them to withdraw. The 5th Iowa Cavalry was in the Union advance and seems to have extinguished the fire. Some of Wilson's cavalry crossed and continued the chase. The pike from Pulaski ended at the bridge, so travel was again very difficult past that point. The Confederate rear guard followed the main army along the barely passable roads. The Federals pursued Forrest and Hood toward Lamb's Ferry and Bainbridge, about eight miles upstream of Florence. While at Pulaski, the Federals took prisoner the 200 or so patients at the Confederate hospital there and found the two cannons in Richland Creek.[27]

Because Wilson's large cavalry was pressing and pushing him into the Confederate wagon train, Forrest took position seven miles below Pulaski and made another stand, this time at Anthony's Hill, also known as King's Hill. Forrest was to hold the ground until Hood was across Sugar Creek, 14 miles away. On Christmas afternoon, Forrest's cavalry ambushed Wilson there with the aid of infantry and three guns of Morton's artillery, pushing him back half a mile. The Confederate losses were about 15 killed and 40 wounded, as opposed to 150 Federals killed or wounded and 50 taken prisoner. This action was needed to buy more time for Hood to reach the Tennessee River, build his

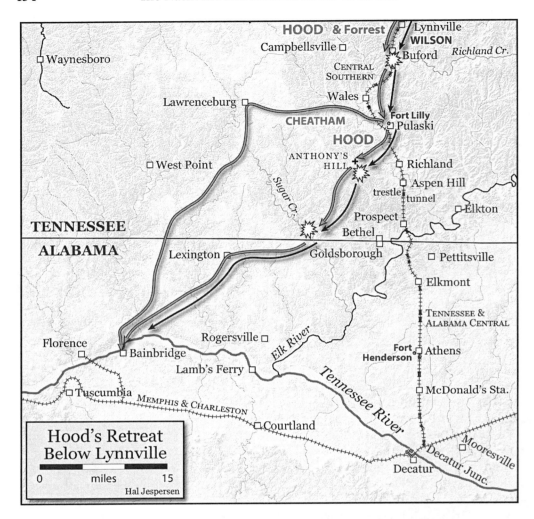

Map 11—Hood's Retreat below Lynnville, Tennessee (map by Hal Jespersen, www.cwmaps. com).

pontoon bridge and cross. During the fight at Anthony's Hill, the 3rd Illinois attacked General Jackson's men at Pulaski and saved two locomotives that were being burned. About 20 miles south of Pulaski, Hood was burning approximately 20 wagons loaded with ammunition, apparently using the animals from that wagon train to pull his pontoon wagons instead.[28]

Most of the retreat/chase was now behind the men and animals. That was a good thing because every creature has its limit, and the grueling journey was taking a heavy toll. Hood's men were generally poorly clothed, many were without blankets, only about half were armed and a third of his infantry had no shoes. In spite of their efforts to cover their feet with whatever was available, the ice and frozen ground cut many of the men and left them with bloody feet. Many had become ill and had to stay behind at one point or another.

The road to Sugar Creek had mud up to about the horses' knees, plus ice. The mud and ice stiffened their legs. Thousands of horses in both armies could not continue.

Many lost their hooves, or were undernourished and exhausted, collapsing by the way not to rise again. The hard, wintry weather created a shortage of forage for the animals pulling Hood's pontoon train. In this territory devoid of sustenance for the animals, the Union cavalry had traveled so fast that they were far ahead of their forage wagon train. Their horses were getting weak, as well, but most kept up the chase.[29]

Forrest arrived at Sugar Creek, just below Minor Hill, at about midnight on the twenty-fifth and camped there. Wilson kept up the chase and was nearly to Minor Hill by sunrise of the twenty-sixth. Wood tried to stay close to the cavalry, camping on Christmas night six miles below Pulaski on the Lamb's Ferry Road. At 8:30 on the morning of the twenty-sixth, Forrest ambushed Wilson at Sugar Creek, routing and pursuing them two miles. He estimated 150 Union men and 400 Union horses dead. Forrest stayed another two hours before moving on late that afternoon.[30]

At about 11 a.m. on Christmas Day, while Forrest was about to ambush Wilson at Anthony's Hill, Hood and his main army were arriving at the Tennessee River. They would cross on the shoals about a mile west of Shoal Creek at Bainbridge Ferry. The site was between Lamb's Ferry and Florence. Lamb's Ferry was near Rogersville, about midway between Decatur and Florence.

Confederate engineers had started working on the pontoon bridge the day before and Hoods' men got to work on it, as well. There had not been enough pontoons to cross the river, but Captain Robert L. Cobb, an experienced pontonier, Col. Windes and a company of the 3rd Confederate Engineers saved the day and perhaps the army. On November 23, Gen. Granger had started withdrawing the federal garrisons from Athens, Decatur and Huntsville and moving them via the M&C toward Stevenson. On the twenty-fifth, the Federals were evacuating Decatur. Under the cover of their gunboats and shore batteries, they took up the large pontoon bridge there and burned a large store house filled with provisions, abandoned saddles and some pontoon boats. Windes saved 15 of the pontoons. Hood sent Cobb to collect them and, if possible, float them down the river to Hood's crossing site. Cobb was successful, delivering them on December 24. The pontoons were waiting for Hood when he arrived. It was so important that they acquire additional pontoons that, in case Cobb was unsuccessful, Hood had ordered Stewart to send 200 men early on the twenty-fourth back toward Pulaski to retrieve some of the estimated 15 damaged and abandoned Confederate pontoons that had been left along the Pulaski road. It is not clear if Stewart returned with any pontoons.

The road from Pulaski to Bainbridge and, to a lesser degree, between Pulaski and Nashville contained the evidence of Hood's frantic retreat. It was strewn not only with pontoons and dead animals, but also burning and abandoned wagons, limbers (two-wheel carts that were attached behind a piece of artillery to carry ammunition), small arms and other supplies.[31]

Reality was sinking in for Thomas. By land, he was not going to catch Hood before he laid his pontoon bridge and started crossing. If the Federals were to stop him, it would have to be from the river. On the twenty-sixth Wilson resorted to felling trees along Sugar Creek so they would float into and down the Tennessee and hopefully destroy Hood's pontoon bridge. That afternoon, having learned that Hood's infantry had arrived at the river and was crossing at Bainbridge, Wilson halted his pursuit. There was no further fighting between Sugar Creek and the Tennessee River.[32]

It appears that delivery of the 15 pontoons from Decatur enabled the Confederates to complete the pontoon bridge, allowing them to cross and discouraging Wilson from continuing pursuit. Without those stolen pontoons (or pontoons from another source) and with Hood not able to cross, it is very likely that Wilson and Wood would have continued the chase all the way to the river. In that case, there would have been at least two scenarios. Hood could have tried to ford many of his troops but left some of his men, wagon trains and artillery behind and perhaps sunk pontoons and dumped wagons and artillery into the river. Or he might have decided to put up a fight with his back to the river, much like the Federals did at Franklin. In that event, Hood would most likely have been forced to surrender, with thousands taken prisoner and perhaps many killed. The depleted Army of Tennessee would have suffered another damaging and demoralizing defeat that we would be writing and talking about today.

Presstman, Cobb and the Confederates finished laying the bridge of about 80 pontoons before sunrise on the twenty-sixth. Though the current put a significant bow and strain on the bridge, the wagon train started crossing that morning and the bridge performed well. Movement across it was slow, with only a few wagons or guns going at a time. The Confederates must have considered themselves fortunate that the river was low and slow enough to allow them to construct the bridge without lengthy delays and that the bridge did not break during the crossing. Much of Hood's wagon train was over the river by dark that day. By late on the twenty-seventh, Hood had crossed his trains and about 17,000 soldiers. Forrest crossed late that night and early on the twenty-eighth. Finally, Stewart's Corps and Walthall's infantry, who had been protecting the crossing, went over on the morning of the twenty-eighth, at which time the pontoons were cut loose at the north end. Because he had 78 pontoons with him a couple of days later, Hood must have removed the pontoons and carted them off.[33]

In the meantime, Admiral Lee's two Union gunboats had threatened to come up the river to destroy the bridge and, in fact, got about two miles past Florence but never closer than two to three miles from the crossing site. Stewart's and Cheatham's batteries on the river did not allow them further. Neither the felled trees nor the gunboats were able to damage the pontoons.[34]

It had taken two full days to make this crossing—the final one for the Army of Tennessee.

All five key factors had gone the Confederates' way. First was the Federals' two-day pontoon-related delay at the Duck. The other four were due to a little luck and good planning by the Confederates. Forrest's strong rear guard was critical in restraining and delaying the Federals three times. Col. Windes and Capt. Cobb had furnished the final 15 pontoons of the 80 needed to cross the river. Having experienced engineers at the crossing site allowed assembly of a structure that would hold up under the strains of the wagon trains, artillery and the river current. Finally, the Confederate artillery had ruined the Federals' plan to destroy the bridge with their gunboats.

It is interesting to compare the paths taken by the armies during Hood's retreat with the path of the N&D. Hood and the Federals traveled essentially north to south, predominantly east of the N&D. They were not far from the railroad until they had crossed Richland Creek and the railroad on the south side of Pulaski and headed southwest. The armies crossed several of the waterways that the railroad crossed but not as many. From Nashville to just below Pulaski, the railroad crossed 21 significant waterways: the Little Harpeth, Spencer Creek, the Harpeth, West Harpeth, five times over Carter Creek, four times over Rutherford Creek, the Duck, Fountain Creek, Robertson Fork Creek, Pigeon Roost Creek and four times over Richland Creek. This must have

11. Chasing Hood

Wagon Train crossing a pontoon bridge (Library of Congress).

been considered the optimal, reasonably flat route that made sense in financing, constructing and operating the railroad. It was also good railroad design for the track of the N&D to be as straight as possible. This kept the construction cost down and allowed the trains to travel at a higher speed while reducing the risk of overturning, shifting of their loads or both. The armies, however, were not constrained by those considerations. They were free to travel by whatever route was suitable for the troops, cavalry and wagons and met their military goals.

Hood was motivated to take the quickest route across the Tennessee River. His path required only 12 significant crossings: the Little Harpeth, Spencer Creek, the Harpeth, the West Harpeth, the east-west reach of Rutherford Creek, the Duck River east of Columbia, Fountain Creek, Robertson Fork Creek, Richland Creek twice (one above and one below Pulaski), a tributary of Pigeon Roost Creek and, finally, Sugar Creek. Unlike the N&D, Hood did not have to cross Carter's Creek five times, nor make three of the four crossings at Rutherford Creek and only made two of the four at Richland Creek. However, he did have to cross Sugar Creek. That made for nine fewer crossings, which meant a lot less concern about high water, the condition of bridges or the laying of pontoons.

During the retreat, repair of the N&D had continued to be a priority and Federals were being sent down it as far as it was open. On December 26, Chief Engineer Wright had reported that Carter's Creek Bridge No. 5, the most southern of the railroad crossings over the creek, was complete except for laying the track. Construction on Rutherford Creek Bridge No. 1 was to commence on the morning of the twenty-seventh. It was nearly complete on the twenty-eighth and the bridge at No. 2 was underway. On the twenty-seventh, the 47th Missouri Infantry was planning to go by rail the next day to be stationed at Pulaski. They reached the Duck River but, because the bridge there had not yet been rebuilt, had to march the rest of the way. The 48th Missouri and another Missouri regiment would have to do the same. On the twenty-eighth, Thomas reported that the Duck trestle bridge should be completed on the twenty-ninth, so the pontoons could soon be taken up and sent to Elkton to be laid across the Elk River. On the 28th, Pvt. Garner crossed the pontoon bridge at the Duck and helped build the trestles on the south side and a "block house" there. He reported in his diary that the bridge was finished on January 10, and that it was washed away that night and rebuilt between January 13 and 15. The bridges on the N&D would not be completed until February 1865.[35]

On the twenty-eighth, Wood reached Lexington, Alabama, just across the Tennessee state line and 30 miles from Pulaski. The next afternoon, Thomas called an end to the chase. The failure to catch Hood had been due largely to the lack of bridges and pontoons along the whole route and the terrible road conditions between Pulaski and the river, which slowed the Federals. On December 30, Thomas announced the end of a successful campaign. Smith had reached Pulaski on the twenty-seventh and Schofield was directed to halt in Columbia. Thomas was back in Nashville on January 4.[36]

In late December, Thomas had directed Gen. Steedman to threaten the Confederates' railroad communications west of Florence. He was to travel cross-country from Franklin to Murfreesboro, then on the N&C to Stevenson. At Stevenson, he would be joined by Brig. Gen. Granger and the troops that had been garrisoning at Huntsville, Decatur and Athens. Steedman was to be in overall command and to travel on the M&C and put troops to reoccupy the positions in northern Alabama that had been evacuated during Hood's advance. The remainder were to cross the Tennessee River, travel north and damage the N&D to keep Hood from moving men or materials south on it. Steedman and a division of USCTs reoccupied Decatur for the Federals on the twenty-seventh and had started out to northern Alabama when he learned that Hood had already escaped over the Tennessee. There was no point in destroying the railroad. Presumably, some of Steedman's men did reoccupy the key positions in northern Alabama.[37]

Forrest took his cavalry to Corinth, arriving on December 29. Hood marched down the relatively high and dry roadbed of the M&C. On the twenty-eighth, he continued from the Tennessee River toward Tupelo. At Decatur, some of Steedman's group was joined by Col. W.J. Palmer and his 15th Pennsylvania Cavalry with their attachments from the 2nd Tennessee and the 10th, 12th and 13th Indiana Cavalries. In a minor sequel to the retreat, on the evening of the twenty-eighth, with Palmer in command, they moved west from Decatur past Courtland and then along Hood's line of retreat in Mississippi. Hood's train of 200 wagons and 78 pontoons had passed Leighton on December 30, headed toward Columbus, Mississippi. Palmer attacked at Russellville, then pressed on and, on the thirty-first, captured and destroyed the poorly guarded train 10 miles past Russellville. The next day, January 1, 1865, Palmer surprised a Confederate supply train just east of Tupelo, burning its 110 wagons. Because the roads were so bad and the materials could not be taken north, he burned the train and killed about 500 mules. Palmer then returned to Decatur on the sixth.[38]

On December 31, Hood issued a circular with orders for disposition of his army. He and his remaining men arrived at Tupelo on January 9. Hood, having commanded the Army of the Tennessee since July 18, 1864, gave up command on the fifteenth. Lt. Gen. Richard S. Taylor, brother-in-law of Jefferson Davis and the only son of President Zachary Taylor, took command for a short time. Hood bid his men adieu on the twenty-third. The spirit of the men of the Army of Tennessee was now largely broken and the Army no longer an effective organization.[39]

12

In the Wake

It seems appropriate to refer to what Hood, Forrest and the Federals left behind after their engagements along the N&D from September through December 1864 as a wake. Burials and mourning. Broken homes. Wounds and chronic illness. Amputations and disfigured men. Prison camp. Physical destruction. The troops, the families, the region and the nation had to deal with catastrophic loss.

From the time of his departure from Florence to the start of the Battle of Franklin, Hood had already lost 1,295 men. Schofield's estimate of Confederate casualties resulting from the November 30 Battle of Franklin was 6,252, including 1,750 dead and buried upon the field, 3,800 injured and in hospitals at Franklin, and 702 captured and taken to Nashville. He also estimated that the federal loss at Franklin on the thirtieth was 2,326, including 189 killed, 1,033 wounded and 1,104 missing or captured. Later analysis shows that 400 to 450 Federals died or were mortally wounded at Franklin.

At Nashville, the Confederates experienced a loss of about 6,000, including approximately 1,500 killed or wounded and 4,500 missing or captured, while the Federals suffered about 3,057, including 387 killed, 2,558 wounded and 112 missing or captured. An estimated 1,000 Confederates were captured at Franklin on December 17. Those numbers do not include the dead and wounded or many of the men captured on both sides during the retreat.

On December 27, 1864, William Hoffman, federal Commissary-General of Prisoners for most of the war, reported to Stanton that approximately 8,000 Confederate prisoners were taken at Franklin and Nashville. It has been estimated that of the 38,000 or so men who crossed the Tennessee River with Hood in mid–November, only about half did so again in late December.[1]

Most of the men wounded at Franklin had been left there. Many of them could not be reached in the field in time to save them or could not be moved because they were so badly injured. Others were lost or forgotten in the darkness. In the aftermath of the battle, virtually every available building nearby was used as a makeshift hospital for the wounded and sick, both Confederate and federal. One count was of 44 buildings used as temporary hospitals, three for the Federals and the remainder for Confederates. Even this number was not sufficient. Therefore, many had to be treated in cloth tents in freezing weather. On December 1, while federal troops were burying the dead in Franklin, the federal Fourth Army Corps' Medical Director had already sent hospital train Number 2 from Nashville to Brentwood. Surely, this was but one of several. It would be a few more days before trains could bring to Nashville the wounded Union troops who were ready to be moved from the communities below Franklin.

The Federals took many wounded Confederates to Nashville for care and as prisoners. They started with prisoners in the Franklin area and proceeded southward as the railroad was being reopened. On December 19, following the Battle of Nashville and with the railroad operating again as far as the Harpeth River Bridge at Franklin, Surgeon John H. Brinton, U.S. Volunteers, Superintendent and Director of U.S. General Hospitals in Nashville, was ordered to set aside a hospital for the Confederate wounded with directions that no visitors be allowed. That same day, an order was sent for federal troops to scour the country from Brentwood Heights to Spring Hill and bring to Franklin all wounded Confederates who were in a condition to travel. Those in Franklin were to be brought to the Confederate hospital in Nashville as transportation would bear. On the 22nd, about the day that the bridge over the Harpeth was again open, Surgeon Orson Q. Herrick, Fourteenth Corps, was ordered to gather the wounded from Columbia and the surrounding countryside and bring them to Nashville as soon as the railroad was open that far. On the twenty-seventh, there were 1,068 wounded Confederates still in Nashville hospitals, with 550 more expected to arrive soon from Franklin and another 200 remaining in Franklin until they were able to be transported. The next day, Herrick received instructions to bring to Nashville all the wounded Confederates from the Pulaski area as soon as possible. During this period, probably because of the shortage of adequate care in Franklin, many of the wounded Confederates there were put aboard trains in Franklin and taken to Columbia and other points. On December 30, Brinton was directed to use the Confederate surgeons as needed in treating the wounded Southerners; they were to be compensated for their efforts.[2]

On December 18, Gen. Thomas had ordered that all the damaged sections of N&D be rebuilt. This was to include, of course, track, bridges and trestles. It was a priority to get the railroad back into working order all the way to Decatur Junction as soon as possible. This meant fixing 6,000 to 7,000 feet of damaged or destroyed bridges and trestles. At that time, track as far as the Harpeth River in Franklin was within one day of reopening. It was also ordered that a permanent wagon bridge be built in Franklin at the site of the original one, but it was reported back that the bridge had already been built. On the nineteenth, Wright had four large parties working on the railroads. One group was assigned to the N&D, starting below Nashville and progressing southward. They were following the Federal Army as rapidly as possible as they chased Hood. Two of the work forces were assigned to the N&C between Nashville and Stevenson, one working in each direction.[3]

The bridges and trestles along the N&D had suffered tremendous damage in late 1864. Forrest and his men were responsible for much of it in September and October. They seem to have destroyed nearly all of the structures below Athens, those in Athens and between Athens and Pulaski (including the Richland Creek Bridge just south of Pulaski), none north of Pulaski until Carter's Creek, almost all on Carter's Creek and those between Spring Hill and Franklin, except at the Harpeth.

Because the N&D was open between Nashville and Pulaski at that time, it appears that after Forrest's fall raids the Federals had rebuilt or repaired the 10 damaged bridges in that stretch of track by the end of November. The bridges that did not need repair were probably the four on Rutherford Creek, one or two on Carter's Creek, at the Harpeth and at Brown's Creek. It is not clear whether the bridges at Spencer Creek and the Little Harpeth had been damaged and required work.

In November and December, Hood did a great deal of damage to the N&D above Lynnville on his way north. He had destroyed almost all of the bridges and trestles between Lynnville and Brentwood and wrecked about six miles of track. He also destroyed most of the blockhouses along that same stretch, many of which Union forces had repaired or rebuilt in the weeks following Forrest's raids.

As for Schofield, he was near the railroad when he left Pulaski on his way to Spring Hill but did no damage to the N&D except for burning the bridge at the Duck River. As the two armies moved north from Columbia, the majority of both were to the east of the railroad until they were near Thompson's Station where they encountered the N&D again.

A review of what happened to the bridges and trestles is a bit tedious but necessary and, hopefully, enlightening. The bridges and trestles between Columbia and Pulaski are something of a puzzle. Forrest did not go there but in early October sent Wheeler and Lyon to destroy them. It is not clear how much damage they did. Richland Creek Bridges Numbers 1, 2 and 3 were probably destroyed by Lyon or Wheeler at that time and rebuilt in the next month or so. When Hood came north in November, most of his army arrived at Columbia and went north, so he did not attack them. Buford and Cheatham encountered the N&D farther south at Lynnville and could have destroyed the trestles at Culleoka, Gracey's, and Robertson Fork when they came north. However, those trestles were probably destroyed by Lyon or Wheeler in October or by Hood during the December retreat. Harris Trestle was not destroyed after February 1864. There is a good chance that Pigeon Roost and Richland Creek Bridges Numbers 1, 2 and 3 were among those washed out in early 1865.

In October and November, the Federals rebuilt the bridges as far south as Pulaski and were sending trains there in November to supply Schofield. The Confederates rebuilt the Duck River railroad bridge, which Schofield had burned, and others after November 30 to supply them at Nashville. Neither Hood nor the Federals burned the Harpeth River Bridge on December 1. Hood needed it to supply him at Nashville and it was still standing when he arrived at Franklin on December 17 and burned it. The bridges at Spencer Creek and the Little Harpeth seem to have been open on December 1 because hospital trains were running from Franklin to Brentwood and must have been open by the sixth because by then Hood was running trains from his camps south of Nashville to Pulaski.

On about December 20, a federal inventory of damaged bridges showed that all five on Carter's Creek and at least one on Rutherford were damaged or destroyed. It is not clear when those bridges were damaged. It was either by Hood coming up in November or retreating in December, probably the latter. The condition of the West Harpeth Bridge on December 20 is not clear. Also, it is not clear when or how the Pigeon Roost Bridge was damaged once after February 1864. The bridges and trestles between Pulaski and Franklin that seem to have avoided significant damage in November and December are Harris, probably some at Rutherford Creek, perhaps Richland Creek Bridge Numbers 1 through 4 and maybe Pigeon Roost. It is not clear when the bridges at Hurricane Creek, Lytle's Creek and the two between the West Harpeth and Carter's Creek were built. It does not appear that they were damaged after construction, so they either survived the Battles of Franklin and Nashville or were built after those battles.

On January 28, 1865, Leonard H. Eicholtz, Assistant Engineer of the Military Division of the Mississippi, reported that he had finished a trestle a mile south of Campbell's Station, which would have been Gracey's Trestle, and ran a trainload of material to the next trestle at Robertson Fork Creek. Reconstruction was completed to Pulaski on

12. In the Wake

February 10. That same day, William McDonald, in charge of rebuilding the tunnel trestle, reported that he was making good progress with that trestle and should be finished by the night of the eleventh. Repairs on the N&D were finished on February 12.[4]

On January 17, 1865, Thomas had ordered that Granger re-occupy Athens, Sulphur Creek Trestle and the stations between the Elk River and Decatur. With the blockhouses in that area burned, the garrisons needed to be much larger than before until new houses were built. Being short on men, Granger requested 1,500 infantry and 500 cavalry for Decatur, an officer and 30 men for each of the four blockhouses between Decatur and Athens, 150 infantry and 150 cavalry for Athens, 150 infantry and 20 cavalry for Sulphur Creek Trestle, and an officer and 30 men for each of the three blockhouses between Sulphur Creek and the Elk River. The normal configuration for the blockhouses built from this time on was octagonal, the shape which had always been considered the most effective. Another reason to build the octagonal structures was that improvement had been made in their construction. The mortises and tenons at the odd-angle joints had been replaced by simple joints connected by spikes. Construction of new blockhouses, probably some for general military purposes and some for the railroad, was still ongoing in June, with several more yet to be built.

The damages caused a shutdown of the N&D from mid–November until February. However, it did not have a significant impact upon the war. Specifically, it had not affected Sherman on his "March to the Sea" or when he was in South Carolina because he already had stored plenty of supplies and was not relying on the N&D at that time. The damage did create delays in deliveries and required that the track be frequently repaired and that the bridges and trestles be repaired multiple times, but none of the destruction had a significant influence on the outcome of any of the major fighting between Nashville and Decatur.

Even after the Confederates had departed, there always seemed to be a structure to rebuild. On February 23, it was reported that Rutherford Creek Bridge Numbers 2 and 3, and 50 feet of the Duck River Bridge had washed away that afternoon. On February 25 and again on March 3, most of the bridges along the N&D were damaged or destroyed by heavy rains.[5]

There was a lot of bridge and trestle work done that spring. On March 25, the bridges over the Duck and Elk Rivers were completed. The other damaged bridges were quickly rebuilt and some were subsequently reconstructed one or two more times, apparently with trestles, before eventually being replaced by permanent truss bridges. Wright's Table 2 does not include these replacements. One source reported that, of the 21 locations that had truss bridges originally built by the N&D, 12 were replaced that spring and the trestles were replaced by temporary structures.

The N&D and other railroads in Middle Tennessee were again firmly under Union control and well-guarded. With Hood, Forrest, Buford and Wheeler gone, the risk of attack on the railroads was greatly reduced. The N&D had an eerie air of relative calm about it for the first time in about three years.

On April 9, 1865, Gen. Robert E. Lee surrendered. Though there would be several other future surrenders, this one essentially signaled the end of the 48-month war. Troops would remain in Middle Tennessee for a few more months. The federal garrison in Franklin, for example, did not depart until that September.

13

After the War

For a while, the Federals kept a significant display of force along the railroad. In May and June 1865, the 61st Illinois Regiment of Infantry Volunteers was headquartered in Franklin and stationed along the entire length of the N&D to guard it. They, the 111th USCT, who were stationed at Pulaski, and the 175th Ohio were among the last regiments with a major presence along the track.

The railroad's role in supporting the Federals was rapidly diminishing. In fact, at this time, one of the primary uses of the N&D was in transporting paroled Confederate prisoners back home to the South. On June 19, Thomas declared that there was no longer a need to strongly guard the N&D, so the 175th Ohio was relieved. The blockhouses were then manned by a small number of troops to guard mainly against burning by citizens who were sympathetic to the Confederacy.

Brig. Gen. Zebulon B. Tower, Inspector General of Fortifications, Military Division of the Mississippi, inspected the forts and blockhouses along the N&D. On June 10, he reported to Thomas a description of the forts, as follows:

The Forts: At Athens, there was Fort Henderson, about half a mile from the depot. It was essentially a work of five bastions enclosing a space about 300 feet long by 200 feet wide. There were embrasures for 13 guns. The fort was in good order but needed a small magazine for ammunition storage. One company seemed sufficient to hold it.

At Pulaski, there was "something approaching an enclosed work" on a distant hill, probably the remains of Fort Lilly. However, it was not a usable fort at that time. Perhaps a stockade enclosing barracks would be as good a defense as a fort.

At Columbia, the defenses were very imperfect. Fort Mizner, on a high hill overlooking the city, had not been completed. If it were finished and properly garrisoned, it would be sufficient. It was five-sided with three small bastions. The interior had no magazine and was in bad condition. If the garrison in Columbia was kept large, there would be no need to finish the works. However, it seemed good policy to have a strong work overlooking such a large town. The fort should be finished, a magazine added and a battery of six guns placed within.

At Franklin, Fort Granger was on the north bank and about 100 feet above the Harpeth River. It was about 700 feet long but narrow and featured two bastion fronts looking northward. The wood works were somewhat rotten and broken in many places. The bomb-proof consisted of two apartments, one of which was probably used as a magazine, and leaked badly. The fort had essentially been dismantled, with both guns and their gun platforms having been removed. There was a small detachment living in tents within the fort. A single company should be adequate to occupy and keep the fort in order. There was a small redoubt on a hill, Roper's Knob, about 1¼ mile from the fort, looking into it. Other batteries were constructed on prominences north of Franklin, but they had long been abandoned.

The Blockhouses: The line was well defended by blockhouses and stockades. Since December, construction on two more had commenced. Most of the blockhouses along the N&D were destroyed by Hood during his invasion. When Hood retreated, their reconstruction was started under the direction of Majors Willett and O'Connell. The houses between Nashville and Columbia were mostly complete. Between Columbia and Pulaski, the materials were ready. Little has been done between Pulaski and Decatur. Because a large portion of the country between Decatur and Pulaski lay in the river bottom, swampy and unhealthy, it did not seem advisable to build a blockhouse at every railroad trestle. It seemed better to place them at the principal bridges and stations.[1]

It is not clear how many blockhouses were built from this time forward. Because the threat of attack on the railroads was diminishing, so was the need for the houses. The railroads would be returned to their owners on September 15 of that year. Tower gave great credit to Col. Merrill and his assistant, Maj. Willett, for building the double-cased blockhouses and for their oversight during the past year of the railroad defenses in the Department of the Cumberland.

Overall, the USMRR did a good job of managing the captured railroads, including the N&D, N&C and M&C. However, it was the managers and the thousands of other men who made the railroads such an asset for the Federals. Nashville was one of the cities to headquarter a USMRR office. From there, John B. Anderson played as large a role as anyone. He was Master of Transportation in charge of repairs on the N&D from March to November 1862, Railroad Superintendent in the Department of the Cumberland from November 1862 to October 1863 and General Manager over the railroads in the new Military Department of the Mississippi from October 1863 to February 1864. Adna Anderson took over for him that February and held that position until seemingly late 1864. W.J. Stevens later served in that capacity and W.W. Wright took over as chief engineer in the Construction Division of the Military Division of the Mississippi. In 1864, Stevens had become Superintendent of all of the railroads running out of Nashville. He was succeeded by A.W. Dickerson at the same time that W.R. Gifford became superintendent of the Nashville-Decatur-Stevenson lines.

The Federals were quite thorough in their summarizing and reporting of what had transpired during the war, certainly more so than the Confederates. This is partly because many Confederate records did not survive the war and Federals were more likely to document their activities than the Confederates who were trying to move forward after defeat. Significant reports regarding the USMRR were prepared by McCallum, Stevens, Wright and others. They indicate the magnitude of the activities and expenses related to operation of the local railroads during the war.

Brev. Brig. Gen. McCallum's report on the USMRR stated that, to meet the demand for locomotives and cars out of Nashville, 21 engines and 195 cars were impressed from Kentucky in April through June of 1864, most coming from the L&N. Deliveries of new engines and cars were impressive from February 1864 through May 1865, with 140 engines and 2,573 cars delivered to Nashville. These numbers underscore the important role that Nashville played in supplying federal forces by rail.

On July 1, 1865, W.J. Stevens, General Superintendent of the USMRR, Division of the Tennessee, reported that, at both the fiscal year start of July 1, 1864, and year end of June 30, 1865, the length of the N&D was 120 miles. In that 12-month period, nine complete water tanks were built on the railroad, as well as houses and shops for 100 workers at Decatur Junction. Those houses and shops were destroyed by the Federals in December 1864 when Hood advanced on Nashville, presumably to prevent them from being used to support Hood. They were later rebuilt. The Nashville machine shop employed an average of 916 men that year. Also during the year, Mr. Herrick made improvements to a wrecking car that allowed him to quickly lift pieces of a wrecked train. That car had lifted 530 wrecked freight cars and 16 wrecked engines between January 1 and June 30 and returned them to Nashville. Four-hundred-forty-six tons of new iron rail (about nine miles of rail or four-and-a-half miles of track) had been placed on the line. Eight thousand linear feet of trestle had been constructed on the N&D. In addition to that large amount of temporary trestlework, 2,145 feet of bridges had been built by Post, Skidmore and Company and Boomer. He confirmed that, except for the high trestlework in Nashville, the flood waters of 1864 had washed out all the bridges along the N&D at least once. During Hood's movements in November and December 1864, many of the bridges had been destroyed by fire at least once, as well.[2]

On February 8, 1866, McCallum reported that, based only upon requisitions of the Army-wide quartermaster's department for the year ending June 30, 1865, about 284,000 troops and 232,000 tons of stores had been transported in about 43,400 cars. The busiest months were October and November 1864. A total of about 54,000 cars were sent through Nashville during the year. The average number of men employed by the Nashville division of the USMRR was about 13,000.[3]

On April 24, 1866, Assistant Adjutant-General Thomas M. Vincent submitted to Gen. McCallum records of the N&D for the period February 1864 through September 1865. Those records stated that the average monthly payroll for both the Construction Corps and the Transportation Corps of the USMRR was about $25,000. No labor was shown for the Construction Corps during the months of February through October 1864 or June through September 1865, which seems to indicate that work done during those months was performed by troops. By far, the busiest month for the Construction Corps was January 1865 in which 1,320 men were employed and that month's payroll was about $78,000. This reflects the extensive rebuilding of the railroad after Hood's retreat. For the Transportation Corps, by far the biggest month was December 1864, in which an unreported number of workers earned over $125,000. This shows the great volume of activity related to the Battles of Franklin and Nashville. The second busiest month was January 1865 at about $32,000. In that 20-month period, the Union used 2,732 tons of iron rails (enough to lay about 54 miles of rail or 27 miles of track), 136,000 pounds of chairs (through which the spikes were driven to attach the rails to the ties), 204,000 pounds of spikes and 120,840 cross ties, for a total cost of about $416,000. The labor total for both Corps for the 20-month period was nearly $693,000, with an additional $549,000 in contract work on bridges. The contract work would have included much of Boomer's construction on the trestles and bridges.

On May 26, 1866, McCallum reported to Quartermaster General Bvt. Maj. M.C. Meigs, "In the beginning of the war military railroads were an experiment and although some light as to their management had been gleaned by the operations of 1862 and 1863, yet so little progress had been made that the attempt to supply the army of General Sherman in the field, construct and reconstruct the railroad in its rear, and keep pace with its march was regarded by those who had the largest experience, and who had become most familiar with the subject, as the greatest experiment of all. The attempt to furnish an army of 100,000 men and 60,000 animals with supplies from a base 360 miles distant by one line of single-track railroad, located almost the entire distance through the country of an active and vindictive enemy, is without precedent in the history of warfare." Though this statement addresses the N&C, not the N&D, it emphasizes the importance and difficulty of keeping all railroads, including the N&D, open for use by the armies of both the Federals and Confederates during the Civil War.

The March 1866 Catalog of Locomotives, U.S. Military Railroads—Division of the Mississippi was compiled by John C. Meginnis, General Engine Dispatcher. It reported a summary of locomotive transactions of the Nashville Department which states that: in 1862, six had been purchased and 23 captured; in 1863, 20 purchased and 10 captured; and in 1864, 152 purchased and 15 captured. That made a total of 178 locomotives purchased and 48 captured. In 1865, after the war had ended, 149 of the 178 locomotives that had been purchased were sold and all 48 that had been captured were returned to the companies that had owned them.[4]

On April 24, 1866, Chief Engineer Wright submitted his final report to McCallum on work performed in the Military Division of the Mississippi since February 1864. He submitted a table (see Table 2 in Appendix C) that listed 41 bridges or trestles on the N&D at the end of the war. He stated that the N&D had been reopened in March 1864 after much work was done at an unknown cost by soldiers under the command of General Dodge. Fifteen water stations had been added along the N&D since March 1864, as follows: one each at the Little Harpeth, West Harpeth, Pulaski, near the tunnel and at McDonald's Station, and two each at Franklin, Carter's Creek, Lytle's Creek, Lynnville and Elkmont. Twenty-two miles of track had been rebuilt after Wheeler's raids in September and seven-and-a-half miles after Forrest's raids between Athens and Pulaski in September and October 1864. Wheeler's damages were repaired very quickly, whereas Forrest's were not fixed until February 1865. Eight thousand feet of sidings (short stretches of parallel tracks to allow other trains to pass) were built at Eaton Depot-Nashville Junction, over 1,000 feet each at Columbia, Athens and Decatur Junction and lesser amounts at Brentwood, Franklin and Prospect.[5]

On May 26, 1866, McCallum reported that for the USMRR during the years 1862 through 1865, 313 locomotives had been purchased or built and 106 captured by the Union for a total of 419, not including those borrowed or impressed into service from the Northern railroads. During that same period, only six locomotives had been lost or destroyed. Also, 5,111 cars had been purchased, 55 built, 409 captured and 755 others already available, for a total of 6,330, again not including those obtained from the North. Of those cars, 1,045 were eventually lost or destroyed.

Reporting on regional activity in the Military Division of the Mississippi indicates that, from about October 1863 to about September 1865, the division purchased 194 engines and captured another 66, purchased 2,257 cars and captured another 126, sold 193 engines and returned 65 to the owners and sold 2,847 cars and returned 101 to the owners. Also, McCallum reported that the maximum number of men employed in the Military Division of the Mississippi at any one time was just over 17,000, that the division operated 260 engines, 3,383 cars and 1,201 miles of track, built or rebuilt 26 miles of bridge or trestle, laid or relaid 641 miles of track and expended approximately $29 million during the war. The transportation division had about 12,000 of the 17,000 men and the construction division, the remaining 5,000. He also reported that compared with 9,555 feet of bridge and trestle originally on the N&D, 14,720 feet were rebuilt after

February 1864, which is an average of each structure being rebuilt about one-and-a-half times. On the N&C, for the same time period, 10,543 feet of bridge were rebuilt with 12,236 feet, an average of less than one and two-tenths times, indicating that the N&D's structures were damaged more than those on the N&C. He also stated that 163,680 feet of track (31 miles of the 122-mile route) on the N&D had to be rebuilt.[6]

Another aspect of the railroads and their activity during the war is the various elements of the N&D and how they fared during the war.

The Bridges and Trestles: The major damages to those structures along the N&D occurred in several phases.

- In February 1862, Col. John Scott destroyed most crossings from Nashville to just short of the Elk River. They were rebuilt later that year.
- Many bridges and trestles were destroyed in two other spans of time in 1862.
- By the fall of 1863, virtually every bridge between the last crossing over Carter's Creek and the Tennessee River, including most of the ones repaired in 1862, had been destroyed by either the Confederates or nature. All of those were repaired or replaced by February 1864, with many of them again soon worked on by Boomer.
- In September and October 1864, Forrest's raids destroyed most of the bridges between Athens and Pulaski and between Columbia and Franklin.
- In November and December 1864, a large number of bridges totaling 7,055 feet were destroyed by both the Confederates and the Federals.[7]
- Most of the bridges and trestles that had been rebuilt by February 12, 1865, when the latest round of repairs on the N&D was complete, were damaged or destroyed by heavy rains on February 25 and again on March 3.

In addition to those six periods, throughout the war many structures were destroyed by Confederates or guerrillas in numerous, small attacks or washed out by heavy rains.

From February 1864 until the end of the war, all of the bridges over Carter's Creek and Rutherford Creek were rebuilt at least twice, and the bridge over the Harpeth River in Franklin was rebuilt twice and partially rebuilt twice. The Duck and all bridges over Richland Creek were rebuilt twice and the Elk three times. Most of the other bridges were rebuilt once and some were never destroyed again during the war. During the period, the bridges at Carter's and Rutherford Creeks were, on average, rebuilt twice and partially rebuilt twice. The Harris, Culleoka, Gracey's and Robertson Fork Creek trestles, Pigeon Roost Creek, Tunnel Trestle, and all the bridges and trestles south of the Elk River were, on average, rebuilt once.

A detailed review of the damages to the bridges at the Harpeth, Duck and Elk Rivers and the grand trestle at Sulphur Creek reveals approximately how many times each was repaired or rebuilt during the war. The following discussion does not include replacement of any of the structures by the federal government in the spring of 1865.

The Harpeth River Bridge seems to have been repaired or rebuilt at least eight or nine times. Three of these were due to damages inflicted by the Confederates, four or five by high flows and one when Boomer replaced it with trusses in early 1864. Three or four of these events—a burning by Hood, two washouts and perhaps Boomer's work—occurred after February 1864. The Wright report indicates that after February 1864 the Harpeth River bridge was rebuilt twice and repaired twice; this aligns well with the estimate of three or four.

The bridge over the Duck seems to have had major work at least 11 or 12 times. Two were due to damage by the Confederates, one by the Federals, three or four by high flows, one when Boomer replaced the north trestles that had not been damaged, and four of unknown cause but most likely by either the Confederates or high flows. Four or five of these events—a burning by Schofield, burning by Hood and two or three washouts—occurred after February 1864. The Wright report indicated that the Duck was rebuilt twice after February 1864, so that report seems not to include repairs to the washouts.

The Elk River Bridge seems to have been rebuilt or had a major repair at least eight or nine times. Four of those were due to damages inflicted by the Confederates, three were from high flows and the cause of the other one or two is not clear. Three (a burning by Buford and two washouts) occurred after February 1864. The bridge was rebuilt in May 1864 after being washed out in December 1863. The Wright report shows that it was rebuilt three times after February 1864, which agrees with the three reported during the war.

Sulphur Creek Trestle fared better than the structures to the north. It seems to have been rebuilt only three times, in each instance because of destruction by the Confederates. The Federals rebuilt it in the spring of 1863, Dodge rebuilt it in early 1864 and the Federals did so again in about November 1864 after Forrest had burned it on his raid that September. Wright reported that it was rebuilt once after February 1864 which aligns fairly well with what was reported during the war.

The Track: The total amount of N&D track that had to be repaired during the war is difficult to determine. About 30 miles seem to have been damaged by Forrest, Wheeler and Buford in September and October 1864 and about six miles by Hood and others that December. In addition, there were numerous other attacks upon shorter stretches of track. The total repaired length, including sections that were repaired more than once, but not including the track that lay on the damaged bridges and trestles, seems to have been between 50 and 70 miles of the 122-mile line.

The Blockhouses: The houses along the N&D do not seem to have fared any better than the bridges. Though they were reasonably effective deterrents to small attacks on the bridges and trestles, they did not fare well when hit by a prepared and determined foe. Like the bridges, trestles and track, they sustained a great deal of damage in September through December 1864. In addition to the 17 or 18 houses that Forrest and others destroyed in September and October, it appears that another 18 to 20 were destroyed in November and December during Hood's campaign. In November and December, Cheatham and Buford may have burned the three houses at Culleoka and Gracey's. In addition to the four houses the Federals burned at Rutherford Creek in November, Hood seems to have burned the four along Richland Creek, the two at the Duck, the house at the West Harpeth and probably all five at Carter's Creek. Assuming there had been some raids on blockhouses by other than Forrest, Hood and the other key Confederates, approximately 45 houses had to be rebuilt because of attack. And assuming 36 houses originally built, that is an average of about one-and-a-quarter times per house in the nine months from April through December 1864 during which they were vulnerable to attack. The railroad certainly had been embattled.

The Pontoons and Pontoon Bridges: The best way to summarize the pontoons may be to state that they were critical to support the armies when crossing a major waterway and that the Confederates won the battle of the pontoons. They, more than the Federals, had pontoons when and where they needed them. The primary examples of this were the Federals' poor management of pontoons when needing to cross the Harpeth in late November 1864 and when chasing Hood the following month, as opposed to Hood's success in having them when needed during his December retreat.

It is interesting to see what the four key figures did after the war. Not surprisingly, all were successful in railroading or engineering.

In March 1865, Col. Innes was made Bvt. Brig. Gen. of U.S. Volunteers for gallant and efficient service. He was often described as an "efficient and energetic railroad man." When the Union-held railroads were turned over to the companies on September 15, 1865, those companies needed to find leaders who were experienced and loyal to the Union. General Thomas had the final say regarding the boards that were to direct the railroads and would certainly have looked favorably upon Innes for a position. The N&C and Nashville and Northwestern Railroads (N&NW) appointed Innes superintendent of both railroads. In addition to those responsibilities, in December 1867 he was elected President and a director of the new Tennessee and Pacific (T&P) Railroad that was planned to run from Knoxville through Nashville and Memphis to Jackson, Mississippi. However, he was soon accused of mismanaging money and state bonds for the N&NW. Because of a lack of trust in Innes, work on the T&P was stopped for several months during the federal investigation. Innes resigned as president in October 1868 and returned to Grand Rapids that fall to work as an insurance and real estate agent. Construction on the T&P started in July 1869 but only the 29 miles from Lebanon to Nashville were completed before the company encountered significant financial difficulty. He was the Michigan Commissioner of Railroads from 1883 to 1884 and became president of the Valley City Street and Cable Car Railway in 1887. Innes was very active in the Freemasons for much of his life. He died in 1893.[8]

After resigning from the military in May 1866, Gen. Dodge became chief engineer for the Union Pacific Railroad and a leading figure in the construction of the Transcontinental Railroad. He was elected to Congress from Iowa's Fifth District, serving from 1867 to 1869, and was successful in that role but did not enjoy it and chose not to run for reelection. Now focusing on the Transcontinental Railroad, he became perhaps more responsible than anyone else for completion of the Union Pacific's 1,085 miles from Council Bluffs to Promontory Point, Utah, where the ceremonial golden spike was placed. Dodge gave much credit for the rapid construction to the heads of his work force units—all former army officers—who managed the 10,000 workers. The 1,912-mile railroad was built by three companies, including the Union Pacific, between 1863 and 1869, with its eastern end being in Council Bluffs. Actually, the final segment of the railroad—the bridge across the Missouri River between Omaha and Council Bluffs—was not completed until 1873. From 1860 until then, passengers had to travel by boat across the river to continue their journey. Dodge resigned from the Union Pacific in January 1870, then accepted the position of chief engineer for the Texas and Pacific Railroad. He moved to Marshall, Texas, and started building towards San Diego. However, the venture suffered from the September 19, 1873, "Black Friday" and ensuing world-wide panic. From 1873 to 1884, he was associated with Jay Gould in railroad development of the Southwest, building more than 9,000 miles of track. During the 1880s and 1890s, he was chief engineer or president of several other railroad companies. Over his lifetime, he was president of seven railroads and nine railway construction companies and about 20,000 miles of track were laid under his direction, perhaps making Dodge number one in that category. In 1906, Gen. Dodge left active railroading and returned to Council Bluffs. He had amassed a fortune well in the millions of dollars. In 1915, he was diagnosed with colon cancer from which he died the next year. He is buried in Council Bluffs.[9]

Mr. Boomer supplied trusses for the Transcontinental Railroad and, therefore, again crossed paths with Gen. Dodge who was chief engineer for the Union Pacific. In 1868, seeing the future in iron bridges, Boomer built the Iron Bridge Works in Chicago which would eventually cover more than three acres under roof. Two years later, Boomer, Stone and others started the original version of the American Bridge Company (ABC) of which Boomer was president. That company built a great deal of iron and combination wood-iron bridgework but struggled. It would not be until 1900 that twenty-eight steel companies joined to form the new version of ABC in Chicago, a venture that became the major corporation that exists today. By that time, the use of steel in bridges, which started with the combination bridges in the mid-nineteenth century, had made wooden bridges virtually obsolete. He died from a cerebral hemorrhage at age 54 and is buried in Chicago. One of his grandchildren was Lucius M. Boomer who, with Thomas Coleman Dupont, owned hotels including the Waldorf-Astoria.[10]

Col. Merrill was continuously engaged in military work for the government after the war. He was promoted to regular major in March 1867 and was chief engineer under Sherman from 1867 to 1870. In 1870, he was placed in charge of the improvement of the Ohio River, a responsibility he maintained until his death. One of the most notable projects he built was the Chanoine wicket movable dam at Davis' Island, five-and-a-half miles below Pittsburgh which, at that time, was the largest movable dam in the world. Further advancements would be to lieutenant colonel in 1883 and then to brevet colonel. Merrill also published several technical documents, including *Truss Bridges for Railroads* (1870). In January 1873, he married Margaret Spencer with whom he had 10 children. Colonel Merrill died unexpectedly of heart failure in 1891 while on a train en route to a government project in Shawneetown, Illinois.[11]

The Civil War had left many people in the South suffering financially. One form of loss was the taking by Union forces of assets belonging to Southern residents. In an Act of March 3, 1871, the Executive Branch of the U.S. Government established the Southern Claims Commission which allowed Union sympathizers who had lived in Southern states during the war to apply for reimbursement of property losses due to U.S. Army confiscations during the war. Only about a third of the total dollar amount of the claims was approved. Some of the typical and more interesting claims from each county through which the N&D ran are presented in Appendix E. An example is Lewis Hobart who claimed $4,324 for property taken in Decatur where he had lived for many years. Before the war, he had worked on the railroad, at removing houses and farming. In early 1864 when Gen. Dodge ordered nearly all the citizens of Decatur to leave, Mr. Hobart left his belongings and horses to the Union Army. He said Dodge gave residents a choice of moving north or south, and he later relocated north to Franklin where he built bridges until near the close of the war. Federal troops took down his two-story house, two stables, carriage house, work/blacksmith shop, brick smoke house and four small houses for their brick and lumber. Some of it was used for fortifications and some to build "shanties" for the soldiers. They also took 27 hogs, 7,620 rails, 12,000 feet of plank and some sawed timber they planned to use on blockhouses. There was testimony both for and against his being a Union man, therefore his award was only $882. After relocating to Franklin, he hauled supplies for the U.S. Government and built bridges. He filed another claim stating that he lost two mules there. He said that on November 30, 1864, the Union Army took from him all they could use, destroying what they could not take. Mr. Hobart claimed that soldiers in an artillery battery camped near his stable took his mules early on the night of the thirtieth because there was a shortage of animals to pull wagons and artillery. Following the Battle of Franklin, he treated a number of wounded Union soldiers and built bridges under quartermaster LeDuc. One was over the Harpeth River for the government to allow Union soldiers to cross and chase Hood. In this case, he was determined to be a Union man and was awarded $250 of his $350 claim.

General Order No. 20 of August 8, 1865, mandated that all captured railroads be transferred to their original owners. Per the order, for the railroads to be returned, the companies needed to establish boards that were loyal to the Union. General Thomas was responsible for approving the boards. Thomas approved the T&A's board on about September 4. The top man for the N&D was John W. Potter, who would be assisted by George Bruce. The president and secretary of the T&A, CS and T&AC were John S. Claybrooke and Francis Hardeman, Thomas Martin and John Baird, and James W. Sloss and John T. Tanner, respectively. To aid the companies, President Andrew Johnson ordered that the southern railroads had the right to purchase military railroad property that was on hand in the government at prices fixed by a board of appraisers. They would also have the opportunity to buy excess government railroad equipment at full price and, later, at auction at reduced prices. In general, there would be plenty of locomotives to meet the demand and even an excess which was auctioned at typically about half of the appraised value. In probably 1865 or early 1866, the T&A, CS and T&AC bought at auction from the government four locomotives, 73 box cars, 12 hand-lever cars and various other items for a total of $58,300. Those four engines seem to have been the *Decatur*, *Pulaski*, *John Childe* and *Davidson*. A couple of years later, those engines would be under N&D ownership as Nos. 5, 9, 10 and 11, respectively. The companies had 12 months to repay, unless agreed otherwise. The railroads were to carry mail and other government property, with the expenses to be credited against their debt. The government deemed it essential that, for the N&D to be successful, repairs be made on it. Because of this and because the government believed the N&D was very well run and respectful of its debt, the companies were granted repayment extensions. The extensions included those to January 1, 1867, and again to November 30, 1867.[12]

The government did not intend to charge the railroads for any repairs they had made to the roads but, on the other hand, took the position that they were not responsible for any of the damage they had done. The government considered that these two balanced each other. They claimed that they had left the N&D in better condition than when they took it over, and that the railroad companies would be indebted to them for the amount of any purchases. That did not mean, however, that the four companies were in a position to repay their debt quickly.

Compared to their pre-war status, the four railroad companies were financially weak, in poor physical condition and needed equipment. The passenger and freight houses near Broad in Nashville had been removed or destroyed, and the depot grounds at Summer Street had been covered by a huge warehouse, the Taylor Depot, which stored military goods. The N&D machine shops, engine house and tools had been removed and the structures taken down. The N&C machine shops had been taken by the Federals for their use. Heavy use of the tracks from March 1862 to September 1865 had the rails badly worn, and though the worst rails had been replaced, some still needed to be. Also, much of the track that was damaged had been re-laid in a hurried, temporary,

13. After the War

wartime-like manner. The Federals had taken the railroad iron that was stored at Nashville and Columbia. Nearly all of the depots, water tanks and other appurtenances along the line had been removed or destroyed and had not been rebuilt by the Federals. Most of the bridges and trestles had been destroyed and replaced, the trestles first by temporary structures and then better ones. However, the new structures were inferior in quality to the original ones. One report stated that of the 21 truss bridges that were in place before the war, 12 were rebuilt by the federal government in the spring of 1865 and the rest had been left with temporary trestles. The bridge at the Duck River was a deck bridge which was so low that it could be washed away by high water. Rather than raising it, it was replaced with a steel structure higher above the river. Steel became the preferred material when many of the other wooden bridges were replaced. The line to Mount Pleasant had been taken up by the Federals and not replaced. And nearly all of the N&D's locomotives and cars had been lost or destroyed. The *Franklin* was blown up while in federal use and the *Columbia* was worn out and useless. Remains of the *Franklin* were at the Nashville yard. There was much work to do on the N&D.[13]

The railroad companies needed locomotives and cars. On August 8, 1865, the date of the order, the T&A bought three government engines, USMRR Nos. 124, 182 and 184, for a total of $51,000. That same day, they purchased 34 box cars for a total of $28,084, 14 flat cars for a total of $9,100 and one passenger car for $2,000. The T&A's total purchase amount was $90,184. The federal government had purchased engine No. 124 for $20,600 on July 13, 1864, as five-foot gauge for use in the South. After the war the T&A bought it for $17,250. No. 182 was purchased new by the Federals on August 4, 1864, for $20,600. It had been repaired in Nashville in January 1865 before the T&A bought it later that year for $16,750. No. 184 had been purchased by the Federals on September 24, 1864, for $20,600. It was repaired in Nashville in March 1865 and then was sold to the T&A for $17,000.

The government returned to the companies the railroad equipment that they could prove was theirs. This included six locomotives, a portable engine, a turntable and foundation, a boiler iron punch and a cylinder boring machine, all of which had been captured. The six locomotives were the *Franklin, Luke Prior,* No. 22 (probably the *Nashville*) and Nos. 6 (*Williamson*), 69 (*Maury*) and 99 (*Thom. Buford*).

The *Nashville* (which became N&D No. 1) had been repaired in Nashville by the Federals in 1864 and 1865, and the *Williamson* (N&D No. 6) had been repaired by the Federals in Memphis in February 1863, transferred to Nashville on March 10, 1864, and repaired in Nashville in March 1865. They had been put in operating order after the war. The *Thom. Buford* and the *Maury* were in working order, also. The *Thom. Buford* was identified by the Federals as USMRR No. 99, the *Gen. McPherson,* and later sold to the N&D in 1866, becoming N&D No. 7. It had been repaired in Nashville in 1864 and 1865. The *Maury* was identified by the Federals as USMRR No. 69, the *Gen. Logan* and later sold to the N&D in 1866, becoming N&D No. 8. It had been repaired in Memphis in December 1862.

The other two of the six engines were the *Franklin* and *Luke Pryor* which were useless, as was the *Columbia* which was sitting in Memphis and not worth the cost required to bring it to Nashville. The *Giles* and *Pulaski* seem to have been leased or otherwise in the possession of other railroads, the *Giles* having been leased to the Alabama and Tennessee River Railroad in 1863. Those two engines had been turned over to the quartermaster at Meridian, Mississippi, in 1865.

In the Military Department of the Mississippi, 65 engines and 101 cars were returned to the various railroad companies that had originally owned them.

The N&D was considering purchasing 15 engines and 200 cars from the government. However, not all railroads in the state needed engines and cars. For example, the N&C had 60 locomotives, 600 cars and a vast amount of railroad material and did not need it all, so a large portion would be among the auctioned items.[14]

Locomotive purchases were a bit of a problem because some engines were desired by more than one company. In general, however, there was plenty of supply to meet the demand and there was even an excess which was auctioned off at typically a reduced cost. Of the 226 locomotives in the Nashville Department, the Federals put up for sale 149 of the 178 that had been purchased and brought into the city.

The T&A purchased at least one other federal locomotive plus pumps, water tanks, cord wood and houses along the road and at Nashville for a total of $18,364. The engine had been purchased from the builder on August 12, 1862, for $9,900 as USMRR Department of Virginia No. 55, the *Washington* (one of several named *Washington*). It was sent to Columbus, Kentucky, on September 12, 1862, then to Memphis where it was repaired and converted to 5-foot gauge. Next, it went to Nashville on March 16, 1864, as USMRR Division of the Mississippi No. 111, the *Washington*. Then it was sold to the N&D for $12,000. The total indebtedness of the T&A to the government was about $108,700.[15]

The T&A, N&D, CS and T&AC purchased approximately $108,700, $71,000, $77,200 and $84,100, respectively, in surplus inventory, all of which was transferred on September 15, 1865. The T&A's $108,700 probably included the $90,184 they had spent on August 5.

General Thomas returned the railroads to their respective companies (the N&D, T&A, CS and T&AC) on September 15, 1865—all the way from Nashville to Decatur Junction—three-and-a-half years after they were taken by the Federals. The companies were again operating independently to their mutual benefit.

That September, N&D President J.W. Sloss went to Washington on behalf of the railroads to present their case for compensation for the damages to the railroad, but the request was not approved. One compensation they had hoped for was for the government to replace or pay to replace the line between Columbia and Mount Pleasant. The N&D turned to the state for assistance. The Tennessee legislature helped the railroad by appropriating and issuing $300,000 of State bonds to help rebuild bridges and put the road in good running order. By June 30, 1866, the accumulated amount the N&D owed the state had risen to $1,378,000.

On September 4, 1866, Sloss requested an indefinite extension of debt for all four companies. That request was not approved, but on December 1, 1866, Alexander Bliss, Col. Quartermaster's Department in charge of the Fourth Division, allowed the railroads to begin two years of monthly payments on January 1, 1869, at an annual interest rate of 7.3 percent. As of December 1, 1866, the federal debt of the T&A, N&D, CS and T&AC was about $81,000, $105,000, $57,000 and $62,000, respectively. Some debt had apparently been transferred from the T&A to the N&D.

The embattled railroad from Nashville to Decatur, the corporate venture that was fully operational for 17 months and then, for three-and-a-half years, was a weapon used by the federal government against the Confederacy, had been returned to its owners. The companies made significant repairs to the railroad. By early 1866, depots had been built at Carter's Creek, Spring Hill and Thompson's Station, a 40- by 162-foot freight depot had been built at Nashville and Engines Number 1 (the *Nashville*) and Number 6 (the *Williamson*) had been rebuilt at a total cost of about $3,000. The bridges and trestles were in good condition and a new bridge was to be built over the Little Harpeth. By June 30, 1866, Engines Number 10 (the *John Childe*), 124, 182 and 184 were also in good running order. The companies had purchased the equipment they needed and made the necessary repairs.

Because management of the railroad companies felt that one long railroad could operate more efficiently and profitably than three short ones, the three companies and the N&D had drafted an agreement on September 27, 1865, to combine the four companies into a single corporation, the Nashville and Decatur Railroad Company. The agreement was amended and approved by the boards on October 23 and the Tennessee State Legislature on April 19, 1866, pending approval by the legislature of the State of Alabama. It was initially to be in effect until January 1, 1867. Under the agreement, the companies would continue to own property that they possessed and pay their own road and other local expenses, keep an accounting of their individual receipts, expenses, assets and liabilities, and possess their own locomotives but share the rolling stock. The assets were divided as fairly as possible. The T&A had bought more than its share of property and would continue to own that property. The net earnings of the N&D would be used first to reduce the debt to the bonds then the debt to the U.S. Government, and the balance, if any, would be passed on to the individual railroads to reduce their debt. At that time, the Mount Pleasant branch had no cross ties or rails. If the government provided funds to pay for that, the money was to go to the N&D. Stockholders exchanged their stock in the individual railroads for stock in the N&D. The company would build a machine shop in Nashville and share mutual expenses like the machine shop, with each one's share being its percentage of the overall receipts. The new machine shop, machinery and tools ended up costing $70,200. It was agreed that, until such time when it was determined otherwise, the T&A would receive 31/65 of the earnings, the CS 21/65 and the T&AC 13/65. These fractions were not proportional to the lengths of the railroads and seem to have been based upon their respective anticipated earnings. The last segment of N&D track that connected to Broad, however, was still occupied by the U.S. Government for its locomotives and cars, so for some time the N&D had to use the track and depot of the N&C, which was inconvenient to both railroad companies. As of June 30, 1866, the tracks were in good condition but needed some new iron, and the N&D's depot grounds were still occupied by government warehouses, so the N&D was renting offices and had built a temporary freight house.

Considering the poor condition of the land through which the railroad passed, the scarcity of livestock to help cultivate the land and the sudden loss of "cheap" labor, the railroad's receipts from passenger and freight traffic were healthy. Since returning to business in September 1865, the company had made a profit every month through June 1866, and the companies were optimistic about the future.

Tennessee rejoined the Union on July 24, 1866, and Alabama did later, on July 13, 1868. The railroad was back to work fulfilling the dream of its founders—moving people and goods profitably during Reconstruction, growing their business and building a stronger region in a reuniting nation.

Appendix A

*Early History of the Three Railroads
Composing the N&D*

The Tennessee and Alabama Railroad (T&A) came into being on January 23, 1852, by an Act of the State of Tennessee General Assembly. The act created the railroad all the way to the Alabama state line, thus including the future Central Southern (CS) Railroad. The primary initial shareholders of the T&A included Robert Buford, W.P. Cannon, John T. Fleming, Brice Hughes, Johnson Jordan, Jr., A.C. Mayberry, Henry G.W. Mayberry, John McGavock, Nicholas Perkins, Thos. Perkins, Absalom Thompson and Jas. H. Wilson. Williamson County residents had already been subscribing to the railroad as early as January 1851. At that time, the estimated cost of the road was $15,000 per mile.[1]

The First Annual Meeting of the President and Board of Directors of the T&A was conducted on July 19, 1853. The meeting was held at the Company Office on Main Street in Franklin, near the Franklin Inn. The report of that meeting showed that the board members selected that day were John S. Claybrooke as President, Samuel Henderson, Elijah Thompson, Thomas F. Perkins, Frank Hardeman, Peter A. Perkins, Thomas Parkes, James H. Wilson, John McGavock, M.G.L. Claiborne, Jefferson Martin, Claiborne H. Kinnard, William P. Cannon and Johnson Jordan. Claybrooke, a Williamson County railroad visionary, would be president of the company throughout the Civil War. Two-hundred-fifty copies of the report were made and distributed to the stockholders.[2]

The report of the meeting states that in September 1852, the T&A had hired Captain John Childe as Chief Engineer and Adna Anderson as Resident Engineer. The company's charter required the road to pass by way of Franklin and Spring Hill, near Columbia and Mount Pleasant to the Alabama state line and then in the direction of Florence, Alabama. The track would never be extended to Florence. A major goal was to have 30 miles of road graded, the bridges and masonry complete and cross ties furnished. At that point, the company would be entitled to state aid or to the bonds of Tennessee for $2,000 per mile to pay for the rails and machinery.

On September 25, the engineers and their assistants started examining the countryside and running survey lines. Two survey lines were run from Nashville to Franklin, one to the east of the other. The company selected the eastern one, by way of Brown's Creek and Atkinson's Gap, which was just north of Brentwood. Work above Atkinson's Gap commenced immediately and, as of the date of the Annual Meeting, the first four-and-five-eighths miles had been prepared for construction. The contract for that construction was let on November 19 and work commenced on December 1.

Two additional surveys were run south from Franklin, one to the east of the other, both ending four miles beyond Columbia. The western route, by way of North's Mill, Gidding's Gap, through the western part of Spring Hill and then two miles west of Columbia, was selected. That route and the line from Atkinson's Gap to Franklin were put under contract on February 14, 1853, all to be ready to receive cross ties and track by March 1, 1854.

A "Contract for Graduation" executed on February 17, 1853, provides some insight into the price of roadbed preparation. The contractors, A.C. and Henry G.W. Mayberry who were also shareholders in the railroad, were to prepare the 12,000 feet of route in Section 22 of the T&A in Williamson County. The location of that section is not known. Work was to be completed by February 1, 1854. Unit prices were fifteen-and-a-third cents per cubic yard for earth excavation, 85 cents per cubic yard for rock, 55 cents per cubic foot for loose rock and six-and-a-half cents per linear foot for clearing and grubbing.

In March 1853, the citizens of Davidson County voted 56 percent to 44 percent in favor of subscribing stock in four railroads, including $200,000 for the T&A. By July, the amount subscribed in the T&A was $725,300 by individuals plus an additional $20,000 from the town of Franklin and the $200,000 from Davidson County. John Claybrooke led a group of about 30 local citizens to provide Franklin's initial $20,000 capital for the railroad. The subscriptions of Franklin and Davidson County were made payable in bonds. The board's goal was by July 1854 to have locomotives and cars running along the 30 miles of road from Nashville to Spring Hill and to have placed contracts for the additional locomotives and cars to have that section in complete operation. It was anticipated that the length of the entire road would be about 112 miles.[3]

As of July 1853, the contract to prepare a one-and-a-half mile stretch near Spring Hill for cross ties and rail, required to meet the 30-mile requirement, had not yet been contracted. However, in June the twenty-eight-and-a-half miles of road from the future connection with the Nashville and Chattanooga Railroad in Nashville to about Spring Hill had been put under contract for grading, bridging and a portion of the masonry. Grading was quickly commenced. The two-mile stretch nearest Nashville was to be ready to receive track by February 1, 1854. The estimated cost of getting the twenty-eight-and-a-half miles ready to receive English iron was $287,103. $206,249 of that was for grading and masonry, $30,139 for ballasting, $20,715 for cross ties and $30,000 for station grounds, right-of-way and miscellaneous.

Contracts for delivery of the cross ties for the first 30 miles were to be closed in July 1853. It seems that John McGavock furnished lumber for some of the cross ties. This is plausible because there was a sawmill on the property of Carnton, his house in Franklin. The mill was located, aptly, on Saw Mill Creek. All bridging had been contracted to Maxwell, Briggs and Company of Knoxville, who was ready to start work when called upon.

By July 1853, preliminary surveys had also been completed for the remaining southern portion of the route. That stretch passed just east of Mt. Pleasant, going up Buckner's Branch of Bigby Creek. From the summit near there, two routes were being considered, both of which had a southwesterly heading and intersected the Alabama state line well west of the railroad's eventual path to Athens. Negotiations were underway for the connection with other railroads being constructed in Alabama, Mississippi, Louisiana and West Tennessee. The path of this southern section would be selected at a later date. Because the direction of the road was changed from southwesterly to southerly, it is obvious that neither of the southwesterly routes was selected.

The company intended to contract for the track and completion of the road from

Appendix A

Franklin to Mount Pleasant as soon as possible. When that work was completed, there would be 53 miles of finished road. At that time, the company would be entitled to state aid in the amount of $400,000. In January 1854, Chief Engineer Childe said the estimated cost of building the road had increased to $12,000 per mile from his previous estimate. This was due to higher costs of iron, cars, engines and labor. Apparently, his previous estimated cost had been well below the initial estimate of $15,000 per mile.

The board decided to construct the road to be more substantial than the minimum, thinking that the reduction in long-term expenses would more than justify the increased initial cost. They were convinced that there would be a handsome return on investment by connecting, directly or indirectly, with the other railroads in the regions previously listed. Anticipated benefits of the T&A included that it would provide an efficient connection between Middle Tennessee and the port of New Orleans, and that it would connect with the Memphis and Charleston Railroad which would form the most direct connection between Middle Tennessee and the rich cotton lands of Arkansas.

The T&A's construction timeline was:

- May 27, 1854—the balance of the iron for its first 30 miles was to arrive soon.
- As of June 9, 1854—the track was expected to be completed to Spring Hill by that fall and trains were expected to be traveling to Franklin by September.
- About September 17, 1854—the T&A bridges had been completed.
- March 6, 1855—the first train from Nashville pulled into Franklin. From that date, a mail/passenger train and a freight/passenger train were to run round trip between Nashville and Franklin daily.
- September 1, 1856—trains were running round trip between Nashville and Thompson's Station.
- February 10, 1857—proposals were due for 13 miles of grading, masonry and bridges from Spring Hill to opposite Columbia.
- June 1857—Irish workers threw down their shovels in protest over being paid $1.10 a day; they wanted $1.25.
- July 1858—iron was being brought in for the stretch between Thompson's Station and Columbia and it was hoped that the road would be open to the Duck by December.
- August 18, 1858—passenger and passenger/freight trains were running round trip daily between Nashville and Thompson's Station.
- February 19, 1859—trains were coming within three miles of Columbia.
- Mid-April 1859—trains were making round trips daily to the Duck.
- May 26, 1859—the bridge over the Duck was nearly finished.
- July 4, 1859—trains were expected to be running round trip daily between Nashville and Columbia by this date.
- It is not clear when the road was completed to Columbia or Mount Pleasant.
- September 1859—there was a new stage line to take passengers from the end of the road near Columbia to Athens; total time from Nashville was 19 hours and the cost was $7.00.
- June 3, 1860—there were two passenger trains and one freight train making daily round trips; one passenger train ran to Decatur Junction and the other ran to Columbia and connected with trains that ran to Mount Pleasant and Pulaski. The tunnel did not open until November 1860, so wagons had to be used to get around Madry's Ridge.

Appendix A

The T&A seems to have had seven locomotives: the *Franklin* and the *Columbia* (obtained in August 1854), the *Gov. Broome* (June 1857, named for the Florida governor), the *Nashville* (August 1857), the *John Childe* (October 1858, named for the chief engineer on the design of the T&A), the *Williamson* (February 1859) and the *Davidson* (July 1859). They appear to have bought the *Giles* from the CS in 1866. The *Gov. Broome* was sold to the Fernandina and Cedar Keys Railroad in Florida. The T&A sold the *Davidson* and the *John Childe* to the N&D in 1868.[4]

The first passenger depot in Franklin seems to have been built in 1854–55. A temporary passenger depot was there in the late 1860s. In the 1870s, a permanent frame passenger depot was built just north of the existing freight depot. That makes at least three nineteenth-century wooden passenger depots. When that depot was replaced in 1901 by the Louisville & Nashville Railroad (L&N), successor to the T&A and N&D, the old depot was "moved back" to a location a bit farther from the tracks and the new one built at the site of its predecessor. It opened on November 26, 1901, and was demolished in about 1959. The first depot in Columbia was built in 1859, a new one in 1877 and the present one in 1903.[5]

The original Franklin freight depot seems to have been built by the T&A in about 1858. It would have had a track siding. During the Civil War, it was probably used primarily to receive and store private commercial goods and for storage of military supplies. It seems to have been partially burned on December 17, 1864. A new brick freight depot was built and is still standing. It was announced in the August 2, 1873, *Nashville Union and American*, dateline August 1, that in Franklin, "a large brick depot has been built at this place by the Louisville and Nashville and Great Southern Railway Company."[6]

In early 1862, the Federals built another freight depot at Franklin, probably just north of Fort Granger and adjacent to the railroad where it would have been protected by the encampment that had been on the north side of the Harpeth River since early to mid–1862. The area around Fort Granger was known to have warehouses. The sketch of the 1863 hangings of Confederate spies Williams and Peters at the encampment shows what appears to be a warehouse. Because the railroad carried both military and private freight, there would have been a need for both the T&A and federal freight/supply depots. Civil War maps show the T&A freight depot as well as what appears to be a passenger depot. Forrest burned a depot in June 1863 which was probably the Union supply depot.

In Nashville, there was a T&A/N&D freight depot with a yard, shops and roundhouse. It was located where the railroad met the N&C, about 1,500 feet east of Fort Negley at about the intersection of present-day Chestnut Street and Fourth Avenue South. The original Nashville T&A passenger depot was at the northern terminus of the railroad near the intersection of Sixth Avenue and Broadway, about a mile northwest of the yard. In May 1867, the railroad approved removal of that depot and the track between the depots and construction of a new passenger depot two miles to the southeast adjacent to the freight depot on Chestnut Street. A large N&C depot was located in Nashville in the valley near the intersection of Tenth Avenue and Church Street. It had warehouses, shops, stables, a coal yard and a roundhouse.[7]

There are no antebellum or Civil War–era depots still in place on the T&A. Several post-war depots exist, and replicas have been built in recent years at Thompson's Station and Lynnville. The freight depot at Franklin and the depots at Columbia, Elkmont, Athens and Decatur were constructed by the L&N.

Appendix A

The Central Southern (CS) Railroad was chartered on November 30, 1853. Its offices were in Columbia. Thomas Martin was its president during the Civil War. The railroad was built better than most in the South, with heavy T-rail rather than the more common strap iron affixed to the cross ties. Instead of untreated local pine or poplar, it used out-of-state red cedar ties which were treated with a preservative. It had stone ballast rather than the usual dirt fill. The designers increased the grades to a maximum of sixty-eight-and-two-thirds feet per mile, reducing the amount of fill required and, thus, the cost of construction. The savings on fill paid for the stone ballast.[8]

Because the railroad was located a mile east of old Lynnville, the town relocated eastward to be along the track. For the same reason, Prospect was moved a mile to the northeast.

There was only one tunnel on the N&D. It was 20 feet tall by about 15 feet wide and through 1,233 feet—nearly a quarter mile—of limestone at Madry's Ridge in southern Giles County. Though there was a lot of work to do along the 122 miles from Nashville to Decatur Junction, the feature requiring the greatest effort to construct was this tunnel. It was excavated from both ends. The goal was that the two segments would align perfectly, the two crews of workers would break through the last bit of rock separating them, cheer and share pleasantries, and the excavation would be about done. This was not easy or exacting work. Pre-Civil War tunneling was slow and dangerous. Holes were drilled into the rock using a star drill, a bar four to eight feet long that was held by one man as another hit the end with a sledgehammer. A number of holes were drilled, then black powder was placed in each hole with fuse. Black powder was used to blast the rock because dynamite had not yet been invented. The holes were packed with clay to keep more of the blast energy within the rock and not out the hole. The fuse was lit, and everyone got back for the explosion. Then the blast rubble was removed, and the process repeated countless times. The tunnel reportedly had two recesses cut into its walls that would offer safe shelter to men who could not get out before an oncoming train whistled and rolled through.

Because the approach to the north entrance to the tunnel at the ridge was over rough, sloping terrain, an 822-foot-long wooden trestle was built. The trestle allowed the track to climb to the optimal elevation on the ridge, thus reducing the tunnel's length. There were at least two lime kilns at the tunnel, one near each end. The north one is still in place. Bits of limestone from the tunnel excavation were burned to make quicklime, which was used in making cement, mortar, whitewash and other products.

The tunnel would be the last piece of the railroad to be completed and its opening was eagerly awaited. The track had been completed to the north and south sides of the ridge in about early 1860. From that time until the tunnel was completed, this was the only break in the track. Trains had to stop there, unload and have their cargo or passengers transported by stagecoach or wagon around the ridge to be placed on another train on the other side.

As of January 14, 1860, the approaches to the tunnel were nearly complete and 557 feet of it had been carved out from the north side and 339 feet from the south. Once the remaining 337 feet were completed, the floor would have to be prepared for the track and the track laid. At one time, the tunnel excavation was expected to be completed in April 1860 and the track laid in May. At that rate, it seems that the tunneling would have commenced in about April 1859. The tunnel and its track were not completed, however, and the railroad open to the state line until November 21, 1860, when the last track was laid at Prospect Station. So, it seems that construction of the tunnel took about 19 months. The delay in completion was largely due to the two segments being several feet off-line from each other, requiring additional excavation that put a slight curve in the tunnel and the track. On November 22, the first train ran all the way from Nashville to Decatur Junction. Ballasting of the track, however, continued for about another month.[9]

The CS's construction timeline was:

- 1855—Road surveys were completed.
- 1857—Construction had begun.
- March 1857—Major Thomas Buford, President of the railroad, predicted that the entire CS should be ready for iron by the time the T&A was complete to Columbia.
- February 19, 1859—grading to Pulaski was mostly complete.
- About April 1859—tunnel excavation starts.
- June 22, 1859—track laying started at Columbia.
- September 15, 1859—Dodson's Gap cut was finished.
- October 1859—the first locomotive rolled from Columbia to Lynnville, which had a turntable, switch and small depot.
- November 2, 1859—grading was complete as far south as Pulaski, several small bridges were finished and the 120-foot bridge over Robertson Fork Creek was completed as was a 160-foot bridge over Richland Creek. Three more bridges remained to be built—two over Richland Creek (180 feet long each) and one over Pigeon Roost Creek (50 feet). Also, track laying had been completed twenty-three-and-a-quarter miles to Reynolds' Station and construction of the engine house at Columbia for four engines had been started.[10]
- About December 1859—the line was open to Reynolds' Station and the Elk River Bridge had been completed.
- January 14, 1860—the track had been laid from the Elk River to the state line. The remaining 12 miles were to be laid by the end of March. Also, 14 miles had been ballasted in Maury County and nine miles in Giles County.[11]
- January 25, 1860—track was completed as far south as Pulaski. At that time, a turntable was being constructed there.
- November 21, 1860—tunnel construction was completed and the railroad was open.

In early 1859, the CS had one engine, the *Giles*, and five flat cars. Eventually, it would add four more engines, the *Pulaski* in May 1859, the *Thom. Buford* in March 1860, the *Maury* in April 1860 and the *Decatur* in May 1860. The *Thom. Buford* was named after the first president of the railroad, who was from Lynnville and had died in 1859. It pulled the first train from Nashville to Pulaski. The *Maury* and *Thom. Buford* were taken for use by the USMRR, returned to the CS in 1865, rebuilt by the N&D and renumbered without names. In 1866, the CS sold the *Decatur, Maury* and *Thom. Buford*. The *Giles* was leased to the Alabama and Tennessee River Railroad in 1863, surrendered to the Federals in 1865, returned to the CS that same year, sold to the T&A in 1866 and later sold to and renumbered by the L&N. Almost all of the CS track south of Pulaski was abandoned in 1986.[12]

The Tennessee and Alabama Central (T&AC) Railroad was chartered on December 19, 1853. James W. Sloss was president of the company through the Civil War. He would

Appendix A

also be president of the Nashville and Decatur while it was being incorporated in 1865 and after the incorporation in April 1866, which combined the three railroads. In 1852, work had started on the Memphis and Charleston Railroad's Tennessee River bridge at Decatur. The first train crossed the bridge in 1855.[13]

The T&AC's construction timeline was:

- Mid-March 1856—the road was graded nearly all the way from Decatur Junction to Athens.
- March 26, 1858—the first rail was laid.
- May 16, 1858—the track was expected to be open from Decatur Junction to Athens by July 4. From there, it would connect to Columbia by stagecoaches.
- July 28, 1858—trains were running on the portion that had been completed, which was about as far north as Sulphur Creek.
- October 18, 1858—enough iron had been purchased to finish the railroad.
- Late December 1858—the road was open from Decatur Junction to Athens and grading was complete north of Athens.
- Fall of 1859—the line reached Elkmont.
- Sometime in 1860—the track was open all the way from Decatur Junction to the state line.

The first engine on the tracks was the *Luke Pryor*, named for the man who, with Thomas Hobbs, was primarily responsible for bringing the T&AC to Alabama. Other engines used by the railroad were the *Limestone* and the *Jack Mason*, which was named after prominent Athens citizen Captain Jack Mason. The *Limestone* was leased to the Savannah, Albany and Gulf Railroad through the Confederate Government. The fate of the *Jack Mason* is unclear.[14]

The railroad was abandoned in April 1986. In 2010, a 10.2-mile stretch of the abandoned right-of-way in Limestone County that had been converted to the Richard Martin Rails to Trail was designated a National Recreation Trail. The trail crosses several bridges and the site of the former Sulphur Creek Trestle.

It seems that the goal of the three companies was to have the track open from Nashville to Decatur in early to mid–1860. However, misalignment of the tunnel created a delay of several months until late November of that year. Though not pleased with the delay in completion, the railroad companies could be proud that, on August 14, 1860, it was reported that there had not been any accident of consequence involving loss of life or limb on the entire 122 miles in the past five years. That seems to be extremely unusual for construction and operation in the railroad business.

The track through Davidson, Williamson, Maury and Giles Counties, Tennessee, is in essentially the same location today as it was during the war. This cannot be said, however, for Limestone County, Alabama. There, the track has been relocated to the west at the extreme southern end of the N&D, just above Decatur.

On November 22, 1860, the same day the first train ran all the way to Decatur Junction, the three railroad companies agreed to operate independently yet cooperatively under the name of the Nashville and Decatur (N&D) Railroad, extending 122 miles from Nashville to Decatur Junction. They shared their stock, which at that time consisted of 36 box cars, 14 stock cars, 26 platform cars and 11 passenger and baggage cars. It would not be until after the war, on April 19, 1866, that an act passed, which was subsequently ratified and confirmed by another act passed on March 8, 1867, thus officially forming the new company. The Nashville and Decatur Railroad Company would begin corporate service under that new name on January 1, 1868.[15]

On May 4, 1871, the N&D leased to the L&N Railroad Company for 30 years its road, franchises and appurtenances, and took over a contract allowing it to pass over the road and bridge at the Tennessee River at Decatur. The lease did not include the road from Columbia to Mount Pleasant. The L&N took possession of the N&D on July 1, 1872, thus starting the 30-year lease period. Another lease was put in place on October 18, 1899. That lease was for 999 years and became effective on July 1, 1900. Through a number of corporate transactions, the L&N was controlled by the Atlantic Coast Line Railroad, then owned by the Seaboard companies which merged with the Chessie System to form the present-day CSX Transportation.[16]

On May 30, 1886, the entire length of the N&D's track was changed from 5'0" gauge to the Northern standard of 4'8½". The track and Madry's Ridge tunnel continued to see heavy use until about 1912, when the 96-mile-long section of the Lewisburg and Northern Railroad (Lew&N) was completed from Athens, Alabama, to Brentwood, Tennessee, where it connected to the existing L&N line. Its construction included Radnor Yard and Radnor Lake in Nashville. The lake is now the centerpiece of Radnor Lake State Park. The new line was funded by the L&N, which took the Lew&N stock as partial payment. Because the L&N owned the former N&D, there was no competition between the parallel lines. The new line essentially paralleled the old one, running a maximum of 20 miles east of it along a route that was straighter and flatter. The new route allowed much heavier loads to be run more quickly than before. Once the Lew&N was open, all major freight and passenger traffic was shifted to it. However, local trains continued rolling along the old N&D. In October 1915, the Lew&N was absorbed by the L&N. The last passenger train ran on the old N&D track in 1966 or 1967. With rolling stock increasing in size, by the 1980s much of it could not pass through the Madry's Ridge tunnel, so the L&N (then the Seaboard System Railroad) abandoned some of the track between Pulaski and Athens which included the tunnel.[17]

Appendix B

Civil War–Era Railroads, Communications and Pontoon Bridges

A primary invention of America's Industrial Revolution was the steam engine. There were many applications for it, one of which was the steam-powered locomotive that was already in use when the Civil War broke out. Before 1830, every soldier engaged in battle got where he needed to be on foot, with the aid of an animal or by water. Supplies were transported in the same manner. Within just three decades all that changed, with steam-powered locomotives transforming the logistics of warfare. Though there was a significant cost associated with maintaining and operating the locomotives and cars and keeping the tracks open and safe, supply trains pulled by locomotives were a vast improvement over those pulled by animals. The animals had to eat, and their food had to be brought along with them or collected from the countryside. So, additional animals were needed to supply them and those animals needed food, too. Also, the animals had to be fed when not in use whereas locomotives did not and caring for them was a huge effort. The primary advantage of the steam locomotive, however, was that in terms of energy consumption it was 10 times as efficient as the animals. In addition, locomotive trains traveled five times as fast as wagon trains. This advantage in speed meant that more men and supplies could be delivered in a given amount of time and the men would arrive less fatigued and the food fresher.[1]

Civil War–era engines were much smaller and lighter than today's diesel locomotives, weighing about 16 to 22 tons as opposed to 100 to 200 tons today. They burned wood and used a lot of water. In fact, the need for water was even greater than that for wood. Coal was being tried in the North as an alternative fuel but did not come into common use until the mid–1860s. Many engines ran without tender cars during the war, so the crews had to stop and reload their trains with wood and water at the stations that were separated by only a few miles along the track. The tender cars that were in use typically carried only enough wood and water for about 50 miles. The engines could pull up to about 10 to 12 cars, depending upon how heavily the cars were loaded, and ran at up to about 15 miles per hour.[2]

Locomotives were designed to run in reverse, a critical capability in war. It gave the operators an opportunity to escape capture if the track or bridge ahead of them was blocked or damaged. However, they ran much better forward than in reverse. Turntables and wyes were placed at various locations along the N&D. They allowed trains to be turned around and run in the opposite direction. The wye was a triangle-shaped junction of three tracks. Decatur Junction was one. There was another at Columbia and there must have been one where the N&D connected with the N&C at Nashville. There were turntables at the Elk River, Pulaski and Lynnville. The Nashville yard and Columbia had roundhouses for servicing engines. The one at Columbia was due south of the town square.

Most of the USMRR locomotives were identified by numbers. Many had names like *Firefly*, *Exeter* and *Buffalo*, or titles like *President* and *Secretary*. Some were named for government officials, Union officers and railroad officials like *Gen. Meigs*, *E.M. Stanton* and *D.C. McCallum*. Box cars were wooden and could carry about 35 soldiers. When needed, they would travel with 70 soldiers to a car, including those sitting on top, or with 75 or more prisoners crammed in and unable to sit. Passenger cars could seat about 50. Artillery would normally travel on flat cars and ammunition was often spread among several manned box cars.[3]

There were several types of trains. Passenger/freight trains were the most common. Construction trains carried rail, ties and any other materials to the site where work was being performed. Wrecking trains were fitted with appliances needed for clearing wreckage from the track and repairing certain damages to the locomotive and cars.

While the N&D was under military control, the federal government generally attempted to still have rail service available for passengers, commercial business and mail delivery. This required the presence of stations along the track. There was a large number of them to encourage business along the line and to provide ample locations for the locomotives to take on more water and wood. The stations and their water tanks and stores of wood were attractive targets for the Confederates. There were many interruptions in service due to damage to the water tanks and wood stores. Stations came and went over time, depending on the need for them.

The railroad operated via telegraph communications. Professor Samuel F.B. Morse had patented his electromagnetic telegraph system in 1837, but it would not be until 1843 that Congress tested the device. In 1844, the directors of the Baltimore & Ohio Railroad allowed Morse to run a line parallel to their track provided they could use it free of charge. That same year, the world's first telegraph service was opened on May 24, but it would be several years before the technology was used to control railroad traffic. The telegraph became gradually better understood and accepted by other railroads until the two innovations were inseparable. The first telegraph lines were designed to be of insulated copper laid underground in a lead pipe in a two-inch-wide, 20-inch-deep trench. This was no easy feat. A team of 16 oxen was needed to pull the special plowshare that cut the trench. Heavy stone ballast or rock was encountered often enough to eventually bring the wire up and string it on poles. By 1861, about 50,000 miles of commercial lines had been run in the U.S. Most business was conducted by the American Telegraph Company whose system ran north to south along the east coast and Western Union who operated from the east coast to California. At that time, the Army had no telegraph component, so the federal government relied on the companies for their communications.

Telegraph poles and lines, set back near the boundary of the railroad right-of-way, ran alongside the track the entire length of the N&D. Western Union owned the system. In April 1861, the U.S. Military Telegraph Corps (USMTC) was formed. Simon Cameron summoned Thomas A. Scott to Washington to be Assistant Secretary of War and manage the railroads and telegraph services for the Army. Scott, in turn, called on Andrew Carnegie to recruit telegraphers and linemen for the USMTC. At the outset, there were only 2,000 telegraph operators in the country, about 100 of whom were women.

Appendix B

Anson Stager was Captain, Assistant Quartermaster and Superintendent of the USMTC. At age 21, he had been put in charge of the first telegraph office in Lancaster, Pennsylvania. He became superintendent of the "National Lines" in Cincinnati and in 1856 was the first general superintendent of the Western Union Company. On May 27, 1861, Stager was appointed superintendent of the lines in the Department of the Ohio. On November 11 of that year, he took charge of the Telegraph Corps, serving in that capacity until 1868. After the war, he was president of Western Electric, the Chicago Telephone Company and the Western Edison Company.

In January 1862, the USMTC was placed under control of the Secretary of War. It employed about 1,200 civilian men, 150 of whom were trained to operate the telegraph. As with USMRR personnel, the operators and the men who were building the telegraph lines during battles sometimes faced great danger. Every important cavalry expedition was accompanied by telegraph operators who also worked to tap the Confederates' wires. The men were mostly age 16 to 22. It is estimated that 12 of them were killed in the war, 23 died from disease, 10 were wounded, and 154 captured. The Corps constructed nearly 16,000 miles of main lines plus 1,000 miles of field wires connecting the different divisions of each army and the fortifications. In 1864, the Corps operated 8,623 miles of military lines. There were about 6.5 million military telegrams sent during the war, an average of 4,500 per day.[4]

Early in the war, Capt. Samuel Bruch was assistant manager of the telegraphs for Kentucky and Tennessee. As the Union advanced through Nashville in February 1862, telegraph lines were repaired by the Southwestern Telegraph Company. The company was to continue operation of the lines, but they did not have the means to do so. Therefore, Bruch took them over and the agency operated them. He suffered from a shortage of good builders and operators and, when guerrillas were prevalent, from a number of his operators being captured, robbed and paroled. The lines from Nashville to Columbia had been damaged by the Confederates and were repaired in March through June 1862. In April and May, Bruch built 75 miles from Columbia to Decatur, but not without great difficulty. He did not have sufficient labor in that lower stretch, and his entire building party was captured and all of his wagons and materials destroyed. Only the foreman, Thomas Keenan, escaped. Keenan helped get another party together and the work continued. Those 75 miles of line were abandoned from mid–August through September 1862 when Gen. Buell's army retreated. After about the first of September, Kentucky and Tennessee were overrun by guerrillas, and it was impossible to keep the lines up. For a while, only the offices in Bowling Green and Nashville were kept open, though they had no outside communication.

Train delays were common. Attacks by Confederates and raids by guerrillas and Southern sympathizers along the roads caused numerous delays and much damage to the trains. Sometimes the Confederates would destroy track or bridges ahead of and behind a train so it would be trapped and raided. To protect the trains when traveling in areas of active fighting, guards often rode atop the cars. Breaks in the line were common and when they occurred, the Federals usually had to rely on wagons to move men and cargo around the break to where the track was intact. The locomotives sometimes ran out of water. If the crew was lucky, they could carry some in buckets from a nearby creek. Another problem arose when soldiers bathed and washed their clothes in a creek that supplied water to a downstream railroad water station. That could create foaming boilers which required the train to stop to replace the water. Sometimes, nature created a delay. Though this incident occurred on the L&N about ten miles north of Nashville, and not on the N&D, it is interesting to note that, on May 6, 1867, a train was brought to a stop by mass of caterpillars that had accumulated on the track. The train could not continue until the insects were swept off.[5]

Accidents occurred frequently. Most were not serious or fatal, only creating a delay. Some wrecks were caused by intoxicated employees, but most were due to inexperienced or negligent operators. Many were caused by rebels displacing rails or placing obstructions on the track. At times, the Confederates would remove the spikes but leave the rails, hoping the next Union train would run off the track and roll off the road. To avoid a head-on collision, trains had to get to the designated siding before another one came the opposite way. There was a shortage of sidings in the South, which made it harder to maintain schedules and avoid such crashes. When a siding was not nearby and there was a possibility that another train might approach, a flagger would sometimes run ahead of his train to warn the oncoming one. In cold weather, the switches could freeze, increasing the chance of a collision. With few fences, cows were often a problem even with the presence of a cowcatcher. Hitting a cow could send the engine and cars off the track. Axles could break and engines explode. Heavy rains could cause bridge abutments to collapse. Bridges or trestles could be washed out or damaged or destroyed by the enemy.

To reduce losses caused by a damaged bridge, it was common practice for the troops aboard a train in territory subject to attacks to walk across bridges. On the N&D and some other railroads, bridges had been burned and temporary trestles constructed in their place. Those trestles were sometimes shaky. To avoid injury or loss of life, the engineer would often send the fireman across the trestle to catch the engine. The engineer would give the locomotive enough steam to carry itself and the train to the other side where the fireman got on it while the engineer walked across. It was not uncommon

Train wreck (Library of Congress).

for trains to be overloaded. Those trains had a greater risk of derailment. As an indication of how common accidents were, the general manager of the Department of the Mississippi reported 12 accidents in the period of July 1–25, 1864. Five were collisions, four involved trains running off the track, one was burned by Confederates, one engine burst a flue and one ran off the track because guerrillas had taken up a rail.[6]

The conductor was captain of the train. He maintained the schedules, tried to avoid collisions, ensured that cars were put off at the correct locations and that the right cars were attached to the train and collected passengers' tickets. He usually carried a pistol to tame a rowdy passenger or deal with robbers. Like many others who worked for the railroads, his skills kept him from being drafted into the war. In fact, many young men sought refuge as railroad employees. Some soldiers hated the railroad men because they thought they were cowards not to fight. However, railroad work meant long hours, and was hard and dangerous, not unlike what the soldiers experienced.[7]

The Southern rails were typically not of the best quality steel, and the bridges were usually hastily constructed with light materials. The N&D was an exception, being better constructed before the war than most. Trains in the South traveled at an average speed of about 15 mph and seldom faster than 25. To reduce the risk of derailment, Gen. Sherman reported that in the summer of 1864 he ordered his trains from Nashville to Chattanooga to be run at 10 mph. That speed limit was not uncommon for freight trains at the time. In fact, before 1870 the N&C did not allow their freight trains to travel at greater than 10 mph or passenger trains at greater than 15. The trains traveled mostly on inverted T-shaped rails like today's, but because the weights and speeds were so much less in the nineteenth century, the rails weighed only 50 to 65 pounds per yard, compared to at least 130 pounds per yard today. Rail was at a premium during the war and was sometimes scavenged from a less important track to support a more important one. For instance, in 1863 all the track iron, spikes and cross ties were taken from the 12-mile-long N&D branch between Columbia and Mount Pleasant for use in repairing main lines, building sidetrack and in naval construction. The branch was rebuilt in 1888.[8]

Civil War–era rails were either attached atop and perpendicular to the cross ties or to stringers that ran parallel to the rails and were attached to the ties. Cross ties were typically not treated to resist rot and were almost always placed directly on the soil. Non-treated ties placed on soil lasted only about five years and were expensive and difficult to replace. The N&D was one of the few railroads to have ties placed on stone ballast. They were often set more closely together to compensate for a poor foundation.[9]

From 1850 through 1860, railroad business was the largest growth industry in the nation. During that period, 26,300 miles of new track were laid and about 3,800 locomotives, 6,400 passenger and baggage cars and 88,600 freight cars were bought. There were many new railroads and they were able to choose their own gauge, the distance measured between the inner faces of the rails. The 4'8½" (56.5 inch) gauge had been adopted by more new railways than any other and would become the standard, but before standardization there was discord. By the mid–1860s, the eastern half of the U.S. and Canada were divided into nine major regions defined by their prevalent gauges, ranging from 56.5" to 6'0". Only three were dominated by the 56.5" gauge. Track in the South, in the region east of the Mississippi except for North Carolina and in part of Virginia, typically used 5'0". Because of the variation in gauges, the traveling range of trains in the Confederacy was somewhat limited. At the points where the gauges changed, cars were lifted to the other track by a steam hoist and placed on wheels of the other gauge. In the North, axles that could be adjusted in length were sometimes used. The 5'0" lines were the slowest to convert to 56.5". In fact, the amount of 5'0" gauge actually doubled between 1865 and 1885 because of new construction and some conversions from the others. However, 1,000 miles in the South converted to the 56.5" gauge in 1881 and 1882, followed by the remaining 15,000 miles in 1885 and 1886.[10]

On May 30, 1886, major changes were made to the track gauge of the former N&D and other railroads. On that day, the N&D's track gauge was changed from 5'0" to the Northern standard of 4'8½". Some other lines went to 4'9" which was compatible with the lines that were at 4'8½". To make this adjustment along the many miles of the N&D and other railroads, one rail was loosened from its ties, slid over 3½" and reattached. The gauge change allowed the rapid and efficient passage of freight and passengers past where the lines of one gauge had connected with a line of the other. This aided the recovery of the South and the nation.[11]

Bridges and trestles were made almost exclusively of wood, though some bridges contained steel structural elements. Many of the bridges built along the N&D in 1864 consisted of Howe trusses, which are characterized by vertical steel or iron tension rods located between one set of cross pieces and the next. To speed construction, in some instances the bents and other structural components were prefabricated and sent to the site ready to put in place. Duplicate components for the bridges were sometimes prepared in the likely event that the bridge was damaged or destroyed. Bridges built on-site had to be constructed without complicated machinery. The necessary tools included axes, cross-cut saws, spiking mauls, augers, ropes, block and tackle, timber-rollers, scaffolding plank and, if available, sets of balance beams and some carpenter's tools. Ox teams were often used for transportation of materials over land. The construction team typically traveled by train, using flat cars for materials and stock cars for the animals.[12]

To build a typical bridge, a team of men would cut nearby timber, flatten it on two sides and have it taken to the bridge site while framers and raisers were clearing the banks. The raisers would rig and run their balance beams at both ends of the bridge. Framers would frame and put a truss together on the ground, ready to be launched into the stream or raised into place from the ground. By the time a truss was put together, the levelers would be ready to give the exact dimension for cutting off the support posts which had been augered into the ground. Meanwhile, the raisers would have their balance beams ready to raise the truss into position. This was repeated, working from both shores at once until all trusses were in place. If building across a large stream, another team would have constructed a temporary ferry upstream of the bridge. The ferry was used for floating trusses for the middle section of the bridge into position for raising. While the skeleton of the bridge was being put into position, a team was busy bracing it at the points of greatest stress and another team was placing the cross pieces between the trusses and then the track stringers. The stringers were always overlapping. The final steps were laying the track by attaching common cross ties perpendicular to the stringers with long spikes and then spiking the rails to the ties. Building a trestle was similar, but involved working primarily or solely from land, augering in bents and installing heavy timbers rather than trusses.[13]

Culverts on the N&D were originally made of hand-placed stone or brick. There are references to culverts on the N&D being burned, so it appears that the original stone culverts, if damaged or destroyed, were sometimes replaced by wooden ones. Preformed culverts were also available at the time, typically round, made of clay or steel and up to 48 inches in diameter. However, it does not appear that they were used on the N&D.

Although pontoon bridges and fords did not have much of an association with the railroads, it is important to discuss them. A pontoon bridge is not a bridge in the common sense of the word because it does not span what it is crossing. Rather, it is a floating platform that bridges the space between one side of a water body and the other. Pontoons are the vessels that provide the buoyancy required to support the weight of what is crossing. During the Civil War, nails were not used when assembling a pontoon bridge. The components were lashed together to make the structure easier to assemble, remove and reuse and give it the flexibility required to move with the load on it, and adapting to the current and the rise and fall of the water. Though rubber and other materials were used in making pontoons, the most common types in the Western Theater seem to have been canvas-covered or solid wood, usually about 22 feet long. The wooden ones were especially heavy and a burden to transport, but durable. Rosecrans had conceptualized a lightweight, strong, folding pontoon that was easier to transport and install than those commonly in use. Thomas put that type of pontoon into production late in the war. They were built in the engineer workshops in Nashville under the supervision of Major Willett. The boats, called "Cumberland pontoons," were used by Sherman in his Atlanta Campaign. A typical pontoon could support several thousand pounds, depending on its dimensions. Troops were not to march in unison across a pontoon bridge because the impact of the stepping could submerge the boats. Transporting all that was required to construct pontoon bridges required several types of carriages: pontoon wagons, chess wagons to carry the planking, tool wagons and forge wagons that carried the anchors and extra iron for the bridge. Hundreds of horses or mules were required to pull all of these wagons.

Building a pontoon bridge of wooden boats required several sequential steps. After selecting the location for the crossing, the abutment crew prepared the approaches and abutments. Pontoon wagons were pulled nearby, and the boat crew unloaded some pontoons, rowed a boat a bit upstream, dropped an anchor and drifted the boat into the correct position. Each boat had an upstream anchor while only alternate boats had one downstream. The balk crew placed the balks (heavy timbers) from the abutment onto the boats as the boats were placed farther into the body of water. The balks connected the boats and supported the planking that was the traffic surface. As the boats were placed, they were roped together by the lashing crew using iron cleats, hooks and other iron pieces that were attached to the wooden components. Then the chess crew covered the balks with flooring and sometimes lay dirt, straw or brush atop the boards to dampen the noise and protect the boards. The rail crew came behind, placing the wooden curbs.

On most pontoon bridges, it was likely that all six crews were working simultaneously for much of the construction time, especially if the abutments and approaches needed a lot of work. The bridge had to be maintained constantly, keeping it clean, making sure it was staying intact and removing flotsam from the anchor cables and the upstream side of the pontoons. Also, because the boats leaked, they had to be bailed out periodically. If there was sufficient time to do so, the bridge would be removed in the reverse fashion in which it was assembled. However, if the army needed to move quickly with the bridge, one way of doing so was to have a crew row to the far side and start cutting some of the heavy timbers and anchor cables. This would allow the bridge to drift to the near bank for faster disassembly.[14]

Fording an undefended waterway was another way of crossing it. Ideally, before using a site as a ford, an engineer or other experienced military man would assess it for good approaches that, without much or any reworking, would allow wagons and artillery access to and from the water. The bed needed to be reasonably firm and not covered with rocks of too large a size. Obviously, the depth and swiftness of the water were important. A cavalryman could pass in about five feet of water, an infantryman in four and a loaded wagon in about two-and-a-half. Gen. Forrest and some other commanders would not be deterred by water that was a bit deep for artillery. They would sometimes swim horses and their riders across and then pull the guns by attaching them to a double team with ropes. The guns got submerged but could be cleaned up. The ammunition could be carried over in small boats, brought over by cavalrymen or distributed to the men and carried over their heads. If the waterway was a bit fast, cavalrymen could be placed downstream to catch an infantryman who had been swept away by the current. At times, the largest men would form two lines across the waterway, with each man connected to the next with their guns to create a lane though which the smaller men could pass. Even the finest crossing sites, however, could become very difficult to cross, especially for artillery and wagons, after much of the army had already crossed and turned the path into deep, soft mud.[15]

Appendix C
*Locating the Crossings
and Fortifications in Mid–1864*

Although most sites on the N&D that had a bridge or trestle at the beginning of the war still had a structure at the close of the war, some structures were built at new locations as the war progressed. Wright's report of bridges and trestles, including his Table 2, confirms this. Similarly, the form of fortification protecting the railroad's bridges and trestles varied as time went by, evolving from encampments to stockades and, finally, to blockhouses. Due to these dynamics, a date needed to be selected at which time a "snapshot" was taken of the railroad. Because the blockhouses are such an interesting aspect of the N&D and quite a bit is known about them, the author selected July 1864, after most of them were in place, for this snapshot. For that point in time, the author attempted to identify the locations of the major crossings and the fortifications at those crossings.

It was not difficult to identify most of the crossings along the N&D during the Civil War that required a bridge or trestle. However, determining the locations of all the blockhouses was a challenge and is not without uncertainty.

There are many locations along the N&D where the original track crossed significant waterways or wide, deep areas that did not have a large waterway. The methods of crossing these two types of low areas are very different.

To cross a waterway, either a culvert or a bridge would have been used. At a larger waterway such as a river or major creek, a bridge would have been the most appropriate structure. At the minor waterway crossings that did not have enough flow, height or width to warrant a bridge, a culvert placed in fill would probably have been constructed.

At crossings that were characterized more by height and width than flow, a trestle was the best structure. During the war, the Federals often hastily built a temporary trestle where there had been a bridge in order to get the railroad open again, intending to come back before the rainy season and build a bridge. Trestles along the N&D were also often built at the approaches to large bridges, like at the Duck and Elk Rivers, and at crossings of less than 17 feet height, like Low Trestle, and wide, swampy areas in northern Alabama.[1]

The terms "bridge" and "trestle" are often mistakenly used interchangeably. However, they are very different structure types. A bridge was used to span the area being crossed whereas a trestle had its foundation within the area being crossed. Of course, long bridges often had one or more pier within the waterway. The main reasons that trestles are not generally best suited for crossings that can have a significant flow are that rushing water can scour the foundation or apply excessive lateral force to the structure, and debris can be carried down the waterway and become caught by the structure, backing up the water like a dam and putting a horizontal load on the trestle for which it was not designed. These factors can cause the trestle to be washed out. At some sites, it would not have been clear whether to use a long embankment or a long trestle. This seems to have been the case at the first tributary of South Fork Fountain Creek, just south of Culleoka, where an embankment was used although a trestle could have been justified, as well.

The reports by Dodge and Wright, especially Dodge's Table 1 and Wright's Table 2, provide valuable information about the locations of the bridges and trestles. The Dodge list starts with bridge No. 6 at the southernmost crossing over Carter's Creek. That implies that there were only five bridges north of that crossing. With five crossings and five bridges over Carter's Creek, one would think that there was only one crossing north of Carter's Creek. However, there were five. Brown's Creek, the Little Harpeth, Spencer Creek, the Harpeth and the West Harpeth were all north of bridge No. 6, and each had a bridge, so it is not clear why Dodge's first bridge is No. 6.

The author compared those two tables to identify the crossings that were in both and those that were in one but not the other. It is important to realize that, if a bridge or trestle was in Wright's earlier list but not Dodge's later one, the reason could be that the structure was present in November 1863 but did not need repair. Pigeon Roost Creek is an example of this. A bridge had been constructed there by the CS railroad and seems to have been in operating condition when Dodge performed his November inventory. It needs to be noted that Wright generally shows the bridges built higher and longer than Dodge.

Many of the bridges and trestles that Dodge and Boomer had rebuilt by May 1864 were damaged between June and November 1864 and destroyed again by the retreating Confederates that December. All were repaired again starting that December, with many being lengthened and heightened. Wright Bridges Nos. 6, 7, 18 and 19 seem to be among the bridges that were built over smaller creeks where it appears there was no bridge before. Nos. 6 and 7 were north of the stretch of track where Dodge worked. The crossings at Nos. 18 and 19 probably had culverts in late 1863. Their bridges were built after Dodge completed his work. All four of these structures seem to have been built after the initial 36 blockhouses were completed.

MapQuest and the CSX System Map at *www.csx.com* were used to confirm the locations that Dodge and Wright presented in their tables and to look for other streams and low areas that might have warranted a bridge or trestle. No such features were identified, so the Wright and Dodge tables seem to list all of the significant crossings. MapQuest shows the waterways in more detail than the CSX website and shows the current location of the track, but not the railway between Pulaski and Athens that has been abandoned. The CSX site shows the current track, the abandoned rights-of-way and most of the waterways. Some of the minor streams that existed in the 1860s may not show up on these maps because they could have been filled or relocated. However, this is not a problem because they are not significant to this analysis.

A key factor is determining the need for a trestle is topography. Where there is a lengthy section with a great difference in elevation from the track to the ground surface below, a trestle was usually constructed. Topography was obtained from U.S. Topo—the National Map and ArcGIS-Tennessee and was assumed not to have changed significantly since the war.

Appendix C

The author drove from Nashville to Decatur Junction to see as many crossings as practicable. He visited all that were reasonably close to a roadway. In some cases, he could not get access to a crossing and had to settle for a visit to a nearby point on the waterway suitable for determining its potential flow rate and width. Seeing these sites helped him to understand which crossings would have required a bridge and which a trestle. In all cases in which the author visited a site where it was known that a bridge or trestle had been constructed, the need for that type of structure was confirmed.

Some sites identified in the Dodge and Wright tables were difficult to locate. The exact location of the Swan Creek Bridge, about four-and-three-quarters miles north of Athens, is still not known and locations of the Harris and Gracey's Trestles were not apparent but were later determined. The National Archives and Records Administration (NARA) had two maps showing some of the bridges, trestles and defenses along the N&D between Carter's Creek and Decatur. Those maps showed the locations of the Harris and Gracey's trestles. Though there are no legend, date or information about the creator of the maps, Orlando M. Poe's name is on the back. Poe oversaw the 1st Michigan as they were building blockhouses on the N&C. Many maps were created under his direction, and he was an avid collector. Those two maps were probably not prepared by or for him, but more likely were in his collection and later donated to NARA. The maps appear to have been produced in 1864.[2]

Results of the analysis are presented in Table 3. The research identified 77 waterway crossings in Tennessee and 14 in Alabama. For each crossing, available literature and topography were reviewed and a judgment made regarding the need for a culvert, bridge or trestle in mid–1864. At that time, there seem to have been 37 bridges and trestles on the N&D, including bridges at Brown's Creek and Spencer Creek but not including the trestles that were approach structures for the larger bridges. The table lists the significant crossings and some of the many crossings that had culverts. The second column notes whether a bridge or trestle is thought to have been used at the site. The only listed bridge at an underpass is the extant one just north of the Harpeth River Bridge in Franklin. The third column shows the crossing number per the Dodge and Wright tables. The fourth column shows the number of times, according to Wright's table, the structure was rebuilt or repaired between February 1864 and the end of the war.

It is more difficult to locate the blockhouses than the bridges and trestles, primarily because of conflicting reports about them, a shortage of information on the specifics of many of the houses and difficulty in understanding the numbering system for the houses in Tennessee.

There is evidence that in mid–1864 there were blockhouses at all of the major bridges and trestles along the N&D, except the few that had a fort or large stockade in the immediate vicinity. Lt. Burroughs reported on June 29, 1864, regarding the N&D, "Thirty-six block-houses all single thickness, with a water tank at each one. One-half of the tanks were placed inside. Twelve block-houses need covering with earth."[3]

The significant forts, some of which negated the need for a blockhouse, were: Fort Negley in Nashville, built in the fall of 1862; Fort Granger at Franklin, built in the spring of 1863; Fort Mizner at Columbia; Fort Lilly at Pulaski, built in the spring of 1862; the fort at Sulphur Creek, still not completed in the fall of 1864; Fort Henderson at Athens, completed in early 1863 but seems to have been reconfigured in 1864; and the two forts with an earthworks in Decatur built in the spring of 1864. There were also four large, open stockades (larger than a blockhouse yet smaller than the main forts) at: Camp

Brentwood, built in the spring of 1863; Fort Palmer at Culleoka, built by the summer of 1862; Lynnville, built in the spring of 1864; and the Elk River. Most of the forts and stockades were garrisoned much of the time. Once all were completed, they provided the Federals a major fortification at an average of about every 12 miles along the N&D. This provided nearby support for a blockhouse that was under attack. It is fairly clear from the report by Lt. March that in September 1864 there were 11 blockhouses along the N&D in Alabama, probably the same ones that had been built earlier in that year. It is important to note that all 11 were on the N&D, none on the M&C below Decatur Junction. With that assumption and assuming a total of 36 houses, there would have been 25 blockhouses in Tennessee.

There can be confusion with the term "stockade." Along the N&D, there were at least two different types of stockades. One was the relatively small, open fortification constructed at key points along the railroad to protect them before blockhouses were built. The other was a larger, open fortification such as those at Brentwood, Culleoka, Lynnville and the Elk. To add to the confusion when studying the railroads, the terms "block house" and "stockade" are sometimes mistakenly used interchangeably in Civil War reports and on maps created during the war.

The 36 blockhouses were in place by mid–1864. At that time, the emphasis had been on improving upon the stockades by using heavier structures that had roofs. Lt. Burroughs was an officer and an engineer who would be knowledgeable about the difference between a blockhouse and a stockade. Given his knowledge of defenses and specific mention of the roofs, it seems certain that all 36 were to have roofs. Therefore, it is reasonable to think that there are no stockades among the 36. There is no known existing complete list of the blockhouse locations along the N&D. However, there is an April 8, 1864, list, presented in *The War of the Rebellion: A Compilation of the Official Records of the Union and Confederate Armies*, of the bridges and trestles along the N&C. Each of them already had or was to get a blockhouse. In that list, the crossings are numbered. One would expect that if, seemingly, all of the major crossings on the N&C had blockhouses, the same would be the case with the N&D. This supports the thought that the 36 "block houses" reported by Lt. Burroughs on the N&D were true blockhouses.[4]

When trying to determine the locations of the houses on the N&D in mid–1864, it was assumed that: (1) every bridge or trestle had at least one blockhouse unless there was sufficient evidence to indicate that a substantial fort or stockade was nearby, (2) because the range of rifled muskets was about 300 to 600 feet, bridges or trestles longer than that would have had a blockhouse on each end, whereas the short ones would need only one house, and (3) the houses were located where seemingly reliable reports indicate they were. Because of the lengths of their crossing structures, it appears that the Duck River, Culleoka, Tunnel Trestle and Sulphur Creek each had two houses. At the crossings where two houses were built, they were located near the opposing ends and on opposite sides of the track. *Report No. 7, Official Records of the War of the Rebellion*, Series I, Volume 39, Page 518 was used to locate the 11 blockhouses in Alabama. It seems there was an error in that report because it should state that House Numbers 8 and 9 were at Sulphur Creek Trestle.

There are very few references to blockhouses north of Spring Hill. The N&C list shows a house as close to Nashville as Mill Creek crossing No. 1, which was about eight miles from the center of the city. The next crossing to the west on the N&C was a bridge at Brown's Creek. There is no known record of a blockhouse being there, probably because it was near enough to Nashville and Fort Negley. The Brown's Creek crossing on the N&D probably did not have a house because it, too, should have been adequately protected by the fortifications in the city. The fact that Wright's table shows that the N&D bridge at Brown's Creek was not destroyed after February 1864 seems to confirm this.

The 1st Michigan built houses in March through June 1864, not far behind Dodge who built bridges from November 1863 through February 1864. Therefore, there should not have been any or many bridges added between the end of Dodge's work and the end of the 1st Michigan's. This means that the crossings with bridges shown in Wright's later table but not in Dodge's should not have been built early enough to get a blockhouse built by the 1st Michigan. That is another assumption used in developing Table 3.

It is difficult to determine the numbering sequence for blockhouses on the N&D in Tennessee. The report by Lt. March indicates that the blockhouse numbering system in Alabama was sequential, starting at Decatur Junction. Reports on the houses in Tennessee indicate that their numbers increase from north to south. However, it does not appear that the numbers were applied sequentially. For instance, the house at the southernmost crossing of Carter's Creek is often referred to as Number 6 and the Poe maps show Carter's Creek houses as Numbers 2 through 6. However, the next house to the south was the northernmost house on Rutherford Creek that was often referred to as Number 9. This makes mysteries of the locations of house Numbers 7 and 8.

Another example of non-sequential numbering is that the houses along Richland Creek are often referred to as Numbers 13 through 16. However, there were a bridge and blockhouse at Pigeon Roost Creek, which is between the third and fourth bridges along Richland Creek. One might expect that its number would be between 13 and 16. Additional confusion comes about because, in April 1865, the 46th Wisconsin Infantry had companies on the N&D at Blockhouse Numbers 37 and 38 and at Number 39 at Decatur Junction. That strongly suggests that the numbering system changed over time and that blockhouses were added near the end of the war and implies the presence of 36 houses in mid–1864.

The houses at Rutherford Creek are often referred to as Numbers 9 through 12. At Richland Creek the houses were often referred to as Numbers 13 through 16. However, if that is true and the numbering was sequential, there would have been no houses between the southernmost crossing of Rutherford Creek and the northernmost of Richland Creek. That does not make sense because literature refers to several houses in that area.

The blockhouses at the various crossings of Rutherford Creek are a good example of the confusion in numbering of the houses. The structure at bridge No. 1 is identified as house Number 9 by Jacob Sigmund and other literature but as stockade Number 7 on the Poe map. The house at the next bridge downstream is referred to as stockade Number 9 by Poe's map, house Number 10 by other literature and house Number 11 by Jacob Sigmund. The structure at bridge No. 4 is identified as stockade Number 11 on the Poe map, house Number 12 by other literature and house Number 13 by Jacob Sigmund.

There are other unresolved questions about the houses. For instance, the one at the northernmost crossing of Carter's Creek is often referred to as house Number 2. There is reference to a house at the West Harpeth River which should, therefore, have been Number 1. However, Spencer Creek probably had a blockhouse as well. This needs to be resolved.

Appendix C

More research is needed to determine how the houses were numbered and to more confidently determine the locations and number of blockhouses in Tennessee.

In the absence of a theory about the numbering system, the author presents the unproven theory that the houses might have been numbered in the order of their construction. The houses were being built at the same time that Boomer was constructing the Howe trusses. It is possible that the Federals made a priority of building the houses at the sites that were first receiving the new trusses. Harris, Culleoka and Gracey's were trestles that would not have required the Howe trusses. Spencer Creek, being north of Franklin, and Pigeon Roost Creek may not have gotten Howe trusses and thus been lower priority for houses. If that were the case and the work at the Duck were a higher priority than at Rutherford Creek, then West Harpeth could have had house Number 1, Carter's Creek had Numbers 2 through 6, Rutherford Creek had Numbers 9 through 12, Duck had Numbers 7 and 8 and Richland Creek had Numbers 13 through 16. Those numbers align fairly well with the blockhouse numbers that have been reported. The numbers for the houses at Tunnel Trestle and the Elk, as well as at the other "low priority" structures in Tennessee, could have been 17 through 25. By the time the 1st Michigan and Boomer got to Alabama, there may have been so few trusses left to install that the Alabama numbering system of 1 through 11 was left intact.

Rather than build off the inconsistent blockhouse numbering found in literature, the author created a system starting with "TN-1" in Table 3. The fifth column shows the type of fortification that seemed to be at each site in mid–1864 and indicates whether any blockhouses are thought to have been there. One take-away from the table is that it lists 37 bridges and trestles along the N&D (including Spencer Creek) at each of which the Federals seem to have had some form of protection—one or more blockhouse, a large stockade or a fort. The reason that Spencer Creek is thought to have had a blockhouse is that the 3rd Kentucky Cavalry was headquartered there in August 1862. They would not have been there if there had not been a bridge. The creek is large enough to warrant a bridge and, hence, a house. Also, there is reference to a blockhouse between Franklin and Nashville; it is very possible that this is the house at Spencer Creek. An argument against there being a house at that site is that house Number 6 was at Carter's Creek Bridge No. 5, which implies that there was only one house north of Carter's Creek and that might have been at the West Harpeth.[5]

In mid–1864, Boomer would have finished replacing many of the trestles with bridges. It is not known how many of the 37 structures at that time were bridges and how many were trestles. Perhaps there were 23 bridges and 14 trestles. Of the 37, one (Low Trestle on Swan Creek) seems not to have had a blockhouse, four seem not to have needed a blockhouse and four seem to have had two houses, so the estimated number of blockhouses is 36, with 25 in Tennessee and 11 in Alabama.

The goal of the analysis was not to justify the number of blockhouses at 36 but, rather, to start from scratch and make an educated estimation of the number of houses. In fact, for about two years during the writing of the book, the author's number was 37. That was reduced by one when he realized that there did not seem to have been a railroad-type blockhouse near the north end of the bridge and trestle at the Elk River. The final result of 36 is encouraging because it is the same number reported by Lt. Burroughs.

A goal of this book is to help the reader understand and appreciate the features of the old railroad and the events that occurred along it. Much about the 122 miles of track has changed. The wooden trestles have been replaced by fill and the wooden bridges, by steel. All of the blockhouses and original depots are gone. A great deal of the original cut and fill work is still apparent, though much of the embankment is higher than the original. Nearly all of today's track and embankment are in the original locations. The tunnel is, of course, still there.

For those who want to get out and see the locations of some of the former features, the crossings that are nearest a road are: (1) the Brown's Creek bridge site in Nashville; (2) the Harpeth River railroad bridge near the intersection of First Avenue South and South Margin Street in Franklin; (3) and (4) railroad bridges at Carter's Creek Bridges Nos. 1 and 5 that had blockhouses; (5) the railroad bridge at Rutherford Creek Bridge No. 4 that had a blockhouse; (6) and (7) the railroad embankments (that were trestles) at Harris and Gracey's that each had a blockhouse; (8), (9) and (10) the railroad embankments (that were trestles) at Culleoka, Tunnel Hill and Sulphur Creek that each had two blockhouses; (11) the Elk River Bridge that had a blockhouse; (12) the Swan Creek Bridge at Redus Hollow Road that had a blockhouse; (13) the bridge (now a covered bridge) at Mill Creek that had a blockhouse; and (14) the railroad bridge at Town Creek in Athens that had a blockhouse on the hill on the other side of the highway. Other interesting features are: (15) and (16) at Franklin, the Underpass Bridge just north of the Harpeth River and the stone abutments of the wagon bridge on First Ave. N; (17) the stone remains of the wagon bridge over Richland Creek near the intersection of S 3rd and W Cemetery Streets in Pulaski; and (18) the north end of the track at Delaney Road, just north of Athens.

Table 1. Dodge's Bridges and Trestles Built November 1863 through February 1864[6]

Dodge Bridge No.	Bridge Name	Length (feet)	Height (feet)
6	Carter's Trestle	225	32
7	Rutherford Creek, No. 1	120	19
8	Rutherford Creek, No. 2	208	19½
9	Rutherford Creek, No. 3	272	29
10	Rutherford Creek, No. 4	272	52
11	Duck River (2 spans Howe truss, 2-span trestle)	609	70
12	Harris trestle	198	30
13	Calleoka (Culleoka) trestle	1,008	39
14	Grace's (Gracey's) trestle	630	43
15	Robertson's trestle	112	17½
16	Richland Creek, trestle No. 1	192	27
17	Richland Creek, trestle No. 2	176	29
18	Richland Creek, trestle No. 3	168	32
19	Richland Creek, trestle No. 4	360	34½
20	Tunnel Hill trestle	720	39
21	Elk River Bridge trestle (rests on seven cribs)	615	36½
22	Mill Creek trestle	315	30

Dodge Bridge No.	Bridge Name	Length (feet)	Height (feet)
23	Sulphur Springs trestle	525	73
24	Athens trestle	96	7
25	Athens trestle	132	11
26	Athens trestle	72	11½
27	Swan Creek trestle	360	12
28	Swan Creek trestle	114	11
29	Swan Creek Swamp trestle	200	9
30	Junction trestle	240	15

Table 2. Wright's Bridges and Trestles Built After February 1864[7]

No.	Location	Height (feet)	Length (feet)	Remarks	Rebuilt (feet)
1	Brown's Creek	12	38	Not destroyed	—
2	Little Harpeth	14	74	—	—
3	Spencer's Creek	17	38	—	—
4	Big Harpeth	38	187	Rebuilt twice and partly rebuilt twice	454
5	West Harpeth	13	58	—	—
6	Near Spring Hill	12	53	—	—
7	Spring Creek	15	21	—	—
8	Carter's Creek, No. 1	18	112	Rebuilt twice and partly rebuilt twice	286
9	Carter's Creek, No. 2	21	184	Rebuilt twice and partly rebuilt twice	470
10	Carter's Creek, No. 3	20	94	Rebuilt twice and partly rebuilt twice	235
11	Carter's Creek, No. 4	20	94	Rebuilt twice and partly rebuilt once	228
12	Carter's Creek, No. 5	30	235	Rebuilt twice and partly rebuilt twice	587
13	Rutherford's Creek, No. 1	26	130	Rebuilt three times and partly rebuilt twice	455
14	Rutherford's Creek, No. 2	27	265	Rebuilt twice and partly rebuilt three times	723
15	Rutherford's Creek, No. 3	30	295	Rebuilt twice and partly rebuilt three times	811
16	Rutherford's Creek, No. 4	50	270	Rebuilt twice and partly rebuilt twice	676
17	Duck River	72	627	Rebuilt twice	1,254
18	Lytle's Creek	14	22	—	—

Appendix C

No.	Location	Height (feet)	Length (feet)	Remarks	Rebuilt (feet)
19	Hurricane Creek	14	22	—	—
20	Harris Trestle	29	232	—	—
21	Kalioka (Culleoka) Trestle	37	1,130	Rebuilt	1,130
22	Grace's (Gracey's) Trestle	42	637	Rebuilt	637
23	Robinson's (Robertson) Forks	18	126	Rebuilt	126
24	Richland Creek, No. 1	32	160	Rebuilt twice	320
25	Richland Creek, No. 2	37	180	Rebuilt twice	360
26	Richland Creek, No. 3	35	180	Rebuilt twice	360
27	Pigeon Roost Creek	12	50	Rebuilt	50
28	Richland Creek, No. 4	41	315	Rebuilt twice	630
29	Tunnel Trestle	38	822	Rebuilt	822
30	Elk River	40	625	Rebuilt three times	1,875
31	—	10	48	—	—
32	Mill Creek	30	330	Rebuilt	330
33	White Sulphur	71	570	Rebuilt	570
34	Mud Creek	5	62	Rebuilt	62
35	Mud Creek	9	102	Rebuilt	102
36	Athens Creek	10	134	Rebuilt	134
37	Athens Creek	11	64	Rebuilt	64
38	Swan Creek	11	340	Rebuilt	340
39	Swan Creek	11	129	Rebuilt	129
40	Black Creek	6	225	Rebuilt	225
41	Junction Trestle	16	275	Rebuilt	275
	Total		9,555	Total	14,720

Total bridging—9,555 feet

Amount rebuilt—14,720 feet

Total built by Government—24,275 feet, or 4 miles 3,155 feet

Appendix C

Table 3. Crossings and Fortifications on the N&D in Mid–1864

Location, Waterway, or Feature	Needed a Bridge, Trestle, or Culvert See Note 1	Dodge/Wright Structure Nos. See Note 2	Wright's Notes on Rebuilding from Feb. 1864 to Apr. 1865	Fortification Type in Mid-1864	Misc. See Note 3
Downtown Nashville				Fort Negley and three other fortifications	1900 L&N Union Station is still here. T&A had freight and passenger depots here
Brown's Creek (just N of Berry Road)	Bridge	Not on Dodge list/1	Not destroyed	No BH See Note 4	
Davidson/Williamson County line and Brentwood					Post was on hill in town. Brentwood RR Station was here
Little Harpeth River (Just N of Concord Road)	Bridge	Not on Dodge list/2		No BH Camp Brentwood (a stockade) was probably still here in 1864	
Concord Road					Owens Station was here
Moore's Lane					See Note 5
Spencer Creek (Baugh Branch on MapQuest; just S of Mack Hatcher Parkway)	Bridge	Not on Dodge list/3		BH TN-1 (*Author's list*)	One mile north of Fort Granger. See Note 6
Underpass just N of Liberty Creek; no waterway.	Small bridge. See Note 7			Was in the camp at Fort Granger	
Harpeth River in Franklin	Bridge	Not on Dodge list/4	Rebuilt twice and partly rebuilt twice. See Note 8	Fort Granger overlooked the bridge. No BH	The 1873 L&N freight depot is still here. See Note 9
A small creek at Collin's Farm	Stone culvert (not visible)				See Note 10

Appendix C

Saw Mill Creek (trib. of Harpeth, near Carnton)	Minor (had an 8 × 10 ft arch tunnel)				
W. Harpeth River (Just S of West Harpeth Road)	Bridge	Probably No. 1 but not on Dodge list/5		BH TN-2	West Harpeth Depot was here
TN 840					
Thompson's Station					Thompson's RR Station was here. Replica L&N depot built in 1993
Williamson/ Maury County line					
Spring Hill					Spring Hill RR Station was northwest of town on Depot Street
Two tribs. of McCutcheon Creek (on Beechcroft just SW of Depot Street). The 2 tribs are one-half mile apart.	Both tribs. have minor flow. Bridges were probably built after mid–1864	None/6 and None/7		No BHs	
Trib. of Carter's Creek	Minor				Carter's Creek Station was near here. See Note 11
Carter's Creek No. 1 (Just SW of the curve in today's Carter's Creek Pike)	Bridge	2/8	Rebuilt twice and partly rebuilt twice	BH TN-3 Near Redoubt No. 1	
Carter's Creek No. 2 (NW of the 90-degree turn in today's Frye Road)	Bridge	3/9	Rebuilt twice and partly rebuilt twice	BH TN-4	Smith's Station near here. See Note 12
Carter's Creek No. 3 (W of the 90-degree turn in today's Frye Road)	Bridge	4/10	Rebuilt twice and partly rebuilt twice	BH TN-5	Only about 1,200 feet between this bridge and bridge No. 4

Location, Waterway, or Feature	Needed a Bridge, Trestle, or Culvert See Note 1	Dodge/Wright Structure Nos. See Note 2	Wright's Notes on Rebuilding from Feb. 1864 to Apr. 1865	Fortification Type in Mid-1864	Misc. See Note 3
Carter's Creek No. 4 (Just SW of bridge No. 3)	Bridge	5/11	Rebuilt twice and partly rebuilt once	BH TN-6	
Dark's Mill Road					Dark's Mill Station and the mill were here
Carter's Creek No. 5 (Near the turn in today's Carter's Creek Pike)	Bridge	6/12	Rebuilt twice and partly rebuilt twice	BH TN-7	Near confluence of Carter's and Rutherford Creeks
Rutherford Creek No. 1	Bridge	7/13	Rebuilt three times and partly rebuilt twice	BH TN-8	Only about 1,000 feet between this bridge and bridge No. 2
Just above Rutherford Creek Bridge No. 2				Maybe a fort. See Note 13	
Rutherford Creek No. 2 (Just N of Theta Pike)	Bridge	8/14	Rebuilt twice and partly rebuilt three times.	BH TN-9	
Rutherford Creek No. 3 (Just S of Theta Pike)	Bridge	9/15	Rebuilt twice and partly rebuilt three times	BH TN-10	Near Ashton's Mill
Rutherford Creek No. 4 (just N of Rock Products Road)	Bridge	10/16	Rebuilt twice and partly rebuilt twice	BH TN-11	
Duck River	Bridge	11/17	Rebuilt twice. See Note 14	2 BHs. BHs TN-12, -13	Duck River Station was just north of here
Columbia				Fort Mizner on Mt. Parnassus. See Note 15	T&A ended and CS RR started here, except that T&A had a leg to Mount Pleasant. 1903 L&N depot is still here

Appendix C

Lytle Creek (Just S of Hwy 50)	Minor.	None/18 Culvert per O.M. Poe maps		
Goose Creek (Just N of Kinzer Lane)	Moderate flow. Large culvert			
Hurricane Creek at Glendale (bridge and embankment)	Borderline flow (Culvert in early 1864)	Not on Dodge list/19	Bridge built later with a BH. See Note 16	Hurricane RR Station was here. A small stockade was at Hurricane Switch at Glendale
Long Tom Branch (Just north of Glencoe Road)	Trestle. Minor flow, but a wide, low area	12/20 Harris Trestle	BH TN-14	See Note 17
Culleoka				Pleasant Grove Station was near here. See Note 18
Fountain Creek (On S side of Culleoka)	Trestle	13/21 Culleoka Trestle	Rebuilt once	BHs TN-15, -16 A stockade, 2 BHs and Fort Palmer
Trib. of South Fork Fountain Creek (just south of Graham Road)	Minor	See Note 19		
Trib. of South Fork Fountain Creek (Just N of Martin Hollow Road)	Minor	See Note 20		
Campbell's Station				
Trib. of South Fork Fountain Creek	Culvert per Poe			
Trib. of South Fork Fountain Creek (aka S Fork of Campbell's Station Branch; one and three-quarters miles, by road, south of Campbell's Station)	Trestle. Minor flow. Long and high	14/22 Gracey's Trestle	Rebuilt once	Across street from Evergreen Cemetery where Mr. Gracey is buried
Maury/Giles County line				

| | | | Bridge and BH probably built later | |

Appendix C

Location, Waterway, or Feature	Needed a Bridge, Trestle, or Culvert See Note 1	Dodge/Wright Structure Nos. See Note 2	Wright's Notes on Rebuilding from Feb. 1864 to Apr. 1865	Fortification Type in Mid-1864	Misc. See Note 3
Lynnville					L&N RR Station rebuilt in 1998 is still here. A turntable was here
Robertson Fork Creek (four-tenths mile SE of Lynnville)	Trestle	15/23 Robertson Trestle	Rebuilt once	No BH Per Poe, 80-foot by 80-foot stockade	
Buford Station					
Richland Creek No. 1 (between Buford Station Rd and Clear Creek Rd) See Note 22	Bridge	16/24	Rebuilt twice	BH TN-18 See Note 23	Near Buford Station
Reynolds' Station					
Richland Creek No. 2 (Just NW of Shady Lane Road; near Columbia Hwy and Walters Rd.)	Bridge	17/25	Rebuilt twice	BH TN-19	Reynolds' RR Station was about ½ mile N of the Richland Creek Bridge No. 2
Richland Creek No. 3 (SW of turn in Old Campbellsville Road)	Bridge	18/26	Rebuilt twice	BH TN-20 See Note 24.	
Wales					Wales RR Station
Pigeon Roost Creek (Just E of Wales) Enough flow for a bridge	Bridge	Bridge but no Dodge number/ 27	Rebuilt once	BH TN-21	
Pulaski				Fort Lilly	Pulaski L&N Station was here; demolished in 1969. See Note 25
Hwy 64					See Note 26

Richland Creek No. 4 (SW of Hwy 31 and 500 feet west of Prospect Rd)	Bridge	19/28	Rebuilt twice	BH TN-22 See Note 27	Richland Station (aka Rockland) was about two miles N of here. A very isolated site
Tunnel Trestle (at Petty Branch Road)	Trestle. No flow but steep and undulating	20/29	Rebuilt once	BHs TN-23, -24 2 BHs	Trestle passed over where short stone tunnel now is on Petty Branch Rd.
Tunnel					Tunnel through crest of Madry's Ridge
Prospect, TN					Prospect RR Station was here
Elk River (Just west of Veto Rd)	Bridge plus long approach trestle on south side	21/30	Rebuilt three times. See Note 28	BH TN-25 Probably 1 BH. See Note 29	
TN/AL State Line (Giles County, TN and Limestone County, AL)				Blockhouse numbering stops here for both TN and AL	CS RR ended and T&AC started here. State Line RR Station was near here
Trib. of Mill Creek at Redus Hollow Road	Bridge. Moderate flow. See Note 30	Bridge but no Dodge number/ 31		BH Number 11	Two miles into AL at the Park just east of the Elk River
Mill Creek	Bridge (aka "Holt's Trestle")	22/32	Rebuilt once	BH Number 10	One third mile S of the park
Elkmont, AL					1887 L&N Station has been renovated and is here. See Note 31
Sulphur Creek (1 mile S of Elkmont)	Trestle (Low flow; very wide, low area)	23/33 (Highest trestle on the N&D)	Rebuilt once	BH Numbers 8 and 9 2 large blockhouses. See Note 32	Hays Mill was about two miles S of Sulphur Creek and ¾ mile N of Wright No. 34

Appendix C

Location, Waterway, or Feature	Needed a Bridge, Trestle, or Culvert See Note 1	Dodge/Wright Structure Nos. See Note 2	Wright's Notes on Rebuilding from Feb. 1864 to Apr. 1865	Fortification Type in Mid-1864	Misc. See Note 3
Swan Creek (Either side of Huber Rd, east of Hays Mill Rd) Seems to have also been called Mud Creek.	Trestle ("Low Trestle") Swampy area. See Note 33	None/34. 5 feet high, the lowest trestle on the N&D.		Perhaps no BH.	This trestle would have been between 3,300 and 4,700 feet N of Wright No. 35
Swan Creek (just SE of Hays Mill at Elkmont Rd)	Trestle. See Note 33	24/35	Rebuilt once	BH Number 7	This site is four miles N of Athens
Athens				Fort Henderson	Restored 1928 L&N depot is here. See Note 34
Town Creek (in Athens, 1,000 feet N of Hwy 72)	Trestle	25/36	Rebuilt once	BH Number 6 (On hill just west of the bridge)	Athens RR Station still there. Track is now on a high embankment. Only about 1,200 feet north of the next crossing
Trib. of Town Creek which is a trib. of Swan Creek (Just SE of Hwy 72 at Jefferson St SE)	Trestle. Tiny flow now. See Note 35	26/37	Rebuilt once	BH Number 5	About ¼ mile south of the Town Creek blockhouse
Trib. of Old Schoolhouse Branch of Swan Creek (Swampy area one third mile S of Roy Long Rd)	Trestle	27/38	Rebuilt once	BH Number 4	McDonald's Station and Tanner were between Old Schoolhouse and Spring Creeks
Spring Creek (Just N of Nuclear Plant Rd)	Minor flow. Probably a culvert	See Note 36			

Appendix C

Spring Creek (just south of the Spring Creek crossing above)	Minor			
Trib. of Tennessee River (just SW of Stewart Rd at Ingram Road)	Minor flow. Swampy			Foote's Station was near here
Swan Creek (large flow)	Trestle	28/39	Rebuilt once	BH Number 3
Pryor Creek, a trib. of the Tennessee River. See Note 37	Trestle. Swampy; moderate flow	29/40	Rebuilt once	BH Number 2
Trib. of Pryor Creek	Minor flow			Hobbs Station was near here
Swampy area at the N corner of Decatur Junction	Trestle (aka Junction Trestle)	30/41	Rebuilt once	BH Number 1
Decatur Junction. See Note 38	Minor			T&AC ended here where it met the M&C. Junction Station was here
Lake in swampy area. See Note 39	Trestle (on the M&C, not N&D)			See Note 40
Tennessee River (Limestone and Morgan County line)	See Note 41			There was a depot on the north side of the river
Decatur				Earthworks with Forts Nos. 1 and 2	Renovated 1905 L&N RR Depot is here

Notes to Table 3

1. "Minor" in the second column means there does not seem to be enough flow at this site to require a bridge or trestle.
2. Bridge numbers from two reports. Gen. Dodge's report of rebuilt bridges, February 1864; bridge Nos. 1–5 were not included his report. Also from Wright's report of April 24, 1866, of bridges built between February 1864 and the end of the war.
3. Railroad stations are as of March 1864.
4. Nashville's forts were probably adequate protection, similar to the situation on the N&C.
5. Mallory Station was on present-day Mallory Station Road. It was a siding for farmers to load, not a depot. There was a nearby pond that supplied water to the locomotives.
6. Troops were stationed here in August 1862. There should have been a blockhouse here, though there is not specific reference to one.
7. Though there may have been others, this is the only listed bridge at an underpass. Bridge now has cut stone abutments and steel girders. In the 1860s, it would have been lower and of timber.
8. Harpeth River Bridge seems to have been rebuilt or had a major repair eight or nine times during the war.
9. The Franklin passenger depot was just north of the freight depot.
10. 300 feet SE of the crossing of Lewisburg Pike, at a very high embankment. The low area is very limited in length, so track was probably originally built on fill, not a trestle.
11. Carter's Creek Station was about one-third mile N of here on Cleburne Road, just N of Butler Road.
12. There were two blockhouses and a 150-foot railroad bridge at Smith's Station. These could be Carters Creek Bridge No. 2 and Blockhouses Numbers 2 and 3 which would have been only about 2,000 feet apart. Smith's Station was not in use in 1864, but nearby Carter's Station was.
13. This was probably the "fort" at Rutherford Creek. Poe's maps show "Stockade No. 8" at this location that may be the "fort."
14. Duck River Bridge had two spans with Howe trusses plus trestles on both ends. It seems to have been rebuilt or had a major repair 11 or 12 times during the war.
15. Mt. Parnassus is on the NW side of Columbia. That site now has water tanks.
16. Borderline flow; it is not obvious to the author that a bridge or trestle was required. A culvert was originally built here. There was a damaged culvert at this site in January 1863 and probably still a culvert in early 1864. Blockhouse built later would have been octagonal. At some time, there was a small stockade at Glendale with 25 to 50 men.
17. Trestle was named for nearby resident Henry Harris.
18. Culleoka was approximately the point where open, cultivated country was to the north and hilly, forested country to the south.
19. The original grade would probably have been much lower. There is a very long, fairly high embankment (at least 420 by 35 feet). A trestle could have been justified here.
20. This site needed a long, low embankment. Not high enough for a trestle.
21. Named for nearby resident J.B. Gracey. Cut stone culvert which replaced the trestle is still present. The Tennessee Division of Archeology documented the earthworks footprint of a square blockhouse. This long trestle may have needed two houses, but musket range was probably 300 to 600 feet, so one could have sufficed. This stretch between Columbia and Pulaski does not seem to have been attacked in September through December 1864, so the last blockhouse here would probably have been square, not octagonal.
22. Near confluence of Richland and Robertson Fork Creeks, across from current Milky Way Farm.
23. Richland Creek blockhouses were known as Numbers 13 through 16.
24. Probably on western corner of intersection.
25. Fort Lilly, a Union earthwork on Fort Hill on the northern edge of town, protected the garrison. Wagon bridge crossed during Hood's retreat is near intersection of South 3rd and West Cemetery Streets.
26. End of the track is just north of Hwy 64. Hick's Cut (now collapsed) is just N of Hwy 64.
27. House was at NE corner of crossing.
28. Elk River Bridge seems to have been rebuilt or had a major repair eight or nine times during the war.
29. Probably one blockhouse on the south side of the Elk, plus two forts on the north side. One fort would have been the "Elk River fort" which may have been the large blockhouse with some earthwork on the hill just west of the Elk River railroad bridge.
30. Not on Dodge's list, so most likely a bridge that was there that Dodge did not have to rebuild. Trestle per Poe and Wright.
31. The depot is a Senior Citizens Center.
32. The site also had a fort. Typo in the Official Records says blockhouse Numbers 7 and 8.
33. Bridge No. 35 is known to have had a blockhouse. Bridge Nos. 34 and 35 were on what was sometimes called "Mud Creek" during the war. This is perhaps because Mud Creek is a major tributary of the Swan, though to the east of the N&D.
34. The rail now stops just north of Athens at Piney Chapel Road.

35. Flow may be less now because of development.
36. Dodge reported that Spring Creek was "out" in November 1863. Probably had a culvert at that time.
37. The relocated section of the N&D is here. Original crossing of Pryor Creek was about one mile NW of intersection of Hwy 31 and Hammons Road, well away from the current crossing. Though it was not a tributary of Swan Creek, Dodge called it Swan Creek Swamp Trestle. Wright called it Black Creek. The Civil War crossing was northeast of the current crossing. The old T&AC diverged in a curve from the existing track 0.7 mile south of the large Swan Creek, ran to the southeast, curved again, tied into the north end of Sandy Road and ran south (paralleling the existing track) to Decatur Junction. Some of this old route is still visible in aerial views. The existing L&N track is shorter and straighter than the original T&AC track.
38. Decatur Junction was in a partially swampy field, which is now the Swan Creek Wildlife Management Area just NW of the Decatur Day Use Park and the intersection of Hwys. 31 and 72.
39. Was called Swan Lake which is now submerged by the Tennessee River and is under the railroad bridge. Per Poe maps, a ferry was there.
40. A blockhouse was here but it was not on the N&D and would not have been included in Lt. March's reported 11 houses or in Lt. Burroughs' 36 houses.
41. Bridge was on the M&C. It had been burned and not yet rebuilt in mid–1864.

Appendix D
Troops Protecting the Railroad

The following entries are far from complete but indicate the large number of regiments that guarded the railroad and the frequency with which they were reassigned.

February through August 1862: Company A, 78th Pennsylvania Infantry was protecting the railroad at Carter's Creek and then Columbia. Company B was at the West Harpeth and then Columbia from March through June. Company C was at Franklin and then Columbia from March through June. Company E was at Rutherford Creek in March and April. Company F was at Franklin and then Columbia from March through August. Company H was at Columbia in July and August. Company K was at Rutherford Creek in March and April, Columbia in May and June, and the Elk River in July and August.

March 1862: the 38th Indiana Infantry was stationed at Camp Meriweather (not certain of its location) one mile from Franklin.

March 22, 1862: the 79th Pennsylvania Volunteers was being reassigned as follows: Headquarters and three companies to the Harpeth River near Franklin, one company at the Little Harpeth, one at the West Harpeth, three at Carter's Creek and two to Rutherford Creek. From the 7th Pennsylvania Cavalry, four companies were to report as follows: a sergeant, corporal and eight men to join the infantry at the Little Harpeth River, a lieutenant and 39 men to join the three companies of infantry at Carter's Creek and a lieutenant and 20 men to join the two companies of infantry at Rutherford Creek. Also, Col. Price and his 21st Kentucky Volunteers were to report to Duck River.

March through June 1862: Col. Lewis D. Campbell and the 69th Ohio Volunteer Infantry were along the N&D. In April, Companies D and H were near Franklin, A and E at Rutherford Creek, B at the Little Harpeth, F, I and K at Carter's Creek and G at the West Harpeth. In May, C, D and H were at Franklin, A and E at Rutherford Creek, B at the Little Harpeth, F and I at four bridges on Carter's Creek, G at the West Harpeth and K at the Duck River. In June, E and G were at Carter's Creek, A and I at Franklin and the remainder at Nashville.

April 1862: the 18th Ohio Infantry and the 4th Ohio Cavalry patrolled the countryside and guarded the N&D and the M&C from Athens to the Limestone Railroad Bridge between Decatur and Huntsville.

June 30, 1862: Col. Marcellus Mundy of the 23rd Kentucky Infantry, stationed at Pulaski, was ordered to send two companies from Pulaski to Reynolds and two to the Elk River. Cross-dresser private Marian McKenzie, with the military name of Henry Fitzallen, was a member of that regiment for a brief time.[1]

July 1862: The 1st Kentucky Cavalry had two companies at the bridges between Franklin and Columbia and one company at the Duck.

Appendix D

July 8, 1862: Brig. Gen. James Negley assigned companies of the 78th Pennsylvania to Reynolds' Station, Lynnville and Culleoka. The 7th Pennsylvania Cavalry was to have one company at Franklin.

Early July 1862: the 19th Illinois was relieved by Turchin's Eighth Brigade and was to guard the railroad from Nashville through Decatur to Huntsville. The regiments were commanded by Gen. Mitchel and would relieve guards now on the lines, except at Huntsville, Decatur, Athens, the Elk River, Pulaski, Reynolds, Columbia and Nashville. The 5th Kentucky Cavalry at Columbia was to proceed immediately to Murfreesboro. Also, the 35th Indiana was relieved from, and the 78th Pennsylvania Infantry, 1st Kentucky Cavalry and 4th Indiana Battery were assigned to, the Seventh Brigade. Headquarters, two regiments of infantry, two sections of artillery and five squadrons of cavalry were assigned to Athens. A third regiment of infantry, one section of artillery and one squadron of cavalry were to be posted on the north side of the river at Decatur. The 78th Pennsylvania was to send two companies to Columbia, four to the Elk River, two to Pulaski and two to Reynolds. The last two were to join the two at Pulaski as soon as the railroad was repaired, and guards were posted at the bridges. A few days later, Major Fry rescinded that order and ordered Gen. William Negley to have the 78th Pennsylvania post two companies at Franklin, four at Columbia, two at Pulaski, two at the Elk River and two on the north side of the Tennessee River.[2]

Mid–July 1862: after the Union suffered significant losses in McMinnville, Gen. Buell sent Gen. Nelson and his division from Athens, up the railroad to Nashville and down the N&C to Murfreesboro to guard the rails and minimize further damages. Also, Major Fry reported that the 1st Wisconsin Infantry and 38th Indiana would soon arrive in Athens. On the seventeenth, Fry told Brig. Gen. Mahlon D. Manson, commander of a brigade in the Army of the Ohio and camped near Athens, that Buell had ordered him to send a brigade under Col. William B. Hazen to help rebuild the railroad up to Reynolds. He needed four regiments to be posted as follows: one at the Elk, one on the north end of the tunnel, one at Butterworth on the south side of Richland Creek and one at two-and-a-half miles south of Reynolds' Station on the north side of Richland Creek.[3]

July 31, 1862: Fry ordered the 74th Ohio Infantry at Nashville to guard the bridges and build stockades between Nashville and Columbia to protect the bridges and guard the important points. Five companies from the 74th Ohio were to go to Franklin to guard the bridges in that area. Their headquarters were in Franklin under the command of Col. Granville Moody, where Company C was stationed. Also, two companies of the 78th Pennsylvania were to go to the bridge at the Elk and two to Pulaski. It was critical that the remainder of the 78th guard any point requiring it between Reynolds' Station and Columbia.

Early August 1862: four companies of the 3rd Kentucky Cavalry were ordered from Athens to Pulaski. The 74th Ohio was posted as follows: one platoon at Brown's Creek, one platoon at the Little Harpeth River, one at Spencer Creek (headquarters of the regiment), two companies at the Harpeth River near Franklin, one platoon at the West Harpeth River, three companies at Carter's Creek (to be posted midway between Carter's Creek Bridge Nos. 1–5, with guards at East Bridge), two companies on Rutherford Creek (to guard the four bridges and to be stationed midway between Bridge Numbers 1 and 4) and one company at the Duck River (with one platoon stationed at the east side). Also, the 78th Pennsylvania Volunteers were to be stationed as follows: three companies at Columbia, one on the south end of the Duck River railroad bridge and the two just relieved by the 74th Ohio are to march to Columbia. Wolford's cavalry was to report to Reynolds' Station except that one of his companies was to report to Columbia.[4] Note—In July and August 1862, the stockades were built along the N&D. Prior to that, the railroad had been protected by camps.

September 1862: the 74th Ohio Infantry, headquartered in Franklin, was guarding the N&D between Nashville and Columbia. Note—the absence of references to federal guards being on the railroad from October 1862 through February 1863 seems to indicate that the bridges and trestles along a portion of the N&D had been damaged by the Confederates in the fall of 1862 and that the Federals did not repair them when they returned late that fall; so, there were no bridges and trestles to guard and the railroad was not in operation during those five or so months.

March 3, 1863: Company A, 92nd Illinois Infantry, took a train on the N&D from Nashville to Franklin. 92nd Companies B, D, F, G, H, I and K and 96th Companies A, B, C, D, F, G, H, I and K were in Franklin in March and April guarding the N&D. They fought Van Dorn on March 10.

March 27, 1863: Company C, 96th Illinois Infantry, marched from Franklin to Brentwood to construct earthworks to protect the N&D track and bridge.

May through August 1863: the 14th Michigan Infantry was headquartered in Brentwood and guarding the N&D between Nashville and Franklin. In late June 1863, the 2nd Michigan Cavalry was guarding the railroad between Nashville and Columbia. Note—The lack of guards south of Franklin from March through part of the summer of 1863 reflects the control that Van Dorn and the Confederates had of the railroad from Spring Hill to the south.

By October 1863: the 39th Iowa had several companies at Reynolds' Station, including two guarding the railroad and three operating the two gristmills, grinding flour and meal.

November 1863: the 18th Missouri Infantry was at Culleoka, except for Company B which was three miles to the north, C at Prospect, F at Lynnville and H at Gracey's Trestle. In December, they were still at Culleoka, except for B at Harris Trestle, C at Prospect, F at Lynnville and H at Gracey's.

November 11, 1863: Col. M.M. Bane, commander of 51st Illinois Infantry, Third Brigade, Second Division, Sixteenth Army Corps, was to move on the twelfth with his brigade to or near Reynolds' Station or Buford Station and camp in positions to best protect the local railroad bridges (some of which were then under repair), guard the railroad from Wales to Lynnville and put the railroad back into running order. Also, Dodge ordered Col. J.W. Fuller, brigade commander, to take his 27th Ohio Infantry on the N&D to camp at Prospect. They were to guard the railroad from the Elk River to Athens and repair that section of the railroad, including the Elk River Bridge.

November 12, 1863: the 81st Ohio Infantry arrived at Pulaski and were still there in February. Company A, under First Lt. David S. Van Pelt, was ordered to Wales to guard the railroad and protect bridges; they were still there in February. As of November 27, Companies B, E, F, G and K had been stationed at Sam's Mills, Tennessee (six miles northeast of Pulaski) under Maj. Frank Evans, running the grist and flour mills to furnish flour and lumber for Dodge's command. It seems that those companies were still there in early March 1864.[5]

November 1863 through at least February 1864: Company A, 14th Michigan Infantry, was stationed at Fort Granger doing garrison duty and guarding the N&D.

December 1863: The N&D was guarded by two brigades under Brig. Gen. Robert S. Granger (Union Commander of the District of Alabama), one under Brig. Gen. Starkweather in Pulaski and the other under Col. Sipes of the 7th Pennsylvania Cavalry in Columbia.

January 19, 1864: Brig. Gen. Thomas W. Sweeny, Commander Second Division, was instructed that: he send a company from Pulaski to relieve the 39th Iowa at Richland Creek near Reynolds' Station; the 39th Iowa will relieve the 18th Missouri, establish headquarters at Culleoka and guard the bridges now guarded by the 18th Missouri; the company of the 39th Iowa at Morris' Mills and the company guarding the bridge north of Reynolds' Station will remain; and the 18th Missouri will be posted at Pulaski.[6]

January 21, 1864: Dodge's headquarters and some of his companies from the 39th Iowa Infantry moved north from Reynolds' Station to Culleoka. Two companies were placed to protect the railroad bridges.

Appendix D

January 26, 1864: the 39th Iowa Infantry joined the regiment at Culleoka doing garrison duty and working on fortifications which consisted of a large stockade and rifle pits, both of which were to protect the long trestle.

January 27, 1864: the 18th Missouri was at Reynolds' Station guarding the bridge over Richland Creek and was to join their regiment at Pulaski as soon as possible.

February 29, 1864: Company G of the 39th Iowa returned to Culleoka. They had been constructing stockades and earthworks in January.

March 1864: The Union sent surplus troops from Maj. Gen. Thomas via the N&D to relieve Gen. Douglas' troops between Columbia and Decatur.

Early March 1864: Companies G and K, 81st Ohio Volunteer Infantry, were at Sam's Mills (six miles northeast of Pulaski), D at Gracey's Trestle, B, E and F at Nance's Mills, Tennessee (near Cornersville) and H and I at Culleoka. On March 12, Companies A, C, D, G, H and I under Lt. Col. Robert Newton Adams went from Pulaski to Lynnville to relieve the Third Brigade which had been guarding the railroad. They built a formidable stockade at Lynnville. One company was to go to the N&D bridge above Reynolds' Station to relieve Capt. Dykeman's 39th Iowa Infantry Volunteers and the larger force was to go to Culleoka.[7]

March 14, 1864: Dodge ordered Col. Dewey, 3rd Alabama Colored Troops (later named the 111th USCT), to guard the bridge between Athens and the low trestle and to patrol the railroad daily from a point halfway to Athens to another point mid-way between the Elk River and the trestle south of the state line.

March 16, 1864: Dodge ordered the 50th Illinois to proceed to and camp at Decatur Junction in relief of Gen. Stevenson's troops.

March 20, 1864: Dodge telegraphed Lt. Col. James L. Donaldson, Chief Quartermaster of the Department of the Cumberland, to move the 64th Illinois by the earliest possible train from Nashville to Decatur.

March 30, 1864: Dodge ordered Gen. Kenner Garrard, Commander, Second Cavalry Division, Army of the Cumberland, to Columbia and Lynnville, relieving Gen. Sweeny who was to report to Athens. Garrard was to occupy the country and guard the railroad in that area. Note—The movement of troops increasingly to the south between November 1863 and March 1864 reflects the presence of Gen. Dodge's trestles that needed protection.

March and April 1864: 1st Michigan Companies A, F, G and H were at blockhouses along the N&D and Companies E, I, L and M at Bridgeport near the M&C and N&C. Company A was at Columbia in March and April, E at Bridgeport from November 1863 through June 1864, F at Brownsboro, Alabama (near Huntsville), seemingly for at least part of March and April, G at Athens in March and April, H at Rutherford Creek in March and April, I and L at Bridgeport from November 1863 through April 1864 and M at Bridgeport in April.

April 1864: The 9th Ohio Cavalry (dismounted) went to Pulaski for guard duty.

April 18, 1864: the 81st Ohio Infantry was relieved by the 7th Pennsylvania Cavalry and moved to Pulaski.

May 13, 1864: Dodge told Sherman that the railroad was in great danger and that his troops were along the railroad holding it from Lynnville to Athens.

Late May 1864: Jacob Sigmund, First Lt., Company E, 7th Pennsylvania Cavalry, was at Lynnville for a week. On June 1, he left the bridge at Buford Station to take charge of his company of 139 men. Twenty-three were mounted, armed with Spencer carbines and doing scout and other duties, 34 were doing guard duty at Gracey's trestle and 11 were unarmed and in the band. The majority, about 70, were cripples and convalescents and without weapons. They departed on about August 1, taking rail cars to Columbia. On the third, he received orders to take 48 men up the rail to Blockhouse Numbers 9 and 10 to relieve the 2nd Michigan Cavalry, who were to report to Franklin. His headquarters was at house Number 10. Sgt. S.B. Darrah and house Number 13 were about three-quarters of a mile away. Corp. Wasson was only about 150 yards away, on the opposite side of Rutherford Creek at house Number 11.[8]

May and June 1864: the 15th Pennsylvania Cavalry was in Nashville guarding trains passing through the city. The 9th Indiana Cavalry was stationed at Pulaski.

May until at least August 1864: several companies of the 10th Indiana Cavalry and the 79th Indiana Infantry were stationed at Pulaski guarding the railroad and bridges. The 10th then moved to Decatur through about October.

June 1864: Company C, 106th USCT was stationed at Athens guarding the trestles on the N&D. In July and August, they were garrisoning house Numbers 4 and 5 near Athens. Note—the presence of troops all along the N&D from March through June 1864, when the 1st Michigan was building blockhouses to replace stockades, reflects the Federals' desire to better protect Dodge's existing trestles and Boomer's new bridges.

July and August 1864: the 2nd Michigan Cavalry was guarding the N&D from Nashville to Rutherford Creek. They were at Franklin, except Company A was near Brentwood, B, G, K and M were near Carter's Creek, C was at Carter's Creek, E was at the West Harpeth and F, H and L were at Nashville.

August 13, 1864: Company E, 9th Indiana Cavalry took positions at house Numbers 15 and 16 on Richland Creek and also at the Lynnville stockade. That stockade protected the rail station and eliminated the need for a blockhouse at Robertson Fork Creek trestle which was a few hundred yards to the southwest.

September 1864 through February 1865: Companies A through H and K, 75th Pennsylvania Infantry were stationed at Franklin, the West Harpeth River and Brentwood.

September 4, 1864: Wheeler's cavalry attacked the rail just south of Lynnville Station where the 9th Indiana Cavalry was guarding the crossing at Robertson Fork Creek.

September and early October 1864: Alabama Blockhouse Numbers 2 (at Pryor Creek), 3 (at Swan Creek) and 4 (at a tributary of Old Schoolhouse Branch) were garrisoned by a total of about 100 men from the 111th USCT under the command of Capt. James Henry. House Number 5 (a mile south of Athens at a tributary of Town Creek) was garrisoned by 40 to 50 men of the 106th USCT under First Sgt. H.C. Weaver. Number 6 (on the west side of the trestle across Town Creek) was garrisoned by Capt. A. Poe and 40 men of the 106th USCT. Number 7 (at Swan Creek about four miles north of Athens) was garrisoned by 25 men from Company K of the 111th USCT under Lt. J.J. Phifer. At Sulphur Creek Trestle, the fort, redoubt and house Numbers 8 and 9 were defended by: about 470 men from the 110th and 111th USCT, who also manned the blockhouses, Eli Lilly and the 196 men from the 9th Indiana Cavalry, 300 from the 3rd Tennessee Cavalry and perhaps some troops from other regiments. In Tennessee, the house at Richland Creek Bridge No. 4 was defended by Col. Hillery J. Walker and 45 men of his 111th USCT. The 9th Indiana Cavalry was guarding blockhouses north of Pulaski. Second Lt. E.F. Nixon, Company E, 7th Pennsylvania Cavalry was in charge of house Numbers 3, 4 and 5 on Carter's Creek.

September 27, 1864: Although many men in the 175th Ohio were being pulled back to the north, those who had been manning the four blockhouses at Rutherford Creek remained there (they had replaced the 7th Pennsylvania). Forrest made a nominal attack on them but did not take the houses or any prisoners there.

October 1864: the 175th Ohio Infantry was garrisoning Blockhouse Numbers 9 through 12 along Rutherford Creek. Captain William P. Wolf was in command of those houses and was set up in house Number 11.

Appendix D 217

October 9, 1864: the 7th Pennsylvania Cavalry and 4th Michigan Cavalry had 450 men stationed at blockhouses along the N&D. Company E, 7th Pennsylvania Cavalry had been at house Number 10 since about August. By about early November, they had been relieved by the 175th Ohio Infantry.[9]

October 11, 1864: the 175th Ohio Infantry was headquartered in Columbia and defending blockhouses on the railroad between Franklin and Pulaski. Two companies were posted at house Numbers 13 and 14 (crossings No. 1 and 2 at Richland Creek) and Companies B and D were sent to house Numbers 15 and 16, respectively.

October 17, 1864: troops of the 175th Ohio rode the N&D from Nashville to Columbia to garrison the town and guard the bridges and trestles north and south of Columbia.[10]

October 19, 1864: troops of Company D, 9th Indiana Cavalry were relieved of duty at house Numbers 13 and 14. They were taken by rail to Nashville and replaced several days later by men of Companies E and G, 175th Ohio at house Numbers 13 and 14, respectively. This conflicts with the October 11 date above.

October 22, 1864: Gen. Granger reported to Maj. Gen. Thomas the stationing of his troops. In Decatur: 102nd Ohio Infantry, eight companies of 10th Indiana Cavalry, 2nd Tennessee Cavalry, Battery A of 1st Tennessee Artillery, Battery F of 1st Ohio Light Artillery and Battery D of 2nd Illinois Artillery. This was a total of 1,745. At Athens and in blockhouses in Huntsville: 73rd Indiana Infantry and one company of the same regiment at Triana (about 20 miles upstream the Tennessee River from Decatur). That total was 360. At Pulaski: four companies of 10th Indiana Cavalry and detachments of the 106th, 110th and 111th U.S. Colored Infantry (three companies total). At Columbia and from Gracey's Trestle to Thompson's Station: a detachment of First Brigade, Second Cavalry Division, totaling 997 men; a detachment of Second Brigade, Second Cavalry Division, 558 men; and a detachment of Third Brigade, Second Cavalry Division, 682 men.

October 23, 1864: Granger, headquartered at Decatur, had the 73rd Indiana Infantry, 13th Wisconsin Veteran Volunteer Infantry and parts of the 11th, 12th and 13th Indiana Cavalry on the railroad from Athens to Stevenson, and about 1,800 men at Decatur. The 29th Michigan Infantry had been ordered to report to Decatur for duty and Granger took every available man from Huntsville to help in Decatur.

October 29, 1864: Col. Sipes, 7th Pennsylvania Volunteer Cavalry, in Columbia had about 1,300 cavalrymen garrisoning the town and occupying numerous blockhouses along the railroad. Some of those men departed for Nashville that day.

October 31, 1864: the 175th Ohio Infantry was guarding the railroad between Franklin and Pulaski. They were there when Hood attacked and captured three blockhouses.

By late October 1864: several hundred men of the 175th Ohio were based in Columbia and had exclusive garrison responsibility for the N&D. Troops from Company A were sent to guard Harris trestle, about 54 from I to Culleoka, K to Gracey's and F to the Lynnville stockade (replacing the 9th Indiana Cavalry).[11]

By mid–November 1864: the 175th Ohio manned at least eight blockhouses north of Columbia. On November 19, some of the troops from Company C were stationed at house Number 5 which had recently been rebuilt after Forrest's raid.

November 20, 1864: the 22nd Indiana Battery was to go by rail on the twenty-first to Columbia to report to Ruger.

November 24, 1864: Company D, 175th Ohio Volunteer Regiment, stationed at house Number 16 south of Pulaski, found themselves in the path of Hood's advance and were captured. They may have been the first captured in Hood's march. That same day, troops of Companies B and E at house Number 15, just north of Pulaski, were captured. On November 25, Company G at house Number 14, near Reynolds' Station, was captured. Troops from Company E at house Number 13 escaped.[12]

November 30, 1864: 20 men of Company E, 75th Pennsylvania were captured by Hood at the West Harpeth River blockhouse.

November and December 1864: Companies A through I and K, 111th Ohio Infantry were stationed at Columbia. Ruger's division would be headed north toward Spring Hill on November 29, and some from the 111th Ohio were ordered to stay behind to guard the railroad bridge over the Duck River and the nearby fords until nightfall. By 3 p.m. on the twenty-ninth, those troops were the only force between the Confederates and house Numbers 9 through 12 at Rutherford Creek. Those houses were under the command of Capt. W.P. Wolf, Company G, 175th Ohio Infantry who was set up at house Number 11.[13]

December 1864 through March 1865: The 75th Indiana Infantry Regiment, Company C, was stationed at Franklin doing provost duty and guarding the T&A. They were under the command of Lt. Col. Alvin Von Matzdorff.

December 24, 1864: 400 men of the 175th Ohio were ordered back to Columbia to retake the town and occupy the blockhouses (or their former sites if burned) between Columbia and Franklin. They continued this duty until June 1865. They were the only unit still in the area that had earlier manned the blockhouses on the N&D. Men from Company H occupied house Number 12 and Company G was to take Number 11, which had been burned by the Federals in November, rebuilt by the Federals and not burned by Hood on his way south.

December 27, 1864: the 47th Missouri Infantry was planning to go by rail the next day to Columbia, then march to be stationed in Pulaski. The 48th Missouri was to do the same on the twenty-ninth. Another Missouri regiment would go soon.

January 17, 1865: Thomas ordered that Granger reoccupy Athens, Sulphur Creek Trestle and the stations between the Elk River and Decatur. With all of the blockhouses burned, the garrisons were to be much larger than before until the houses (probably octagonal) were rebuilt. With a shortage of men, Granger requested 1,500 infantry and 500 cavalry for Decatur, an officer and 30 men for each of the four blockhouses between Decatur and Athens, 150 infantry and 150 cavalry for Athens, 150 infantry and 20 cavalry for Sulphur Creek Trestle, and an officer and 30 men for each of the three blockhouses between Sulphur Creek Trestle and the Elk River.

January and February 1865: the 106th USCT was stationed at Athens.

April 1865: the 46th Wisconsin Infantry was stationed at Athens, except that Company D was at Mill Creek Trestle, G was at blockhouse Number 39 at Decatur Junction on the T&A (from mid–February until the end of April), H was at Mud Trestle on the T&A, I was at Sulphur Creek Trestle (end of April through the end of June) and K was at blockhouse Numbers 37 and 38 on the T&A.[14]

March through June 1865: Company D, 111th USCT was at Pulaski and the 61st Illinois Infantry Volunteers were guarding the N&D between Nashville and Columbia with headquarters in Franklin. All companies of the 61st were in Franklin, except for the following. In March, Company B was at "stockade" Number 1, H was at stockade Number 2 and K at stockades Numbers 3, 4 and 5. In April, C and I were at Fort Granger, B was still at stockade Number 1, H still at stockade Number 2 and K still at Spring Hill at Numbers 3, 4 and 5. In May, B was still at Number 1, C and I still at Fort Granger, H still at Number 2 and K still at Numbers 3, 4 and 5. In June, B was at Numbers 10 and 11, C still at Fort Granger, H at Number 2 and Spring Hill and K at Numbers 3 through 9. Note—these "stockades" were actually blockhouses.

May and June 1865: the 61st Illinois was headquartered in Franklin and guarding the entire length of the N&D.

June 19, 1865: Thomas declared that there was no longer a great need to strongly guard the N&D, so the 175th Ohio was relieved. The blockhouses were then manned by a small number of troops to mainly guard against burning by Confederate-leaning citizens.

Appendix E
The Southern Claims Commission

From 1871 to 1873, the Southern Claims Commission received and evaluated numerous claims from residents in Tennessee, Alabama and other states who claimed to have had property taken by Union forces during the war, but without compensation. The claim process was very thorough. The claimants had to answer 80 standard questions and bring a number of witnesses to vouch that they had been sympathetic to the Union. Some of the typical and more interesting claims made by residents in the five counties through which the N&D ran, plus Morgan County and Decatur, are presented below.[1]

Morgan County, Alabama

Lewis Hobart claimed $4,324 for property taken in Decatur during the war. He was from Quincy, Massachusetts, and had lived for many years in Decatur. Before the war, he had worked at removing houses, farming and working on the railroad. While Gen. Dodge was stationed in Decatur in March 1864, nearly all the citizens of Decatur were ordered to leave. Hobart left his belongings and horses to the Union Army. He said Dodge gave residents a choice of moving north or south, and he relocated north to Franklin. Federal troops took down his two-story house, two stables, carriage house, work/blacksmith shop, brick smoke house and four small houses for their brick and lumber, hauling them off in wagons. Some of the materials were used for fortifications and some to build "shanties" for the soldiers. They also took 27 hogs, 7,620 rails, 12,000 feet of plank and some sawed timber they planned to use on blockhouses. There was testimony both for and against his being a Union man, therefore his award was only $882.

Limestone County, Alabama

Charles E. Tucker was a self-described poor farmer who lived a mile southeast of Athens on his 80-acre property. Twenty acres were cultivated, and the rest was timber. That was not the best place to live during the war, as numerous regiments marched back and forth through Athens and near his home. Mr. Tucker is a good example of the way many locals were treated during the conflict. On January 24, 1873, he made a claim for damages that was partially approved. He reported that he had lost 700 pounds of beef, 3,000 rails, planking, 70 cords of wood, flour, corn, potatoes, fruit, two cattle and a donkey. It just so happens that Mr. Tucker was a house carpenter who worked during the war for a contractor, getting out cross ties for the N&D. Born in 1808, he had lived in Athens since 1838, was 53 years old when the war started and was never in the military service. Mr. Tucker was not happy when federal Col. Jessie Phillips took wood for fires and for building quarters for his men. Col. Campbell of the 110th USCT and Col. Cummins of the 39th Iowa came to forage. Campbell took planking to place on the ground to run his cannon to and from portholes. Turchin and 15 men came to Mr. Tucker's farm. Though Tucker told them he was very poor and needed what he had to care for himself and his family, it didn't matter. They spent an hour there, killed two cattle and hauled them away on mules and took rails to build stock lots, loading it out on wagons. In February 1864, some of Gen. Dodge's men took timber for fuel. On January 1, 1865, while chasing Hood out of Tennessee, Gen. Wilson took Mr. Tucker's prize mule because one of his men was afoot. Of his $887 claim, $647 was allowed.

Emily Frazier (Fraser) was a "colored" woman. She stated that she had lost four hogs, two mules and a horse. Before the war, she had been enslaved to William Richardson, a lawyer in Athens who died in 1866. She was allowed to accumulate property in her own right and did so. She raised hogs and had a mule and a horse when the Federals came to Limestone County in 1863. They took the hogs and when they left the area, they stole the other animals. She obtained an order from Col. Campbell to pursue the men to Decatur to get her animals back. Ms. Frazier tried but was unable to do so. The horse was taken by a cavalryman when Col. Wade retreated from Athens after the arrival of Hood; Wade had come in after Forrest captured Campbell's men. The man promised to return it to her but did not. Ms. Frazier was industrious, baking cakes and pies and selling them to the Union troops, doing wash and running wagons. After the war, she had a house and lot, two milk cows, two horses, two oxen and hogs, all in her name. Ms. Frazier claimed $526 and received $40. She received no money for the horse because it was not used for military purposes. It is not clear why she was paid nothing for the mules.

Giles County, Tennessee

Anna Bright and Fannie Bramlett filed a claim for the loss of many thousands of pounds of hay, 70 sheep, 4,250 pounds of pork, beef, bacon, potatoes, corn, firewood, six mules and two mares. They had a 1,000-acre farm four miles north of Pulaski, almost all of which was cultivated. Fannie's husband had died before the war, leaving Fannie a married daughter and three young daughters, including Anna, who had since married. All but the married daughter were heirs. On May 6 and 11, 1862, Forage Master White, by order of G.M. Williams of the 23rd Kentucky Infantry, stole the first lot of hay and corn. From May 17 through July 26, 1862, Quartermaster Williams, encamped at Pulaski, took hay, corn and firewood (mostly hay) on 16 different dates. Also on July 26, the 17th Kentucky Cavalry took hay, as did the 1st Kentucky Cavalry on July 31. A mule was taken by the 5th Tennessee Cavalry on July 26, 1863, and another by the 18th Missouri Mounted Infantry on December 12, 1863. The remaining mares and mules were taken on September 15, 1863, by Col. Eli Long of the Second Division, U.S. Cavalry. Fodder was taken by the 81st on November 13, 1863. It was determined that the women were sympathetic to the Union. Their claim filed in May 1872 in the amount of $3,018 was approved for $2,554.

Hannah Harville was a poor widow whose husband had died in 1859, leaving her with 10 children. She could neither read nor write and rented the farm she was working. It was on Hurricane Creek in western Giles County. The farm had several lots, one of which was 12 acres. She claimed that corn, pork and hay were taken. Her Confederate-leaning neighbors called her children "little Yankee devils." She saw Gen. John T. Croxton's men take her goods. They stayed in the area for three days and then left for Pulaski. On September 12, 1864, Alexander Marshall signed, as Captain Battery G, First Brigade, First Division Cavalry, that his men had taken from her 700 pounds of shelled corn. She also had a receipt of that same date from H.W. Walker, Forage Master, 2nd Michigan Cavalry for his taking of 45 bushels of corn. Ms. Harville was found to be loyal to the Union. $375 of her claim in the amount of $403 was paid.

Maury County, Tennessee

Elizabeth T. Pillow lived on 360 acres near Columbia. Her husband, William Pillow, died as a prisoner of war to the Confederates on December 23, 1864. Numerous witnesses testified on her and her husband's behalf, including Gen. William Negley who had written that her husband was a fine Union man. Mr. Pillow had been a prominent Union man who was consulted by local Union officials. He was arrested and taken prisoner by Hood's command. Gen. Schofield was encamped about a mile from her farm. She lost 2,000 bushels of corn, 7,000 bundles of oats, 4,000 bundles of fodder, 8,600 feet and 2,600 foot-inches of lumber, 1,900 feet of siding, 16 hogs and 2,500 pounds of pork. Much of the lumber and siding came from a dwelling, smoke house and stable that were dismantled, the materials being used to build living quarters. Her goods were taken by Schofield's command between November 20 and December 24, 1864, moved to the east bank of the Duck River and used by the Fourth, Sixteenth and Twenty-third Army Corps. From her claim in the amount of $3,249, the award was reduced to $2,324 because her requested amount was determined to be high. Then came the determination of loyalty. She had nine children, including one daughter who had died years before and two sons who joined the Confederate Army. With the aid of Federals, those two sons were removed from service and seemingly sent north as prisoners of war. It was decided that there were 10 shares, two for her and one each for the eight living children. With those two sons not loyal to the Union, her award was reduced by an additional two-tenths. It was determined that she and her husband were loyal to the Union, and she received $1,859.

Rosanna Bolton lived in Columbia and was a Union supporter. She had lost three horses, two in July 1864 and the other that December. Her husband had been in the Confederate Army for 15 months but deserted and died in June 1864. After his death, she bought the first two horses that were used to haul wood for the railroad that was run by the government. While it seemed that those two were taken for use by the Union, it was not clear that the Union had used the third even though it had been taken by a federal soldier. She filed a claim in the amount of $450 and received $240.

Williamson County, Tennessee

Lewis Hobart, who had moved from Decatur to Franklin, filed another claim stating that he lost two mules there. He said that on November 30, 1864, the day of the Battle of Franklin, the Union Army took from him all they could use and destroyed what they could not take. Mr. Hobart claimed that soldiers in an artillery battery camped near his stable took his mules early on the night of the thirtieth because there was a shortage of animals to pull wagons and artillery. While in Franklin, he hauled supplies for the U.S. Government. He said that Confederates had taken oats and corn from him, calling him "a damned Yankee." After the Battle of Franklin, he treated a number of wounded Union soldiers and built bridges under quartermaster William G. LeDuc, including a bridge over the Harpeth River for the government that allowed Union soldiers to cross and chase Hood. On December 20, after Hood had retreated south of Franklin, he was working on a bridge when he saw a wagon train returning from the front and heading for Nashville. The train was under the command of LeDuc. He saw his mules in a team and demanded them back but was refused, being told he could follow them to Nashville and get them there. However, he was in charge of a work force of 150 men and could not go. Hobart sent a man to Nashville who returned with nothing. One of Hobart's witnesses was Edward Wells, a conductor for the N&D. Mr. Wells confirmed that Mr. Hobart's stable was near or on the battlefield and said he had seen the mules in LeDuc's train. In this case, he was determined to be a Union man and was awarded $250 of his $350 claim.

James Crockett had 310 acres four miles south of Brentwood, only a quarter mile from a Union camp. When he made his claim on January 8, 1872, he was 80 years old and had lived on the property since about 1822. He claimed that the Union Army, mostly Rosecrans command, had taken 450 barrels of corn and large quantities of hay, fodder and bacon in late 1862 and early 1863. Also, two horses had been taken by Gen. Stanley's men. His witnesses included G.M.C. and Nelson Mallory, James P. Moore and an enslaved man, George Crockett. He was found to be loyal to the Union. His claim of $2,572 was approved for $1,066. Separately, he was awarded $1,375 for eight horses and two mules that had been taken by Gen. Hatch's command on December 1, 1864.

Catherine W. Crockett filed a claim on April 12, 1872, for losses at her farm three-and-a-half miles south of Brentwood on Wilson Turnpike. At that time, she was 76 years old and had lived on her property for 50 years. She had been confined to her home during the war, said she was loyal to the Union and had several witnesses speak on her behalf. In December 1862, Rousseau's men, who were camped near her farm, had taken corn, hay, fodder, oats, 7,000 rails and two mules. In February 1863, Steedman's men, also camped nearby, took corn, hay, 9,000 rails, 5,000 feet of plank and a horse. Later, one of her horses was taken to Mizner of the 14th Michigan Infantry in Franklin. The plank was to be used for tent floors and then as fuel for fires. The rails were to be burned to warm the soldiers. On December 4, 1863, Edwin Paschall wrote to Gen. Granger on her behalf that Rousseau and Steedman had taken nearly all of her fences and that she feared the cutting of nearby timber which would leave her unable to rebuild the fences. On December 19, Granger replied that he would protect not only the timber, but all of her property. Her claim in the amount of $2,965 was approved for $1,752.

Charles Primm had been blind for many years and owned a 75-acre farm near Nolensville. He claimed that he had lost two horses, 500 bushels of corn, 5,000 bundles of fodder, 1,800 pounds of pork, 65 bushels of potatoes, and another four horses and a mule. In December 1862, foragers took all but two horses. Those two seem to have been taken by Croxton's Cavalry in the fall of 1864 when Gen. Thomas was retreating to Nashville. Mr. Primm was determined be loyal to the Union. However, the Commission thought there was so much military activity near his farm that the horses could have been taken by the Confederates. Therefore, they did not pay for the horses which, at $750, was about half of his claimed amount. Of his $1,695 claim, $570 was awarded.

Davidson County, Tennessee

On May 10, 1871, Cynthia H. (Mrs. Aaron V.) Brown filed a claim. She was the widow of Aaron V. Brown, the Postmaster General in Washington, D.C., who had died in 1859. Mrs. Brown lived south of Nashville in her place "Melrose" which was near the present-day Woodlawn Cemetery. She had a plantation near Helena, Arkansas, of which 500 acres were cultivated, 400 of that in corn. The Federals took 30 cattle, 10,400 pounds of fresh pork, 22,500 pounds of bacon, 25 mules, 16,000 bushels of corn and 32,000 pounds of fodder. Some of the cattle were shot, skinned and taken off in wagons while others were driven away. Most of it was taken on July 15, 1862, by order of Gen. Curtis. The corn was taken in the fall of that year. She was wealthy and claimed to be a supporter of the Union. Mrs. Brown said she opened her house to Union officers the day their Army reached Nashville on February 20, 1862. She claimed that her home was a social headquarters for federal officers and that she fed thousands of U.S. soldiers. Gens. Buell, Rosecrans and Thomas gave her safeguards and passes and allowed her to keep guns and ammunition while all those around her were seized. President Johnson, Governor Brownlow and Generals Rosecrans, Mitchel, Wood, Granger and others were entertained at her home. She allowed Gen. Smith's Illinois regiment to move from a low, damp location to camp on her dry lawn, thus saving much sickness. She had many witnesses testify on her behalf, including Mr. J.B. Pillow of Columbia, and some to testify against her regarding her loyalty to the Union. On December 15, 1879, a Special Commission of the Claims Commission was convened at the Commercial Hotel in Nashville to review her case. Following the hearings, it was determined that her award would be a reduced amount because four men of position in Nashville claimed that she had sympathized with the Confederates. The only Confederate known to have entered her house was Gen. Hood near the end of the war, presumably in December 1864. With Hood below Nashville, the Confederate main lines south of her and Hood's pickets north of her, she let Hood take fence rails and a barn for firewood because the men were poorly clothed, shod and sheltered. It seems that these actions did not help her case. Of her $9,967 claim, she was awarded $1,869. Equal amounts were claimed by and awarded to her husband's heirs.

John McGavock claimed that the Union Army had taken 6,000 cedar rails, 6,000 oak rails, 2,500 feet of plank, corn, 5,000 bundles of oats, five tons of hay, sugar, molasses, 1,200 pounds of flour, 10 head of cattle, three mules, two horses, a mare, fencing and timber on 37 acres of land. He also asked for $300 rent for the Union's use of his house as a hospital and use of his barns and stables, and for damages to his house and furniture. He stated that Gen. Mitchel had ordered Col. Cahill to take cattle and timber and that much of his goods were taken by and for Illinois and Indiana regiments. He reduced his initial claim from $12,604 to $10,964 and was awarded $3,507. The documentation does not state where his land was and does not give details about how the final award was determined, other than that he was found to be "a noted Rebel."

Appendix F
The 1901 Franklin, Tennessee, L&N Passenger Depot

It is not clear when the Tennessee and Alabama Railroad (T&A) built the first railroad passenger depot in Franklin. One source indicates that the first such depot was built in 1854–55 in preparation for the opening of the railroad and a better one constructed in the 1870s. The original depot was probably burned and rebuilt at least once during the Civil War. Several maps of the Battle of Franklin in November 1864 show a passenger depot near the freight depot. It is not clear how many passenger depots were there before the Louisville and Nashville Railroad (L&N) built theirs in 1901.

A T&A freight depot was probably built at Franklin when the railroad was new. Col. Scott may have burned it in February 1862. With the Union controlling the railroad later in February, they would have wanted freight depots along the track and built them in Franklin, then in Columbia and other places. Those military depots would have been built not for the convenience of the T&A but for the armies. The one in Franklin seems to have been on the north side of the Harpeth River near Fort Granger. It was probably built about a year before the fort. It appears that Forrest burned that Union freight depot on June 3, 1863, and that the Federals rebuilt it by June 10. That building may have stood for the remainder of the war. A map showing that depot has not been found. On December 17, 1864, Gen. S.D. Lee partially burned a depot as the Confederates passed south through Franklin. That depot would have been on the south side of the Harpeth River and was probably a T&A freight depot that is no longer standing. It is not clear how many T&A freight depots were there before the present one was built. After the war, a more modern freight depot was constructed, almost certainly the one that is there now. A newspaper article of September 27, 1873, reported that the L&N had erected a warehouse and reconstructed the depot houses in Franklin.

The Civil War–era passenger depot was located just east of the intersection of present-day First Avenue South and South Margin Street in downtown Franklin. It was about 150 feet north of, and on the same side of the tracks as, the existing freight depot. In 1901, it was "moved back" and a new one constructed by the L&N on the same site. Its footprint size (using the building's maximum dimensions) was approximately 75 feet parallel to the tracks by approximately 37 feet perpendicular to the tracks. Presumably, the old depot was moved back to keep it operational during construction of the new building and so the new one could be built on the same site relative to the freight building and tracks. That depot opened on November 26, 1901, and was demolished in about 1959.

The building floor plan is shown in the following drawing. The structure was wood

Appendix F

1901 L&N Railroad Passenger Depot, Franklin, Tennessee (Williamson County Historical Society).

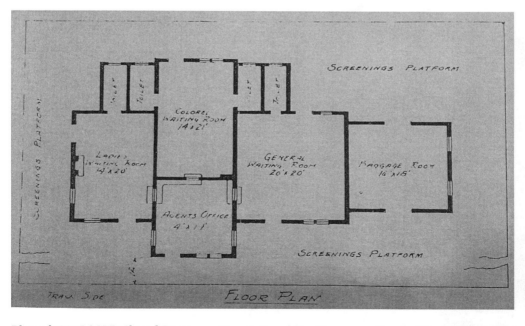

Plan of 1901 L&N Railroad Passenger Depot, Franklin, Tennessee (Louisville and Nashville Railroad Company Records, University Archives and Records Center, University of Louisville, Louisville, Kentucky).

frame with weather boarding and a slate roof. Its interior usable area was approximately 1,900 square feet. Features included an agent's office, general waiting room with toilet, ladies' waiting room with toilet, colored waiting room with two toilets, two coal fireplaces and chimneys, a baggage room and a large screenings (crushed rock) platform. Around the entire structure, except for a portion of the northwest side, there was an overhanging roof larger than the building footprint.

A new version of the depot would be a wonderful asset and attraction for Franklin. If the original site is developed for commercial use, it would be good for the City of Franklin Board of Mayor and Aldermen to encourage the developer to incorporate a "passenger depot" into their plans. Although the original location is the ideal place for a rebuilt structure, it could be situated at another site near the tracks.

There are numerous potential uses for the building. Rather than being a museum or strictly a renovated depot, it might better serve as a community meeting venue, visitor's center or office space. Depending on how it is used, this project could support tourism, be a source of revenue and increase the sense of community. The building could be outfitted with railroad memorabilia to tell the stories of the 1901 depot and earlier passenger depots, the role they and the original freight depot played in the Civil War, the L&N Railroad and the Franklin-Nashville Interurban.

There is a resurgence of interest in the big steam locomotive, with several currently in operation and more restorations planned or underway. Perhaps one of them could periodically come through Franklin or be here for the ribbon cutting.

Chapter Notes

Chapter 2

1. James B. Jones, "Study Unit No. 4, Early Railroad Development in Tennessee, 1820s–1865" (Nashville: Tennessee Historical Commission).

2. "American Railroad Journal" (New York: D.K. Minor, 1832), January 14, 1860, p. 24; Jones, "Study Unit No. 4."

3. Segment of a map of the N&D showing the location of Decatur Junction; credited to Orlando M. Poe. Stack 330, Record Group 77, Records of the Office of the Chief of Engineers Series: Civil Works Map File. National Archives and Records Administration; College Park, MD.

4. Robert Huhn Jones, *Disrupted Decades: The Civil War and Reconstruction Years.* Cartography by Bernhard H. Wagner (New York: Scribner, 1973).

5. Douglas H. Galuszka, *Logistics in Warfare: The Significance of Logistics in the Army of the Cumberland During the Tullahoma and Chickamauga Campaigns* (San Francisco: Pickle Partners, 2015).

6. Walter T. Durham, *Nashville, The Occupied City: 1862–1863* (Knoxville: University of Tennessee Press, 2008); Signage at Fort Negley, Nashville, Tennessee; Frank Harrison Smith, *Frank H. Smith's History of Maury County, Tennessee* (1969).

7. Durham, *Nashville, The Occupied City.*

8. Ibid.; Eva Swantner, *Military Railroads During the Civil War* (Alexandria, VA: Society of American Military Engineers, 1929); United States, Robert N. Scott, H. M. Lazelle, George B. Davis, Leslie J. Perry, Joseph W. Kirkley, and Frederick Crayton Ainsworth, *Official Records of the Union and Confederate Armies 1861–1865* (Washington, D.C.: National Archives, National Archives and Records Service, General Services Administration, 1959), Series 1, Volume 7, p. 429; John Miller M'Kee, "The Evacuation of Nashville," *Nashville Banner*, June 14, 1904, p. 45; Gen. Rice A. Pierce, "Gray Chieftain Tells How Forrest's Men Kept Wizard from Leading in Last Fight," *Nashville Tennessean*, July 16, 1934, p. 2.

9. Durham, *Nashville, The Occupied City*; Douglas Anderson, "Nashville Felt Real Panic as Exaggerated Rumors of Fort Donelson Fall Spread," *Nashville Banner*, January 4, 11 and 18, 1931.

10. Ezra Stearns Papers, James S. Schoff Civil War Collection, William L. Clements Library, University of Michigan, Ann Arbor, MI.

11. OR, Series 1, Volume 32, part 3, p. 279; OR, Series 1, Volume 32, part 3, p. 311.

12. Swantner, *Military Railroads*; Lt. Col. Irby W. Bryan, *Civil War Railroads: A Revolution in Mobility* (Carlisle Barracks, PA: U.S. Army War College, 2001); OR, Series 3, Volume 2, p. 795; OR, Series 3, Volume 4, part 2, p. 883.

13. Swantner, *Military Railroads.*

14. Lenette Taylor, *The Supply for Tomorrow Must Not Fail: The Civil War of Captain Simon Perkins, Jr., Union Quartermaster* (2014).

15. Swantner, *Military Railroads*; "Records Relating to the U.S. Military Railroads," 43, No. 2 (National Archives, Summer 2011); Stewart H. Holbrook, *The Story of American Railroads* (New York: Dover, 2016).

16. "Records Relating to the U.S. Military Railroads"; OR, Series 1, Volume 52, part 1, p. 228.

17. United States, D.C. McCallum, and James B. Fry, *Reports of Bvt. Brig. Gen. D.C. McCallum: Director and General Manager of the Military Railroads of the United States, and [of James B. Fry] the Provost Marshall General; in Two Parts* (Washington, D.C.: G.P.O., 1866); U.S. House of Representatives, "Affairs of the Southern Railroads" (1867); Christopher R. Gabel, *Railroad Generalship: Foundations of Civil War Strategy* (Fort Leavenworth, KS: U.S. Army Command and General Staff College, 2014).

18. OR, Series 3, Volume 5, p. 982.

19. Swantner, *Military Railroads*; Bryan, *Civil War Railroads.*

20. OR, Series 3, Volume 5, p. 1000.

21. OR, Series 3, Volume 5, p. 1001.

Chapter 3

1. Robert Dunnavant, *The Railroad War: N.B. Forrest's 1864 Raid Through Northern Alabama and Middle Tennessee* (Athens, AL: Pea Ridge Press, 1994); Dunnavant, *The Railroad War.*

2. OR, Series 3, Volume 5, p. 537.

3. Mark Hoffman, *My Brave Mechanics: The First Michigan Engineers and Their Civil War* (Detroit: Wayne State University Press, 2007).

4. Albert Baxter, *History of the City of Grand*

Rapids, Michigan: With an Appendix—History of Lowell, Michigan (New York: Munsell & Company, 1891), 586.

5. Charles R. Sligh, *History of the Services of the First Regiment Michigan Engineers and Mechanics, During the Civil War, 1861–1865* (Ann Arbor: University Microfilms International—Books on Demand, 1989).

6. Daniel F. O'Connell, "Union and Confederate Engineer Operations in the Civil War," *Essential Civil War Curriculum*. Internet.

7. Hoffman, *My Brave Mechanics*; Galuszka, *Logistics in Warfare*; O'Connell, "Union and Confederate Engineer Operations"; "1st Michigan Engineers and Mechanics," *Military Images* 22, no. 5 (2001), 19; Sligh, *History of the Services of the First Regiment*.

8. Galuszka, *Logistics in Warfare*.

9. "1st Michigan Engineers and Mechanics," *Military Images*; Sligh, *History of the Services of the First Regiment*.

10. Sligh, *History of the Services of the First Regiment*.

11. Hoffman, *My Brave Mechanics*.

12. Dunnavant, *The Railroad War*.

13. Taylor, *The Supply for Tomorrow*.

14. Smith, *History of Maury County*; Park Marshall, "Bridges of Franklin," *The Review-Appeal*, January 3, 1929.

15. John Beatty, *Citizen Soldier: An Account of the American Civil War by a Union Infantry Officer of Ohio Volunteers Who Became a Brigadier General* (Gardners Books, 2007); John Knox and B. E. Breedlove, *A History of Morgan County, Alabama: Surname Index* (Decatur, AL: Morgan County Board of Revenue, 1966).

16. Thomas Hubbard Hobbs and Faye Acton Axford, *The Journals of Thomas Hubbard Hobbs: A Contemporary Record of an Aristocrat from Athens, Alabama Written between 1840, When the Diarist Was Fourteen Years Old, and 1862, When He Died* (Tuscaloosa University of Alabama Press, 1976); Robert Parham, "The Court Martial of Colonel John B. Turchin: The Sack of Athens, Alabama, May 2, 1862" (Decatur, AL); Friends of the Archives. "Athens, Limestone County, 1861–1865" (Athens, AL).

17. Parham, "The Court Martial"; Robert Henry Walker, *History of Limestone County, Alabama* (Athens, AL: Limestone County Commission and Robert Henry Walker, Jr., 1973), 107–116.

18. Charlotte S. Fulton, "Holding the Fort, A History of Trinity School in Athens, Alabama, 1865–1870" (Athens, AL).

19. Parham, "The Court Martial"; Walker, *History of Limestone County*.

20. Beatty, *Citizen Soldier*.

21. Ira S. Owens, *Greene County Soldiers in the Late War: Being a History of the Seventy-Fourth O.V.I....* (Bethesda, MD: University Publications of America, 1993); Diary of John H. McPherson, Co. C, 74th Regiment, OVI, Filson Historical Society, Louisville, KY.

22. Faye Acton Axford, *"To Lochaber Na Mair": Southerners View the Civil War* (Athens, AL: Athens Publishing Co., 1987), 141; OR, Series 1, Vol. 16, Part I, p. 603.

23. Hoffman, *My Brave Mechanics*.

24. OR, Series 1, Volume 16, part 1, p. 325; OR, Series 1, Volume 16, part 2, p. 37; OR, Series 1, Volume 16, part 2, p. 38.

25. Ezra Stearns Papers.

26. Hoffman, *My Brave Mechanics*; OR, Series 1, Volume 16, part 2, p. 117.

27. Smith, *History of Maury County*; OR, Series 1, Volume 16, part 2, p. 233; OR, Series 1, Volume 16, part 2, p. 110.

28. Hoffman, *My Brave Mechanics*; OR, Series 1, Volume 16, part 1, p. 248.

Chapter 4

1. W. E. Merrill, "Block-houses for Railroad Defense in the Department of the Cumberland," *Sketches of War History 1861–1865, Papers Read before the Ohio Commandery of the Military Order of the Loyal Legion*, Volume 3, 1890.

2. Owens, *Greene County Soldiers in the Late War*; Diary of John H. McPherson.

3. OR, Series 1, Volume 16, part 2, p. 194.

4. OR, Series 1, Volume 16, part 2, p. 198.

5. Bob Duncan, "Defending the Indefensible," *Columbia Herald*, date not known; OR, Series 1, Volume 16, part 2, p. 192.

6. Dunnavant, *The Railroad War*.

7. OR, Series 1, Volume 3, part 1, p. 260.

8. Park Marshall, "Bridges of Franklin," *Journal of the Williamson County Historical Society* (Franklin, TN: WCHS, 1997), vol. 28, p. 107.

9. Signage at Fort Negley, Nashville, Tennessee.

10. OR, Series 1, Volume 23, part 1, p. 26; OR, Series 1, Volume 23, part 1, p. 10.

11. Hoffman, *My Brave Mechanics*.

12. *Ibid.*

13. OR, Series 1, Volume 23, part 2, p. 732.

14. John R. Scales, *The Battles and Campaigns of Confederate General Nathan Bedford Forrest, 1861–1865* (2017); Editors Mobile Advertiser and Register, no title, *Mobile Advertiser and Register*, June 25, 1863, p 2; OR, Series 1, Volume 30, part 4, p. 713; OR, Series 1, Volume 32, part 2, p. 647.

15. Historical marker at Fort Granger, Franklin, Tennessee.

16. Galuszka, *Logistics in Warfare*; Phillip M. Thienel, *Mr. Lincoln's Bridge Builders: The Right Hand of American Genius* (Shippensburg, PA: White Mane Books, 2000).

17. Scales, *The Battles and Campaigns*; Thomas Jordan, J.P. Pryor, and Ezra J. Warner, *The Campaigns of Lieut.-Gen. N.B. Forrest, and of Forrest's Cavalry, with Portraits, Maps, and Illustrations* (Dayton, OH: Morningside House, 1995); "92nd Mounted Illinois Infantry Regiment History," The Illinois Civil War Project, Internet; Charles A. Partridge, *History of the Ninety-Sixth Regiment*,

Illinois Volunteer Infantry (La Crosse, WI: Brookhaven Press, 2005).

18. Scales, *The Battles and Campaigns*; Jordan, Pryor and Warner, *The Campaigns*.

19. Scales, *The Battles and Campaigns*; OR, Series 1, Volume 23, part 1, p. 188; OR, Series 2, Volume 5, p. 493; Ryan Powers, "The Life and Times of Worshipful Brother Elisha Bourne Basset" (2011,) Internet; OR, Series 1, Volume 23, part 1, p. 105.

20. Scales, *The Battles and Campaigns*; OR, Series 1, Volume 23, part 1, p. 222.

21. Scales, *The Battles and Campaigns*; Jordan, Pryor and Warner, *The Campaigns*.

22. Smith, *History of Maury County*; Rick Warwick, "The Civil War as Seen through the Female Experience," *Journal of the Williamson County Historical Society* (Franklin, TN: WCHS, 2008), 128; "Hanged as Spies," *Nashville Banner*, December 18, 1884, p. 2; Col. George C. Porter, "Execution as Spies of Two Confederate Officers, Col. Orton Williams and Lieut. Walter Peter," *Nashville Banner*, February 24, 1912, p. 38.

23. Quartermaster Simon Perkins Collection, Summit County Historical Society of Akron, Ohio, Special Collections Division of the Akron-Summit County Public Library.

24. Quartermaster Simon Perkins Collection.

25. Ralcon Wagner, Nashville, Tennessee; personal communications.

26. OR, Series 1, Volume 30, part 2, p. 223.

Chapter 5

1. Walter W. Pyper, *Grenville Mellen Dodge and 19th Century America: Growing Pains of a Man and a Nation* (Princeton: Pyper, 1960).

2. OR, Series 1, Volume 31, part 3, p. 38.

3. Ulysses S. Grant and John Y. Simon, *The Papers of Ulysses S. Grant. Vol. 9* (Carbondale: Southern Illinois University Press, 1982).

4. W.H. Chamberlin, *History of the Eighty-First Regiment Ohio Infantry Volunteers, During the War of the Rebellion* (Whitefish, MT: Kessinger, 2007); Dunnavant, *The Railroad War*.

5. Mabel Baxter Pittard, "The Coleman Scouts," *Rutherford County Historical Society Publication No. 13* (Murfreesboro, TN, 1979).

6. Grenville M. Dodge. Dodge Papers, Council Bluffs Public Library, Special Collections; Pyper, *Grenville Mellen Dodge*; Holmes W. Kendall, "Sam Davis Death," *The Tennessean*, February 7, 1926, p. 8; David Meagher of Giles County, Tennessee; personal communications.

7. OR, Series 1, Volume 31, part 3, pp. 119–121.

8. OR, Series 1, Volume 31, part 3, p. 169.

9. Dodge Papers, Council Bluffs Public Library; OR, Series 1, Volume 31, part 3, p. 161; OR, Series 1, Volume 31, part 3, p. 120.

10. OR, Series 1, Volume 31, part 3, p. 325; Grant and Simon, *The Papers of Ulysses S. Grant. Vol. 9.*

11. OR, Series 1, Volume 30, part 3, p. 279. OR, Series 1, Volume 39, p. 153; OR, Series 1, Volume 30, part 3, p. 279.

12. Dodge Papers, Council Bluffs Public Library.

13. *Ibid.*

14. *Ibid.*

15. Keith F. Davis and George N. Barnard, *George N. Barnard, Photographer of Sherman's Campaign* (Kansas City: Hallmark Cards, 1990); James A. Hoobler Photo Collection, Tennessee State Library and Archives. Box 6, Folder 12; Photo No. 165-C-989.jpg, Bridge at Harpeth River, National Archives and Records Administration; College Park, MD; Photo No. 165-C-991.jpg, Bridge at Rutherford Creek No. 4, National Archives and Records Administration; College Park, MD; Photo No. 165-C-987.jpg, Bridge at the Duck River, National Archives and Records Administration; College Park, MD.

16. Dodge Papers, Council Bluffs Public Library; Letters Received by the Commission Branch of the Adjutant General's Office. 1863–1870. Roll 252, 1866, D2—D182, National Archives Microfilm Publication M1064.

17. Dodge Papers, Council Bluffs Public Library; OR, Series 1, Volume 31, part 3, p. 220; Grant and Simon, *The Papers of Ulysses S. Grant. Vol. 9.*

18. Dodge Papers, Council Bluffs Public Library; OR, Series 1, Volume 31, part 3, p. 325; OR, Series 1, Volume 32, part 2, p. 111; OR, Series 1, Volume 31, part 2, p. 367; OR, Series 1, Volume 31, part 3, p. 286.

19. Letters Received by the Commission Branch.

20. OR, Series 1, Volume 32, part 2, p. 451.

21. Dodge Papers, Council Bluffs Public Library; Photo No. 165-C-992.jpg, Trestle at Culleoka, National Archives and Records Administration; College Park, MD.

22. James A. Hoobler; Dunnavant, *The Railroad War*.

23. Dunnavant, *The Railroad War*; OR, Supplement, Part 2, Series 33, p. 105.

24. Dodge papers, Council Bluffs Public Library; Friends of the Archives, *Athens, Limestone County, 1861–1865* (Athens, Alabama).

25. Dodge papers, Council Bluffs Public Library.

26. *Ibid.*

27. OR, Series 3, Volume 5, p. 988.

28. Dodge Papers, Council Bluffs Public Library; OR, Series 1, Volume 32, part 3, p. 151.

29. Dodge Papers, Council Bluffs Public Library; J. R. Perkins, *Trails, Rails, and War: The Life of General G.M. Dodge* (New York: Arno Press, 1981); Robert Dunnavant, *Decatur, Alabama: Yankee Foothold in Dixie, 1861–1865* (Athens, AL: Pea Ridge Press, 1995); Letters Received by the Commission Branch.

30. Dunnavant, *The Railroad War*; OR, Series 3, Volume 5, p. 984; OR, Series 3, Volume 5, p. 985.

31. Dodge Papers, Council Bluffs Public Library; OR, Series 3, Volume 4, part 2, p. 965.
32. OR, Series 3, Volume 4, part 2, p. 883.

Chapter 6

1. Kimberly A. Chase, *In Their Own Words: The Abernathy (Eason, Rivers, and Tarpley) Slaves of Giles County, Tennessee* (2014).
2. Tina Jones, "From Slaves to Soldiers and Beyond—Williamson County Tennessee's African American History," Franklin, Tennessee. Internet.
3. OR, Supplement, Part 2, Series 77, p. 190; Tina Jones, "From Slaves to Soldiers."
4. Tina Jones, "From Slaves to Soldiers."
5. L. Thomas, Adjutant General, "Camp for Contrabands," *Nashville Daily Union*, February 11, 1864, p. 1.
6. Historical Marker at Fort Granger, Franklin, Tennessee; "Samuel Boyd Map of Franklin, Tennessee, April 10, 1863," from Tina Jones, Franklin, Tennessee; Kelly Fisk Hamlin, Giles County, Tennessee, personal communications.
7. Margaret E. Wagner, Gary W. Gallagher, and Paul Finkelman, eds., *The Library of Congress Civil War Desk Reference* (New York: Simon & Schuster, 2009).
8. David Meagher and Amy Murrell Taylor, *Embattled Freedom: Journeys Through the Civil Wars Slave Refugee Camps* (Chapel Hill: University of North Carolina Press, 2020).
9. Ibid.
10. *Ibid*.
11. Kelly Fisk Hamlin, Pulaski, Tennessee, personal communications; David Meagher, Giles County, Tennessee. Notes from Samuel H. Stout, head of Gen. Bragg's Medical Corps.
12. David Meagher.
13. "Sixth Annual Report of the Board of Directors of the Central Southern Railroad Company to the Stockholders, 1861," from Hathi Trust Digital Library; David Meagher.

Chapter 7

1. Swantner, *Military Railroads*; HQ Military Division of the Mississippi, "General Orders No. 6," April 6, 1864; OR, Series 1, Volume 32, part 3, p. 174; OR, Series 1, Volume 32, part 3, p. 241; OR, Series 1, Volume 32, part 3, p. 279; OR, Series 1, Volume 32, part 3, p. 311.
2. Swantner, *Military Railroads*; Dunnavant, *The Railroad War*; "East Tennessee Historical Society Publication," No. 23 (ETHS, 1951), 58.
3. Merrill, "Block-houses for Railroad Defense."
4. Hoffman, *My Brave Mechanics*; Merrill, "Block-houses for Railroad Defense."
5. Hoffman, *My Brave Mechanics*; Merrill, "Block-houses for Railroad Defense"; Col. W.E. Merrill, "Blockhouses—Federal Means of Protecting Communication," *Sketches of War History 1861–1865, Papers Read before the Ohio Commandery of the Military Order of the Loyal Legion*, Volume 3, 1890.
6. Merrill, "Block-houses for Railroad Defense."
7. Hoffman, *My Brave Mechanics*; OR, Series 1, Volume 32, part 1, p. 14; James M. Sligh letters, Sligh Family Collection, Michigan in the Civil War, Folder 14, pp. 9–10, 14–15. Barton Historical Society, University of Michigan.
8. Dodge papers, Council Bluffs Public Library; Jacob Sigmund Collection, Manuscript Group 222, Pennsylvania State Archives, Harrisburg, PA.
9. OR, Series 1, Volume 32, part 3, p. 331.
10. Jacob Sigmund Collection; OR, Series 1, Volume 38, part 4, p. 640.
11. Hoffman, *My Brave Mechanics*.
12. Dunnavant, *Decatur, Alabama*; OR, Series 1, Volume 39, part 2, p. 20.
13. Jacob Sigmund Collection.
14. James M. McPherson, *The War That Forged a Nation: Why the Civil War Still Matters* (2017).
15. Jacob Sigmund Collection.
16. OR, Series 1, Volume 54, part 2, p. 155.
17. "Regimental Order No. 4," *National Tribune*, April 4, 1895, p. 1, col. 6.

Chapter 8

1. Scales, *The Battles and Campaigns*.
2. Dunnavant, *The Railroad War*.
3. OR, Series 1, Volume 39, part 1, p. 518.
4. Scales, *The Battles and Campaigns*.
5. OR, Series 1, Volume 39, part 1, p. 519.
6. Scales, *The Battles and Campaigns*.
7. OR, Series 1, Volume 39, part 1, p. 518; OR, Series 1, Volume 39, part 1, p. 542.
8. Scales, *The Battles and Campaigns*; Bennie McRae, Jr., "Lest We Forget, African American Military History" (Athens, AL).
9. Scales, *The Battles and Campaigns*; McRae, "Lest We Forget"; Fulton, "Holding the Fort."
10. Scales, *The Battles and Campaigns*.
11. *Ibid*.
12. OR, Series 1, Volume 39, part 1, p. 518.
13. OR, Series 2, Volume 8, p. 109.
14. OR, Series 1, Volume 39, part 1, p. 533. Scales, *The Battles and Campaigns*.
15. Scales, *The Battles and Campaigns*.
16. *Ibid.*; OR, Series 1, Volume 39, part 1, p. 544; OR, Series 1, Volume 39, part 2, p. 474.
17. Scales, *The Battles and Campaigns*.
18. *Ibid*.
19. Tina Jones, "From Slaves to Soldiers"; Glenn Robins, *They Have Left Us Here to Die: The Civil War Prison Diary of Sgt. Lyle G. Adair, 111th U.S. Colored Infantry* (Kent: Kent State University Press, 2014).
20. Jordan, Pryor and Warner, *The Campaigns*; OR, Series 1, Volume 39, part 2, p. 878.
21. OR, Series 1, Volume 39, part 1, p. 545; Taylor, *Embattled Freedom*.
22. Dunnavant, *The Railroad War*.

23. Scales, *The Battles and Campaigns*.
24. *Ibid.*; Eric A. Jacobson and Richard A. Rupp, *Baptism of Fire: The 44th Missouri, 175th Ohio, and 183rd Ohio at the Battle of Franklin* (Franklin, TN: O'More Publishing, 2011); Eddy Davison, *Nathan Bedford Forrest: In Search of the Enigma* (Gretna, LA: Pelican, 2019); Jordan, Pryor and Warner, *The Campaigns*.
25. Scales, *The Battles and Campaigns*.
26. OR, Series 1, Volume 39, part 1, p. 546.
27. Jordan, Pryor and Warner, *The Campaigns*; Dunnavant, *The Railroad War*; OR, Series 1, Volume 39, part 3, p. 41; OR, Series 1, Volume 39, part 1, p. 547.
28. Tennessee Historical Commission, *Tennessee Civil War Sourcebook* (October 1864); OR, Series 1, Volume 39, part 1, p. 508.
29. Scales, *The Battles and Campaigns*; Jacobson and Rupp, *Baptism of Fire*; Davison, *Nathan Bedford Forrest*.
30. Ulysses S. Grant and John Y. Simon, *The Papers of Ulysses S. Grant. Vol. 12* (Carbondale: Southern Illinois University Press, 1982), 306; Scales, *The Battles and Campaigns*.
31. Tina Jones, "From Slaves to Soldiers."
32. NARA, College Park, MD; RG77, Nashville and Decatur (Rds. 191); Tennessee Division of Archaeology, Nashville, Tennessee. Inventory of Archaeological Sites. Site No. 40MU516, p. 4.
33. Scales, *The Battles and Campaigns*; Dunnavant, *The Railroad War*.
34. OR, Series 1, Volume 39, part 1, p. 507.
35. Jerry O Potter, *The Sultana Tragedy: America's Greatest Maritime Disaster* (Gretna, LA: Pelican, 1992).
36. Robert P. Williams, "Rivaled Loss of the Titanic," *Nashville Banner*, April 27, 1912, Part Two, 16.

Chapter 9

1. Robert Parham, "Hood's Demonstration in Front of Decatur, Alabama, October 26–29, 1864, After Action Reports" (Decatur, AL).
2. *Ibid.*
3. John Bell Hood, *Advance and Retreat* (Classics U.S., 2013); Scales, *The Battles and Campaigns*; James R. Knight, *Hood's Tennessee Campaign: The Desperate Venture of a Desperate Man* (2014).
4. Mary Ann Harris Gay, *Life in Dixie During the War, 1861–1865* (2013).
5. Scales, *The Battles and Campaigns*.
6. *Ibid.*; OR, Series 1, Volume 39, part 1, p. 613; Grant and Simon, *The Papers of Ulysses S. Grant. Vol. 12*.
7. Jacobson and Rupp, *Baptism of Fire*.
8. *Ibid.*
9. Terry and Nancy's Ancestors, "Capt. Robert Linah Cobb," Family History Section. Internet.
10. Thomas B. Van Horne, *History of the Army of the Cumberland: Its Organization, Campaigns, and Battles, Written at the Request of Major-General George H. Thomas.... Volume II* (Forgotten Books, 2015); Scales, *The Battles and Campaigns*.
11. Van Horne, *History of the Army of the Cumberland*; Scales, *The Battles and Campaigns*.
12. Van Horne, *History of the Army of the Cumberland*; Scales, *The Battles and Campaigns*; OR, Series 1, Volume 45, part 1, p. 358.
13. Jacobson and Rupp, *Baptism of Fire*.
14. Van Horne, *History of the Army of the Cumberland*.
15. Hood, *Advance and Retreat*; Van Horne, *History of the Army of the Cumberland*; Scales, *The Battles and Campaigns*.
16. Scales, *The Battles and Campaigns*; OR, Series 1, Volume 45, part 1, p. 32.
17. Van Horne, *History of the Army of the Cumberland*; Jacob D. Cox, *Battle of Franklin, Tennessee, November 30, 1864: A Monograph* (2019); Jacobson and Rupp, *Baptism of Fire*; OR, Series 1, Volume 45, part 1, p. 1107; Jacob Dolson Cox, *The March to the Sea Franklin and Nashville* (2017).
18. Title not available. *Sketches of War History 1861–1865, Papers Read before the Ohio Commandery of the Military Order of the Loyal Legion*, Volume 3, 1890, p. 44.
19. "Joseph T. Garner Family Tree," Ancestry.
20. Jacobson and Rupp, *Baptism of Fire*; A.P. Cutting, "This is How it Was," *National Tribune*, March 22, 1894.
21. "Fighting Them Over," *The National Tribune*, April 19, 1900, p.3 ; Jacobson and Rupp, *Baptism of Fire*.
22. Wesley S. Thurstin, *History of the One Hundred Eleventh Regiment Ohio Volunteer Infantry* (Columbus: Ohio Historical Society, 1988).
23. Hood, *Advance and Retreat*.
24. *Ibid.*
25. *Ibid.*; Scales, *The Battles and Campaigns*.
26. Van Horne, *History of the Army of the Cumberland*.
27. Scales, *The Battles and Campaigns*; Jamie Gillum, *The Battle of Spring Hill: Twenty-Five Hours to Tragedy* (2004).

Chapter 10

1. Gay, *Life in Dixie*.
2. Van Horne, *History of the Army of the Cumberland*.
3. Marshall, "*Bridges of Franklin*"; Cox, *Battle of Franklin*.
4. Cox, *Battle of Franklin*.
5. *Ibid.*; Thienel, *Mr. Lincoln's Bridge Builders*.
6. Cox, *Battle of Franklin*.
7. Wiley Sword, *The Confederacy's Last Hurrah: Spring Hill, Franklin, and Nashville* (2017); OR, Series 1, Volume 45, part 1, p. 342; OR, Series 1, Volume 45, part 1, p. 1170.
8. OR, Series 1, Volume 45, part 1, p. 32.
9. Van Horne, *History of the Army of the Cumberland*; Sword, *The Confederacy's Last Hurrah*.

10. *Ibid.*; Cox, *Battle of Franklin*; OR, Series 1, Volume 45, part 1, p. 432.

11. John McElroy, "Franklin and Nashville," *The National Tribune*, March 9, 1911, p. 1; Cox, *The March to the Sea*.

12. Cox, *Battle of Franklin*; Jacobson and Rupp, *Baptism of Fire*; Sword, *The Confederacy's Last Hurrah*.

13. Sword, *The Confederacy's Last Hurrah*; Cox, *Battle of Franklin*.

14. Hood, *Advance and Retreat*; OR, Series 1, Volume 45, part 1, p. 358.

15. Hood, *Advance and Retreat*.

16. Van Horne, *History of the Army of the Cumberland*; OR, Series 1, Volume 45, part 1, p. 32; OR, Series 3, Volume 5, p. 502.

17. Van Horne, *History of the Army of the Cumberland*; Cox, *Battle of Franklin*; OR, Series 1, Volume 45, part 1, p. 74; OR, Series 1, Volume 45, part 1, p. 117; OR, Series 1, Volume 45, part 1, p. 1172.

18. Cox, *Battle of Franklin*; Rick Warwick, "Reminiscences of a School Girl during the War between the States," *Journal of the Williamson County Historical Society* (Franklin, TN: WCHS, 2008), 17; Sword, *The Confederacy's Last Hurrah*; David R. Logsdon, *Eyewitnesses at the Battle of Franklin* (Nashville: Kettle Mills Press, 2000), 69–70; OR, Series 1, Volume 45, part 1, p. 151.

19. Park Marshall, "Confederate Artillery," *Nashville Banner*, December 5, 1928, p. 8.

20. Van Horne, *History of the Army of the Cumberland*; Eric A. Jacobson and Richard A. Rupp, *For Cause & for Country: A Study of the Affair at Spring Hill & the Battle of Franklin* (2008); Sword, *The Confederacy's Last Hurrah*; OR, Series 1, Volume 45, part 1, p. 126; OR, Series 1, Volume 45, part 1, p. 317; Cox, *The March to the Sea*.

21. OR, Series 1, Volume 45, part 1, p. 721.

22. Cox, *Battle of Franklin*.

23. Van Horne, *History of the Army of the Cumberland*; Ulysses S. Grant and John Y. Simon, *The Papers of Ulysses S. Grant. Vol. 13* (Carbondale: Southern Illinois University Press, 1982), 53.

24. Hood, *Advance and Retreat*; Park Marshall, "The Battle of Franklin," *Journal of the Williamson County Historical Society* (Franklin, TN: WCHS, Spring 1993), 116.

25. Hood, *Advance and Retreat*; OR, Series 1, Volume 45, part 2, p. 656; Cox, *The March to the Sea*; Collection of Civil War Telegrams, Travellers Rest, Nashville, Tennessee.

26. Cox, *The March to the Sea*; Grant and Simon, *The Papers of Ulysses S. Grant. Vol. 13*, p. 87.

27. Paul H. Stockdale and John McGlone, *The Death of an Army: The Battle of Nashville and Hood's Retreat* (Murfreesboro, TN: Southern Heritage Press, 1992).

28. Signage at Fort Negley, Nashville, TN.

Chapter 11

1. Franklin Battlefield, City of Franklin, Tennessee, homepage.

2. Scales, *The Battles and Campaigns*.

3. Marshall, *Bridges of Franklin*.

4. Derek Smith, *In the Lion's Mouth: Hood's Tragic Retreat from Nashville, 1864* (Mechanicsburg, PA: Stackpole Books, 2011); Hood, *Advance and Retreat*; Sword, *The Confederacy's Last Hurrah*; OR, Series 1, Volume 45, part 1, p. 706; OR, Series 1, Volume 45, part 2, p. 232; OR, Series 1, Volume 45, part 1, p. 690.

5. Smith, *In the Lion's Mouth*; Michael Thomas Smith, *The 1864 Franklin-Nashville Campaign: The Finishing Stroke* (Santa Barbara: Praeger, 2014); Sword, *The Confederacy's Last Hurrah*.

6. OR, Series 1, Volume 45, part 1, p. 1251; Park Marshall, "The Battle of Franklin," *Journal of the Williamson County Historical Society* (Franklin, TN: WCHS, Spring 1993). 120.

7. Stockdale and McGlone, *The Death of an Army*; Smith, *The 1864 Franklin-Nashville Campaign*; Sword, *The Confederacy's Last Hurrah*; Smith, *History of Maury County*; OR, Series 1, Volume 45, part 2, p. 214.

8. Smith, *In the Lion's Mouth*.

9. Van Horne, *History of the Army of the Cumberland*; OR, Series 1, Volume 45, part 1, p. 157.

10. Stockdale and McGlone, *The Death of an Army*; Smith, *In the Lion's Mouth*.

11. Van Horne, *History of the Army of the Cumberland*.

12. *Ibid.*

13. Stockdale and McGlone, *The Death of an Army*; Van Horne, *History of the Army of the Cumberland*.

14. Stockdale and McGlone, *The Death of an Army*; Smith, *In the Lion's Mouth*; Van Horne, *History of the Army of the Cumberland*; OR, Series 1, Volume 45, part 1, p. 32; OR, Series 1, Volume 45, part 1, p. 42; OR, Series 1, Volume 45, part 1, p. 578.

15. Stockdale and McGlone, *The Death of an Army*; Smith, *In the Lion's Mouth*; Scales, *The Battles and Campaigns*.

16. Stockdale and McGlone, *The Death of an Army*; Smith, *In the Lion's Mouth*.

17. Smith, *In the Lion's Mouth*.

18. Stockdale and McGlone, *The Death of an Army*; Smith, *In the Lion's Mouth*.

19. Stockdale and McGlone, *The Death of an Army*.

20. Stockdale and McGlone, *The Death of an Army*; Smith, *In the Lion's Mouth*; Scales, *The Battles and Campaigns*.

21. Smith, *In the Lion's Mouth*.

22. Scales, *The Battles and Campaigns*; Smith, *In the Lion's Mouth*; Stockdale and McGlone, *The Death of an Army*; Van Horne, *History of the Army of the Cumberland*; Smith, *History of Maury County*.

23. Smith, *In the Lion's Mouth*; Van Horne, *History of the Army of the Cumberland*; OR, Series 1, Volume 45, part 2, p. 310.

24. Stockdale and McGlone, *The Death of an Army*.

25. OR, Series 1, Volume 45, part 1, p. 361.

26. Stockdale and McGlone, *The Death of an Army*; Smith, *In the Lion's Mouth*; Scales, *The Battles and Campaigns*; OR, Series 1, Volume 45, part 1, p. 42.
27. OR, Series 1, Volume 45, part 1, p. 603; OR, Series 1, Volume 45, part 1, p. 32.
28. Stockdale and McGlone, *The Death of an Army*; Smith, *In the Lion's Mouth*; Scales, *The Battles and Campaigns*.
29. Stockdale and McGlone, *The Death of an Army*.
30. Scales, *The Battles and Campaigns*.
31. Stockdale and McGlone, *The Death of an Army*; Smith, *In the Lion's Mouth*; OR, Series 1, Volume 45, part 1, p. 32.
32. Smith, *In the Lion's Mouth*; Scales, *The Battles and Campaigns*; Van Horne, *History of the Army of the Cumberland*.
33. Smith, *In the Lion's Mouth*; Scales, *The Battles and Campaigns*; William Bruce Turner, *History of Maury County, Tennessee* (Nashville: Parthenon Press, 1955).
34. Smith, *In the Lion's Mouth*.
35. OR, Series 1, Volume 45, part 2, p. 283.
36. Smith, *In the Lion's Mouth*; Van Horne, *History of the Army of the Cumberland*; OR, Series 1, Volume 45, part 1, p. 32.
37. OR, Series 1, Volume 45, part 1, p. 32
38. Stockdale and McGlone, *The Death of an Army*; Smith, *In the Lion's Mouth*; Scales, *The Battles and Campaigns*.
39. Smith, *In the Lion's Mouth*.

Chapter 12

1. OR, Series 3, Volume 5, p. 502; Hood, *Advance and Retreat*.
2. OR, Series 2, Volume 8, p. 56.
3. OR, Series 3, Volume 5, p. 29.
4. OR, Series 3, Volume 5, p. 989; OR, Series 3, Volume 5, p. 536; OR, Series 3, Volume 5, p. 45; OR, Series 1, Volume 49, part 1, p. 688.
5. OR, Series 1, Volume 49, part 1, p. 758.

Chapter 13

1. OR, Series 1, Volume 49, part 2, p. 978.
2. OR, Series 3, Volume 5, p. 84; OR, Series 3, Volume 5, p. 88.
3. OR, Series 3, Volume 5, p. 588.
4. John C. Meginnis, "Descriptive Catalog of Locomotive Engines compiled for U.S. Military Railroads—Division of the Mississippi, 1862–1864."
5. OR, Series 3, Volume 5, p. 939.
6. Affairs of Southern Railroads; Henry V. Poor, "Manual of the Railroads of the United States" (New York: H.V & H. W. Poor, 1870).
7. OR, Series 3, Volume 5, p. 536.
8. Baxter, *History of the City of Grand Rapids*.
9. Pyper, *Grenville Mellen Dodge*; Poor, "Manual of the Railroads."
10. John Carbutt, *Biographical Sketches of the Leading Men of Chicago: Photographically Illustrated* (Chicago: Wilson, Peirce & Co., 1876).
11. Margaret E. Merrill, "William E. Merrill," *Professional Memoirs, Corps of Engineers, United States Army and Engineer Department at Large* 9, No. 48 (Society of American Military Engineers in JSTOR, 1917), 639–642.
12. Affairs of Southern Railroads; "The Tennessee and Alabama Road," *Tennessean*, October 19, 1865, p. 2.
13. Dunnavant, *The Railroad War*.
14. "The Tennessee and Alabama Road," *Tennessean*.
15. Richard M. Hochadel, "Locomotives of the Civil War U.S. Military Railroads," Yahoo group message board; Meginnis, "Descriptive Catalog of Locomotive Engines."

Appendix A

1. "The Rail Road," *Nashville Union and American*, June 20, 1854, p. 2; "The Railroad," *Nashville Union and American*, September 17, 1854, p. 3; Jill Knight Garrett, *"Hither and Yon": The Best of the Writings of Jill K. Garrett* (Columbia, TN: Maury County Historical Society, 1999); Thomas T. Taber III, "Antebellum American Railroad Compendium, 1830–1860," Book Number 1 (Muncy, PA).
2. "Report of the President and Directors of the Tennessee and Alabama Rail Road Company, to the Stockholders at their First Annual Meeting, July 19, 1853," Carnton, Franklin, Tennessee.
3. Rick Warwick, "Historical Markers of Williamson County, Tennessee: A Pictorial Guide" (Hillsboro, 1999).
4. Affairs of Southern Railroads.
5. Tennessee Historical Commission, "National Register of Historic Places Determination, Tennessee and Alabama Railroad Freight Depot, Williamson County, TN," March 20, 2000; Garrett, *"Hither and Yon."*
6. "Williamson County Items," *Nashville Union and American*, August 2, 1873, p. 4, col. 2.
7. Ralcon Wagner, Nashville, Tennessee; personal communications.
8. *American Railroad Journal*; John Tunstall, "History of the Central Southern Railroad" (Lynnville, TN).
9. Dunnavant, *The Railroad War*; *American Railroad Journal*; "Railroad Consolidation," *Tennessean*, October 28, 1860, p. 3.
10. "The Central Southern Railroad," *Nashville Union and American*, January 8, 1860, p. 3.
11. American Railroad Journal.
12. Affairs of Southern Railroads.
13. Axford, *To Lochaber*; "Tennessee and Alabama Railroad," *Tennessean*, February 19, 1859, p. 2; "New Route of Travel Opening," *Tennessean*, May 16, 1858, p. 3; "Good News!" *Daily Nashville*

Patriot, October 18, 1858, p. 2; Walker, *History of Limestone County*.
14. William H. Jenkins and John Knox, *The Story of Decatur, Alabama* (Salt Lake City, filmed by the Genealogical Society of Utah, 1979); Affairs of Southern Railroads.
15. "Sixth Annual Report of the Board of Directors of the Central Southern Railroad Company to the Stockholders, 1861," Hathi Trust Digital Library.
16. Dunnavant, *The Railroad War*; Edward W. Hines, "Corporate History of the Louisville and Nashville Railroad Company, and Roads in the System" (1905).
17. Ralcon Wagner, Nashville, TN; personal communications.

Appendix B

1. Galuszka, *Logistics in Warfare*; Gabel, *Railroad Generalship*.
2. Bryan, *Civil War Railroads*.
3. Swantner, *Military Railroads*; Bryan, *Civil War Railroads*.
4. Title not available. *Sketches of War History 1861–1865, Papers Read before the Ohio Commandery of the Military Order of the Loyal Legion on the United States*. Volume 2, p. 392; OR, Series 1, Volume 52, part 1, p. 479.
5. Swantner, *Military Railroads*; "Caterpillars," *Union and Dispatch*, May 8, 1867.
6. N.J. Bell and James Arthur Ward, *Southern Railroad Man: Conductor N.J. Bell's Recollections of the Civil War Era* (DeKalb: Northern Illinois University Press, 1993); Swantner, *Military Railroads*.
7. Bell and Ward, *Southern Railroad Man*.
8. OR, Series 3, Volume 4, p. 963.
9. E.G. Campbell, "The United States Military Railroads, 1862–1865, War Time Operation and Maintenance," *Journal of the American Military History Foundation* 2, No. 2. (1938), 70–89.
10. Bryan, *Civil War Railroads*; Douglas J. Puffert, "The Standardization of Track Gauge on North American Railways, 1830–1890," *The Journal of Economic History* 60, no. 4 (Cambridge University Press, 2000), 933–960.
11. Kincaid Herr, "The Big Switch—A Great Day on Tennessee's Railroads," *Nashville Tennessean Magazine*, October 9, 1955, p. 26.
12. Campbell, "The United States Military Railroads."
13. *Ibid*.
14. Robert Niepert, "Civil War Pontoon Bridges," Internet.
15. Earl B. McElfresh, *Maps and Mapmakers of the Civil War* (New York: Harry N. Abrams, in association with History Book Club, 1999).

Appendix C

1. Jacobson and Rupp, *Baptism of Fire*.
2. NARA, College Park, MD; RG77, Nashville and Decatur (Rds. 191).
3. OR, Series 1, Volume 38, part 4, p. 640.
4. OR, Series 1, Volume 32, part 3, p. 290.
5. Grenville M. Dodge, "Use of Block-Houses During the Civil War," *The Annals of Iowa* 6, Number 4 (1904), 297–301.
6. OR, Series 1, Volume 32, part 2, p. 451.
7. OR, Series 3, pt. 5, p. 939.

Appendix D

1. OR, Series 1, Volume 16, part 2, p. 79.
2. OR, Series 1, Volume 16, part 2, p. 110.
3. Thomas B. Van Horne, *History of the Army of the Cumberland: Its Organization, Campaigns, and Battles, Written at the Request of Major-General George H. Thomas....* Volume I (Forgotten Books, 2015); OR, Series 1, Volume 16, part 2, p. 172.
4. OR, Series 1, Volume 16, part 2, p. 262; OR, Series 1, Volume 16, part 2, p. 261.
5. OR, Supplement, Part 2, Series 33, p. 105.
6. Letters Received by the Commission Branch of the Adjutant General's Office. 1863–870. Roll 252, 1866, D2—D182, National Archives Microfilm Publication M1064.
7. OR, Supplement, Part. 2, Series 33, p. 105; OR, Series 1, Volume 32, part 3, p. 57.
8. Jacob Sigmund Collection.
9. Jacobson and Rupp, *Baptism of Fire*.
10. *Ibid*.
11. *Ibid*.
12. *Ibid*.
13. "Fighting Them Over," *The National Tribune*.
14. OR, Supplement, Part 2, Series 89, pp. 49–53.

Appendix E

1. Fold3.

Bibliography

Official Publications

"Report of the President and Directors of the Tennessee and Alabama Rail Road Company, to the Stockholders at their First Annual Meeting, July 19, 1853," Carnton, Franklin, Tennessee.

"Sixth Annual Report of the Board of Directors of the Central Southern Railroad Company to the Stockholders, 1861," HathiTrust Digital Library.

U. S. House of Representatives. "Affairs of the Southern Railroads" (1867).

United States, Robert N. Scott, H.M. Lazelle, George B. Davis, Leslie J. Perry, Joseph W. Kirkley, and Frederick Crayton Ainsworth. *Official Records of the Union and Confederate Armies 1861–1865* (Washington, D.C.: National Archives, National Archives and Records Service, General Services Administration, 1959).

United States, D.C. McCallum, and James B. Fry. *Reports of Bvt. Brig. Gen. D.C. McCallum: Director and General Manager of the Military Railroads of the United States, and [of James B. Fry] the Provost Marshall General; in Two Parts* (Washington: G.P.O., 1866).

Manuscripts and Records

Dodge, Grenville M. Dodge Papers. Council Bluffs Public Library, Special Collections.

"1st Michigan Engineers and Mechanics." *Military Images* 22, no. 5 (2001).

Hobbs, Thomas Hubbard, and Faye Acton Axford. *The Journals of Thomas Hubbard Hobbs: A Contemporary Record of an Aristocrat from Athens, Alabama...* (Tuscaloosa: University of Alabama Press, 1976).

Letters Received by the Commission Branch of the Adjutant General's Office. 1863–1870. Roll 252, 1866, D2–D182, National Archives Microfilm Publication M1064.

McPherson, John H., Co. C, 74th Regiment OVI. Diary. Filson Historical Society, Louisville, KY.

Meagher, David. Notes from Samuel H. Stout, head of Gen. Bragg's Medical Corps. Giles County, Tennessee.

National Archives and Records Administration, College Park, MD. Civil Works Map File. Record Group 77.

Quartermaster Simon Perkins Collection, Summit County Historical Society of Akron, Ohio, Special Collections Division of the Akron-Summit County Public Library.

"Records Relating to the U. S. Military Railroads" (National Archives: Summer 2011), Vol. 43, No. 2.

Sigmund, Jacob. Collection, Manuscript Group 222, Pennsylvania State Archives, Harrisburg, PA.

Sligh, James M. Letters, Sligh Family Collection, Michigan in the Civil War, Folder 14, Pages 9–10, 14–15. Barton Historical Society, University of Michigan.

Stearns, Ezra, Papers. James S. Schoff Civil War Collection, William L. Clements Library, University of Michigan, Ann Arbor.

Travellers Rest. Collection of Civil War Telegrams, Nashville, Tennessee.

Newspapers

Daily Nashville Patriot. "Good News!" October 18, 1858.

Mobile Advertiser and Register. June 25, 1863.

Nashville Banner. Anderson, Douglas, "Nashville Felt Real Panic as Exaggerated Rumors of Fort Donelson Fall Spread," January 4, 11 and 18, 1931.

Nashville Banner. "Hanged as Spies," December 18, 1884.

Nashville Banner. Marshall, Park, "Confederate Artillery," December 5, 1928.

Nashville Banner. M'Kee, John Miller, "The Evacuation of Nashville," June 14, 1904.

Nashville Banner. Porter, Col. George C., "Execution as Spies of Two Confederate Officers, Col. Orton Williams and Lieut. Walter Peter," February 24, 1912.

Nashville Banner. Williams, Robert P., "Rivaled Loss of the Titanic," April 27, 1912.

Nashville Daily Union. Thomas, L., Adjutant General, "Camp for Contrabands," February 11, 1864.

Nashville Union and American. "The Central Southern Railroad," January 8, 1860.
Nashville Union and American. "The Rail Road," June 20, 1854.
Nashville Union and American. "The Railroad," September 17, 1854.
Nashville Union and American. "Williamson County Items," August 2, 1873.
The National Tribune. Cutting, A.P., "This is How it Was," March 22, 1894.
The National Tribune. "Fighting Them Over," April 19, 1900.
The National Tribune. McElroy, John, "Franklin and Nashville," March 9, 1911.
The National Tribune. "Regimental Order No. 4," April 4, 1895.
Review-Appeal. Marshall, Park, "Bridges of Franklin," January 3, 1929.
The Tennessean. Holmes, W. Kendall, "Sam Davis Death," February 7, 1926.
The Tennessean. "New Route of Travel Opening," May 16, 1858.
The Tennessean, Pierce, Gen. Rice A., "Gray Chieftain Tells How Forrest's Men Kept Wizard From Leading in Last Fight," July 16, 1934.
The Tennessean. "Railroad Consolidation," October 28, 1860.
The Tennessean. "Tennessee and Alabama Railroad," February 19, 1859.
The Tennessean. "The Tennessee and Alabama Road," October 19, 1865.
The Tennessean Magazine. Herr, Kincaid, "The Big Switch—A Great Day on Tennessee's Railroads," October 9, 1955.
Union and Dispatch. "Caterpillars," May 8, 1867.

Articles and Periodicals

"American Railroad Journal" (New York: D.K. Minor, 1832), January 14, 1860.
Campbell, E. G. "The United States Military Railroads, 1862–1865, War Time Operation and Maintenance." *Journal of the American Military History Foundation* 2, no. (1938).
Dodge, Grenville M. "Use of Block-Houses During the Civil War." *The Annals of Iowa* 6, no. 4 (1904).
"East Tennessee Historical Society Publication" 23 (ETHS, 1951).
Friends of the Archives. "Athens, Limestone County, 1861–1865" (Athens, AL).
Fulton, Charlotte S. "Holding the Fort, A History of Trinity School in Athens, Alabama, 1865–1870" (Athens, AL).
Garner, Joseph T. Family Tree, Ancestry.
Hines, Edward W. "Corporate History of the Louisville and Nashville Railroad Company, and Roads in the System" (1905).
Hochadel, Richard M. "Locomotives of the Civil War US Military Railroads." Yahoo group message board.
Jones, James B. "Study Unit No. 4, Early Railroad Development in Tennessee, 1820s–1865" (Nashville: Tennessee Historical Commission).
Jones, Tina. "From Slaves to Soldiers and Beyond—Williamson County Tennessee's African American History." Franklin, Tennessee. Internet.
Marshall, Park. "The Battle of Franklin." *Journal of the Williamson County Historical Society* (Franklin, TN: WCHS, Spring 1993).
Marshall, Park. "Bridges of Franklin." *Journal of the Williamson County Historical Society* (Franklin, TN: WCHS, 1997), vol. 28.
McRae, Jr., Bennie. "Lest We Forget, African American Military History" (Athens, AL).
Meginnis, John C. "Descriptive Catalog of Locomotive Engines compiled for U.S. Military Railroads—Division of the Mississippi, 1862–1864."
Merrill, Col. W.E. "Blockhouses—Federal Means of Protecting Communication." *Sketches of War History 1861–1865, Papers Read before the Ohio Commandery of the Military Order of the Loyal Legion* 3 (1890).
Merrill, Margaret E. "William E. Merrill." *Professional Memoirs, Corps of Engineers, United States Army and Engineer Department at Large* 9, no. 78 (Society of American Military Engineers in JSTOR, 1917).
Merrill, W.E. "Block-houses for Railroad Defense in the Department of the Cumberland." *Sketches of War History 1861–1865, Papers Read before the Ohio Commandery of the Military Order of the Loyal Legion* 3 (1890).
Niepert, Robert. "Civil War Pontoon Bridges." Internet.
"92nd Mounted Illinois Infantry Regiment History." The Illinois Civil War Project, Internet.
O'Connell, Daniel F. "Union and Confederate Engineer Operations in the Civil War." *Essential Civil War Curriculum.* Internet.
Parham, Robert. "The Court Martial of Colonel John B. Turchin: The Sack of Athens, Alabama, May 2, 1862" (Decatur, AL).
Parham, Robert. "Hood's Demonstration in Front of Decatur, Alabama, October 26–29, 1864, After Action Reports" (Decatur, AL).
Pittard, Mabel Baxter. "The Coleman Scouts," *Rutherford County Historical Society Publication No. 13* (Murfreesboro, TN, 1979).
Poor, Henry V. "Manual of the Railroads of the United States" (New York: H.V. & H. W. Poor, 1870).
Powers, Ryan. "The Life and Times of Worshipful Brother Elisha Bourne Basset" (2011). Internet.
Puffert, Douglas J. "The Standardization of Track Gauge on North American Railways, 1830–1890." *Journal of Economic History* 60, no. 4 (2000).
Sketches of War History 1861–1865, Papers Read before the Ohio Commandery of the Military Order of the Loyal Legion. Title not available. Volume 3 (1890).
Sketches of War History 1861–1865, Papers Read before the Ohio Commandery of the Military Order of the Loyal Legion on the United States. Title not available. Volume 2.

Bibliography

Taber, Thomas T., III. "Antebellum American Railroad Compendium, 1830–1860." Book Number 1 (Muncy, PA).

Tennessee Division of Archaeology, Nashville, Tennessee. Inventory of Archaeological Sites. Site No. 40MU516.

Tennessee Historical Commission. "National Register of Historic Places Determination, Tennessee and Alabama Railroad Freight Depot, Williamson County, TN." March 20, 2000.

Terry and Nancy's Ancestors. "Capt. Robert Linah Cobb." Family History Section. Internet.

Tunstall, John. "History of the Central Southern Railroad" (Lynnville, TN).

Warwick, Rick. "The Civil War as Seen through the Female Experience." *Journal of the Williamson County Historical Society* (Franklin, TN: WCHS, 2008).

Warwick, Rick. "Historical Markers of Williamson County, Tennessee: A Pictorial Guide" (Hillsboro, 1999).

Warwick, Rick. "Reminiscences of a School Girl during the War between the States." *Journal of the Williamson County Historical Society* (Franklin, TN: WCHS, 2008).

Books

Axford, Faye Acton. *"To Lochaber Na Mair": Southerners View the Civil War*. Athens, AL: Athens Publishing Co., 1987.

Baxter, Albert. *History of the City of Grand Rapids, Michigan: With an Appendix—History of Lowell, Michigan*. New York: Munsell & Company, 1891.

Beatty, John. *Citizen Soldier: An Account of the American Civil War by a Union Infantry Officer of Ohio Volunteers Who Became a Brigadier General*. Gardners Books, 2007.

Bell, N.J., and James Arthur Ward. *Southern Railroad Man: Conductor N.J. Bell's Recollections of the Civil War Era*. DeKalb: Northern Illinois University Press, 1993.

Bryan, Lt. Col. Irby W. *Civil War Railroads: A Revolution in Mobility*. Carlisle Barracks, PA: U.S. Army War College, 2001.

Carbutt, John. *Biographical Sketches of the Leading Men of Chicago: Photographically Illustrated*. Chicago: Wilson, Peirce & Co., 1876.

Chamberlin, W.H. *History of the Eighty-First Regiment Ohio Infantry Volunteers, During the War of the Rebellion*. Whitefish, MT: Kessinger, 2007.

Chase, Kimberly A. *In Their Own Words: The Abernathy (Eason, Rivers, and Tarpley) Slaves of Giles County, Tennessee*. 2014.

Cox, Jacob D. *Battle of Franklin, Tennessee, November 30, 1864: A Monograph*. 2019.

Cox, Jacob Dolson. *The March to the Sea Franklin and Nashville*. 2017.

Davis, Keith F., and George N. Barnard. *George N. Barnard, Photographer of Sherman's Campaign*. Kansas City: Hallmark Cards, 1990.

Davison, Eddy. *Nathan Bedford Forrest: In Search of the Enigma*. Gretna, LA: Pelican, 2019.

Dunnavant, Robert. *Decatur, Alabama: Yankee Foothold in Dixie, 1861–1865*. Athens, AL: Pea Ridge Press, 1995.

Dunnavant, Robert. *The Railroad War: N.B. Forrest's 1864 Raid Through Northern Alabama and Middle Tennessee*. Athens, AL: Pea Ridge Press, 1994.

Durham, Walter T. *Nashville, The Occupied City: 1862–1863*. Knoxville: University of Tennessee Press, 2008.

Friends of the Archives. *Athens, Limestone County, 1861–1865*. Athens, Alabama.

Gabel, Christopher R. *Railroad Generalship: Foundations of Civil War Strategy*. Fort Leavenworth, KS: U.S. Army Command and General Staff College, 2014.

Galuszka, Douglas H. *Logistics in Warfare: The Significance of Logistics in the Army of the Cumberland During the Tullahoma and Chickamauga Campaigns*. San Francisco: Pickle Partners, 2015.

Garrett, Jill Knight. *"Hither and Yon": The Best of the Writings of Jill K. Garrett*. Columbia, TN: Maury County Historical Society, 1999.

Gay, Mary Ann Harris. *Life in Dixie During the War, 1861–1865*. 2013.

Gillum, Jamie. *The Battle of Spring Hill: Twenty-Five Hours to Tragedy*. 2004.

Grant, Ulysses S., and John Y. Simon. *The Papers of Ulysses S. Grant. Vol. 12*. Carbondale: Southern Illinois University Press, 1982.

Grant, Ulysses S., and John Y. Simon. *The Papers of Ulysses S. Grant. Vol. 13*. Carbondale: Southern Illinois University Press, 1982.

Grant, Ulysses S., and John Y. Simon. *The Papers of Ulysses S. Grant. Vol. 9*. Carbondale: Southern Illinois University Press, 1982.

Hoffman, Mark. *My Brave Mechanics: The First Michigan Engineers and Their Civil War*. Detroit: Wayne State University Press, 2007.

Holbrook, Stewart H. *The Story of American Railroad*. New York: Dover, 2016.

Hood, John Bell. *Advance and Retreat*. The Classics, 2013.

Jacobson, Eric A., and Richard A. Rupp. *Baptism of Fire: The 44th Missouri, 175th Ohio, and 183rd Ohio at the Battle of Franklin*. Franklin, TN: O'More Publishing, 2011.

Jacobson, Eric A., and Richard A. Rupp. *For Cause & for Country: A Study of the Affair at Spring Hill & the Battle of Franklin*. 2008.

Jenkins, William H., and John Knox. *The Story of Decatur, Alabama*. Salt Lake City: Filmed by the Genealogical Society of Utah, 1979.

Jones, Robert Huhn. *Disrupted Decades: The Civil War and Reconstruction Years*. Cartography by Bernhard H. Wagner. New York: Scribner's, 1973.

Jordan, Thomas, J.P. Pryor, and Ezra J. Warner. *The Campaigns of Lieut.-Gen. N.B. Forrest, and of Forrest's Cavalry, with Portraits, Maps, and Illustrations*. Dayton, OH: Morningside House, 1995.

Knight, James R. *Hood's Tennessee Campaign: The Desperate Venture of a Desperate Man*, 2014.

Knox, John, and B. E. Breedlove. *A History of Morgan County, Alabama: Surname Index*. Decatur, AL: Morgan County Board of Revenue, 1966.

Logsdon, David R. *Eyewitnesses at the Battle of Franklin*. Nashville: Kettle Mills Press, 2000.

McElfresh, Earl B. *Maps and Mapmakers of the Civil War*. New York: Harry N. Abrams, in association with History Book Club, 1999.

McPherson, James M. *The War That Forged a Nation: Why the Civil War Still Matters*. 2017.

Owens, Ira S. *Greene County Soldiers in the Late War: Being a History of the Seventy-Fourth O.V.I...* Bethesda, MD: University Publications of America, 1993.

Partridge, Charles A. *History of the Ninety-Sixth Regiment, Illinois Volunteer Infantry*. La Crosse, WI: Brookhaven Press, 2005.

Perkins, J. R. *Trails, Rails, and War: The Life of General G.M. Dodge*. New York: Arno Press, 1981.

Potter, Jerry O. *The Sultana Tragedy: America's Greatest Maritime Disaster*. Gretna, LA: Pelican, 1992.

Pyper, Walter W. *Grenville Mellen Dodge and 19th Century America: Growing Pains of a Man and a Nation*. Princeton: Pyper, 1960.

Robins, Glenn. *They Have Left Us Here to Die: The Civil War Prison Diary of Sgt. Lyle G. Adair, 111th U.S. Colored Infantry*. Kent: Kent State University Press, 2014.

Scales, John R. *The Battles and Campaigns of Confederate General Nathan Bedford Forrest, 1861–1865*, 2017.

Sligh, Charles R. *History of the Services of the First Regiment Michigan Engineers and Mechanics, During the Civil War, 1861–1865*. Ann Arbor: University Microfilms International—Books on Demand, 1989.

Smith, Derek. *In the Lion's Mouth: Hood's Tragic Retreat from Nashville, 1864*. Mechanicsburg, PA: Stackpole Books, 2011.

Smith, Frank Harrison. *Frank H. Smith's History of Maury County, Tennessee*.1969.

Smith, Michael Thomas. *The 1864 Franklin-Nashville Campaign: The Finishing Stroke*. Santa Barbara: Praeger, 2014.

Stockdale, Paul H., and John McGlone. *The Death of an Army: The Battle of Nashville and Hood's Retreat*. Murfreesboro, TN: Southern Heritage Press, 1992.

Swantner, Eva. *Military Railroads During the Civil War*. Alexandria, VA: Society of American Military Engineers, 1929.

Sword, Wiley. *The Confederacy's Last Hurrah: Spring Hill, Franklin, and Nashville*. 2017.

Taylor, Amy Murrell. *Embattled Freedom: Journeys Through the Civil War's Slave Refugee Camps*. Chapel Hill: University of North Carolina Press, 2020.

Taylor, Lenette. *The Supply for Tomorrow Must Not Fail: The Civil War of Captain Simon Perkins, Jr., Union Quartermaster*. Kent: Kent State University Press, 2014.

Tennessee Historical Commission. *Tennessee Civil War Sourcebook*. October 1864.

Thienel, Phillip M. *Mr. Lincoln's Bridge Builders: The Right Hand of American Genius*. Shippensburg, PA: White Mane Books, 2000.

Thurstin, Wesley S. *History of the One Hundred Eleventh Regiment Ohio Volunteer Infantry*. Columbus: Ohio Historical Society, 1988.

Turner, William Bruce. *History of Maury County, Tennessee*. Nashville: Parthenon Press, 1955.

Van Horne, Thomas B. *History of the Army of the Cumberland: Its Organization, Campaigns, and Battles, Written at the Request of Major-General George H. Thomas....* Volume I. Forgotten Books, 2015.

Van Horne, Thomas B. *History of the Army of the Cumberland: Its Organization, Campaigns, and Battles, Written at the Request of Major-General George H. Thomas....* Volume II. Forgotten Books, 2015.

Wagner, Margaret E., Gary W. Gallagher, and Paul Finkelman, eds. *The Library of Congress Civil War Desk Reference*. New York: Simon & Schuster, 2009.

Walker, Robert Henry. *History of Limestone County, Alabama*. Athens, AL: Limestone County Commission and Robert Henry Walker, Jr, 1973.

Other

Boyd, Samuel. Map of Franklin, Tennessee, April 10, 1863," from Tina Jones, Franklin, Tennessee.

Fold3

Franklin Battlefield, City of Franklin, Tennessee homepage.

Hamlin, Kelly Fisk, Giles County, Tennessee; personal communications.

Meagher, David, Giles County, Tennessee; personal communications.

Signage at Fort Granger, Franklin, Tennessee.

Signage at Fort Negley, Nashville, Tennessee.

Wagner, Ralcon, Nashville, Tennessee; personal communications.

Index

Numbers in *bold italics* indicate pages with illustrations

Acklen, Adelecia 42
Acklen, Joseph A.S. 42
Adair, Lyle 110
Adams, Emil 75
Adams, John 140
Adams, Robert Newton 215
African Americans 53
Agricultural and Mechanical College of Mississippi 124
Akins, S.B. 110
Akron, Ohio 59
Alabama 3, 7, 16, 21, 29, 30, 42, 46, 48, 51, 65, 71, 73, 78, 81–84, 86, 87, 93, 97, 100, 103, 104, 109, 116, 117, 120–122, 126, 152, 158, 159, 175, 177, 178, 183, 193, 195–198, 219
Alabama Cavalry, 53rd 75
Alabama Colored Infantry: (1st) 65; (2nd) 73, 82; (3rd) 73, 83, 110; (4th) 82
Alabama Infantry, 19th 71
Alabama State Legislature 175
Allegan, Michigan 56
Allegheny Mountains 7
American Bridge Company 171
American Telegraph Company 186
Anderson, Adna 24–26, 80, 91, 165, 177
Anderson, John B. 25, 26, 31, 43, 48, 50, 54, 61, 62, 67, 68, 165
Anderson, Robert 124
Andersonville Prison 117, 126
Andrews, James J. 37
Anna, Illinois 37
Annapolis and Elk Ridge Railroad 22
Anthony's Hill 153–155
Appalachian Mountains 23
Appomattox 17
ArcGIS-Tennessee 194
Arkansas 16, 63, 120, 179
Arlington Estate 17
Arlington National Cemetery 17, 71
Armstrong, Frank 55, 57
Army and Navy Club 92
Army Corps: (4th) 124, 160; (16th) 1, 83, 214; (23rd) 135, 221
Army of Central Kentucky 18

Army of Kentucky 49, 93
Army of Mississippi 122
Army of Tennessee 49, 51, 52, 71, 121, 123, 124, 128, 129, 152, 156, 159
Army of the Cumberland 25, 49, 53, 56, 59, 91–93, 126, 127, 144, 215
Army of the Mississippi 18
Army of the Ohio 18, 21, 33, 37, 40, 45, 46, 60, 91, 92, 126, 127, 144, 213
Army of the Tennessee 61, 66, 91, 126, 159
Ashe, William 26
Ashton's Mill 151, 204
Ashwood Hall 128
The Athenaeum 127
Athens, Alabama 22, 38, 40–43, 45–47, 49, 50, 52, 61–63, 65–67, 69, 71, 73, 75, 76, 78, 81–83, 97, 99, 101, 103–109, 112, 114, 117, 122, 123, 155, 158, 161, 163, 164, 167, 168, 178–180, 183, 184, 194, 195, 199–201, 208, 210, 212–220; *see also* The Sack of Athens
Atkinson's Gap 177, 178
Atlanta, Georgia 5, 20, 25, 34, 37, 56, 61, 63, 66, 71, 80, 90, 91, 92, 100, 101, 103, 114, 121, 122, 124, 131, 135, 191
Atlantic Coast Line Railroad 184
Auton, Lawrence W. 57, 58

Bailey, Lieutenant 75
Bainbridge, Alabama 150, 153, 155
Baird, John 172
Baird, John P. 56–58
Baltimore, Maryland 36
Baltimore and Ohio Railroad 22, 186
Bane, M.M. 65, 214
Barley, W.J. 119
Barnard, George N. 69–71
Barnard, R.W. 86
Barnes, L.B. 87
Bassett, Elisha 55, 56
Battle Ground Academy 1
Battle of Atlanta 100
Battle of Chickamauga 45, 49, 53, 71, 121, 122, 124, 127

Battle of Decatur 82, 123
Battle of Franklin 1, 3, 56, 92, 125, 135, *136*, 142, 160, 172, 222, 224; *see also* Cox, Jacob D.; Franklin, Tennessee; Schofield, John M.
Battle of Mills Springs 21
Battle of Nashville 17, 81–84, 121, 124, 127, 144, 161; *see also* Nashville, Tennessee; Thomas, George H.
Battle of Spring Hill 129, 134; *see also* Cox, Jacob D.; Forrest, Nathan Bedford; Hood, John Bell; Spring Hill, Tennessee
Battle of Stones River 45
Battle of Sulphur Creek Trestle 36; *see also* Forrest, Nathan Bedford; Lilly, Eli; The *Sultana*
Beach, Captain 123
Beatty, John 41, 147
Beaufort, South Carolina 37
Beauregard, P.G.T. 124, 143
Beechlawn 128
The Belmont Mansion 42
Benham and Company 99
Bickford, Chaucla 101
Bigby Creek 178
Black Creek 201, 211
Blacks 2, 4, 18, 53, 67, 68, 78, 81, 84–87, 101, 104, 106
Blair, Austin 31
Bliss, Alexander 174
blockhouse (large) 30, 50, *95*, 142, 210
blockhouse (small, at railroad crossings) 2–5, 30, 33, 34, 86–88, 90, 91, 93, 94, *95*, *96*, 97–102, 104–117, 121, 125, 127–132, 134, 143, 150, 152, 153, 158, 162–165, 169, 171, 193–199, 202, 210, 215–219; author's numbering system in Tennessee 193, 202; at Culleoka 115, 130; at Gracey's 115, 210; at Harris 115, 127, 130; locations of 202; at Richland Creek Crossing No. 4 110, 127, 216; sketches by Merrill 195; at Spencer Creek 210; at Sulphur Creek 207; summary of damages to 169; at the Elk River

239

Index

210; at Tunnel Hill Trestle 111; at West Harpeth 131, 218
Blockhouse No. 1 (Alabama) 104
Blockhouse No. 2 (Alabama) 104, 216
Blockhouse No. 3 (Alabama) 104, 216
Blockhouse No. 3 (Carter's Creek) 113, 216
Blockhouse No. 4 (Alabama) 104, 216
Blockhouse No. 4 (Carter's Creek) 113, 216
Blockhouse No. 5 (Alabama) 107, 216
Blockhouse No. 5 (Carter's Creek) 113, 216
Blockhouse No. 6 (Alabama) 107, 216
Blockhouse No. 6 (Carter's Creek) 113
Blockhouse No. 7 (Alabama) 108, 216
Blockhouse No. 7 (Tennessee) 210
Blockhouse No. 8 (Alabama) 108
Blockhouse No. 8 (Tennessee) 210, 216
Blockhouse No. 9 (Alabama) 108
Blockhouse No. 9 (Rutherford Creek) 100
Blockhouse No. 9 (Tennessee) 216
Blockhouse No. 10 (Alabama) 110
Blockhouse No. 10 (Rutherford Creek) 100
Blockhouse No. 11 (Alabama) 110
Blockhouse No. 11 (Rutherford Creek) 132
Blockhouse No. 12 (Rutherford Creek) 128
Blockhouse No. 13 (Richland Creek) 127, 217
Blockhouse No. 14 (Richland Creek) 127, 217
Blockhouse No. 15 (Richland Creek) 127, 217
Blockhouse No. 16 (Richland Creek) 217
Blockhouse No. 19 101, 102
Blockhouse No. 37 197, 218
Blockhouse No. 38 197, 218
Blockhouse No. 39 197, 218
Blockhouse Nos. TN-1 through TN-25 (author's numbering system) 193, 202
Bloodgood, Edward 54, 55
Bolton, Rosanna 221
Boody, Stone and Company 63
Boomer, Lucius B. 2, 3, 31, *62*, 63, 67–75, 90, 97, 98, 101, 136, 166, 168, 169, 171, 194, 198, 216; *see also* Howe, William
Boomer, Lucius M. 171
Boomer Bridge Works 4, 63, 67
Booth, John Wilkes 24, 120
Borden, Baker 31
Bosque Bonita Farm 103

Bowers, Theodore S. 84
Bowling Green, Kentucky 19, 41, 187
Brady, Matthew 69
Bragg, Braxton 18, 41, 49, 52, 53, 58, 64, 122, 136
Bramlett, Fannie 220
Brentwood, Tennessee 50, 55–58, 139, 141, 142, 147, 160, 162, 167, 177, 184, 196, 202, 214, 216, 222
Brentwood Hills 140, 161
Brice's Crossroads 19, 103
bridge (railroad) 1–5, 7, 9, 20, 22, 24, 26, 28, 29–31, 33–57, 59–63, 65–76, 78, 79, 81, 84, 86, 87, 90, 91, 93–102, 104, 107, 108, 110–117, 121, 122, 124–130, 132, 136–141, 143, 145–148, 150–153, 158, 161–163, 165–171, 173–175, 177, 179, 182–185, 187–190, 193–208, 210–218, 222; author's table of locations 202; Dodge's table of locations 199; summary of damages to 168, 169; Wright's table of locations 200
bridge (wagon) 2–4, 20, 29, 35, 42, 56, 130, 135–139, 141–143, 146–148, 153, 161, 199, 210
Bridgeport, Alabama 33, 50, 67, 76, 215
Bright, Anna 220
Brinton, John H. 161
Brown, Aaron V. 86, 223
Brown, Cynthia H. 223
Brown, Thomas J. 86–88, 111
Brown, William L. 86, 87
Brownlow, William 6, 223
Brown's Creek 161, 177, 194–197, 199, 202, 213
Brown's Ferry 75
Brownsborough, Alabama 112, 215
Bruce, George 172
Bruch, Samuel 187
Buchanan, James 24, 86
Buckingham, C.P. 35
Buell, Don Carlos 18, 20, 21, 33, 35–37, 40, 41, 43, 44, 46–48, 52, 92, 187, 213, 223
Buford, Abraham 102, 103, 109–112, 116, 121, 127, 142, 145, 153, 162, 163, 169
Buford, Robert 177
Buford, Thomas 182
Buford Station 65, 206, 214
Bureau of Colored Troops 81
Bureau of Military Information 64
Bureau of Refugees, Freedmen and Abandoned Property 86
Burnside, Ambrose 53
Burroughs, George 98, 195, 196, 199, 211
Burrow, Washington 18
Butterworth, Tennessee 213

Cahaba Prison 117, 120
Cahill, Colonel 223

Cairo 20
Cairo, Illinois 117
Calhoun Plantation 85
Callender, B.M. 106
Cameron, Simon 24, 31, 186
camp 2, 4, 21, 23, 30, 33, 35, 37, 38, 40, 44, 46, 48, 50, 51, 54, 55, 65, 67, 69, 78, 82–87, 90, 100, 103, 106, 108, 111–113, 116, 132, 133, 143, 145, 147, 149–152, 155, 160, 162, 172, 180, 193, 202, 213–215, 220–223
Camp Brentwood 55, 195, 202
Camp Chase, Ohio 118, 119
Camp Meriweather 212
Camp Owen 32, 33
Camp Stanton 81
Camp Weakley 16
Campbell, Lewis D. 212
Campbell, Wallace 105–107, 220
Campbell's Station 49, 112, 162, 205
Campbell's Station Branch 205
Cannon, W.P. 177
Carnegie, Andrew 186
Carnton 178, 203; *see also* McGavock, John
Carolina Life Insurance Company 27
Carrol 59
Carter, John C. 140
Carter House 1, 135, 138, 140
Carter's Creek 60, 61, 68, 70, 71, 73, 91, 96, 97, 110, 112–116, 125–128, 148, 151, 152, 158, 161, 162, 167–169, 174, 194, 195, 197, 198, 203, 204, 210, 212, 213, 216; station at 60, 113, 203, 210;
Carter's Creek Crossing No. 1, railroad bridge at 113, 199, 203, 213
Carter's Creek Crossing No. 2, railroad bridge at 68, 113, 203, 213
Carter's Creek Crossing No. 3, railroad bridge at 203, 213
Carter's Creek Crossing No. 4, railroad bridge at 204, 213
Carter's Creek Crossing No. 5, railroad bridge at 68, 158, 198, 199, 204, 213
Carter's Creek Pike 57, 138, 147
Castle Morgan Prison 117
Cedar Valley, Ohio 56
Central Southern Railroad 8, 29, 72, 172, 174, 175, 177, 180–182, 194, 204, 207; construction timeline 182
Chalmers, James R. 145
Chapel Hill, Tennessee 19, 112
Charleston, South Carolina 16, 26, 53, 63
Chattanooga, Tennessee 22, 25, 37, 41, 60, 61, 71, 72, 76, 79, 81, 91, 93, 100, 189
Cheairs, Martin 51
Cheairs, Nathaniel 133
Cheatham, Benjamin F. 121, 122,

Index

124, 127, 129, 133, 152, 156, 162, 169
Cheatham, Richard B. 18–20
Cherokee, Alabama 103, 114, 117
Chessie System 184
Chicago, Illinois 62, 63, 72, 73, 171
Chicago Telephone Company 187
Chickamauga, Georgia 45
Chickamauga and Chattanooga National Military Park 124
Chickasaw, Mississippi 148
Childe, John 177, 179
Cincinnati, Ohio 24, 42, 187
Cincinnati College 37
Cincinnati Law School 125
Cist, Henry 99
Claiborne, M.G.L. 177
Clarksville, Tennessee 18, 84
Claybrooke, John S. 172, 177, 178
Cleburne, Patrick 124, 129, 135, 140
Cleveland, Grover 56
Cleveland, Ohio 63
Cobb, Robert L. 155, 156
Coburn, John 54, 55
Coffinberry, Wright 31
Coleman, Captain 146
Coleman, E.C. 64; *see also* Shaw, Henry
Coleman Hill 104
Coleman's Scouts 64
Collins Farm 202
Columbia 48, 128, 173, 180
Columbia, Tennessee 7, 8, 19, 22, 29, 35–37, 47–50, 52, 57, 60–62, 65–68, 72–74, 76, 80, 96, 100, 101, 104, 110, 112, 113, 117, 121, 124–134, 137–140, 142, 147, 149–152, 158, 161, 162, 164, 165, 167, 168, 173, 174, 177–187, 189, 195, 210, 212–215, 217, 218, 221, 223, 224
Columbia Federal Depot 35
Columbia Pike 54, 56, 57, 115, 134, 138, 141, 147, 206
Columbus, Kentucky 174
Columbus, Mississippi 159
conductor 23, 138, 189, 222
Confederate Army 3, 17–19, 51, 103, 123, 124, 133, 140, 152, 221
Confederate Congress 27
Confederate Engineers, 3rd 155
Confederate Office of Exchange 117
Confederate Railroad Bureau 27
Confederate States of America 16, 122
Construction Corps of United States Military Railroad 23, 31, 166
contraband camp 2, 4, 53, 82, **83**, 84–87, 90, 111
Cooper, Duncan B. 72
Cooper, George E. 151
Corinth, Mississippi 18, 41, 61, 62, 71, 143, 147, 159

Cornersville, Tennessee 78, 215
Corps of Scouts 63, 73
cotton 7, 16, 19, 36, 42, 63, 85–87, 119, 121, 179
Cotton Lane 136
Council Bluffs, Iowa 61, 170, 171
County Bridge in Franklin 136–139, 141–143, 146
Courtland, Alabama 7, 159
Cowan, James B. 110
Cox, Jacob D. 125, 127–130, 132, 135, 138–140, 149; *see also* Battle of Franklin
Crittendon, Captain 43
Crockett, Catherine W. 222
Crockett, George 222
Crockett, James 222
Croxton, John T. 221, 222
CSX Transportation 3, 184, 194
Culleoka, Tennessee 45, 50, 65, 72, 74, 75, 78, 98, 113, 115, 127, 130, 162, 168, 169, 194, 196, 198, 199, 201, 205, 210, 213–215, 217
Culleoka-Pleasant Grove Station 205
culvert 30, 50, 110, 131, 190, 191, 193–195, 202, 204–206, 208, 210, 211
Cumberland pontoons 191
Cumberland River at Nashville 7, 16–18, 20, 23, 42, 143
Cummins, Colonel 45, 220
Curtis, General 223
Custer, George A. 97
Custis-Lee Mansion 17
Cutting, A.P. 131
Cypress Creek 114

Dancy Polk House 78
Danville, Virginia 27
Dark's Mill 71, 91, 204
Darrah, S.B. 100, 216
Davidson 172, 180
Davidson County, Tennessee 178, 223
Davis, Jefferson 17, 26, 27, 51, 71, 126, 159
Davis, Jefferson C. 21, 49, 50
Davis, Sam 64, 73
Davis' Ford 129
Davis' Island 171
Dayton, Ohio 127
D.C. McCallum 186
Decatur 172, 182
Decatur, Alabama 1–4, 7, 8, 16, 20, 22, 26, 36–40, 48, 49, 52, 60, 66, 68, 72–75, 78, 82, 83, 91, 99–101, 104–106, 111, 112, 121–126, 143, 144, 155, 158, 159, 163, 165, 171, 174, 180, 183, 184, 187, 195, 212, 213, 215, 217–221
Decatur Junction 8, 9, 14, **15**, 22, 38, 43, 44, 49, 50, 61, 66, 68, 71–76, 78, 82–86, 90–92, 96, 104, 105, 116, 161, 166, 167, 174, 179, 181–183, 185, 195–197, 200, 201, 209, 211, 215, 218
DeHews, Capt. 78

Demonstration at Decatur 123; *see also* Battle of Decatur
Department of Missouri 92
Department of the Cumberland 25, 31, 46, 54, 63, 80–82, 86, 92, 98, 147, 151, 165, 215; *see also* Army of the Cumberland
Department of the Interior 53
Department of the Mississippi 35, 63, 92, 165, 174, 189
Department of the Missouri 61
depot 1, 4, 8, 18–20, 28, 35, 42, 45, 56, 57, 59, 68, **79**, 91, 92, 105, 112, 128, 146, 164, 167, 172–175, 180, 182, 199, 202–204, 208–210, 224–226
Detroit and Milwaukee Railroad 5
Detroit, Grand Haven and Milwaukee Railroad 31
Dewey, Joey A. 97, 215
diary: Garner, Joseph T. 158; Kimball, William H. 34, 51, 96; McPherson, John 42; Turchin, Madame Nadine 37
Dickerson, A.W. 26, 165
District of Nashville 65, 97
District of North Alabama 82, 122
Dodge, Grenville M. 3, 31, 61, **62**, 63–69, 71–76, 78, 80, 87, 89, 90, 93, 94, 96–99, 101, 104, 105, 107, 108, 113, 167, 169–171, 194, 195, 197, 199, 200, 202–208, 210, 211, 214–216, 219, 220
Dodson's Gap 182
Donaldson, James L. 92, 215
Doolittle, Charles C. 122, 123
Douglas, General 215
Driver, William 21
Duck River 16, 35, 36, 42, 47–50, 60, 61, 65–69, **70**, 72–75, 80, 101, 112–115, 121, 125–132, 134, 137, 148–153, 156, 158, 162, 163, 168, 169, 173, 179, 193, 196, 198–200, 204, 210, 212, 213, 218, 221
Dumont, Ebenezer 34
Dunlavy, Lieutenant 110
Dunlop, George 57, 58; *see also* Peters, Walter G.
Dupont, Thomas Coleman 171
Dykeman, Captain 215

Eastport, Mississippi 62
Eaton Depot 167
Edgefield, Tennessee 7, 18, 20, 84
Edgefield and Kentucky Railroad 7
Eicholtz, Leonard H. 162
Eli Lilly and Company 36
Elk River 29, 42–46, 52, 54, 60, 65–69, 71, 73, 75, 76, 81, 84, 86, 90, 97, 101, 105, 108, 110, 111, 114, 116, 117, 158, 163, 168, 169, 182, 186, 193, 196, 198, 199, 201, 207, 210, 212–215, 218
Elkmont, Alabama 68, 110, 167, 180, 183, 207, 208

Index

Elkton, Tennessee 43, 86, 110, 111, 158
Elliott, W.L. 147, 149
Elza, Robert 119
Emancipation Proclamation 81, 101
engine 21, 24, 26, **27**, 28, 37, 47–50, 55, 59, 72, 79, 91, 93, 97, 101, 106, 116, 121, 131, 143, 144, 165–167, 172–175, 179, 182, 183, 185, 186, 188, 189; *see also* locomotive
enslaved Black 4, 16, 18, 19, 31, 40, 49, 53, 64, 72, 80–82, 84–86, 92, 101, 135, 220, 222
Enterprise, Mississippi 36
Episcopal Church 51
Erie Railway 31
Evans, Frank 78, 214
Evans, Henry G. 149
Ewing, Alexander 1
Ewing, Alexander C. 84
Ewing, Andrew 84
Ewing, William 84

Fayetteville, Tennessee 112
Federal Army 81, 161
Figuer's Bluff 53
First Battle of Franklin 56
First Michigan Engineers and Mechanics 5, 20, 21, 31, **32**, 33–35, 43–45, 47, 50, 52, 54, 60, 74, 90, 93–99, 114, 195, 197, 198, 215, 216; *see also* Innes, William P.
Fisk, Clinton B. 86
Fitzallen, Henry 212
Fleming, John T. 177
Flint River at Brownsboro, Alabama, railroad bridge at 112, 215
Florence, Alabama 43, 103, 112, 114, 121, 123, 124, 126, 137, 148–150, 153, 155, 156, 158, 160, 177
Florida 16, 180
Floyd, John B. 20
Fontaine, Jo 72
footbridge 45, 149
Foote's Station 209
ford 35, 43, 54, 103, 110, 129, 130, 136–142, 146–149, 151, 156, 191, 192, 218
Ford's Theater 24
Forrest, Jesse 19, 106
Forrest, Nathan Bedford 2, 19, **20**, 36, 50, 52, 54–59, 71, 76, 82, 83, 87, 96, 98–117, 119–121, 123, 124, 126–129, 133, 134, 137, 140, 142, 143, 145, 149–153, 155, 156, 159–163, 167–169, 180, 192, 216, 217, 220, 224
Fort Donelson 17, 18, 20
Fort Granger 46, 49, 53, 54, 56, 57, 59, 85, 97, 138, 140–142, 146, 164, 180, 195, 202, 214, 218, 224
Fort Henderson 82, 101, 104, 105, 112, 164, 195, 208
Fort Henry 18
Fort Hill 36

Fort Lilly 36, 164, 195, 206, 210
Fort Mizner 66, 164, 195, 204
Fort Monroe 27
Fort Negley 45, 50, 53, 84, 85, 142, 152, 180, 195, 197, 202
Fort Palmer 45, 196, 205
Fort Pillow 19, 106
Fort Rosecrans 54
Fort Sumter 16, 53, 124
Fountain Creek 156, 158, 194, 205
Fox, Captain 51
Fox, Perrin 31
Franklin 40, 59, 173, 180
Franklin, Tennessee 1–4, 8, 21, 22, 35, 42, 46–51, 53–60, 69, 71, 72, 75, 84, 85, 92, 93, 97, 99–101, 112, 113, 121, 122, 124–126, 128, 130–147, 149–152, 156, 158, 160–168, 171, 172, 177–180, 195, 198, 199, 202, 210, 212–214, 216–219, 221, 222, 224–226; map of November 30, 1864, crossings 136
Franklin, Tennessee L&N freight depot 180, 202, 210, 224
Franklin, Tennessee L&N passenger station 1, 4, 180, **225**
Franklin, Tennessee N&D freight station and depot 56, 59, 146, 180, 224
Franklin, Tennessee N&D passenger station 8, 180, 210, 224
Franklin-Nashville Interurban 226
Franklin Pike 53, 130, 135, 136, 138, 142, 144, 146, 147
Frazier, Emily 220
Freedmen 81
Freedmen's Bureau 86
Freedmen's Department of the Army 84, 87
Freeman, Samuel L. 52, 55, 56
Freemasons 170
Frink, Charles S. 138
Frohn, A. 113
Fry, James B. 43, 44, 47, 48, 213
Fuller, J.W. 65, 78, 214
Fusselman, Lieutenant 141

Gallatin, Tennessee 81, 84
Galveston, Texas 49
Garfield, James 41, 57, 58
Garner, Joseph T. 130, 158
Garrard, Kenner 215
Gaubert, C.H. 43
gauge (railroad) 16, 79, 173, 174, 184, 189, 190; standardization on N&D in May 1886 190
Gay, Mary A.H. 124, 135
General 37; *see also* The Great Locomotive Chase
Genl. J.C. Robinson **27**
Gen. Logan 72, 173
Gen. McPherson 72, 173
General Order 40, 49, 52, 84, 91, 93, 172
Gen. Thomas 123

Geneva, New York 66
Georgia 5, 16, 17, 25, 27, 30, 67, 68, 71, 79, 80, 90, 91, 93, 100, 103, 117, 121, 124, 126, 135, 151
Gerry, New York 92
Gettysburg, Pennsylvania 24, 121
Gidding's Gap 178
Gifford, W.R. 26, 165
Gilbert, Charles C. 46
Giles 173, 180, 182
Giles County, Tennessee 4, 8, 76, 87, 88, 181–183, 220, 221
Gist, States Rights 140
Glendale, Tennessee 205, 210
Goose Creek 205
Gould, Jay 170
Gov. Broome 180
Granbury, Hiram B. 140
Grand Rapids, Michigan 5, 6, 31, 170
Grand Rapids and Indiana Railroad 31
Granger, Gordon 49, 56, 57, 60, 223
Granger, Robert 104–106, 122, 123, 155, 158, 163, 214, 217, 218, 222
Grant, Ulysses S. 17, 18, 24–26, 35, 36, 61–63, 67, 68, 72, 73, 75, 125, 126, 142–144, 151
Great Lakes 11th Lighthouse District 114
The Great Locomotive Chase 37; *see also General*
guerrillas 28–30, 34, 35, 40, 42, 45, 47, 60, 65, 72, 81, 91, 93, 97, 99, 125, 168, 187, 189
gunboat 17–20, 114, 123, 155, 156

Halleck, Henry 24, 35, 50, 142, 143
hanging 49, 57, 58, 64, 180; *see also* Auton, Lawrence W.; Davis, Sam; Dunlop, George
Hannon, Moses W. 75
Hardeman, Francis (Frank) 172, 177
Harding Pike 144
Hardison's Mill 112
Harlinsdale Farm 145
Harpers Ferry 130
Harpeth River 1, 3, 35, 42, 46, 47, 49, 50, 53, 55, 56, 59, 60, **69**, 71, 101, 125, 130, 134–143, 145–150, 156, 158, 161, 162, 164, 168, 170, 172, 180, 194, 195, 199, 200, 202, 203, 210, 212, 213, 222, 224
Harris, Isham 18, 19
Harris, Joseph W. 85
Harrison, William 134
Harville, Hannah 220, 221
Hatch, Edward 127, 140, 148, 150, 151, 222
Haupt, Herman 23–25
Hays Mill, Alabama 108, 207, 208
Hazen, William B. 213
Helena, Arkansas 83, 223
Henderson, Samuel 177

Index

Hendersonville, Tennessee 84
Henry, James 104
Herrick, George 166
Herrick, Orson Q. 161
Hillsborough Pike 144
Hobart, Lewis 171, 172, 219, 221, 222
Hobbs, Thomas 183
Hobbs House 78
Hobbs Station 209
Hoffman, William 160
Hoge, George W. 128
Holland, William 110
Hollow Tree Gap 145
Hood, John Bell 3, 19, 56, 59, 61, 63, 71, 81, 82, 84, 87, 96, 99, 103, 110, 115, 120, 121, **122**, 123–135, 137, 139–156, 158–163, 165, 166, 168–170, 172, 210, 217, 218, 220–223; *see also* Battle of Decatur; Battle of Franklin; Battle of Nashville
Hood's retreat 1, 103, 110, 114, 124, 144, 145, 148, 155, 156, 158, 160, 162, 165, 166, 170, 194
Hopkins, Enos 32
Howe, William 67; *see also* Boomer, Lucius B.
Howe Truss 63, 67- 71, 75, 97, 101, 136, 190, 198, 199, 210
Huey's Mill 29, 129
Hughes, Brice 177
Hughes' Ford 56, 140
Hunt, Ralph 85
Hunter, Lieutenant 104
Hunter, Mrs. 60
Hunton, Kinsman A. 21, 44, 93, 94
Huntsville, Alabama 37–42, 44–46, 48, 50, 78, 84–86, 91, 104, 112, 122, 144, 155, 158, 212, 213, 215, 217
Hurd, Mr. 78
Hurricane Creek 11, 12, 50, 162, 201, 221
Hurricane Station 205

Illinois 126, 223
Illinois Artillery, 2nd 123, 217
Illinois Central Railroad 37
Illinois Infantry: (3rd) 154; (9th) 75, 99; (19th) 37, 40, 41, 49, 213; (24th) 37, 40; (38th) 97; (50th) 215; (51st) 214; (57th) 85; (61st) 164, 218; (64th) 215; (73rd) 129; (92nd) 55, 214; (96th) 55, 214; (111th) 72; (112th) 134
Indiana 36, 110, 117, 127, 223
Indiana Battery: (4th) 213; (22nd) 217
Indiana Cavalry: (2nd) 43; (8th) 153; (9th) 36, 101, 108, 110, 111, 216, 217; (10th) 101, 111, 112, 159, 216, 217; (11th) 122; (12th) 122, 159; (13th) 122, 123, 159
Indiana Infantry: (9th) 147; (21st) 36; (31st) 44; (35th) 213; (36th) 20; (37th) 40; (38th) 212, 213;

(65th) 133; (68th) 123; (73rd) 112, 122, 217; (75th) 146, 218; (79th) 140, 141, 216; (84th) 55; (85th) 57; (115th) 55; (120th) 129
Indiana Light Artillery: (15th) 138; (18th) 36; (23rd) 138
Indianapolis, Indiana 36
Industrial Revolution 3, 185
Innes, William P. 3, 5, 6, 31, **32**, 33–36, 47, 54, 94, 96, 98, 99, 170; *see also* 1st Michigan Engineers and Mechanics
Iowa 61, 170
Iowa Cavalry, 5th 153
Iowa Infantry, 39th 65, 75, 214, 215, 220
Iron Bridge Works 171
Irwinville, Georgia 27

Jack Mason 183
Jackson, Andrew 51
Jackson, William "Red" 54, 56, 127, 142, 153, 154
Jackson, Mississippi 170
Jefferson Barracks 118
John Childe 172, 175, 180
Johnson, Andrew 27, 29, 92, 172, 223
Johnson, Ben 8
Johnson, Colonel 109, 111
Johnson, Edward 132
Johnson, Richard W. 132
Johnson's Island, Ohio 64
Johnsonville, Tennessee 84
Johnston, Albert S. 18–20, 29, 122
Jordan, Johnson, Jr. 177
Jordan, Stephen A. 101
Juneteenth 49

Kansas Cavalry, 7th 64
Keenan, Thomas 187
Kelley, Colonel 109, 111
Kentucky 17, 27, 33, 37, 49, 79, 103, 142, 143, 165, 187
Kentucky Cavalry: (1st) 212, 213, 220; (3rd) 198, 213; (5th) 213; (6th) 57; (17th) 220
Kentucky Infantry: (1st) 85; (5th) 65; (7th) 111; (21st) 212; (23rd) 212, 220
Kimball, Nathan 127, 147, 149, 150
Kimball, William H. 34, 51, 96, 97
King's Hill 153
Kingston Springs, Tennessee 7
Kinnard, Claiborne H. 177
Kneeland, Samuel M. 105
Knoxville, Tennessee 91, 114, 170, 178
Koger's Island 114
Kramer, Albert 113
Ku Klux Klan 19

Lake Erie 64
Lamb's Ferry Road 152, 153, 155
Lancaster, Ohio 63
Lancaster, Pennsylvania 187

Lathrop, William H. 106, 109
La Vergne, Tennessee 33, 94, 146, 148
Lawrence County, Alabama 82
Lawrenceburg, Tennessee 114, 127, 152
LeDuc, William G. 151, 172, 222
Lee, Henry III 17
Lee, Robert E. 17, 58, 119, 124, 142, 163
Lee, Samuel P. 147, 148, 156
Lee, Stephen D. 124, 128, 129, 132, 137, 145–147, 151, 224
Leighton, Alabama 38, 159
letters: Garner, Joseph T. 130; Sigmund, Jacob 99; Starnes, James 21; Stokes, Thomas J. 124
Lewis, William T. 117
Lewisburg, Tennessee 112
Lewisburg and Northern Railroad 184
Lewisburg Pike 56, 57, 129, 210
Lexington, Alabama 158
Lexington, Kentucky 103
Libby Prison 56
Liberty Creek 202
Liberty Pike 54
Lillard's Mill 149
Lilly, Eli 36, 108–110, 216
lime kiln 88, 90, 181
Limestone 183
Limestone County, Alabama 109, 183, 207, 220, 219
Limestone Creek 40
Lincoln, Abraham 16, 17, 23, 24, 27, 34, 41, 52, 61, 81, 86, 101, 117, 120, 127
Little Harpeth River 35, 50, 55–57, 59, 156, 158, 161, 162, 167, 175, 194, 200, 202, 212, 213
Little Miami Railroad 37
locomotive 3, 21, 24–26, **27**, 28, 29, 35, 37, 40, 49, 50, 59, 72, 78–80, 90, 93, 104, 116, 131, 143, 153, 154, 165, 167, 172–175, 178, 180, 182, 185–187, **188**, 189, 210, 226; *see also* engine
Logan, John A. 144
Logwood, Colonel 110
Long, Eli 220
Long, J.F. 113
Long Tom Branch 205
Longstreet, Captain 71
The Loop 22, 92, 98, 100
Louisiana 16, 121, 178
Louisiana Cavalry, 1st 29, 40
Louisiana State Seminary of Learning and Military Academy 63
Louisiana State University 63
Louisville, Kentucky 7, 21, 25, 33, 42–44, 49, 63, 72, 143
Louisville and Nashville Railroad 1, 3, 7, 25, 180, 224, 225
Lowell, Ohio 18
Luke Pryor 40, 173. 183
Lynnville, Tennessee 45, 49, 60, 65–67, 98, 99, 101, 105, 125, 127,

Index

152, 154, 161, 162, 167, 180–182, 186, 196, 206, 213–217
Lyon, Hylan 71, 110, 111, 113, 114, 162
Lytle Creek 162, 167, 200, 205

MacLand House 78
Madry's Ridge 2, 4, 8, 16, 43–45, 87–89, 111, 179, 181, 184, 207; *see also* Tunnel Hill
Mallory, G.M.C. 222
Mallory, Nelson 222
Mallory Station 55, 210
Manson, Mahlon D. 213
March, Henry C. 104, 211
March to the Sea 63, 69, 71, 100, 103, 121, 126, 163
Marion, Arkansas 120
Marion and Memphis Railroad 19
Marshall, Alexander 221
Marshall, Michigan 32
Marshall, Texas 170
Martin, Jefferson 177
Martin, Richard 183
Martin, Thomas 36, 153, 172, 181
Martin Female College 36
Martin Methodist College 36
Mason, Jack 183
Matthews, Stanley 21
Maury 72, 173, 182
Maury County, Tennessee 19, 35, 36, 52, 110, 182, 221
Maury Light Artillery 18
Maxwell, Briggs and Company 178
Mayberry, A.C. 177, 178
Mayberry, Henry G.W. 177, 178
Maysville, Kentucky 21
McArthur, John 144
McCall, Captain 75
McCallum, Daniel C. 16, 23–26, 68, 76, 78, 79, 91, 92, 116, 165–167; *see also* United States Military Railroad
McCallum Bridge Company 24
McCartney Hotel 78
McCook, Alexander 60
McCook, Daniel, Jr. 60
McCook, E.M. 43, 44
McCook, John J. 60
McCown, Brigadier General 53
McCoy, Daniel 131
McCutcheon Creek 203
McDonald, William 163
McDonald's Station 104, 167, 208
McEntire House 78
McGavock, John 177, 178, 223; *see also* Carnton
McGavock Cemetery 135
McGaw, J.P. 36
McKay, Alford 110
McKenzie, Marian 212
McMinnville, Tennessee 213
McPhail, Daniel 138, 139
McPherson, James 91
McPherson, John 42
McTaggart, Captain 107

Meagher, David 88, 89
Meginnis, John C. 167
Meigs, Montgomery C. 16, 17, 22, 59, 166
The Melrose House 223
Memphis, Tennessee 7, 19, 27, 72, 76, 118, 119, 170, 173, 174
Memphis and Charleston Railroad 1, 7–9, 22, 25, 26, 28, 36–38, 40, 50, 76, 78, 90, 91, 93, 100, 103, 112, 122, 123, 126, 155, 158, 159, 165, 179, 183, 196, 209, 211, 212, 215
Merchants' and People's Line 117
Merrill, William E. 3, 31, 53, 75, 93, **94**, 95, 96, 99, 105, 165, 171; *see also* blockhouse
Michigan 5, 31, 117, 170
Michigan Cavalry: (2nd) 100, 114, 214, 216, 221; (4th) 101, 217
Michigan Central Railroad 73
Michigan Infantry: (14th) 65, 66, 72, 214, 222; (18th) 106, 107, 123; (19th) 55; (29th) 122, 217
Midbridge, Tennessee 86, 87
Military Division of the Mississippi 23, 25, 26, 67, 69, 80, 90, 114, 140, 162, 164, 165, 167
Military Division of the Pacific 92
Milky Way Farm 153, 210
Mill Creek 46, 66, 68, 71, 83, 84, 97, 110, 178, 196, 199, 201, 203, 207, 218
Miller, Madison 64
Minnis, John 108, 109
Minor Hill, Tennessee 64, 155
Mississippi 16, 27, 36, 51, 63, 82, 83, 103, 124, 126, 159, 178
Mississippi Cavalry, 4th 55,
Mississippi River 17, 19, 23, 63, 117, 120, 189
Mississippi River Squadron 148
Missouri 73, 124
Missouri Artillery, 1st (light) 106
Missouri Infantry: (18th) 214, 220; (24th) 63, 132; (25th) 63; (44th) 128, 131, 132; (47th) 158, 218; (48th) 158, 218
Missouri River 61, 170
Mitchel, Ormsby M. 37, 38, 40–43, 213, 223
Mitchell, John 35
Mizner, Henry R. 32, 65–68, 72, 74, 75, 222
Mobile, Alabama 107, 117
Mobile and Ohio Railroad 126
Montgomery, Alabama 143
Montgomery Bell Academy 64
Montreal, Canada 125
Moody, Granville 47, 213
Moore, James 110
Moreland's Cavalry Brigade 75
Morgan, John Hunt 36
Morgan, Thomas J. 81
Morgan County, Alabama 82, 219
Morris' Mills 214
Morse, Samuel F.B. 186

Morton, Gilbert 123, 153
Morton, James St. Clair 52–54
Morton, John W. 108
Moulton, Alabama 38
Mount Olivet Cemetery 122
Mount Parnassas 204, 210
Mount Pleasant, Tennessee 7, 25, 60, 113, 127, 128, 173–175, 177–179, 184, 185, 204
Mud Creek 97, 201, 208, 210
Mundy, Marcellus 36, 212
Munfordville, Kentucky 127
Murfreesboro, Tennessee 18, 20, 33, 42, 47, 49, 53, 54, 57, 127, 143, 144, 149, 158, 213
Murfreesboro Road 136, 137, 146, 147
Mussel Shoals, Alabama 103, 124, 126

N. Alabama 59
Nance's Mills, Tennessee 78, 215
Nash, J.M. 80
Nashville 21, 59, 173, 174, 180
Nashville, Tennessee 1–5, 7, 8, 10, 16–22, 25, 26, 28, 29, 33–37, 39–50, 52, 53, 55, 57–61, 64, 67, 68, 72, 73, 75, 76, 78–82, 84–88, 91–93, 96, 99–101, 105, 110–112, 121–132, 134–140, 142–151, 155, 156, 158, 160–163, 165–168, 170–175, 177–184, 186–189, 191, 195–199, 210, 212–218, 222, 223
Nashville and Chattanooga Railroad 5, 6, 7, 9, 20, 22, 23, 25, 26, 28, 30, 31, 33, 35, 41–44, 46, 47, 52, 54, 60, 65, 67, 72, 76, 79, 80, 82, 90–92, 94–98, 100, 101, 103–111, 114, 116, 143, 158, 161, 165, 167, 168, 170, 172, 174, 175, 178, 180, 186, 189, 195, 196, 210, 213, 215
Nashville and Decatur Railroad 1, 3, 4, 5, 7–16, 19–23, 25, 26, 28–31, 33–35, 37, 40–44, 46–54, 58, 60–65, 67–72, 74–77, 80–82, 86, 90–98, 100–105, 111, 112, 114, 117, 120, 122, 124, 125, 127–130, 132, 134, 135, 142–144, 146, 150, 152, 153, 156, 158–169, 171–175, 180–186, 188–191, 193, 195–198, 202, 207–220, 222
Nashville and Northwestern Railroad 6, 7, 84, 170
Nashville City Reservoir 142
Nashville N&C freight depot 180
Nashville Pike 35, 139
Nashville Railroad Yard **79**, 173, 186
Nashville T&A freight depot 174, 180
Nashville Union Railroad Station 202
National Archives and Records Administration 2, 15, 69, 70, 74, 115, 116
National Cemetery (Nashville) 34

Index

National Lines 187
Naylor, Captain 123
Negley, James S. 45, 50, 213
Negley, William 36, 37, 47, 48, 213, 221
Nelson, William "Bull" 21, 35, 36, 44, 47, 49, 50, 213
New Albany, Indiana 25
New Orleans, Louisiana 27, 117, 121, 179
New York 16, 49
New York, New York 31, 63
New York & Erie Railroad 24
New York Infantry, 68th 113
Newport, Alabama 103
Newsom's Depot, Virginia 92
Niphonia Fairgrounds 38, 49
Nixon, E.F. 113, 216
North Carolina 1, 16, 122, 189
Northrop, Lucius B. 52
Norwich University 61

Oakland & Ottawa Railroad 31
Oaklawn 133
O'Connell, Major 165
Odd Fellows Hall 141
Ohio 37, 60, 114, 117, 125, 143
Ohio Artillery, 1st 217
Ohio Cavalry: (4th) 212; (9th) 215
Ohio Infantry: (3rd) 38, 41; (6th) 21, 47; (14th) 147; (18th) 38, 40, 212; (19th) 140, 141; (24th) 20; (27th) 65, 78, 214; (35th) 57; (40th) 55; (41st) 20; (43rd) 72; (50th) 125; (51st) 20, 21; (60th) 130; (69th) 212; (74th) 42, 46, 213; (81st) 62, 65, 66, 78, 90, 110, 214, 215; (82nd) 131; (102nd) 101, 106, 107, 123, 217; (111th) 129, 130, 132, 133, 139, 218; (175th) 127, 130–132, 152, 164, 216–218
Ohio Light Artillery, 1st 138
Ohio National Guard Infantry, 183rd 128, 131
Old Schoolhouse Branch 104, 105, 208, 216
Omaha, Nebraska 61, 170
Overton, John 143
Owens Station 202
Owingsville, Kentucky 121

Pacific Railroad Act 61
Palmer, W.J. 159
Paris, Tennessee 121
Parkes, Thomas 177
Parks, Major 68
Paschall, Edwin 222
Pea Ridge, Alabama 87
Peabody, Massachusetts 61
Pennsylvania 17, 45
Pennsylvania Cavalry: (7th) 98, 113, 125, 212–217; (15th) 159, 216
Pennsylvania Infantry: (7th) 113, 131; (12th) 84; (75th) 134, 216, 218; (78th) 45, 48, 212, 213; (79th) 212
Pennsylvania Railroad 22
Perkins, Nicholas 177

Perkins, Peter A. 177
Perkins, Simon 59
Perkins, Simon F., Jr. 58, 59
Perkins, Thomas 136, 177
Perryville, Kentucky 1, 18, 33, 52
Peters, James B. 51
Peters, Jessie McKissack 51
Peters, Walter G. 58, 180
Petersburg, Virginia 53, 142
Petty Branch 87, 207
Phifer, J.J. 108, 216
Philadelphia, Pennsylvania 16, 24, 53
Phillips, Jessie 220
Phillips, Jonathan 84
photography 69–71, 93
Pickens, Samuel W. 105
Pierce, Franklin 27
Pigeon Roost Creek 12, 13, 65, 66, 71, 156, 158, 162, 168, 182, 194, 197, 198, 201, 206
Pillow, Elizabeth T. 221
Pillow, J.B. 221
Pillow, William 221
Pioneer Brigade 31, 39, 52–54, 72, 74, 83, 99, 130, 138, 146, 152
Pittsburgh, Pennsylvania 45, 171
plank (and unplank track) 43–45, 51, 125, 128, 136, 137, 141, 146, 152, 191
Pleasant Grove Station (near Culleoka) 205
Poe, A. 107, 216
Poe, Orlando M. 34, 69, 114, 115, 195, 197, 205, 206, 210, 211
Polk, Andrew J. 128
Polk, Leonidas 122, 124
pontoon 39, *39*, 43, 52, 76, 78, 123, 125, 126, 128–130, 132, 135, 139, 145–148, 150–152, 154–156, 158, 159, 169, 170, 191
pontoon bridge 2–4, 33–36, **38**, 39, 54, 56, 72, 73, 78, 101, 122, 123, 128, 129, 131, 139, 142–152, 154, 155, *157*, 158, 169, 191
pontoon train 39, 52, 129, 146, 148, 150–152, 155
Poppleton, O.O. 117
Port Gibson, Mississippi 51
Post, Skidmore and Company 166
Potter, John W. 172
Powell's Ferry Road 152
Presstman, Stephen 129, 152, 156
Price, Colonel 212
Price, Sterling 38
Pride, George G. 67
Primm, Charles 222
Promontory Point, Utah 170
Prospect, Tennessee 65, 72, 73, 83, 87, 88, 90, 111, 167, 181, 182, 207, 214,
Prosser, A.S. 119
Prosser, William F. 105
Pryor, Luke 183
Pryor Creek 66, 104, 209, 211, 216
Pulaski 172, 173, 182
Pulaski, Tennessee 22, 36, 44, 49, 51, 60, 62, 64–68, 71–74, 76, 82–86, 87, 104, 105, 108, 110–114, 117, 124, 126, 127, 130, 143, 149–156, 158, 161, 162, 164, 165, 168, 179, 182, 184, 186, 194, 195, 199, 206, 210, 212–218, 220, 221
Pulaski turnpike 86, 87, 111, 150, 152, 155

quartermaster 16, 17, 22, 23, 26, 28, 32, 43, 52, 58, 59, 92, 96, 105, 109, 126, 151, 166, 172–174, 187, 215, 220, 222
Quartermaster's Department 23, 85, 166
Quebec, Canada 27

Radnor Yard 184
railroad bridge: at Brown's Creek 161, 194–197, 199, 200, 202, 213; at Carter's Creek Crossing No. 1 200, 203; at Carter's Creek Crossing No. 2 68, 200, 203, 210; at Carter's Creek Crossing No. 3 200, 203; at Carter's Creek Crossing No. 4 200, 204; at Carter's Creek Crossing No. 5 68, 158, 198, 200, 204; at Duck River 36, 47–50, 60, 65–69, **70**, 72–74, 121, 125, 127, 151, 152, 158, 162, 163, 168, 169, 173, 179, 193, 199, 200, 204, 210; at Elk River 29, 42–45, 52, 54, 60, 66–69, 71, 73, 75, 81, 84, 90, 101, 108, 111, 114, 117, 163, 168, 169, 182, 193, 198, 199, 201, 207, 210, 214; at Harpeth River 46, 47, 49, 50, 55, 60, **69**, 71, 101, 136, 137, 141, 150, 161, 162, 168, 199, 200, 202, 210; at Little Harpeth River 35, 50, 55–57, 59, 161, 162, 175, 200, 202; at Richland Creek Crossing No. 1 44, 113, 153, 162; at Richland Creek Crossing No. 2 44, 113, 162; at Richland Creek Crossing No. 3 67, 113, 162; at Richland Creek Crossing No. 4 51, 86, 110, 111, 116, 127, 162; at Rutherford Creek Crossing No. 1 158, 199, 200, 204; at Rutherford Creek Crossing No. 2 163, 199, 200, 204; at Rutherford Creek Crossing No. 3 163, 199, 200, 204; at Rutherford Creek Crossing No. 4 68, **70**, 199, 200, 204; at Spencer Creek 156, 161, 162, 194, 195, 198, 200, 202; at tributaries of McCutcheon Creek 203; at tributary of Mill Creek 207; at West Harpeth River 71, 133, 162, 200, 203
Railways and Telegraph Act 22
Rainey, Robert 146
Ramsey, Captain 146
Rathbone, Henry 24
Reconstruction 6, 92, 175
Reilly, James W. 138

Reynold's Federal Depot 42
Reynolds' Station 42–48, 65, 66, 75, 76, 127, 182, 206, 212–215, 217
Rhinemiller, W. 113
Richardson, William 220
Richland Creek 44, 45, 47, 50, 61, 66, 68, 69, 71, 75, 76, 83, 87, 90, 103, 111, 114, 116, 127, 151–153, 156, 158, 161, 168, 169, 182, 197–199, 201, 206, 207, 210, 213–217; Crossing No. 4, blockhouse at 86, 110, 116, 127
Richland Station 83, 86, 87
Richmond, Virginia 27
Rippavilla 133
Robertson Fork Creek 50, 66, 67, 101, 113, 156, 158, 162, 168, 182, 201, 206, 210, 216
Rochester, New York 24
Rock Island Bridge 63
Rockland Station 111, 207
Rocky Mountains 61
Roddey, Philip D. 48, 72, 75, 104, 144
Roderick 55
Rogersville, Alabama 104, 155
Roosevelt, Theodore 71
Roper's Knob 53, 163
Rosecrans 59
Rosecrans, William S. 18, 31, 33, 36, 52–54, 57, 59, 61, 92, 191, 222, 223
Ross's Ford 103
Rough Riders 71
roundhouse 180, 186
Rousseau, Lovell 65, 67, 68, 104, 112, 222
Route Cipher 65
Ruger, Thomas H. 128, 217, 218
Running Water Creek, Tennessee, railroad bridge at 67
Russellville, Mississippi 159
Russian Empire 37
Russian Guards 37
Rutherford County, Tennessee 64
Rutherford Creek: Crossing No. 1, blockhouse at 197; Crossing No. 4, blockhouse at 199

The Sack of Athens 40
St. Cloud Hill 50
Sam's Mills, Tennessee 214, 215
Santa Fe, Tennessee 16, 128
Savannah, Georgia 63
Savannah, Tennessee 33, 35
Savannah, Albany and Gulf Railroad 183
Saw Mill Creek 178, 203; *see also* McGavock, John
sawmill 33, 65, 73, 74, 86, 90, 113, 178
Sawyer, R.M. 66, 73, 91, 140
schedule 76, **77**
Schofield, John M. 91, 92, 121, 122, 124–135, 137–144, 150, 152, 158, 160, 162, 169, 221; *see also* Battle of Franklin

Scott, John S. 29, 30, 35, 36, 38, 40, 44, 136, 168, 224
Scott, Joseph R. 41
Scott, Thomas A. 22, 186
Seaboard Companies 184
Second Battle of Franklin 142; *see also* Battle of Franklin
Second Battle of Petersburg 53
Selma, Alabama 119
Shaw, Henry 64; *see also* Coleman, E.C.
Sherman, William T. 5, 17–19, 25, 30, 33, 34, 37, 41, 56, 61, 63, 65, 67, 69, 71, 73, 76, 78–80, 90–93, 99–101, 103, 107, 111, 112, 114, 116, 121, 122, 124, 126, 151, 163, 166, 171, 189, 191, 215
Shiloh, Tennessee 18, 35–37, 63, 71, 122, 127
Shoal Creek 114, 155
Shy's Hill 144
Sibley Tent 46
Sigmund, Jacob 98–101, 197, 215
Sipes, William B. 104, 125, 214, 217
Sligh, James M. 96
Sligh, James W. 31
Sloss, James W. 172, 174, 182
Smith, A.J. 124, 128, 141, 150, 152, 153, 158
Smith's Station 68, 72, 203, 210
South Carolina 16, 63, 103, 124, 163
Southern Claims Commission 171, 219
Southern Illinois Hospital for the Insane 37
Southwestern Telegraph Company 187
Sowell's Mill 129
Spalding, George 108, 110, 111
Spanish-American War 71
Sparks, Surgeon 139
Speed, Frederick 119
Spencer Creek 127, 150, 156, 158, 161, 162, 194, 195, 197, 198, 202, 213
Spring Creek 66, 200, 208, 209, 211
Spring Hill, Tennessee 19, 51, 52, 54, 57, 58, 71, 99, 101, 112, 113, 117, 122, 124, 125, 128–134, 138, 143, 147, 149, 150, 152, 161, 162, 174, 177–179, 196, 200, 203, 214, 218
Springfield 59
Springfield, Tennessee 18
spy 53, 58, 64, 65, 73, 180
stagecoach 5, 112, 181, 183
Stager, Anson 187
Stanley, David S. 56, 125–129, 131, 132, 139, 141, 222
Stanley, T.R. 38, 40
Stanton, Edwin M. 23, 24, 29, 41, 78, 160
Starkweather, John C. 104, 105, 108, 214
Starnes, James 55, 57

State Bank Building 78
State Line Station 207
station 5, 16, 23, 29, 30, 40, 42–49, 54, 55, 57, 60, 65, 66, 68, 72, 73, 75, 76, 79, 83, 86, 87, 99, 101, 104, 111–113, 125–129, 131, 133, 153, 162, 163, 165, 167, 174, 178–180, 182, 185–187, 202–210, 213–218
steam dummy 59
Stearns, Ezra 21, 44, 57
Steedman, James B. 49, 147, 158, 159, 222
Steubenville, Ohio 24
Stevens, Vernon K. 7
Stevens, W.J. 26, 76, 165
Stevenson, Carter L. 128
Stevenson, John D. 105, 215
Stevenson, Alabama 7, 22, 25, 26, 37, 42, 59, 91, 92, 100, 101, 122, 144, 155, 158, 161
Stewart, Alexander P. 123, 124, 129, 133, 142, 152, 155, 156
stockade (large) 165, 195, 198; at Culleoka 75, 196, 205, 215; at Lynnville 101, 196, 206, 215–217; at the Elk River 196; at the Little Harpeth River 55, 56, 196, 202
stockade (small, for railroad crossings) 30, 46, **47**, 48, 54, 67, 68, 74, 75, 93, 96, 98, 99, 112, 115, 193, 196, 197, 205, 213, 216
stockholders 175, 177
Stokes, Thomas J. 124, 135
Stone, A.B. 67
Stone and Boomer Company 63
Stone River 123
Strahl, Otho. F. 140
Strange, J.P. 140
Stratford Hall 17
Streight, Abel D. 151
Strickland, Silas A. 125
Sugar Creek 153–155, 158
Sulphur Creek 13, 14, 29, 36, 46, 51, 66, 68, 71, 73, 74, 82–84, 99, 106–108, **109**, 110, 114, 117, 119, 163, 168, 169, 183, 195, 196, 199–201, 207, 216, 218; *see also* Battle of Sulphur Creek Trestle
Sultana 117, **118**, 119, 120
Suman, Isaac C.B. 147
sutler 36, 57, 92
swamp 9, 165, 193, 200, 208, 209, 211
Swan Creek 9, 66, 69, 71, 83, 97, 104, 108, 195, 198–201, 208, 209, 211, 216
Swan Creek Management Area 211
Swayne, Colonel 72
Sweeney, Henry 72
Sweeny, Thomas W. 214, 215
Swords, Thomas 43, 44

Tanner, John T. 172
Tarpley's Shop 111
Tatem, Ezekiel H. 47
Taylor, Richard S. 103, 159
Taylor, Zachary 27, 159

Index

Taylor Depot 172
telegraph 22–24, 37, 38, 40, 47, 48, 55, 57, 60, 68, 72, 104, 112, 125–127, 130, 142, 143, 186, 187, 215
Tennessee 1, 3, 5–7, 16–18, 22, 25, 26, 28, 35, 42, 46–49, 51–54, 56, 58, 61, 63, 64, 67, 71, 79, 81, 84, 86, 87, 93, 97, 111, 117, 120, 121, 123–125, 137, 151, 163, 175, 177–179, 187, 195–198, 216, 219, 220
Tennessee and Alabama Central Railroad 7, 8, 29, 40, 105, 172, 174, 175, 182, 183, 207, 209, 211
Tennessee and Alabama Railroad 7–9, 21, 25, 29, 40, 48, 56, 58, 59, 60, 172–175, 177–180, 182, 202, 204, 218, 224
Tennessee and Pacific Railroad 6, 170
Tennessee Artillery (Fed.), 1st 112, 123, 217
Tennessee Cavalry (Conf.): (2nd) 55; (3rd) 19; (9th) 101; (10th) 155; (11th) 54; (14th) 105; (21st) 106, 114
Tennessee Cavalry (Fed.): (1st) 65; (2nd) 105, 119, 217; (3rd) 105, 108, 119, 216; (4th) 104; (5th) 220; (10th) 125; (12th) 108
Tennessee Division of Archeology 210
Tennessee General Assembly 177
Tennessee Infantry (Conf.): (1st) 64; (3rd) 124; (48th) 149
Tennessee River 7, 8, 19, 22, 37, 38, 42, 50, 60, 62, 73, 75, 76, 82, 84, 103, 104, 110. 114, 121, 123, 126, 127, 143–145, 147, 148, 150, 153, 155, 158–160, 168, 183, 184, 209, 211, 213, 217
Tennessee State Legislature 175
Tennessee Volunteers of African Descent: (2nd) 81; (3rd) 81
Texas 16, 49, 129
Texas and Pacific Railroad 170
Texas Infantry: (4th) 121; (10th) 124, 135
Texas Rangers 21
Thatcher, Stone and Company 63
Third Battle of Franklin 146
Thirteenth Amendment 101
Thom. Buford 173, 182
Thomas, George H. 18, 33, 49, 72, 75, 80, 91–93, 107, 111, 114, 121, 124–128, 130, 134, 137, 140, 142–144, 146–152, 155, 158, 161, 163, 164, 170, 172, 174, 191, 215, 217, 218, 222, 223
Thomas, Lorenzo 85
Thompson, Absalom 133, 177
Thompson, Alice 55
Thompson, Elijah 177
Thompson's Station 54, 55, 125, 126, 129, 131, 133, 162, 174, 179, 180, 203, 217
Thornapple River, Michigan 5
Thurstin, W.S. 132, 139

Titanic 117, 118; *see also Sultana*
Toledo and Wabash Railroad 125
Topographical Department 93
Topographical Engineers 126
Tower, Zebulon B. 164, 165
Town Creek 38, 66, 105, 107, 199, 208, 216
track 7, 9, 16, 21–23, 25, 26, 28–31, 33–35, 37, 40, 41, 43–45, 47–51, 55, 60, 61, 65, 67, 68, 71–76, 78–80, 88, 90, 91, 97, 99–101, 104–107, 112, 114, 116, 117, 121, 125, 131, 132, 139, 152, 158, 161–164, 166–170, 172, 175, 177–190, 193, 194, 196, 198, 199, 208, 210, 211, 214, 224, 226
Transcontinental Railroad 61, 170, 171
Transportation Corps of United States Military Railroad 23, 80, 166
Traveller's Rest 142, 143
trestle 2, 3, 5, 9, 26, 29–31, 33, 34, 41–44, 48, 50, 51, 60–62, 65–76, 90–98, 100–102, 104–105, 107, 108, 113, 114, 116, 117, 124, 126, 136, 148–152, 161–163, 165–169, 173, 175, 188, 190, 193–196, 198–202, 204–211, 214–218; at Carter's Creek crossings nos. 1–4 200; at Carter's Creek crossing no. 5 68, 200; at Decatur Junction 71, 74; at Elk River 77, 110; at Fountain Creek (Culleoka) 45, 50, *74*, 75, 115, 196; Gracey's 65, 100, 114, 115, *116*, 162, 168, 169, 195, 198, 199, 201, 205, 210, 214, 215, 217; Harris 65, 66, *115*, 127, 130, 162, 168, 195, 198, 199, 201, 205, 210, 214, 217; Holt's Trestle 68, 110, 207; Low Trestle 83, 97, 107, 108, 193, 198, 208, 215; at Mill Creek 68, 71, 83, 84, 110; at Robertson Fork Creek 162; at Sulphur Creek 29, 36, 66, 68, 71, 73, 74, 82, 83, 89, 107, 108, *109*, 169, 183, 196; at Swan Creek (south of Athens) 71; at Tunnel 43–46, 66, 67, 72, 83, 86–88, 111, 181, 196, 198
Triana, Alabama 217
Triune, Tennessee 56, 57
Truett, Alpheus 138, 139
Tucker, Charles E. 219, 220
Tullahoma, Tennessee 53, 56, 60, 112, 124
tunnel 203
Tunnel Hill 2, 4, *8*, 16, 30, 43–45, 66–68, 72, 83–84, 86, *88*, *89*, 90, 110, 111, 116, 163, 167, 168, 179, 181–184, 196, 198, 199, 201, 207, 213; *see also* Madry's Ridge
Tupelo, Mississippi 52, 159
Turchin, John B. (Ivan) 37, 38, 40, 41, 49, 104, 213, 220; *see also* The Sack of Athens
Turchin, Madame Nadine 37

turntable 30, 173, 182, 185, 186, 206
Tuscumbia, Alabama 7, 38, 124
Tuscumbia, Courtland & Decatur Railroad 7
Tuscumbia Railway 7
Twining, William J. 130, 135

Union Car and Bridge Works 63
Union Navy 147
Union Pacific Rail Road 25, 170, 171
United States Army 16, 121, 171
United States Army Corps of Engineers 127
United States Artillery, 4th 142
United States Capital 17
United States Cavalry, 4th 56, 149
United States Colored Troops 2, 4, 19, 72, 73, 81, *82*, 85, 88, 90, 96, 106, 107, 114, 117, 159, 164; (12th) 81; (13th) 81; (14th) 81, 123; (40th) 81, 82; (106th) 81, 82, 105, 107, 117, 216–218; (110th) 73, 81, 82, 87, 105, 107, 108, 110, 117, 216, 217, 220; (111th) 73, 81, 82, 87, 104–108, 110, 111, 117, 215–218
United States Congress 22, 23, 27, 45, 52, 86, 101, 170, 186
United States General Hospitals 161
United States House of Representatives 71
United States Military Academy 49, 71, 92, 103, 124, 126, 127
United States Military Railroad 16, 22–26, 28, 31, 40, 48, 72, 76–78, 165–167, 173, 174, 182, 186, 187; *see also* McCallum, Daniel
United States Military Telegraph Corps 186, 187
United States Naval Academy 21
United States of America 16, 22, 24, 37, 80, 105, 119, 122, 123, 171, 175, 186, 189, 222, 223
United States Sanitary Commission 58
United States Topo—The National Map 194
United States Volunteers 161, 170
United States War Department 81
University of Cincinnati 125
University of Mississippi 124

Valley City Street and Cable Car Railway 170
Van Derveer, Ferdinand 57
Van Dorn, Earl 51, 52, 54–56, 58, 214; *see also* Peters, Jessie McKissack
Van Pelt, David S. 214
Vicksburg, Mississippi 63, 103, 117–119
Vincent, Thomas M. 166
Virginia 16, 17, 24, 25, 58, 92, 189
Von Matzdorff, Alvin 146, 218

Index

Wade, A.B. 112, 220
wagon bridge 2–4, 20, 29, 35, 42, 49, 56, 130, 135–139, 141, 142, 146–148, 153, 161, 199, 210
wagon train 33, 40, 42, 43, 55, 123, 129, 130, 132–134, 137–139, 147, 148, 150, 152–156, *157*, 159, 185, 222
Waldorf-Astoria 171
Wales, Tennessee 65, 66, 76, 206, 214
Walker, Hillery J. 111, 216
Walker, H.W. 221
Walthall, E.C. 142, 145, 149, 150, 156
War Department 34, 57, 81
The War of the Rebellion: A Compilation of the Official Records of the Union and Confederate Armies 2, 196
Warfield, Amos 128
Washington 174
Washington, D.C. 17, 24, 34, 50, 78, 93, 174, 186, 223
Washington, Georgia 27
Washington, Kentucky 18
Washington and Lee University 17
Washington Aqueduct 17
Washington College 17
Washington Monument 53
Wasson, Corporal 100, 216
water tank 28, 67, 74, 90, 95, 98, 113, 166, 173, 174, 186, 195, 210
Watkins, Lewis 57, 58
Weaver, H.C. 107, 216
Wells, Edward 222

West Harpeth River 10, 11, 71, 97, 127, 131, 133, 134, 147, 150, 156, 158, 162, 167, 169, 194, 197, 198, 200, 203, 212, 213, 216, 218
West Point 17, 18, 27, 51, 56, 63, 93, 114, 121, 127
Western and Atlantic Railroad 37
Western Cavalry Corps 126
Western Edison Company 187
Western Military Institute 64
Western Theater 25, 33, 63, 103, 114, 120, 126, 151, 191
Western Union Company 186, 187
Westmoreland County, Virginia 17
Westover Plantation 122
Westport, Tennessee 114
Wharton, John A. 33, 57
Wharton, Lieutenant 57
Wheeler, Joseph 33, 71, 101–104, 112, 114, 116, 121, 124, 162, 163, 167, 169, 216
Wheeler Dam 104
Whipple, William D. 98, 147
White Hall 51
white trash camp 87, 90
Whiteside, Tennessee 67
Willett, J.R. 97, 150, 165, 191
Williams, Captain 125
Williams, G.M. 220
Williams, William O. 58, 180
Williamson 21, 59, 173, 175, 180
Williamson County, Tennessee 47, 84, 85, 110, 177, 178, 183, 221

Wilmington and Weldon Railroad 26
Wilson, A.N. 114
Wilson, James H. (federal general) 126, 127, 129, 140, 142, 144, 145, 147–153, 155, 156, 220
Wilson, James H. (T&A shareholder) 177
Windes, Francis M. 114, 155, 156
Winstead, Merideth P.G. 1
Winstead Hill 134, 140, 147
Wintergreen Cemetery 51
Wirz, Henry 126
Wisconsin 93
Wisconsin Infantry: (1st) 213; (13th) 122, 217; (22nd) 54, 55; (46th) 197, 218
Wolf, William P. 132, 216, 218
Wolford, Mr. 213
Wood, Thomas J. 127, 138, 140–142, 145, 147–153, 155, 156, 158, 223
woodyard 29, 85, 112
Worthum, Mr. 72
Wright, J.M. 46
Wright, M. 58
Wright, W.W. 25, 66, 74, 75, 83, 107, 108, 110, 111, 158, 161, 163, 165, 167–169, 193–195, 197, 200, 202, 210, 211
wye 185

Xenia, Ohio 42

Yates, Captain 37
Yates, John B. 96, 97
Yellowstone Expedition 56